The Ark Before Noah

Irving Finkel

The Ark
Before Noah

Decoding the Story of the Flood

NAN A. TALESE

Doubleday

New York   London   Toronto   Sydney   Auckland

Library of Congress Cataloging-in-Publication Data
is on file with the Library of Congress.

ISBN 978-0-385-53711-7 (hardcover)   ISBN 978-0-385-53712-4 (eBook)

MANUFACTURED IN THE UNITED STATES OF AMERICA

1   3   5   7   9   10   8   6   4   2

First American Edition

This book is dedicated, in respectful admiration,
to Sir David Attenborough

Our own Noah

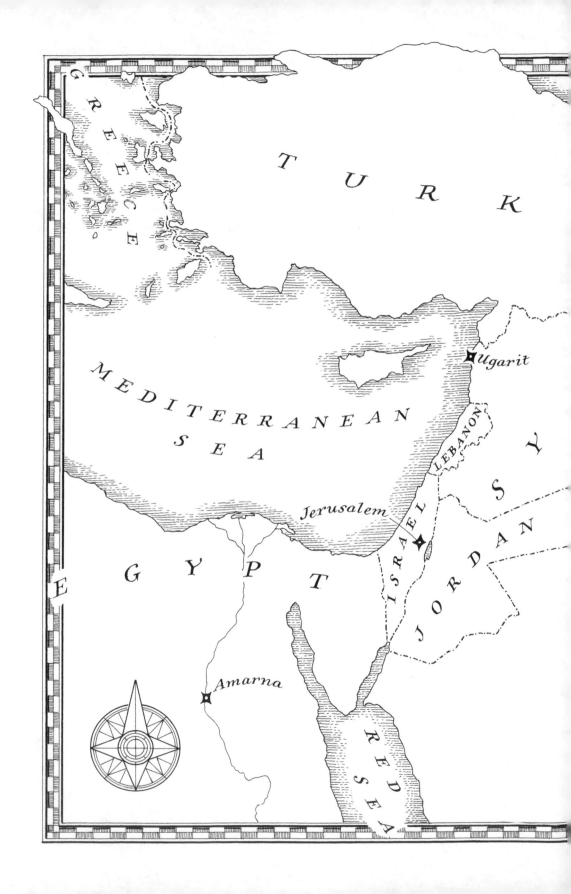

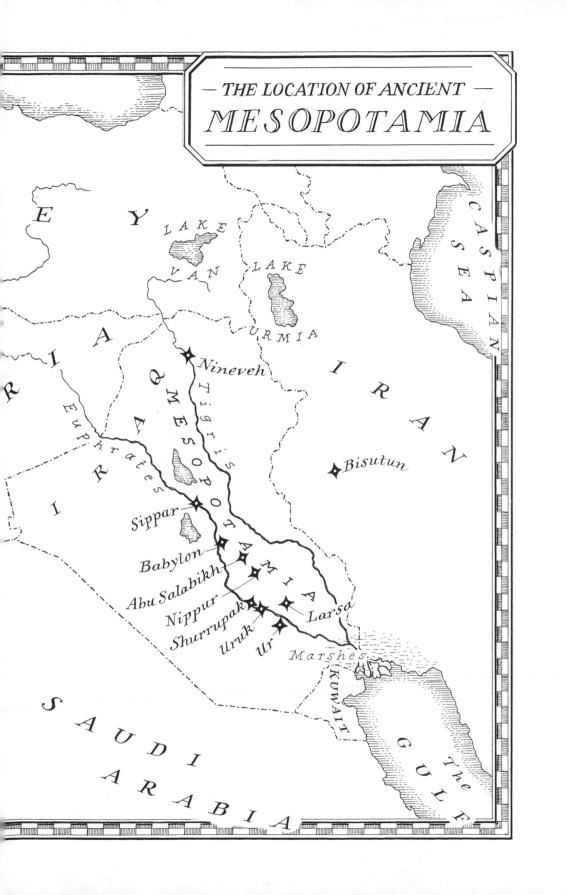

THE LOCATION OF ANCIENT
MESOPOTAMIA

CASPIAN SEA

LAKE VAN

LAKE URMIA

IRAN

Nineveh

Bisutun

MESOPOTAMIA

Tigris

Euphrates

IRAQ

Sippar

Babylon

Abu Salabikh

Nippur

Shurrupak

Uruk

Ur

Larsa

Marshes

KUWAIT

The GULF

SAUDI ARABIA

Contents

I

About this Book

Time's wheel runs back or stops:
Potter and clay endure

Robert Browning

In the year AD 1872 one George Smith (1840–76), a former bank-note engraver turned assistant in the British Museum, astounded the world by discovering the story of the Flood – much the same as that in the Book of Genesis – inscribed on a *cuneiform tablet* made of clay that had recently been excavated at far-distant Nineveh. Human behaviour, according to this new discovery, prompted the gods of Babylon to wipe out mankind through death by water, and, as in the Bible, the survival of all living things was effected at the last minute by a single man. He was to build an ark to house one male and one female of all species until the waters subsided and the world could go back to normal.

For George Smith himself the discovery was, quite plainly, staggering, and it propelled him from back-room cuneiform boffin to, eventually, worldwide fame. Much arduous scholarly labour had preceded Smith's extraordinary triumph, mind you, for his beginnings were humble. Endless months of staring into the glass cases that housed the inscriptions in the gallery resulted in Smith being 'noticed', and eventually he was taken on as a 'repairer' in the British Museum in about 1863. The young George exhibited an outstanding flair for identifying joins among the broken fragments of tablets and a positive genius for under-standing cuneiform inscriptions; there can be no doubt that he was one of Assyriology's most gifted scholars. As his abilities increased he was made Assistant to the famous Henry Creswicke

Rawlinson, and put to sorting the thousands of clay tablets and fragments that had by then entered the Museum. Sir Henry (1810–95) had played an important and adventurous role in the early days of Assyriology and by this time was in charge of the cuneiform publications put out by the Trustees of the British Museum. Smith called one of his working categories *Mythological tablets* and, as the pile of identified material grew, he was slowly able to join fragment to fragment and piece to larger piece, gradually gaining insight into their literary content. The Flood Story that he came upon in this way proved to be but one episode within the longer narrative of the life and times of the hero Gilgamesh, whose name Smith suggested (as a reluctant make-shift) might be pronounced 'Izdubar'.

George Smith thus set under way the cosmic cuneiform jigsaw puzzle that is still in heroic progress today among those who work on the British Museum's tablet collections. A problem that confronted him then – as it sometimes confronts others today – was that certain pieces of tablet were encrusted with a hard deposit that made reading the signs impossible. It so happened that one substantial piece which he knew was central to the 'Izdubar' story was partly covered with a thick, lime-like deposit that could not be removed without expert help. The Museum generally had Robert Ready standing by, a pioneer archaeological conservator who could usually work miracles, but he happened to be away for some weeks. One can only sympathise with the effect this had on George Smith, as recorded by E. A. Wallis Budge, later Keeper of Smith's department at the Museum:

> *Smith was constitutionally a highly nervous, sensitive man, and his irritation at Ready's absence knew no bounds. He thought that the tablet ought to supply a very important part of the legend; and his impatience to verify his theory produced in him an almost incredible state of mental excitement, which grew greater as the days passed. At length Ready returned, and the*

tablet was given to him to clean. When he saw the large size of the patch of deposit, he said that he would do his best with it, was not, apparently, very sanguine as to results. A few days later, he took back the tablet, which he had succeeded in bringing into the state in which it now is, and gave it to Smith, who was then working with Rawlinson in the room above the Secretary's Office. Smith took the tablet and began to read over the lines which Ready had brought to light; and when he saw that they contained the portion of the legend he had hoped to find there, he said, "I am the first man to read that after more than two thousand years of oblivion."

Setting the tablet on the table, he jumped up and rushed about the room in a great state of excitement, and, to the astonishment of those present, began to undress himself!

Smith's dramatic reaction achieved mythological status in itself, to the point that probably all subsequent Assyriologists keep the tactic in reserve just in case they too find something spectacular, although I have often wondered whether Smith might not have suffered an epileptic response to his great shock, for this reaction could be a symptom.

George Smith in 1876 with a copy of his
The Chaldean Account of Genesis.

3

Smith chose a very public platform from which to announce his discoveries: the December 3rd meeting of the Society of Biblical Archaeology in London, 1872. August dignitaries were present, including the Archbishop of Canterbury – since the topic had serious implications for church authority – and even the classically disposed Prime Minister, W. E. Gladstone. The meeting ended late and in unanimous enthusiasm.

For Smith's audience, as it had been for the man himself, the news was electrifying. In 1872 everyone knew their Bible backwards, and the announcement that the iconic story of the Ark and the Flood existed on a barbaric-looking document of clay in the British Museum that had been dug up somewhere in the East was flatly indigestible. Overnight, the great discovery was in the public domain, and no doubt the Clapham omnibus buzzed with 'Have you heard about the remarkable discovery at the British Museum?'

In 1873 the *Daily Telegraph* newspaper stumped up funds to send Smith back to Nineveh to find more pieces of the story. He succeeded in this rather more rapidly than might have been envisaged and, having sent a telegram to announce that he had discovered another missing Flood fragment, his expedition was brought to an expeditious end by the sponsors. It is worth quoting Smith's account of this:

> *I telegraphed to the proprietors of the "Daily Telegraph" my success in finding the missing portion of the deluge tablet. This they published in the paper on the 21st of May, 1873; but from some error unknown to me, the telegram as published differs materially from the one I sent. In particular, in the published copy occurs the words "as the season is closing," which led to the inference that I considered the proper season for excavating was coming to an end. My own feeling was the contrary of this, and I did not send this . . .*
>
> Smith 1875: 100

The 'Daily Telegraph' *tablet DT 42 excavated by Smith at Nineveh.*

Many an archaeologist will have profited from this learning experience, the rule being that if you find something spectacular right at the outset of a season in the field tell no one, least of all your sponsor, until the last week of the funding.

Although Smith was never to learn the fact that this new piece, which he accurately described as 'relating the command to build and fill the ark, and nearly filling up the most considerable blank in the story' (Smith 1876: 7), turned out to belong not to the Gilgamesh series at all, but to a similar, earlier mythological composition concerning the Flood, called after its hero, Atra-hasīs (whom Smith called 'Atar-pi'), as we will see later.

Smith's fame is visible in a charming postage stamp journal called *The Philatelist* that dates to this very period. The 1874 edition contains an oblique tribute to Smith's reputation, in the form of a note under the heading 'The Latest Post-Office Puzzle':

> *The number of foreigners resident in London brings a large quantity of letters from abroad, and the forms which Leicester Square or Soho assume in the addresses of these missives might even cause Mr. George Smith of the British Museum, the interpreter of Assyrian tablets, to tear his locks in despair. But the most curious letter as regards the unintelligibility of the address ever received at the General Post-office, arrived by the last mail from India. The officials and experts could make nothing of the blots, crooks, and fantastic sprawling lines on the envelope, which looked like microscopic photographs of queer insects. Eminent linguists in the British Museum were applied to without avail. The authorities at the India Office were consulted and were equally at fault. Malagasy, Pali and Canarese scholars, and the most learned linguists resident in the metropolis, were as nonplussed as the Oriental pundits by the mystic hand-writing on the wall in the palace of Sennacherib. At last, however, this Chubb-lock of letters was picked by two learned gentlemen residing in Bayswater, who discovered that the address was in the Telugu character, and that the contents were intended for the Ranee, by whom was meant her Majesty the Queen.*

George Smith died young, fairly romantically and, it must be said, probably quite unnecessarily. He expired at Aleppo of shigellosis (or dysentery), traditionally put down to his own stubbornness but probably partly due to neglect by others; his long-suffering and newly bereaved widow Mary, left with their five children, was to struggle with a modest state pension. His ghost is reputed to have called aloud to the German Assyriologist Friedrich Delitzsch at the very hour of his demise while the latter was passing the London street where he had lived. Mary Smith could scarcely have anticipated that her husband's name would remain vibrant today, but it has been indissolubly wedded to the Babylonian *Flood Story* ever since, and rightly so.

George Smith's discoveries led to unease in more than one quarter. It was simply bizarre that a close relative of Holy Writ should emanate from such a primitive, barbaric world through so improbable a medium, to thrust itself uncompromisingly into public consciousness. How could Noah and his Ark possibly have been known and important to the Assyrians of noble Asnapper and the Babylonians of mad, dread Nebuchadnezzar? Worried people over garden fences and in church pews clamoured to have important questions answered. Smith, writing soberly in 1875, ducked none of them, unanswerable though they then were. Two questions that presented themselves at the outset have echoed ever since:

> *Which flood tradition was older?* and *When and how did the transmission of the flood tradition take place?*

The first has long since been answered: cuneiform flood literature is by a millennium the older of the two, however one dates the biblical text – still a difficult problem. As for the second question, this book offers a new answer.

A hundred and thirteen years after Smith's breakthrough, and with far less drama, a British-Museum-curator-meets-amazing-cuneiform-flood-story similar episode befell the author of this book. In 1985 a cuneiform tablet was brought in to the British Museum by a member of the public for identification and explanation. This in itself was nothing out of the ordinary, as answering public enquiries has always been a standard curatorial responsibility, and an exciting one to boot, for a curator never knows what might come through the door (especially where cuneiform tablets are involved).

On this occasion the member of the public was already known to me, for he had been in with Babylonian objects several times before. His name was Douglas Simmonds, and he owned a collection of miscellaneous objects and antiquities that he had inherited from his father, Leonard Simmonds. Leonard had a lifelong eye open for curiosities, and, as a member of the RAF, was stationed in the Near East around the end of the Second World War, acquiring interesting bits and pieces of tablets at the same time. His collection included items from Egypt and China as well as from ancient Mesopotamia, among which were included cylinder seals – Douglas's personal favourite – and a handful of clay tablets. It was just such a selection of artefacts that he brought to show me on that particular afternoon.

I was more taken aback than I can say to discover that one of his cuneiform tablets was a copy of the Babylonian Flood Story.

Making this identification was not such a great achievement, because the opening lines ('Wall, wall! Reed wall, Reed wall! Atra-hasīs . . .') were about as famous as they could possibly be: other copies of the Flood Story in cuneiform had been found since Smith's time, and even a first-year student of Assyriology would have identified it on the spot. The trouble was that as one read down the inscribed surface of the unbaked tablet things got harder, and turning it over to confront the reverse for the first time was a cause for despair. I explained that it would take many hours to wrestle meaning from the broken signs, but Douglas would not by any means leave his tablet with me. As a matter of fact, he did not even seem to be especially excited at the announcement that his tablet was a Highly Important Document of the Highest Possible Interest and he quite failed to observe that I was wobbly with desire to get on with deciphering it. He blithely repacked his flood tablet and the two or three round school tablets that accompanied them and more or less bade me good day.

This Douglas Simmonds was an unusual person. Gruff, non-communicative and to me largely unfathomable, he had a conspicuously large head housing a large measure of intelligence. It was only afterwards that I learned he had been a famous child actor in a British television series entitled *Here Come the Double*

Deckers, and that he was a more than able mathematician and a man of many other parts. The above programme was entirely new to me, as I grew to manhood in a house without a television, but it must be recorded that when I gave my first lecture on the findings from this tablet and mentioned the *Double Decker* series a lady jumped out of her chair with excitement and wanted to know *all about Douglas* rather than the tablet. Many of the original cast became well known; all the episodes of the series have been reprinted.

All I knew then was that this new and unread flood tablet was leaving the precincts and that it was going to require a master-stroke to get it back into my hands so I could read the thing. Douglas appeared periodically in the Department thereafter with other small bags of objects. I never saw him myself, because he only wanted to consult my then-colleague Dominique Collon, who knows everything there is to know about cylinder seals, and who even managed to acquire a few interesting specimens from the Douglas Simmonds Collection for the Museum in 1996. Nothing happened about 'my' tablet until much later, when I spotted Douglas staring at Nebuchadnezzar's East India House inscription in our Babylon, Myth and Reality exhibition in the British Museum early in 2009. I picked my way carefully through the crowds of eager visitors and asked him straight out about it. The seductive quantities of bewitching cuneiform tablets strewn around the exhibition must have had a good effect because he promised to bring his tablet in again for me to examine. And he did.

I discovered that in the meantime Douglas had had the tablet fired in a kiln by someone who knew about such things, and it was now housed in a customised box, so its importance had not really been lost on him. He agreed to leave the tablet on deposit with me, in its box, so that I could work on it properly for as long as I needed to.

Finally alone with the tablet, armed with lamp, lens and freshly sharpened pencil, I got to work on reading it. Decipherment proceeded in fits and starts, with groans and expletives, and in mounting – but fully dressed – excitement. Weeks later, it seemed, I looked up, blinking in the sudden light . . .

*

I discovered that the Simmonds cuneiform tablet (henceforth known as the *Ark Tablet*) was virtually a detailed instruction manual for building an ark. I worked very industriously on that inscription, wedge by cuneiform wedge. Gradually the meaning could be teased out, and I reported in to Douglas now and again what was emerging. Most importantly, he was enthusiastic for me to use the tablet in collaborating on a major new documentary with Blink Films, currently under production, entitled *Rebuilding Noah's Ark*, and, finally, to write this, the present book. Sadly Douglas died in March 2011.

Writing this book has called upon philology, archaeology, psychology, ethnography, boat-building, mathematics, theology, textual exegesis and art history. All this will lead us into an adventurous expedition of our own. What is this ancient *cuneiform* script? And can we sense what these Babylonians who wrote in it were really like? I will clarify exactly what the Simmonds tablet has to say and how it compares with the flood story texts that are already known, and then look at how, after all, the story of the flood passed from Babylonian cuneiform to alphabetic Hebrew and came to be incorporated within the text of the Book of Genesis.

This is a book strongly dependent on ancient inscriptions and what they have to tell us. Most of them are written in the said cuneiform, the world's oldest – *and most interesting* – kind of writing. It has seemed important not only to say what we know but to explain how we know it, and also to make it clear when some word or line is persistently obscure, or open to more than one interpretation. I have tried to keep Assyriological philology to a minimum; some has perforce crept in, but not to the point, I hope, that the true Flood Story detective will be put off. For this is certainly a detective story. I had no idea when I started reading that tablet and writing this book where it was all going to lead me, but it has certainly been an adventure. I found myself facing many unanticipated questions that now had to be answered. To a cuneiform scholar the *Ark Tablet*, if not breathtakingly beautiful, will always be a thing of wonder. I hope that anybody else who reads this book will reach the same verdict.

2

The Wedge between Us

Then I can write a washing bill in Babylonic
    cuneiform
And tell you ev'ry detail of Caractacus's uniform
In short, in matters vegetable, animal, and mineral
I am the very model of a modern Major-General
W. S. Gilbert

The ancient Babylonians believed in Fate, and I suppose it must have been Fate that made me become an Assyriologist in the first place; it certainly seems to have played a hand in the writing of this book. I had decided by the age of nine that I wanted to work in the British Museum. This unswerving ambition was probably not uninfluenced by the curious upbringing to which the five of us children were subjected, for we used to visit the Bloomsbury galleries when it wasn't even raining and there was no glass case in the building against which my nose had never been pressed. At the same time I had a long-running interest in dead and 'difficult' writing, far more interesting than any schoolwork, and vacillated regularly in the weighty choice between ancient Chinese and ancient Egyptian.

When I went off to university in 1969 with my copy of Gardiner's *Egyptian Grammar* held proudly under my arm it was then that Fate intervened properly for the first time. The Egyptologist at Birmingham was T. Rundle Clark, a sedate and well-rounded scholar of cinematic eccentricity who delivered but a single introductory lecture before peremptorily expiring and leaving the department, noisy with new students, bereft in Egyptology. The worried head, Professor F. J. Tritsch, called me into his study to explain that it would take months to procure a new teacher of hieroglyphs and, since I liked such things, why didn't I do a bit of *cuneiform* or *wedge-writing* in the interim with *Lambert* down the hall? Lambert was known not to have much truck with beginners as a rule but, the head thought, might be persuaded to take me on under the circumstances. I and three young women accordingly found ourselves waiting expectantly outside the cuneiform door two days later. It was in this completely accidental way that the Assyriologist W. G. Lambert became my teacher, although at that stage I had no conception of how great a scholar he was, nor of the unclimbed mountains that lay ahead. I had just turned eighteen.

Our new professor hardly said good morning and showed no interest in what our names might be, but chalked three Babylonian words on the blackboard: *iprus, niptarrasu, purussû*, and asked the four of us if we noticed anything about them. There was silence. After boyhood Hebrew it was obvious that the words shared a common 'root' of three consonants, *p*, *r* and *s*. I suggested that. There was a slight nod, and I and the young ladies were then handed two sheets of cuneiform signs which we had to 'learn for Monday', and that, thanks to Fate, was it. The moment we started reading our first Babylonian words in cuneiform writing, '*If a man* . . .' in Hammurabi's *Law Code*, I knew that I was going to be doing Assyriology for good. It was one of those absolutely life-changing instances. No one else in the room knew the fateful inner turmoil that was in progress. But that is what happened to me. Lambert soon proved to be an austere and unforgiving teacher with a tendency to ironic acerbity: one had to take an unspoken vow of dedication and, one by one, the young ladies, unaffected by epiphanies, quietly gave up; before long I was alone with, if I may put it this way, destiny.

Cuneiform! The world's oldest and hardest writing, older by far than any alphabet, written by long-dead Sumerians and Babylonians over more than three thousand years, and as extinct by the time of the Romans as any dinosaur. What a challenge! What an adventure!

I suppose it is in some way a remarkable matter to sit day by day over the dusty writings of the ancient kings of Mesopotamia within a mile or two of Birmingham's Bull Ring and surrounded by useful university departments like French or Mechanical Engineering, but the oddness of it never struck me. Extinct languages that have been deciphered can be learned from grammar books in a classroom like any other, for the *I do, you do, he does* paradigm that comes with Latin, Greek or Hebrew also works for Sumerian and Babylonian.

Apprenticeship in cuneiform, as I soon discovered, actually involves two mountainous challenges: the *signs* and the *languages*. In normal walks of life it is counter-intuitive to separate language from script, for speakers and writers never think in such terms, but a language and its script are as much separate entities as a body and its clothing. Historically, Hebrew language, for example, has often been written in Arabic script, Aramaic occasionally rendered in Chinese characters, and, if necessary, Sanskrit could be carved in runes. Learning a new dead language in a new dead script is what some people might call a double whammy. With cuneiform, it is several degrees worse. Cuneiform script was used (primarily) for two dead languages, Sumerian and Akkadian, and until you read a few words of a tablet you cannot tell which language it is written in. Sumerian, the older language, has no known relative. Akkadian, of which Assyrian and Babylonian are northern and southern dialects, belongs to the Semitic language family and is helpfully related to Hebrew, Aramaic and Arabic, much as Latin is related to Italian and French and Spanish. Sumerian and Akkadian existed side by side in ancient Mesopotamian society and a properly educated scribe had to master both, a principle that still held vigorous sway in Lambert's classroom.

The thing is, too, that these were real languages. The Akkadian verb was fluent and complex, capable of expressing humour, irony, satire and *double-entendre* just like English. Vocabulary, also, was rich in every direction: the miraculous, expensive and confusingly named *Chicago Assyrian Dictionary*, only recently completed and weighing in at five feet of shelving, has tried to document all Akkadian words in (American.) In 1969, when I began my studies, most of the available grammars and dictionaries were in German. The *Akkadisches Handwörterbuch*, for example, grey and monotonous in double columns of small print, was more or less affordable and indispensable, but dependence on it for me meant that I often ended up knowing what an Akkadian word was in German without remembering what the German meant in English. Fellow students reading history or physics seemed to me frankly to be on a cushy ride, and it was a source of only mixed satisfaction when even my friend Andrew Sutherland, who got an outstandingly good First in German, found himself quite unable to tell me what on earth Adam Falkenstein was talking about in his exposition of Sumerian grammar in the 'helpful' little book entitled *das Sumerische*.

Lambert favoured a Holmes-like exactitude in class where uncertainty or ignorance was exposed with a merciless needle. Cribs were forbidden: the naked text had to be in plain view on the table, read out loud, translated exactly, and the grammatical forms analysed. There was absolutely nowhere to hide. This was a school of Assyriology altogether different from that prevailing, say, in Oxford, where apparently even a tutor might rely on notes under the table to navigate through Assyrian royal inscriptions. Another thing they did there during the first weeks – according to my friend Jeremy Black – was to transliterate the opening chapter of *Pride and Prejudice* into syllabic cuneiform signs. This, it was felt, served to introduce students emphatically to the realities of cuneiform writing, for it clarified the impossibility of writing adjacent consonants in a syllabary and focused attention on the lack of 'o', 'f' or 'j' in cuneiform; this exercise resulted in a distilled product such as *tu-ru-ut u-ni-we-er-sa-al-li ak-nu-le-eg-ge-ed*.[1] Lambert had no interest in such infantilia, nor did we ever try writing cuneiform with cross-cut lolly-sticks and Plasticine. One learned one's signs, all of them, and that was

[1] Truth universally acknowledged

that. Years and years later, starting off an experimental evening class in cuneiform at the Museum, I wrote on the blackboard the following inscription in cuneiform signs:

a-a a-am tu-u bi-i ma-ar-ri-id tu-ma-ar-ru. [2]

which sentence was literally true: I really wanted to leave early. It provoked the greatest excitement when the signs were identified in random order by the students from their list and called out one by one so that they could see the sentence finally emerge. I had to think up a completely different sentence, I am happy to say, for the same purpose, when I started another class some years later.

Cuneiform signs, which I think of as jewels in a bowl, full of meanings obvious and subtle, never seemed strange or alien to me, and I practised them endlessly. A red-letter day came when John Ruffle of the Birmingham City Museum gave me a copy of René Labat's wonderful (and at that time utterly unobtainable) *Manuel d'Épigraphie Akkadienne*, in which three millennia of sign forms were clearly laid out across double pages in black ink and all you had to do was remember them. This was the only book I have ever possessed which fell to pieces through use.

Studying the world's oldest writing for the first time compels you to wonder about what writing is, how it came about more than five thousand years ago and what the world might have looked like without it. Writing, as I would define it, serves to record language by means of an agreed set of symbols that enable a message to be 'played back' like a wax cylinder recording; the reader's eye runs over the signs and tells the brain how each is pronounced and the inert message springs into life.

As far as we know from archaeology, writing appeared for the first time in the world in ancient Mesopotamia. The most important point here is not the date, which was in or around 3500 BC, or all the trials and experiments before things really took off,

2 I am to be married tomorrow

but the unromantic fact that writing was bestowed on humanity by ancestors of the Inland Revenue service. The stimulus that set writing on its path was not the urge to create poetry or the desire to record history but the need to accommodate the demands of book-keepers. While the ultimate beginnings of it all remain irretrievable, the first documents which we encounter deal with the practical, large-scale administration of individuals, goods and wages, all carefully documented with names and numbers.

And their preferred medium from the outset was *clay*. Clay at first does seem a strange choice of writing support in a world where others employed wood, parchment, skin, leather or potsherds, but all of these are suitable for writing in ink and serve an entirely different mechanism. Riverside clay was liberally to hand; scribes always knew a source for the best quality requiring least preparation (hence, perhaps, the expression *laughing all the way to the bank*), and the essence of script was crucially intertwined with the quality of clay fabric from the outset. Ancient Mesopotamians, it must be said, knew clay like no one else. The medium lent a depth and sculptural quality to the writing; it is probable that, with a fluent scribe, both left and right hands moved subtly together in the creation of the signs. And what they wrote can last in the ground for ever. Since ancient inscriptions on organic materials tend to perish, we should be doubly appreciative that writing began that day in Mesopotamia on handfuls of beautiful clay and never swerved.

The earliest Sumerian signs, which we can represent in CAPITALS, used in these tablets resemble simple outlines drawn by a four-year-old child: 'to stand' is represented by the outline of a FOOT; a JUG represents 'beer'. A large number of such picture signs came into being which, at first, functioned uncomplicatedly: each sign meant what it looked like. With a bagful of such signs and a handful of other symbols for numbers, it is possible to produce surprisingly complex records of ingoing or outgoing materials, but while the result was a recording system that might satisfy bureaucracy it could scarcely do justice to language. As long as matters were limited to monthly returns, things might have stopped there, but at a certain moment an outburst of explosive creativity meant that, before long, anything, including poetry and history, could be recorded too.

The primary revolution involved the idea that a given sign, representing some object graphically, could also convey the sound of that object's name. For example, the very early sign for 'barley' was EAR-OF-BARLEY. The actual word 'barley' in Sumerian, was še, pronounced something like the syllable *sheh*. The EAR-OF-BARLEY sign now could be put to two different uses: to mean 'barley', or to express the sound of the syllable *sheh* to spell another word or part of a word, where the meaning 'barley' had no relevance, as if writing the beginning of the English word 'shellfish'. The conception that a graphic sign could convey sound isolated from meaning is the Great Leap, for it meant that real and full writing could become possible. A whole system of signs was engendered that in combination could record words, speech, grammar and ultimately narrative literature in Sumerian and Akkadian – as well as other ancient Middle Eastern languages – with all their subtle and complex demands.

Even today we can visualise something of the important issues that must have arisen, such as having to agree on a new sign that hadn't been needed before, or finding a sign to write something that cannot be drawn. No one beyond Lewis Carroll could envision drawing an 'it', for example, but a sign was needed for such an essential word. The solution was to employ an underworked sign that already existed and give that a new meaning. The Sumerian sign JUG was first used to write 'beer' (pronounced kaš) but otherwise had no other use than for jugs. It was this sign that was recruited to write *bi*. So it came about that the JUG sign now had the values *kash*, meaning 'beer', and *bi*, meaning 'it'.

The Sumerian sign KA represents 'mouth', by means of a man's head with the salient part emphasised. The same sign can also be used to write the words DUG_4, 'to speak', ZÚ, 'tooth', KIR_4, 'nose', INIM, 'word', and meaning and pronunciation come from context. This sign, KA, could also function as a box in which a smaller sign inside gives new meanings and new sounds. The small sign, NINDA, meaning 'food', was inserted inside KA to create a new sign, GU₇, which means 'to eat', and A, 'water', was inserted inside KA to create NAG, 'to drink'.

The very early signs before 3000 BC were drawn in firm as-yet-undried clay with a pointed tool much as we use a pencil on paper. Eventually these more or less realistic and often curved drawings were reduced to combinations of straight lines impressed with a specially cut reed or stylus that looked something like a chopstick. In addition, the orientation of the signs was changed and their uses and values considerably increased. The evolved cuneiform proper which resulted is written in signs made up of separate strokes impressed into the clay. Inscribing cuneiform on clay is, therefore, more akin to printing than writing. The characteristic wedge feature is a direct consequence of impressing the signs with a straight-edged writing tool in contrast to drawing with a point, and it is this that led the nineteenth-century decipherers to name the script cuneiform, derived from the Latin *cuneus*, 'wedge'. Each application of the edge of the stylus-tip left a line ending in a wedge-head, be it the top of a vertical, the left end of a horizontal wedge, or a diagonal produced by impressing the corner of the stylus. This feature was, perhaps, accidental, since the original plan was only to replace all sign elements with straight rather than curved lines. The reader's eye sees the bottom of the triangular depression displaced by the stylus, which always appears like some kind of elongated wedge. Broadly speaking there are three primary strokes: horizontal, vertical and diagonal, and you can also find upward diagonal and downward diagonal wedges, but these are really modifications of the horizontal. With these five distinct shapes any cuneiform sign can be written. Neat individual strokes can be produced with a minimal movement of the right hand, ranging principally between due west to due north.

Cuneiform absolutely *cannot be written with the left hand*, and any school candidate who manifested that sinister tendency in antiquity would, no doubt, have it beaten out of him, as has often happened since in human history. I know from personal experience that it is impossible, having conducted countless museum workshops with schoolchildren, armed with clear sign drawings (and the lolly-stick and Plasticine bag). Children (unlike their parents or guardians) are always right on top of the complexities in minutes and dead keen to try it out, but every time about 70 per cent of them turn out to be left-handed. I always say, 'You will have to do it with your right hand then'. The reply is usually, 'I can't write with my right hand,' to which the correct riposte is, 'How do you know you can't write cuneiform with your right hand if you have never ever written cuneiform before?'

'A good scribe,' they said in Sumerian, 'could follow the mouth', which might mean the ability to write at dictation speed or just refer to accuracy. Some cuneiform signs consist of only a few 'wedges'; complex signs can have many. Sign-shapes, structure and the sequence in which wedges should be impressed were fixed by convention, and youthful scribes had to learn them laboriously, much as Chinese characters have to be learned today.

In some sense, it has sometimes seemed to me, cuneiform signs on clay don't really exist, for all that one has to work with is depressions in a clay surface; the depth of each produces sufficient shadow to delineate it for the reader's eye; an ant strolling microscopically across the surface of a tablet would encounter a mine-field of spindly, angular ravines.

Unfortunately for the young apprentice, as the signs became stylised into cuneiform wedges their 'realistic' quality became much diminished, and after three millennia of daily use there were hardly any in which the 'original' graphic significance survived as a clue to meaning. One clear exception is EAR-OF-BARLEY, which is still recognisable for what it is in tablets of the first century AD.

King Hammurabi's Law Code could have been written with first-year students, 3,750 years later, in mind. It is repetitive in structure, lots of the strange words recur, and before long you see that this is codified rational thinking expressed in real language by real people, who can talk to us even though they have been dead for so long:

> *If a man, some of whose property is lost, seizes his lost property in a man's possession, if the man in whose hand the thing belonging to him is seized states, 'A seller sold it to me; I bought it before witnesses' and the owner of the lost property states: 'I will produce witnesses who know my lost property,' if the buyer produces the seller who sold it to him and the witnesses before whom he bought it and the owner of the lost property produces the witnesses who know the lost property, the judges shall examine their statements and the witnesses before whom the sale was made and the witnesses who know the lost property shall declare what they know before a god, the seller is a thief; he shall be put to death. The owner of the lost property shall take his lost property; the buyer shall take the money which he has paid from the house of the seller.*

> *If the buyer does not produce the seller who sold it to him and the witnesses before whom he bought it but the owner of the lost property produces the witnesses who know his lost property, the buyer is a thief: he shall be put to death. The owner of the lost property shall take his lost property.*

> *If the owner of the lost property does not produce witnesses who know his lost property, he is a felon since he has uttered slander; he shall be put to death.*
>
> Code of Hammurabi, Laws 9–12

This is a code that embodied legal principles that prevailed in the background: there is no evidence that judges quoted from it or followed it literally, nor would either guilty party here be facing a death sentence. Hammurabi's masterpiece, like all attempts to tell people how to behave, was written in stone, and the cuneiform signs in which it was recorded were deliberately old-fashioned (in comparison with writing on contemporary, everyday tablets), in order to convey to a reader that the guiding principles and the dynasty that had codified them were eternal. This 'archaising' of type of signs, too, happens to be perfect for the beginner, because they are clear and elegant and often still preserve within themselves something of the remote 'picture sign' from which they evolved.

After about three years of round-the-clock effort, everything becomes clear to the long-suffering acolyte. Reading cuneiform becomes second nature and the wedge, at first painful, becomes a magic bridge to a long-dead world populated by recognisable fellow humans. I would go so far as to recommend Assyriology enthusiastically as a way of life to many, especially when certain points about it are borne in mind. One is the cheerful fact that almost any cuneiform sign can be used in up to four distinct ways:

- *Logograms*, which spell a complete Sumerian word, one sign per word, such as kaš = 'beer', or lugal = 'king'.
- *Syllabograms*, which spell one syllable, such as BA or UG, which usually form part of a word.
- *Phonetic complements*, which are placed next to (or sometimes inside) other signs as a clue to their pronunciation.
- *Determinatives*, which stand in front of or behind words,

without being pronounced, as a clue to their meaning, such as GIŠ = 'wood', or DINGIR = 'god'.

For example, the sign AN, if pronounced 'dingir', is just the Sumerian noun 'god', meaning god; if pronounced 'an' it is a syllable sign to write the sound '*an*'; if it is a phonetic complement it appears after a word ending in -*an*, or if a determinative sign it indicates that the name of a god follows. The reader's decision as to which usage or value applies depends on the context.

The Sumerian language is written partly with logograms (especially nouns), partly with syllabograms (especially verbs and other bits of grammar), and partly with determinatives. Phonetic complements in Sumerian texts occur mostly inside complex signs.

The Akkadian language is written predominantly with syllabograms, based on the premise that to spell words in a retrievable way for a reader of Jane Austen they must be sliced up like a cucumber into their constituent elements, which are expressed in syllabic signs:

ku-ku-um-be-er = cucumber.

Cuneiform signs express syllables, and the slices are 'pushed back together' in order to reconstitute the sound of the underlying cucumber. The majority of cuneiform signs are used for syllables like this. Most syllable signs are simple like AB, IG, EM or UL, or BA, GI, ME or LU, but there are many like DAB, SIG or TUR. Rarer logographic signs with a longer structure, such as BULUG or MUNSUB, can hardly ever be used to spell words syllabically. Spelling with syllables is perfectly comfortable once you have learned the signs, but Akkadian is not always written that way. There is a special Mesopotamian device whereby traditional Sumerian logograms can be liberally used when writing Akkadian, leaving readers to supply the Akkadian equivalent themselves in the correct grammatical form. We are familiar with this process today in the specific case of the sign $, for which the sound 'dollar' is instantly supplied by the reader, who is usually oblivious of (and quite unconcerned with) what the symbol actually means. This substitution technique is central to the writing of Akkadian and is often aided by the use of phonetic complements.

For example, in the *Ark Tablet* with which this book is concerned, the hero Atra-hasīs's name is spelt ᵐ*at-ra-am-ḫa-si-is*, where the cuneiform sign for the number 'I' precedes the personal name as determinative, which we show as ᵐ (short for 'man'), with the other syllables expressed by six straightforward syllabic signs, *at, ra-* and so on.

In contrast the famous words 'destroy (your) house, build a boat' are written *ú-bu-ut* É *bi-ni* MÁ. É and MÁ are old Sumerian logograms, or word signs, for which the corresponding Akkadian words are to be supplied by the reader; these are *bītam*, 'house', and *eleppam*, 'boat', respectively, both in the accusative case. The other Akkadian words *ubut*, 'destroy!' and *bini*, 'build!' are spelled out syllabically.

In itself, syllabic writing is not a complicated matter. Minimal consonantal signs to express English would require a table of 210 signs, which would consist of AB and BA, EB and BE, IB and BI, OB and BO and UB and BU, and so on for the twenty-one non-vowel letters, with a few independent vowels thrown in to be helpful. The cuneiform script, however, was never concerned to achieve helpful simplicity. It is characterised by three idiosyncratic factors:

Idiosyncrasy I

In cuneiform writing, it hardly ever occurs that for a given syllabic sound such as 'ab' or 'du', there is only one sign that has that value. For historical reasons, there are usually several signs; in some cases there are many. For example, the syllabic sound 'sha' can theoretically be written with any one of the following six signs, if not more:

Idiosyncrasy *1*: Multiple signs with one sound

This situation does not mean that all these values were in regular use at any one time. For many signs, syllabic use is fortunately limited, either by period, or genre of text.

Idiosyncrasy 2

In addition, most individual signs have more than one sound value; some, again, have many. Furthermore, things can differ from Sumerian to Akkadian.

SPECIMEN SIGN:

In Sumerian, words:
utu = 'sun'
dingir utu, 'the Sun God'
ud, 'day'
babbar, 'white, shining'
zalag, 'pure'.

In Akkadian, sounds:
ud/ut/ut/utam/tam/ta/sa$_{16}$ /tú/pir/par/laḫ/liḫ/ḫiš.

Idiosyncrasy 2: Multiple values for one sign

Idiosyncrasy 3

When writing conventions were evolving, the earliest scribes tended to draw a box around signs that belonged together to produce meaning and it was up to the reader to put them in order. Such a system is not always free of ambiguity. Later Mesopotamian scribes displayed a different characteristic: all signs in a line touched and they wrote with no gaps between the words. Generally speaking, developed cuneiform is right justified and if there are not enough signs to fill a whole line naturally, gaps appear within the line. Fancy calligraphers such as those in the royal Assyrian library at Nineveh liked to stretch out or distort certain signs to avoid empty space. The realisation that there are no gaps between words is hard to believe for the absolute beginner. One crumb of comfort is that a word could never be divided over two lines.

These cuneatic idiosyncrasies mean that reading involves *first* identifying a given sign, *then* understanding whether it is a logogram, syllabogram, phonetic complement or determinative, and *finally* choosing the correct sound reading if it is a syllabogram. Young scribes like young Assyriologists just had to accept that all cuneiform signs had more than one sound value and all sounds could be represented by more than one cuneiform sign, or, in other words, *Polyvalence is All*. In practice, traditions restricted the use of many signs. Since words are usually spelled in syllables, the eye quickly learns to select readings that produce harmony and correct grammar, discarding unlikely or impossible sequences.

From the very earliest stages Mesopotamian scribes found themselves making lists of words, for it was crucial to establish what the signs were as they developed and were agreed on, both to avoid confusion and to allow them to be taught. We find that mature cuneiform ended up as a fairly tidy set of some six hundred signs that was universally subscribed to by all Mesopotamian writers thereafter. Sign shapes were certainly streamlined, similar signs might coalesce and once in a while a new value was introduced, but one is hard put to point to major innovations or changes over that vast expanse of time once writing was standardised. Any unwieldy proliferation of invented signs at the outset was evidently reined in and controlled, evidently anticipating the chaos that would ensue if all Mesopotamia's cities came up with their own local signs and insisted that they were 'right'. It is hard to credit that this remarkable script discipline would have come about of its own accord. One might imagine a 'summit' at which those who were responsible for the use and dissemination of the new tool would agree between them on what was to be the sign list that everyone would use.

Wedge shape and calligraphic proportion did not remain static over three thousand years of use. Teachers of sign-writing in cuneiform school always promoted the accepted shapes with vigour, and personal style in handwriting had no place at all. Early cuneiform around 2900 BC has long, slim wedges; the first-millennium Assyrian librarians perfected a canon of proportions to such an extent that one library scribe can hardly be distinguished from another without micro-photography, while under the Seleucids in the fourth century BC cuneiform signs leaned so far backwards that they look like dominoes on the verge of collapse.

Some of the first lists to appear came to be copied and recopied by apprentices ever afterwards, such as the 'Names and Professions List', which gives all titles and activities and was still revered at the end of the first millennium BC, even if many of the words were completely out of date. Certain lists concentrated on the signs, arranging them in a learnable sequence by their shape, and analysing pronunciation, composition and ultimately meaning. Others were assembled by subject matter: anything made of wood; anything made of stone; animals, plants or gods. Cuneiform signs could only be brought together by graphic structure or meaning: our default system of alphabetic order would not be possible for another two thousand years. As the linguistic domination of Sumerian declined, Akkadian equivalents to or translations of all the Sumerian words were included. The lists grew, evolved, and were eventually edited into established or even 'canonical' series of texts, the perpetual bread and butter of the scribal colleges. As the centuries unfolded and dynasties rose and fell, the Mesopotamian cultural backbone bent and swayed with changes but the written tradition remained a stable entity. A solid continuum of scribal tradition saw to it that the inherited lore in Sumerian and Akkadian cuneiform was preserved for ever. It was this unique Mesopotamian institution that made it possible for the same list of words to survive from 3000 to 300 BC. Tradition was consciously and deliberately safeguarded and passed on by a winding queue of dedicated scribes to whose hands the whole of knowledge, transmitted by the gods after Atra-hasīs's Flood, was entrusted.

The scribe's responsibility was to ensure anonymous transmission of this heritage without intervention or change. The older a particular tablet the more valued its contents. The core of this heritage was exemplified by the word lists. In them all the words and signs for everything were logically and retrievably stored.

While cuneiform script was used for the writing of the Sumerian and Akkadian languages for three thousand years it was often exported way beyond the home borders by itinerant Mesopotamian scribes, with the result that it came to be used to write Hittite, Hurrian, Elamite, Mitannian and other languages too, while in the second millennium BC Akkadian was widely used as an international language for correspondence, diplomacy and treaties. The flexibility and adaptability of the cuneiform script meant that the sounds, and therefore the grammar and vocabulary of languages completely unrelated to Sumerian or Akkadian, could likewise be reduced to writing and, in the same way, ultimately consigned to posterity. Despite its spiky appearance and undeniable complexities, cuneiform served the civilised world for an unimaginable length of time and, in the same breath, it is *much more fun* than any alphabet.

Reading those first laws of Hammurabi with Professor Lambert led to a thesis on Babylonian exorcistic incantations under the same teacher, and working for three years on the *Dictionary* in the Oriental Institute of the University of Chicago. Then, to my great joy, I was appointed Assistant Keeper in what was then called the Department of Western Asiatic Antiquities at the British Museum. Fate intervened at that point, too, for the intimidating Chairman of the interviewing board was Director David Wilson, a man who I later found referred to cuneiform writing as *chicken scratches* and favoured an attitude of apparent disdain for Assyriology as a way of life. During the interview, something prompted me to bring up my one dose of field experience at the University of Birmingham excavation in Orkney, where I had sat about on the edge of the trench for a month being sarcastic about illiterate civilisations but had happened to make the only real find of the season; a spot of desultory trowel work by me one morning accidentally laid bare a fine Viking sword in a ludicrously good state of preservation. All the other archaeologists present squirmed in unspeakable jealousy at the sight of my find, but as far as I was concerned the thing was uninscribed and therefore not that interesting. As I recounted this incident, David Wilson, unknown to me then as the international authority on the Vikings that he is, leaned forward in excitement to ask a technical question, and I have never quite got rid of the feeling that it was this archaeological fluke that got me the cuneiform job. After signing the Official Secrets Act, I was handed my heavy, passport-to-the-Nation's-treasure key, which is soberly inscribed IF LOST 20/- REWARD.

The tablet collections in the British Museum defied and still defy belief. Cupboards full of shelves laden with Victorian glass-topped boxes house about a hundred and thirty thousand tablets of clay inscribed in cuneiform writing, with three thousand years of wonderful, wedge-shaped messages. Who could ask for more?

3

Words and People

How many miles to Babylon?
Three score miles and ten.
Can I get there by candle-light?
Yes, and back again.

Anon

We ought, being plunged in at the deep end, to consider without delay which part of the world has provided our cuneiform tablets (for they do not, as I think my old professor secretly believed, grow in museums), and hunt for the ancient Sumerians, Babylonians and Assyrians who produced them. At the same time there is the important question of what the old Mesopotamians actually wrote.

The cuneiform homeland is identified under a single, resonant name that in the normal world usually lies buried somewhere at the back of the mind: *Mesopotamia*. Such a resonant name is due to Greek; *meso* means *between*, and *potamus* means *river* (hippopotamus, to the Greek mind, is a 'river horse'). There was a period when junior-school teachers drew the rivers in question on blackboards for their pupils, Euphrates to the left and Tigris to the right, all the while happily reciting *How many Miles to Babylon?* Since the First World War, however, the once familiar name Mesopotamia has been altogether supplanted by that for the same territory today, modern Iraq. The very names of those rivers are half as old as time, recognisable in the unfolding sequence of languages that encapsulate Mesopotamia's history: *buranun* and *idigna* in Sumerian, *purattu* and *idiqlat* in Babylonian, *perat* and *hiddeqel* in Hebrew, *euphrátēs* and *tigris* in Greek, and *furāt* and *dijla* in Arabic.

Like the Nile in Egypt, the twin rivers Euphrates and Tigris were the very lifeblood of ancient Mesopotamia. The fertility and wealth that they bestowed on the world's most expert irrigators had far-reaching consequences, for ancient Iraq became a world stage for the interplay of discovery, invention, trade and politics. We do not know who got there first to harness the waters. Certainly the Sumerians – known best for the Royal Graves that Sir Leonard Woolley uncovered at their capital city, Ur – were early. It is they who, most probably, made the first moves towards writing well before 3000 BC, and it is their language, as we have seen, which was the first to be recorded in the developing cuneiform script. With the advent of Mesopotamian writing, prehistory came to an end and history – acknowledging events and depending on records – became a meaningful term.

Today we know a surprising amount about ancient Mesopotamia. In part this is, of course, due to archaeology, which can analyse graves and architecture and pots and pans, but a deeper understanding of a vanished culture depends inevitably on its written documents. It is from these that we can outline their history and populate it with characters and events; we can observe the populations at work in their daily lives, we can read their prayers and their literature and learn something of their natures. Those on the trail of ancient Mesopotamia through their documents are blessed in their choice of writing medium, for even unbaked tablets of clay can last intact in the ground for millennia.

(The fortunate archaeologist who finds tablets on his excavation will encounter them wet to the touch if they are unbaked, but they will harden sufficiently in the warm, open air to be safely entrusted to the impatient epigrapher within a day or two. It is exciting beyond words to find one of these things actually in the ground, to harvest it like a potato and read it for the first time.)

This survival factor means that the widest spread of documents survives, state and private, much of it ephemeral and never intended for eternity. Startlingly, most of the cuneiform tablets ever written – if not deliberately destroyed in antiquity and not as yet excavated – still wait for us in the ground of Iraq: all we have to do is dig them up one day, and read them.

Digging actually started in the 1840s, and cuneiform tablets were soon forthcoming in great number, long before anyone could understand them. The motive behind the first expeditions was to excavate in the territory where the events of the Bible had been enacted, with the principal idea of substantiating Holy Writ. Excavations were carried out under permit from the Turkish Administration which at that time provided for the export of the finds to London. It was this reality that led to the decipherment of Akkadian cuneiform and the development of the field of Assyriology. To any right-thinking individual the decipherment of cuneiform must rank among the great intellectual achievements of humanity and, in my view, should be commemorated on postage stamps and fridge magnets. The decipherment was only possible, much as with Egyptian hieroglyphs, with the help of parallel inscriptions in more than one language. Just as the Greek translation on the Rosetta Stone allowed pioneer Egyptologists to unlock the version in Egyptian hieroglyphs, so an Old Persian cuneiform inscription at Bisutun in Iran enabled contemporary Babylonian cuneiform of around 500 BC, to be, gradually, understood. This was because the old Persian text was accompanied by a translation into Babylonian. In both cases the spelling of royal names, Cleopatra and Ptolemy in Egyptian, Dariawush (Darius) in Babylonian, provided the first glimmerings of understanding of how these ancient, essentially syllabic sign systems worked.

Without some bilingual prompt of this kind, cuneiform would probably have remained impenetrable for ever. The first identified cuneiform signs, *da-*, *ri-* and so forth, coupled with the suspicion that Babylonian might be a Semitic tongue, meant that decipherment found itself on the right track from early on, and progress followed comparatively rapidly. Crucial brainboxes here were

Georg Grotefend (1775–1853) and Henry Creswicke Rawlinson (1864–1925) for the Old Persian version, and, most importantly, the Irish clergyman Edward Hincks (1792–1866), an unsung genius if ever there was one, who, marvellously, took up cuneiform studies in the hope that they would aid him in his serious work on Egyptian hieroglyphs. Hincks was the first person in the modern world to understand the nature and complexities of Babylonian cuneiform. One persistent cause of confusion was how to tell the difference between Sumerian and Akkadian since they were both written in one and the same script. Some scholars still believed right into the twentieth century that Sumerian was not a real language at all, but a sort of code made up by the scribes. There *were* cuneiform codes, as a matter of fact, but Sumerian was not one of them. Today we have full sign lists, advanced grammars and weighty dictionaries to help us read ancient Babylonian, and similar resources for Sumerian. With these extraordinary advantages created by generations of heroic scholars it is now possible to read the *Ark Tablet* and quite comfortably translate it into English.

The venerable culture of this antique land is something extraordinary, the contributions of which to the modern world often go unnoticed. Every thinking child, for example, has at one time or another asked why minutes and hours are divided into *sixtieths* of all things instead of sensible tens, and why, worse yet, circles are divided into *three hundred and sixtieths*. The reason is the Mesopotamian preference for sexagesimal mathematics, which developed with the dawn of writing and persisted unthreatened by decimal counting. Counting in sixties was transmitted from Mesopotamians to us by serious-minded Greek mathematicians, who encountered Babylon and its records, thoroughly sexagesimal, still alive at the end of the first millennium BC, spotted their potential and promptly recycled them; the consequence is celebrated on everybody's wrist today. Mesopotamia's place on the archaeologist's roll of honour will always be high: out of the ground have come the wheel and pottery, cities and palaces, bronze and gold, art and sculpture. But writing changed everything.

From the earliest times, well before 3000 BC, nomads came to settle in Mesopotamia, attracted by abundance and blending amicably into the resident populations. Some of the newcomers spoke an early form of Akkadian, which, in its Assyrian and Babylonian forms, was to co-exist with Sumerian for more than a millennium until the latter subsided into a purely 'bookish' role, much like Latin in the Middle Ages. Akkadian survived as Mesopotamia's main spoken language altogether for a good three thousand years, evolving as any language must over such a long period, until it was eventually knocked out for good by another Semitic tongue, Aramaic, at the end of the first millennium BC. By the second century AD, as the Pax Romana, or 'Roman peace,' prevailed and Hadrian was planning his wall, the last readers and writers of cuneiform were dying in Mesopotamia, and their distinguished and hallowed script became finally extinct until it was so brilliantly deciphered in the nineteenth century AD.

Third-millennium Sumerian culture had seen the rise of powerful city-states that lived in uneasy collaboration; it took the political abilities of Sargon I, king of Akkad, in about 2300 BC to develop (to the delight of later historians) the first empire in history, stretching far beyond Mesopotamia proper into modern-day Iran, Asia Minor and Syria. His capital, Akkad, probably somewhere near the city of Babylon, gave rise to our modern term for his language and culture, Akkadian.

The break-up of Sargon's empire saw a Sumerian renaissance and the rise to prominence of the city of Ur, famous especially as the birthplace of Abraham. Here a succession of powerful kings like Naram-Sin, or Shulgi supported empires and trading of their own in about 2000 BC without ignoring the claims of music, literature and art, and even boasting of their accomplishments as literati, musicians and men of culture.

Incursions of Semitic Amorite speakers from the west of Mesopotamia proper ushered in a succession of new dynasties, so power came to relocate from the city of Isin to nearby Larsa and ultimately to Babylon, where Hammurabi set up his iconic law-code in the eighteenth century BC, quoted in the previous chapter. The northern 'Iraqi' territory meanwhile saw Assyria establish her own far-flung empire. Assyrian armies, undeterred by hardship, hunted new terrain and tribute, with a string of famous kings like Sargon II, or Byron's Sennacherib – the wolf on the fold – and Great Librarian Ashurbanipal. Babylon, rid of invader Kassites, could ultimately collaborate with the Medes in the East to destroy Assyria for ever; the fateful destruction of Nineveh in 612 BC changed the world for ever and paved the way for the Neo-Babylonian Empire under Nabopolassar and Nebuchadnezzar the Magnificent, the latter of whom plays an important role in this book. Nabonidus, the last native Mesopotamian king, lost his throne to Cyrus the Achaemenid in 539, and then came Alexander, the Seleucid kings and, ultimately, the end of the ancient Mesopotamian world.

*

Once the script had achieved maturity and grown beyond book-keeping, writing was applied with increasing liberality and inventiveness. Key dictionary texts from the early third millennium BC were soon followed by the first Sumerian narrative literature and royal inscriptions; by the closing decades of that millennium private letters accompany the unrelenting flow of administrative record-keeping. Semitic Akkadian texts remain rare before 2000 BC, but before long comes a richer literature in both Sumerian and Akkadian, with the first magical and medical texts and a wide sweep of omen or fortune-telling documents, and an increasing waterfall of economic and official documents, themselves now put in context by codified sets of laws.

We can be sure that from very remote times favourite narratives about gods and men were transmitted orally, but after 2000 BC such works were increasingly committed to writing. As the old Sumerian tongue became hazy or obscure, many classical

texts came to be translated word for word into Akkadian with
the help of the lexical texts. Bilingual or two-language versions
of hymns, spells and stories led the most gifted ancient scholars
in the peace of their academies to undertake sophisticated grammatical studies in which the linguistically unrelated Sumerian
and Akkadian were analytically compared. Some of the most
revealing texts are round, currant-bun school exercises from Old
Babylonian times, which give an open window on the curriculum
that was designed to instil cuneiform literacy and ability in practical mathematics, offering us at the same time a glimpse of
uncommitted pupils and the liberal use of the stick.

Archives of merchant or banking families are often scattered
far and wide due to 'informal' excavation in the nineteenth
century, but working in collaboration, scholars today can recon-
struct awe-inspiring details of marriages, births, deaths and the
price of goods in the market. Those record-keepers would be
utterly astonished if they knew what we get up to today. In the
first millennium we even have, most wonderful of all, cuneiform
libraries, where orderly housekeeping by real librarians meant
that tablets were stored on end in alcoves according to the system.
As both Babylonian language and script began to wind down in
some quarters at the end of the first millennium BC, disciplines
such as astrology and astronomy generated increasingly complex
literature in traditional wedge-shaped form.

Cuneiform tablets that are so precious to us now were usually
just dumped in antiquity or recycled as building fill; only seldom
are they discovered nicely sealed in a datable destruction level
for the benefit of the archaeologist. Tablets in general become
more plentiful with the passage of time, but Assyriological assess-
ments of distribution or rarity are seldom significant; data usually
reflect nothing more than the accident of survival.

The most famous cuneiform library belonged to Assurbanipal
(668–627 BC), the last great king of Assyria, who had a bookish
mind. The royal librarian was always on the hunt for old and new
tablets for his state-of-the-art Royal Library at Nineveh; his plan

was to collect the entire inherited resources. His holdings, now the pride and joy of the British Museum tablet collection, were one of the real wonders of antiquity (far surpassing *gardens* or *lighthouses*), and we can still read Assurbanipal's written orders to certain 'literary' agents who were despatched down south to Babylonia to borrow, purloin or simply commandeer anything interesting that was not already included on the royal shelves:

Order of the king to Shadunu: I am well – let your heart be at ease!

The day you read (this) my tablet, get hold of Shumaya son of Shuma-ukin, Bel-etir, his brother, Aplaya, son of Arkat-ili and the scholars from Borsippa whom you know and collect whatever tablets are in their houses, and whatever tablets as are stored in the temple Ezida; tablets (including): those for amulets for the king; those for the purifying rivers for Nisannu [month I]; the amulet for the rivers for the month Tashritu [month VII]; for the House-of-Water-Sprinkling (ritual); the amulet concerning the rivers of the Sun's decisions; four amulets for the head of the king's bed and the feet of the king's bed; the Cedar Weapon for the head of the king's bed; the incantation 'May Ea and Asalluhi combine their collected wisdom'; the series 'Battle', whatever there might be, together with their extra, single-column tablets; for 'No arrow should come near a man in battle'; 'Walking in Open Country', 'Entering the Palace', the instructions for 'Hand-Lifting'; the inscriptions for stones and . . . which are good for the kingship; 'Purification of a Village'; 'Giddiness', 'Out of Concern', and whatever is needed for the Palace, whatever there is, and rare tablets that are known to you do not exist in Assyria. Search them out and bring them to me! I have just written to the temple-steward and the governor; in the houses where you set your hand no one can withhold a tablet from you! And, should you find any tablet or ritual instruction that I have not written to you about that is good for the Palace, take that as well and send it to me.

The king regarded Babylonian handwriting with disfavour, and so a roomful of trained calligraphers at the capital worked around the clock to produce perfect Assyrian copies of the incoming acquisitions for him. In time the Nineveh libraries grew to contain the richest tablet resources ever put together under one Mesopotamian roof, anticipating, in some measure, the ideas behind the library at Alexandria.

What it would be to spend a week in Assurbanipal's library! The prime fantasy element for the cuneiform reader is that all the individual documents and multi-tablet compositions would have been *complete on the shelves*; *Gilgamesh I–XII* all in a row: none of the library tablets would have been tolerated in broken condition, and, if something untoward happened, they would be recopied. Everything was available in full. This is truly the stuff of dreams, for it is seldom indeed that a perfect cuneiform tablet comes to light, and Assyriologists are conditioned to live with broken fragments and damaged signs, never 'knowing the end of the story'. In Assurbanipal's day scholars who wanted to talk over the interpretation of a thorny phrase occurring in a letter to the king about some ominous occurrence could pull down from the shelves (1) the standard version – *complete*; (2) a variant edition from Babylon or Uruk in the south – *complete*; (3) a highly 'unorthodox' or provincial version from some obscure place that still ought to be consulted – *complete*; and (4) any number of explanatory commentaries, where learned diviners had already recorded their own bright ideas which might bring insight – *complete*. Perhaps they might also have to hand some really venerable tablet, valued even if fragmentary and accorded special care, although the administrators would always be on the lookout for a better copy. Today we can muster bits of all this range of library writings, and it takes a huge leap of imagination to envisage a situation where the only problem for a tablet reader might be to understand the sense of the signs or the meaning of the words. The king's effort at completion in assembling top-quality clay manuscripts meant that the first resources seen by Western decipherers in the middle of the nineteenth century were both the fullest and most easily legible of any that could possibly have been dug up for them.

Nineveh's destruction in 612 BC at the hands of the Medes and Babylonians saw the palatial buildings sacked and burnt, but fire to a clay librarian was not the disaster that it was to Eratosthenes, the keeper of the scrolls. When Assurbanipal's tablets were discovered in the nineteenth century, as deliciously described by Henry Layard, the thousands of broken pieces were mostly in fine condition, fired to crisp terracotta, awaiting decipherment and 're-joining' by generations of patient Assyriologists over the centuries to come. Fortunately many of Assurbanipal's literary treasures existed in several duplicating copies, so that today the wording can sometimes be recovered in full even when none of the source tablets is itself complete. It was this library that contained the Assyrian pieces of *Atrahasīs* and the *Epic of Gilgamesh*, which George Smith was the first to identify and translate.

*

Given what lies in the world's museums and collections it will be a long time before there is a shortage of cuneiform material to work on and there is always a shortage of workers. In the nineteenth century, after decipherment had been achieved, standards for scholarship were set very high. The true giants – usually hothouse trained in Germany – knew their Latin, Greek, Hebrew, Arabic, Coptic, Ethiopic, Syriac and Aramaic before they even *looked* at Babylonian. On top of that they stood tall in other ways and it is astonishing how fast-acquired and deep was their understanding. When I first started work at Chicago in 1976 Erica Reiner, then editor of the *Chicago Assyrian Dictionary*, mentioned one day that her predecessors Benno Landsberger and Leo Oppenheim (later examples of these giants) had both read every cuneiform text published since it all began in 1850 (and, what is more, remembered every line). Today, when cuneiform books, articles and texts are published uninterruptedly, this feat would be beyond anyone's abilities. One consequence of this is that modern scholars tend to limit themselves to one or other language and one or other period with increasingly narrowing perspectives. In Lambert's classroom this nail-buffing, *I-am-a-specialist* idea that we sometimes encountered in visiting scholars was heavily frowned upon and later subjected to derision, for a *real* cuneiformist was expected to read anything and everything in either language, and quickly too. This model stood me in good stead when I got to the British Museum, for that is what has to be done.

And what is it all? I think it is beneficial to see our roomfuls of cuneiform documents at large as falling into five loose categories: *official* (state, king, government, law), *private* (contracts, inheritance, sales, letters), *literary* (myths, epics, stories, hymns, prayers), *reference* (sign lists, dictionaries and mathematical tables) and *intellectual* (magic, medicine, omens, mathematics, astronomy, astrology, grammar and exegesis).

Each single tablet, to a greater or lesser extent, contributes information. Some, like the *Ark Tablet* which is central to this book, offer something astonishing with almost every line of text, others find their niche as part of a broad study, or contribute no more than a couple of signs that can, once in a while, settle a textual debate that has continued for a century. Reading a tablet satisfactorily is like squeezing a bath sponge; the more determined the grip the greater the yield. It is always exciting to get the sense of a cuneiform inscription from so long ago, even when you do it every day; each surviving message is, frankly, miraculous. To paraphrase Dr Johnson, he who is tired of tablets is tired of life.

I have been happily reading cuneiform tablets every day now for about forty-five years. (As Arlo Guthrie would say: I'm not proud. Or tired. I could read them for another forty-five years.) During such prolonged exposure an impression gradually but unavoidably begins to take shape about the long-dead individuals who actually wrote these documents. We can handle their handiwork and read their words and ideas, but, I find myself asking, can one grasp at identity within these crowds of ghostly people for whom, as the poet put it, 'dust was their sustenance and clay their food?' The question finally crystallises into a single, and I think important, problem: *were ancient Mesopotamians like us or not?*

Scholars and historians like to stress the remoteness of ancient culture, and there is an unspoken consensus that the greater the distance from us in time the scanter the traces of recognisable kinship; my elementary school question is usually avoided altogether. As a result of this outlook the past comes to confer a sort of 'cardboardisation' on our predecessors, whose rigidity increases exponentially in jumps the further back you go in time. As a result the Victorians would seem to have lived exclusively in a flurry about sexual intercourse; the Romans worried all day about toilets and under-floor heating, and the Egyptians walked about in profile with their hands in front of them pondering funerary arrangements, the ultimate men of cardboard. And before all these were the cavemen, grunting or painting, reminiscing wistfully about life back up in the trees. As a result of this tacit process Antiquity, and to some extent all pre-modern time, is led to populate itself with shallow and spineless puppets, denuded of complexity or corruption and all the other characteristics that we take for granted in our fellow man, which we comfortably describe as 'human'. It is easiest and perhaps also comforting to believe that we, now, are the *real* human beings, and those who came before us were less advanced, less evolved and very probably less intelligent; they were certainly not individuals whom we would recognise, in different garb, as typical passengers on the bus home.

After decades among the tablets I have become very doubtful that this wall of detachment from individuals who come out of the past is appropriate. We are, for one thing, talking only of the last five thousand years, a mere *dollop* in Time terms, in which snail processes like evolution or biological development have no measurable part. Nebuchadnezzar II ruled at Babylon from 605–562 BC, ascending to the throne 2,618 years before this book was brought into being.

*

How can one actually visualise that interval of time clearly in order to bring the ancient king closer? If thirty-five individuals in a line live for seventy-five years each in historical sequence, the result is a straight run of 2,625 years. Thus a chain like a cinema queue of no more than thirty-five cradle-to grave lives divides us from people who lived and breathed when Nebuchadnezzar was king. This is not, after all, unimaginable remoteness in time past. And we can hardly flatter ourselves that 'we' are any more intelligent than, say, Babylonians who practised mathematical astronomy for a living. There were Mesopotamian geniuses and Mesopotamian numbskulls walking about at the same time.

This issue, whether ancient writers can be accessible and familiar as human beings, affects very seriously how we interpret their writings. I am reluctant to settle for the faraway and unattainable nature of the ancient Mesopotamian mind, the remoteness of which has often been stressed, particularly with regard to religion. In my view humankind shares a common form of starting 'software' which is merely given a veneer by local characteristics and traditions, and I argue that this applies to the ancient populations of the Middle East exactly as it does to the world today. The environment in which an individual exists will contribute formative, possibly dominating pressures; the more enclosed the community the more conformist the individual will be, but, evaluated from a broad perspective, such differences are largely cosmetic, social and in some sense superficial. Take *Pride and Prejudice*. In their outer wrapping, the characters within it do look a bit odd from a very contemporary perspective, with their social mannerisms, codes of behaviour and religious practice, but their *motives, behaviour and humanity* are in every way familiar. So it must be as one vaults backwards in time, and so it is with Shakespeare and Chaucer, and the Vindolanda tablets in demotic Latin, and Aristophanes, and there we are, BC *already*. One species in myriad disguises. In my estimation the old cuneiform writers have to be inspected with the right end of the telescope, the one that brings them *closer*.

If tablet writings are to provide an answer to the question of how accessible Mesopotamians were, it must be granted, of course, that they will always give incomplete information. Far from everyone had a voice. And then a high proportion of our cuneiform documents are official, formulaic and hidebound by tradition, rarely innovative and often manipulative. Assyrian military campaigns, for example, are portrayed on stately prisms of clay as a matter of unimpeded triumph, with huge booty and minimal loss of Assyrian life; such accounts require the same necessary reading between the lines that historians must apply to modern journalism.

The most informative documents will be those of the everyday world, which ought to be impulsive, informal and unselfconscious in comparison. There are two cuneiform categories among these which are undoubtedly the most helpful from this point of view: *letters* and *proverbs*.

Huge numbers of private letters survive, for they come in a particularly durable, fit-in-the-hand size and are not as readily broken as larger tablets. These letters, often exchanged by merchants who were irritated with one another about slow delivery or overdue payment, sometimes allow us to eavesdrop. Flattery – (*I am so worried about you!*) alternates with irony – (*Are you not my brother?*) – spiced with wheedling or threats, and the timeless claim that the letter is in the post occurs endlessly – *I have already sent you my tablet!*

Letters can give us a remarkable picture of people going about their lives, preoccupied with 'money' and mortgages, worried about business, sickness or the lack of a son. From our over-the-shoulder vantage point can come a moment of closeness to an individual, or a sense of fellowship with the harassed – or crafty – person 'at the other end'.

How did cuneiform letters function? The operation was cumbersome and of a slower-paced world. Letters despatched to colleague or foe usually went to a different town as otherwise it would have been simpler to go and talk. The message had to be dictated to a trained scribe, carried from A to B, and read aloud by the recipient's own scribe when it finally arrived. This is explicit from the words that open almost every example: 'To So-and-so speak! Thus says So-and-so . . .' and in the actual Akkadian word for letter, *unedukku*, loaned from the Sumerian u-ne-dug, 'say to him!' Since fluent letter dictation is beyond most people today I think we must imagine a merchant starting off, 'Tell that cheat . . .'; *no, wait a minute*; 'May the Sun God bless you etc. – *ha! curse more like . . . o.k. o.k.; here we go*: When I saw your tablet . . .' The scribe, experienced and patient on a stool, would jot down the main points as they emerged and then produce a finished letter on a proper-looking tablet. Outside on a wall it would dry in the warm air, and then go into a runner's 'post-bag' for delivery.

The sender knows the background: usually we don't. He gets his answer: again, usually we don't.

Those who read other people's correspondence must harvest everything possible: spelling, word forms, grammar and idiom, sign use and handwriting. Squeezing the sponge involves more than the extraction of clear facts; also crucial is inferring, with varying degrees of probability, a good deal more: What led to the letter; what light might it throw on trade, social conditions, crime and immorality, not to mention the person of the writer himself? Such inferences derive from knowledge of contemporary documents seasoned with common sense.

There is an additional useful factor, the Sherlock Holmes principle that, we are told, he wrote up in a magazine called *The Book of Life*:

> *'From a drop of water', said the writer, 'a logician could infer the possibility of an Atlantic or a Niagara without having seen or heard of one or the other.'*
>
> A. Conan Doyle, *A Study in Scarlet*

In my experience, this Niagara principle is of considerable value to the practising Assyriologist. A good case of this is Babylonian surgery. References to surgical practice of any kind are rare in the medical texts. Cataracts were dealt with using a knife and there is a text where infection is released from the chest cavity by some kind of inter-rib incision. But, in comparison with Egyptian medicine across the sands where the Edwin Smith surgical papyrus gives astonishing procedural treatments for injuries and wounds, Babylonian doctors do not measure up. This seems curious. The mighty Assyrian army was constantly in the field. A deterrent clause in an Assyrian political treaty focuses on the reality of battle wounds, with a glimpse of emergency treatment, possibly even self-applied: *If your enemy stabs you, let there be a lack of honey, oil, ginger or cedar resin to apply to your wounds!*

Over the centuries there must have been a very considerable inherited, practical, medical field knowledge: staunching of blood loss, extracting arrows, stitching wounds, and emergency amputations with hot pitch; also important was judging whether a wounded soldier was even worth the saving; all this *stands to reason.* None of our known therapeutic texts sheds light on this, however. So we have to assume either that all medical lore in the army was transmitted, hands-on from expert to tyro, without recourse to written form, or that no such text happens to have come to light. In my understanding it is the second explanation which is true.

Going back to the Niagara principle, an important scribe in the Assyrian capital at Assur once drew up a catalogue of medical compositions available in a library there. He included a section with the following tantalisingly incomplete titles, quoted by their first line:

> *If a man, whether by sword or slingstone . . .*

> *If a man . . . in front of a ship.*

These lost tablets must have dealt not with diseases or demons but, compellingly, with injuries: military, industrial or caused by

45

a goring ox. They give us a glimpse of what was once written down about Mesopotamian wounds, just as happened in ancient Egypt. One day I shall find those tablets.

The richest 'fellow man' vein of writing to pursue is cuneiform proverbs and wisdom literature, some of which go back, surprisingly, into the third millennium BC, and which are a staple of the scribal schools. The Sumerians made use of a device that tends to make right-thinking youths wriggle with impatience:

> *In those days, in those remote days,*
> *In those nights, in those faraway nights,*
> *In those years, in those far remote years,*
> *In those days, the intelligent one, the one of elaborate words,*
> * the wise one, who lived in the country,*
> *The Man from Shuruppak, the intelligent one, the one of*
> * elaborate words, the wise one, who lived in the country,*
> *The Man from Shuruppak, gave instruction to his son –*
> *The Man from Shuruppak, the son of Ubartutu – gave*
> * instructions to his son Ziusudra:*
> * "My son, let me give instructions; let my instructions be*
> *   taken!*
> * Ziusudra, let me speak a word to you; let attention be paid*
> *   to them!*
> * Don't neglect my instructions!*
> * Don't transgress the words I speak!*
> * The instructions of an old man are precious; you should*
> *   comply with them . . ."*

The *Man from Shuruppak* was ruler of the last city before the Flood, and he is addressing his son Ziusudra, the *Sumerian equivalent of Noah in the Bible* (as we will see later!), who built the life-saving ark and obtained eternal life for himself. The instructions that follow are nothing to do with arks or shipbuildings, however, but are precepts from an agricultural culture that promote a kind of ethics that Bendt Alster, the translator, called '"modest egoism" that is, don't do anything to others that may provoke them to retaliate against you'. This was a much-valued composition; the first texts appeared around the middle of the third millennium BC, and it was still being read in first-millennium Assyria and Babylonia, with the benefit of an Akkadian translation which is equally useful for us.

Proverbs, and the wisdom literature that derives from them, thus come in both Sumerian and Akkadian, and pithy, sardonic and cynical *mots* seem to flow naturally in Sumerian. 'Don't laugh with a girl if she is married: slander is powerful' is a rueful example. The word for 'virgin', *kiskilla*, literally means 'pure place', and girls at the beginning of history were most definitely supposed to be a virgin on marriage. One Babylonian roué, arraigned before a judge in about 1800 BC, testified, *I swear that I did not have intercourse with her, that my penis did not enter her vagina*; not, one reflects, the last time someone has got off on that technicality. Mesopotamians were always fearful of slander; it was one of their *things*, and they called it 'evil finger-pointing in the street', but victims could always toss painted clay tongues inscribed with power words into the river as a remedy. King Esarhaddon himself once reflected in a seventh-century letter from Nineveh, 'The oral proverb says: "In court the word of a sinful woman prevails over her husband's"', while a classic of Babylonian wisdom literature advised, 'Do not love, sir, do not love. Woman is a pitfall – a pitfall, a hole, a ditch. Woman is a sharp iron dagger that cuts a man's throat.' One can pass a pleasant hour reflecting on such statements.

What do we know about the scribes themselves?

Unfortunately, not a great deal is known about the scribes themselves. At all periods they were almost invariably male. It is likely that there were scribal families, and that access to formal schooling was limited to such circles. To become a scribe in Mesopotamia required exhaustive training, as we can see from lots of surviving old clay schoolbooks, especially from the Old and Neo-Babylonian periods, about 1700 BC and 500 BC. There is even an entertaining cycle of stories in Sumerian about what happened in the classroom, as much fun to read now as they must have been originally. Making a proper tablet (which is not so simple!) was followed by a strict diet of wedges, signs, proper names, dictionary texts, literature, maths, spelling and model contracts. This training gave a scribal family boy his basic grounding. At this stage he could technically spell and write whatever he wanted, and perhaps the majority would find work as commercial scribes, sitting at the city gate and taking on all comers who needed a bit of writing done when they were selling some land or marrying off a daughter. 'Graduate' students, in turn, would specialise in their chosen field; an apprentice architect would study advanced maths, weight systems (also not so simple!) and how to make things stay up once they were put up, while novice diviners would learn to expound each corner and wrinkle of a diseased sheep's liver. Very often, it seems, such 'professionals' were sworn to secrecy in the process.

Small notations bring the Mesopotamian *ṭupšarru*, or 'tablet writer', even closer. Library and scientific texts sometimes have a line along the top edge in easy-to-miss, minute writing: 'At the word of My Lord and My Lady may this go well!' Such an utterance – for it was probably muttered more than once under the breath as well as inscribed – is very understandable, for cuneiform mistakes had consequences: clay is an unforgiving medium and invisible correction almost impossible. Many a time a scribe, checking over his work, must have sighed wearily and started another tablet; erasures and errors that come through are, generally speaking, conspicuously uncommon. Sometimes, however, a whole line gets omitted, the scribe making a diminutive 'x' mark to indicate the point of omission and writing out the lost signs down the side from a point with another 'x'. To avoid this problem, long or elaborate documents often marked every tenth line at the left side with a small 'ten' sign, confirmed by a line total at the end, since it was as easy for a Babylonian eye to jump a line as it is for a modern copy-typist's and checking aids were very helpful. Sometimes a worried scribe records that he has not seen all the text, or makes a note in similar tiny cuneiform signs to show that the tablet he was copying was broken. There are two degrees: *hepi* (it-was-broken), and *hepi eššu* (a new it-was-broken). In principle the system worked like this. The scribe Aqra-lumur, seated in some institution, is copying out the text of an important tablet. There is a damaged passage that he cannot read with certainty, so he writes *hepi* (it-was-broken) where signs or wedges are abraded. The scribe who makes a copy of Aqra-lumur's tablet takes care to reproduce all cases where his predecessor wrote *hepi*. Thus is set in train a process of transmission whereby any number of scribes preserve as accurately as possible the situation first encountered by Aqra-lumur. Notations like this are revealing, for *hepi* (it-was-broken) is found in places where even we can tell what is missing, highlighting that the scribe's task was to transmit old texts found precisely,

Three generations of scribes record their efforts to transmit an ancient and extremely damaged cuneiform tablet, recording their own names and family names on the reverse.

without imposing himself or his ideas even when the restoration was self-evident. As this line of transmission proceeds it comes about that a subsequent tablet in the chain gets chipped or broken itself. This damage is, so-to-speak, new, and will be indicated by *hepi eššu* (a new it-was-broken). Literary texts often concluded with a colophon that recorded the source of the text and the scribe's name. With very venerable documents these successive colophons were all copied out, so a given tablet might have three of them, in chronological order.

This very sketchy scribal picture – for this is a big topic with sprawling evidence – leads to a separate question:

> *What was the level of literacy in society at large in, say, the first millennium* BC?

Nobody in ancient Mesopotamia ever stood on a street corner soap-box to advocate literacy for all, and, up until recently, Assyriologists have mostly taken it for granted that the ability to read and write was highly restricted in Mesopotamian society. (There is an attractive paradox in the construct of an age-old, highly literary culture in which hardly anyone at any particular time was in fact literate.) I have a suspicion that this evaluation derives ultimately from what King Assurbanipal had to say at home in seventh-century Nineveh. A special note at the end of many of his library tablets recorded boastfully that – unlike the kings who preceded him – he could even read inscriptions from *before* the Flood:

> *Marduk, the sage of the gods, gave me wide understanding and broad perceptions as a gift. Nabu, the scribe of the universe, bestowed on me the acquisition of all his wisdom as a present. Ninurta and Nergal gave me physical fitness, manhood and unparalleled strength. I learnt the lore of the wise sage Adapa, the hidden secret, the whole of the scribal craft. I can discern celestial and terrestrial portents and deliberate in the assembly*

of the experts. I am able to discuss the series 'If the Liver is the Mirror Image of the Sky' with capable scholars. I can solve convoluted reciprocals and calculations that do not come out evenly. I have read cunningly written text in Sumerian, dark Akkadian, the interpretation of which is difficult. I have examined stone inscriptions from before the flood, which are sealed, stopped up, mixed up.

We know, in fact, that Assurbanipal *was* literate, for nostalgically he kept some of his own school texts, but is it justified to conclude from this statement that Assyrian kings otherwise were completely illiterate? For me it is impossible to credit that mighty Sennacherib, accompanying foreign potentates through the halls of his Nineveh Palace where the sculptures were inscribed with his name and achievements, would have been unable to explain a cluster of cuneiform signs on demand. Surely any king worth the name, pulled this way and that by advisors, technicians, diviners and what have you, would need, if only for self-protection, some cuneiform know-how? An educated monarch, moreover, would not do his own writing; there were staff to do all that. But there has been a direct overspill from Assurbanipal's literary boast: And if kings were usually illiterate, how much more so the great unwashed?

This limited-literacy idea is probably compounded by the nature of the cuneiform discipline itself. Assyriologists today have to master absolute shelves of words, grammar and signs. Those who survive indoctrination often feel that the ability to read cuneiform can never be taken for granted in anyone else, *including the ancients*. It is easy, however, to forget that in ancient Mesopotamia everyone already knew (a) the words and (b) the grammar of their own language, even if they were unaware that they knew such things. This left only the cuneiform signs to be mastered. The truth, as has been seen in more recent books, must be that many people knew how to read to some level, or, rather, to the level that they needed. Merchants were in charge of their own book-keeping; some son or nephew had to record all the contracts and loans, and commerce is a great motivator to book learning. It is inconceivable to me that all cuneiform writing was constrained in a professional, those-who-need-to-know box. The real situation to be envisaged is that within a large city there must have been very different levels of literacy. Very few individuals can ever have known all the rarest signs in the sign lists together with all their possible readings, but the number of signs needed to write a contract or a letter was, in comparison, very restricted; some 112 syllable signs and 57 ideograms to write Old Babylonian documents, while Old Assyrian merchants (or their wives) needed even less. Similarly modest was the range of signs needed to inscribe the palace walls of the Assyrians with triumphant accounts of conquest. A parallel might derive from facility in typing in the 1960s. Anyone could type with two fingers but few such people would have called themselves a typist; certificated professionals at the other end of the spectrum who could do dazzling hundreds of words a minute most proudly would, while in between there was a wide range of ability. So it might well have been with sign recognition, many people having a 'little bit' of writing. Probably lots of people knew signs that could spell their own name, as well as those for god, king and Babylon; these were, after all, used everywhere. Letter writers and contract drafters knew what they needed to know, professional men a good deal more, and so forth.

Gods

Mesopotamian gods were everywhere, in sheer number beyond the mastery of all but the most learned of theologians, and man interacted with them, felt confident of their mercy or was needlessly punished by them throughout life. Such a profusion of gods drove the theologians to sort them out; god lists became a major strand of lexical endeavour, and there was a would-be tidiness about it all; small gods were identified or amalgamated with similar ones, or given domestic responsibilities within the household of their seniors.

Literature that touches the divine is abundant: hymns, prayers and litanies, rituals and other temple documents, as well as lists of gods or their sacrificial dues. Many of these, from our point of view, concern *religious* matters, although there was no ancient Sumerian or Babylonian word for 'religion' in today's sense, and man's relationship with the gods affected most aspects of his daily life.

Scholars often find themselves explaining how hard it is to write religious history from cuneiform sources. One reason is the great length of time that is involved, some three thousand years of inscriptions; another is the imbalance in what survives. For some periods there is rather too much evidence, such as thousands of detailed day-to-day Sumerian temple records; for others there is hardly a thing, or manuscripts might be broken, or obscure. Generally speaking, too, we know far more about 'state' or 'official' religion at all periods than about the private belief of individuals. Evidence about religion comes from official monuments and the pious statements of kings, from temple records of ritual and cult, from the incantations and prayers of healers and the esoteric writings of diviners and astrologers. The background to all this is supplied by myths and epics which show the gods in action. The religious calendar wound its way through the year with a network of traditional offerings, recitations and pious activity. When everything was in order and the powerful gods were content, they were to be found in residence in their temples, housed in the cult statues to which the priests attended. Divine anger or displeasure could cause a god such as Marduk to depart from his 'house', the consequences of which were breakdown and disaster. The theft of a cult-statue by an enemy, therefore, was cause for protracted mourning: absence of the statue meant the absence of the god himself. While the congregation of deities was too numerous and often too obscure to have been familiar to any but the most learned divines, everyone had heard of the main gods, and private individuals could feel that the particular god or goddess to whom they had been consecrated at birth looked out for them and was 'there in the background', to see to protection during life. There was, undeniably, something of the business contract underlying this arrangement, which was naturally found to be far from fail-safe. A good individual who fulfilled his obligations should feel confident that he would not fall sick at the hand of demons any more than his business would fail or his flocks fail to reproduce. Poetic incantation literature in the *What-have-I-done-now?* mould suggests a sense of betrayal in suffering, although it was conceded that man could transgress a taboo unwittingly and still be punished for it. Human sorcery was a parallel source of danger, and fear of that and dealing with it are common topics.

Some Mesopotamian gods and goddesses had held sway since the third millennium BC, and all had their level of status and characteristic 'strong points'. The most elevated were attached to the main cities – Enlil to the city of Nippur, or Sin the Moon God to the city of Ur, Abraham's birthplace – while small towns and villages likewise had their 'own' local god or goddess. Many native gods survived the transition from Sumerian to Semitic consciousness with no difficulty, sometimes blending one into another, as when the Sumerian Inanna, goddess of love and war, came to be 'identified' with Ishtar. This process, which allowed the two entities to exist on one level side by side, had the effect of moulding them, at least by the end of the second millennium BC, into what was really one multi-faceted deity, although both names remained in use. Descriptions of individual gods and epithets and achievements which were specific or exclusive to that individual are often hard to trace. The ancient gods and goddesses of Mesopotamia, like their counterparts elsewhere, were modelled on the human race: they were unpredictable, wilful, inscrutable, unreliable and often indulgent, and much of man's attempts to communicate with them took account of such factors in prayer, ritual and behaviour.

In all this time, as is to be expected, the status of the important gods could change and evolve, often due to political circumstances. Marduk was only a little-known god when King Hammurabi first established Babylon as his capital and began his dynasty, more than a millennium before the time of Nebuchadnezzar II. This process was to propel Marduk, god of city and state, into ever-increasing prominence.

Kings professed themselves constantly under the umbrella of divine protection from the most powerful gods, but it is usually impossible to grasp the nature of their own private belief under the wording. It is improbable, too, that the majority of soldiers, merchants and farmers knew a great deal about the gods at large, for the mass of theological data known to us reflects a very minor and closed-in side of religious life in general. In villages one local god and his plump consort would likely feature to the exclusion of most others, but inner religious thoughts or reflections of individuals never made it onto clay. In the large cities things were, at least outwardly, different. Public processions and festivals brought people into closer contact with the gods in statue form or through the annual cycle of their sacred lives, even if the spiritual heart of such activity was carried out in camera. Shrines with images were to be found at city street corners. Large temples must have been refuges for people in need as well as in piety, and cheap clay figures of the type to infuriate the Hebrew prophets were available from vendors who set up stall nearby large temples.

*

Certain 'hallmark' aspects of ancient Mesopotamian life recorded in cuneiform writings do not feature so centrally in other ancient cultures of which we are informed. Let us look at two or three.

1. *Omens: Predicting the Future*

Among such hallmark elements known to us from writings, the quintessential Mesopotamian preoccupation is the restless urge to predict the future. A good percentage of intellectual thought over the best part of three millennia was lavished on the desire to penetrate the veil, fuelled by the conviction that human beings could, everything being equal, obtain the needed information from the gods through well-established procedures. This field of activity generated a vast literature of carefully assembled one-line omens on this pattern:

If A happened, B will happen.

Here the sought-for outcome B, known as the *apodosis*, is deemed to be the consequence of an observed phenomenon, the *protasis* A. One example exemplifies how a diviner operated in about 1750 BC while examining the surface of a freshly extracted liver from a healthy sheep for diagnostic marks:

Protasis: *If there are three white pustules to the left of the gall bladder*
Apodosis: *the king will triumph over his enemy.*

Divination of this sort by animal entrails, especially the liver, was in place at least by the early third millennium BC and persisted unswervingly thereafter. The Sumerian king Shulgi, writing in about 2050 BC, was well up in techniques and responsibilities, and leaves his court diviner standing:

I am a ritually pure diviner,
I am Nintu of the written list of omens!
For the proper performance of the lustrations of the office of
  high priest,
For singing the praises of the high priestess and (their)
  selection for (residence in) the gipar
For the choosing of the Lumah and Nindingir priests by holy
  extispicy,
For (decision) to attack the south or strike the north,
For opening the storage of (battle) standards,
For the washing of lances in the "water of battle",

And for making wise decisions about rebel lands,
The (ominous) words of the gods are most precious, indeed!
After taking a propitious omen from a white lamb – an
   ominous animal –
At the place of questioning water and flour are libated;
I make ready the sheep with ritual words
And my diviner watches in amazement like a barbarian.
The ready sheep is placed in my hand, and I never confuse a
   favourable sign with an unfavourable one.

. . .

In the insides of a single sheep I, the king,
Can find the messages for the whole universe.

The diviner's importance, his range of procedures and the extent of his written resources increased as the centuries unrolled; omens were still vital enough when Alexander was at the gates of Babylon for the priests to forecast his death if he entered the city, correctly as it turned out. Omens could be derived from spontaneous events, such as a gecko falling from the ceiling into one's breakfast cereal, or solicited through deliberate procedure, such as releasing caged birds and watching the patterns they make in flight.

The favoured system, as in the quotation above, was examining the liver (hepatoscopy) or sometimes the other organs (extispicy) of a sacrificed sheep for diagnostic signs which had been left there for the informed expert by Shamash, the Sun God. The decision would be made from the observed phenomena, in strict order of priority according to the importance of the liver part.

Such predictive activities remained a royal prerogative throughout the second millennium BC, but with the arrival of the first millennium different types of divination came within the reach of private – although probably wealthy – individuals. Centuries of specialist celestial observations finally culminated under Greek influence, in personal, contemporary-sounding horoscopes.

The backdrop canvas for significant chance happenings was

nothing less than the whole of heaven and earth. Little in daily life was immune from possible ominous significance, and with truly dramatic phenomena, such as malformed animal and human foetuses, a major stream of literature developed to document all the possibilities.

In the first millennium BC a professional Mesopotamian diviner could take omens by interviewing the client's dead relatives (necromancy), analysing his spontaneous or provoked dreams (oneiromancy), observing the patterns from scattered flour (aleuromancy), incense-smoke (libanomancy) or oil on water (leconomancy), or by tossing stones (psephomancy) or knucklebones (astragalomancy) onto a prepared diagram; there were no doubt many other systems. By Alexander's time the streets of Babylon were probably awash with people who could tell you for a handful of *istaterranus* (as they called the Greek stater coin) via a dozen cunning systems whether you would soon be rich or your wife would produce a son.

The historical origin of the entire Mesopotamian prognostic system has been debated and often considered obscure, but in fact is probably simple and straightforward: a peculiar event on one occasion, such as the birth of a sheep with two heads, coincided with, say, noticeable success in the field of battle. A nuclear collection of carefully noted primary phenomena led in time to the flourishing of a kind of science, according to which there were always trackable markers to events that unfolded on many levels, so that the unusual accompanied by the memorable came to assume the nature of structured dogma: a recurrence of the same phenomenon would imply the same consequences. The core of the principal omen series – whatever the type – must, I think, derive from empirical observation; real occurrences were recorded with their apparent consequences. The desire to cover all eventualities led to major textual extensions in all directions, because analysing spotting on a sheep's gall bladder needed to cover number, colour and position so that a precise result could be forthcoming. In some cases the desire for complete coverage led to absurdity (a sheep with eleven heads) or even technical impossibility (a lunar eclipse at the wrong time of the month) and with all fortune-telling genres the unbridled multi-tablet outpourings of the first-millennium diviners would have astonished their second-millennium forebears.

OMENS – A NIAGARA CASE

In the Vorderasiatisches Museum in Berlin is a uniquely informative, malformed, diviner's *dogfish* in bronze.

The case of the ominous dogfish: a study in bronze.

The right flank shows two fins but the left only one, and it is inscribed with an omen derived from this deficiency and a date:

If a fish lacks a left fin (?) a foreign army will be destroyed.
The 12th year of Nebuchadnezzar, king of Babylon, son of Nabopolassar, king of Babylon.

To the Mesopotamian mind all abnormalities were ominous. Examples from the natural world, especially with misshapen foetuses, animal and human, were taken seriously and probably there was an obligation to report them to the capital, although we might expect that most people buried birth monstrosities of all kinds without a word and pretended they had never happened. Here a dogfish lacking a fin must have been dredged up in a canal at Babylon. The specimen itself would not survive for long, and, rather than pack it in salt, a scale model was produced in clay, and the cuneiform inscription added. We cannot as yet associate a military success with Nebuchadnezzar's twelfth year, but the pairing of abnormality and omen must date from that moment. The fish abnormality and the victory coincide, and the two are instructively bracketed together from then on. The whole was cast in bronze, producing an indestructible record of the abnormality and its event *vis-à-vis* prediction association. The bronze fish that resulted would be a wonderful teaching device for the Diviner's College.

This item is proffered as a fine case of the Niagara principle, whereby a single episode can imply a more widespread occurrence, for while it is at present unique I would infer that modelling abnormalities in bronze for reference was a regular practice on the grounds that, probably, there was a roomful somewhere in the Assyrian or Babylonian capitals of all manner of frightfulness done into metal for apprentices, later greeted with horror and melted down at once by conquering outsiders.

2. Magic and Medicine

Misfortune, sickness and disease were in the main attributed to demonic and supernatural forces, although human witches and malevolent practitioners were an additional threat. Incantations were available to combat most of these problems, either by staving them off or helping to exorcise them. Masters in such procedure called *āshipus* had the know-how to cope with everything from the overdue arrival of a baby to ensuring that a new tavern would turn a good profit. Their stock-in-trade of amulets, spells and rituals is known to us from a surprising number of magical tablets. Such healers worked side by side, and evidently in harmony, with a different group of specialists known as *asûs*, who were more expert in drugs, almost entirely plant-based, and therapeutic treatments.

Most of what we know about Babylonian medicine concerns what Tom Lehrer once lucidly referred to as the 'diseases of the rich'. Almost all of our sources and other relevant medical information originate in major cities such as Ashur or Nineveh in the north of ancient Iraq, or Uruk and Babylon in the south, where healers treated members of the court circle, the high administration and powerful merchant families, as is reflected in the complexity of their ritual and the elaborate and no doubt costly requirements of their *materia medica*. The poor and unimportant, or those who lived in the countryside, would hardly ever encounter the highbrow stream of curative activity as we know it from written tablets, although itinerant doctors and local midwives undoubtedly brought comfort to many, and knew what to do if there was anything that could be done.

Medical praxis in town at its fullest relied on a blend of amulet or incantation with the administration of drugs. Again one is entitled to demand what curative understanding lay behind two thousand years of cuneiform healing documents. The same plants were consistently used for the same condition, and the careful re-copying and collecting of hard-won knowledge into large, many-columned library tablets where all information was arranged in a head-to-foot sequence demands the concession from us that *Mesopotamian treatments were assuredly more beneficial than otherwise*. As Guido Majno put it, most human ailments are self-healing anyway, but there was undoubtedly far more to Babylonian medicine than that. Mesopotamians fled from investigating inside the human body but they knew a good deal from the internal workings of sheep (and disembowelled soldiers) and they were expert observers of exterior manifestations. A good healer would recognise recurrent conditions and know what would in time right itself and what in his drug

61

collection could help among all the astringents, balms, diuretics and emetics. Pharmacological plant knowledge was very extensive and carefully documented. The combination of *āšipu* and *asû* at the bedside of a worried chamberlain's daughter must have been very effective, with swirling incense and muttered imprecations in the shadowy room, a pricey amulet to be pinned at the bed head, and foul-tasting preparations mixed from unspeakable things in vials that went down with reluctance and no doubt came up again soon after.

I think, having been immersed in these fascinating texts for decades, that the ancient Mesopotamian system can be summed up as simultaneously instinctive and observation-based, with a solid underpinning of long-endorsed pharmacological samples, while at the same time a good part of the whole was, unwittingly, placebic. Among it all there was good stuff to learn from them, for the Hippocratic Greeks were by no means above incorporating Babylonian ideas in their new-cast treatises.

MAGIC AND MEDICINE — A NIAGARA CASE

As time went by old magical spells in the Sumerian language were particularly valued by Babylonian exorcists, even though the words themselves were often no longer fully intelligible. Garbled spellings show that sometimes incantations had been learned by rote and written out by ear. A few spells are neither Sumerian nor Akkadian but true *mumbo jumbo*, the more foreign-sounding the better, especially if they come from the East, over the mountains in ancient Iranian Elam. There is an unusual yellowish tablet in large script in the British Museum inscribed with mumbo jumbo lines that were particularly effective for banishing unwanted domestic ghosts:

zu-zu-la-ah nu-mi-la-ah hu-du-la-ah hu-šu-bu-la-ah

These sonorous and outlandish words ending in *-lah* 'sound' like Elamite, and they can be found inscribed on other tablets or carved on obsidian amulets, frequently enough to show that this spell was popular over a long period. Collecting the examples together shows that the first magical word *zu-zu-la-ah* occurs in varying forms: *si-en-ti-la-ah*, *zi-ib-shi-la-ah*, *zi-in-zi-la-ah* and *zi-im-zi-ra-ah*. Neither the exorcist nor his client would have had any idea what these four words meant, but it just so happens that today we have the advantage over them. Around 2000 BC, Sumerian administrators imported fierce mastiffs from Elam over the border where such dogs were bred, and their handlers, who were very probably the only people who *could* handle them, had to come too.

Monthly rations records preserve the name and title of *one such* Elamite dog-handler, *zi-im-zi-la-aḫ*, 'dog warden', provoking, it cannot be denied, a trenchant 'Aha!' For this single name reveals the independent, mundane source of what later became an item of powerful magic. Some old record of Elamite personnel must have been discovered a thousand years or more later during a building operation – for Mesopotamians, unlike certain archaeologists, were always finding old tablets – and eventually brought to someone who could read. The bizarre run of unintelligible names in neat old signs could only be an irresistible spell of great antiquity, and it is not hard to imagine how the tablet itself would have been prized and its message ultimately incorporated into regular exorcistic practice: *Now this is a really old spell from faraway in the East . . . I am not going to pronounce these words aloud for we should only whisper them, but if we write them on a stone and you wear it, or hang it up over there, there will be no more visitations . . .*

There is another odd thing about Mesopotamian magical amulets of stone. The inscriptions are often in truly atrocious handwriting, with cuneiform signs split in half or even divided over two lines, both heinous betrayals of scribal convention. Fortunately the worst specimens have been properly excavated on ancient sites, otherwise everyone would just say they were forgeries. Of course one could argue that these were not the work of scribes as such, but of illiterate craftsmen who engraved the scene on one side and blind copied the text from a master draft on the other. This explanation, however, will not wash. Magical inscriptions conventionally need to be free of error to be effective, and figural carvings on amulets are, in stark contrast to the written signs, often of such a high standard that they showcase the capabilities of craftsmen who could never have been satisfied with shoddy distortion of the signs. Hard stones were never cheap and even people who could not read at all would likely sense that such sloppy writing quality didn't really justify the cost. At the same time, however, cuneiform spells on amulets can employ the rarest sign usages, reflecting highly learned input, and I think there must be another explanation to reconcile such incompatible evidence. Some incantations, like those against the she-demon Lamashtu who preyed on newborn babies, occur on many amulets, which list her seven cover names showing that everyone knew who she was. Perhaps the Babylonians had the idea that, if a common spell were legibly or beautifully written, Lamashtu, who had seen it all before, would recognise it from afar and be undeterred, as it was unfamiliar, whereas she might tell herself that a hard-to-identify incantation with distorted signs and obtuse spellings might be something dangerous, and move away to another house, just to be on the safe side. Identifying a familiar cuneiform inscription from twenty paces is perfectly possible: it is quite fun to do it when visitors bring in a stamped Nebuchadnezzar brick, which can be completely translated into English before it is halfway out of the wrapping.

3. Ghosts

It is an arguable proposition that human beings, whatever they may say, believe in ghosts. With the Babylonians there can be no doubt at all; their attitude to the restless dead is matter-of-fact and unselfconscious, and no one ever quizzically asked a neighbour waiting at a fruit stall if they 'really believed' in them.

Ghosts were a common trouble, for anyone who died in dramatic circumstances or was not properly laid to rest or just felt abandoned by their descendants could come back and hang about disturbingly. At some periods dead family members were buried under house floors, and offerings had to be made to them via a special pipe. Seeing a ghost was troublesome; hearing them speak was much more worrying and the *āšipu* practitioner had a whole bag of tricks for sending ghosts back where they belonged once and for all. A typical ritual involved furnishing a little clay model of the ghost that was to be buried with a partner – male or female as was appropriate – and setting them up with all they needed for the return journey and peaceful retirement when they got there. These rituals, too, are elaborate; one exorcist determined to give clear instructions to a follower included a drawing of a ghost as a guide in making the model (see p. 316).

There was another, more worrying side to ghostly presence. Many diseases and illnesses in the medical omens were attributed to the 'hand' of a god, a goddess or other supernatural entities. Frequently mentioned among these is the Hand of a Ghost, which caused, among other afflictions, hearing problems (by slipping in via the ears) and mental disturbance. Unhappy ghosts whose legitimate needs were not attended to turned vengeful and became much more dangerous.

THE RIGHT END OF THE TELESCOPE

This huge mass of written cuneiform testimony, assorted religious texts, omens, medical and magical texts especially, is chock full of human ideas, for they represent the ways in which sentient individuals tried to make sense of their world and cope with it on all levels. The structure through which their data is presented is formulaic without being synthetic. Mesopotamian ideas, and therefore their sum of knowledge, come down to us in a specific kind of packaging. This packaging is above all practical, for its sole purpose was to present what was inherited from earlier times in usable, retrievable form. Knowledge derived from observation and its amplification was extensive and diverse but the fruit of the whole was never, or hardly ever, subjected to the type of analytical synthesis that a modern person, or an ancient Greek, would take for granted. No statement of principle or theoretical summary comes out of the cuneiform resources at our disposal.

This characteristic provokes the enquiry, difficult to satisfy, of the extent to which such intellectual processes took place at all. My own view is that the intelligent human mind is not always fettered by tradition, and I find it much harder to believe that no Babylonian ever asked himself philosophical or even non-conformist questions and that what we happen to have of the Babylonian mind on clay is all there was. It is far from valueless to consider how Babylonian ideas came about and functioned, and, to some extent, to visualise their practitioners.

There are two principal strands to knowledge storage. One is sign and word lists, which – as already indicated – I would categorise as reference works, the other a more intellectual branch which I would like to call *If-thinking*. Underlying both systems is a tacit principle of *textual balance*.

Lexical compositions are set up so that a word in the left-hand column is equated with another on the right. Lexical lists thus actually look like what they are, the juxtaposed entries neatly opposite one another. (An exception sometimes occurs in school texts when lazier pupils wrote out the whole of the left column before the right column; halfway down, the entries no longer match properly, with very unhelpful results.) Two juxtaposed words in a lexical text, most commonly Sumerian equated with Akkadian, do not necessarily share lexical identity to the point that word A means absolutely the same as B, but the system indicates rather that there is a strong overlap between them: A can and often does translate best as B, *but not always*. The same phenomenon occurs in translating between any two languages today; it is curiously difficult to pair words whose full range of nuanced meaning is identical in both cases.

The desire for balance or equation underpins several categories of Akkadian compilations which begin with the word 'If'. This is no classification invented by me, for there is actually a Babylonian technical word that means 'a composition beginning with the word "if",' – *šummu*. It derives from *šumma*, the normal word for 'if' itself, and we can see that the collected paragraphs of a law collection or diagnostic medical omens were known to librarians as the *šummus*.

Laws in codes such as that of Hammurabi represent the most stripped-down manifestation of the idea:

If a man put out the eye of another man, his eye shall be put out.

One deed or event leads unambiguously and inexorably to its consequence, in this case exemplifying the Bible-like eye-for-an-eye ruling (even if the literal penalty was not always exacted). This is straightforward. The same structural format of 'If A then B', however, applies equally to two much broader fields: divination and medicine.

DIVINING WITH 'IF'

Let us imagine that the king of Babylonia in the second millennium BC was contemplating a punitive raid over the Elamite border to the east. His first move would be to turn to his court diviner to establish whether this projected foray would go over well with the gods and which day would be fortuitous. The diviner's training would lead him to identify sufficient diagnostic data on the various freshly extricated sheep's organs (allowing for the internal hierarchy) to enable him to predict that *the king should be victorious* and *Thursday should be good*.

The diviner's job under such circumstances was always complex: he had to tell the king authoritatively, in accordance with traditional lore and perhaps backed up with reference works, whatever he judged that the king wanted to hear without being obvious about it, and doing so in such a way that he and his colleagues always had a let-out in case of disaster. In a non-Versailles type of court the king, if a powerful man, might be served by a loyal court diviner who would do his best to manoeuvre conscientiously through the pitfalls; at Arabian-Nights Nineveh, where there was an abundance of talented and ambitious diviners with more than one agenda between them, it is not hard to imagine the subtle play of loyalty and testimony that would circle around all state-level omen taking; wonderful letters come out of that courtly world.

HEALING WITH 'IF'

The same formal 'If A then B' structure is fundamental to Mesopotamian healing literature for,

(a) cause-of-symptom analysis by medical omens:

> *If a sick man's body is hot and cold and his attack changes*
> *a lot:*
> *Hand of Sin the Moon God.*
> *If a sick man's body is hot and cold but he does not sweat,*
> *Hand of a Ghost, a message from his personal god.*

(b) nature-of-symptom analysis to prescribe therapy:

> *If a woman has difficulty in giving birth, bray a north-facing*
> *root of 'male' mistletoe, mix in sesame oil, rub seven times*
> *in a downward direction over the lower part of her abdomen*
> *and she will give birth quickly.*

> *If during a man's sickness an inflammation affects him in*
> *his lower abdomen, pulverize together sumlalu and dog's-*
> *tongue plant, boil in beer, bind on him and he will get*
> *better.*

(c) nature-of-symptom analysis to predict outcome:

> *If his larynx makes a croaking sound he will die.*
> *If during his illness either his hands or his feet grow weak,*
> *it is no stroke:*
> *he will recover.*

Predictions vary from 'he will get better' to 'he will die' with many variants in between.

Actually it has worried me for years that cuneiform scholars today invariably translate omen predictions within the 'If A then B' system after the model *the king will triumph over his enemy,* and medical prescriptions are made to promise *he will get better.* How is it that either system could allow certainty? Blithe predictions that someone *will* get better after a calculated interval or even an unspecified interval are probably more than any professional doctor would care to make nowadays. I think we must assume that *all* professional prognostications in ancient Mesopotamia were delivered with such riders as *'in as much as we can judge . . .'* or *'features like this tend to suggest . . .'* The whole process of taking or interpreting omens was, as I see it, delicately orchestrated with immense flexibility and subtlety, both physical and intellectual. We might also realistically assume that any military decision concerning a military plan which derived from omen work would never see the army setting out on a march there and then; level-headed input would always be required from the king's chief of staff, who might privately have a low opinion of 'gut-readers' and much prefer their own sober assessment of arms, armour, chariotry and supplies before agreeing to any departure date.

To attribute such an interpretation to the verb form that provides the 'B' half of all this *If-data* is, in fact, quite permissible, for there is undoubtedly a shortfall in the Akkadian verb with regard to modality. This means that, for example, the verb form *iballuṭ*, 'he will live', or 'he will get better', can sustain a range of nuances that in English are 'he could/might/should/ought to get better'. In today's world all predictions are hedged around with uncertainty or escape mechanisms. I do not see for a moment how things could have been different in ancient Mesopotamia.

There is one unique discussion of these matters in cuneiform by the top people who actually did this work and shouldered very real responsibility. It was published under the title 'A Babylonian Diviner's Manual' by the Chicago scholar A. L. Oppenheim, and to some extent it comes to our rescue. The author quotes the first lines of fourteen completely unknown and rather strange tablets of *terrestrial* omens and eleven of equally unknown *astral* omens. He then writes paragraphs – as if responding to three questions from a persistent interviewer with a microphone (which is, I suppose, what we are) – as follows:

Q. How does your science work?

A. *A sign that portends evil in the sky is also evil on earth; one that portends evil on earth is evil in the sky. When you look up a sign, be it one in the sky or one on earth and if that sign's evil portent is confirmed then it has indeed occurred with regard to you in reference to an enemy or to a disease or to a famine. Check the date of that sign, and should no sign have occurred to counteract that sign, should no annulment have taken place, one cannot make it pass by, its evil consequence cannot be removed and it will happen. These are the things that you have to consider when you study the two collections . . .* [He quotes the titles of the two terrestrial and astral series]. *When you have identified the sign and when they ask you to save the city, the king and his subjects from enemy, pestilence and famine, what will you say? When they complain to you, how will you make the evil consequences bypass them?*

Q. What have you given us in this document?

A. *Altogether 24 tablets with signs occurring in the sky and*

on earth whose good and evil portents are in harmony(?).
You will find in them every sign that has occurred in
the sky and has been observed on earth.

Q. How do you make use of them?
A. *This is the method to dispel them:*

Twelve are the months of the year, 360 are its days.
Study the length of the year and look in tablets for the
timings of their disappearances, the visibilities and the
first appearance of the stars, also the position of the Iku
star at the beginning of the year, the first appearance of
the sun and the moon in the months Addaru and Ulūlu,
the risings and first appearance of the moon as observed
each month; watch the opposition of the Pleiades and
the moon and all this will give you the proper answer.
Thus establish the months of the year and the days of
the months, and do perfectly what you are doing. Should
it happen to you that at the first visibility of the moon
the weather should be cloudy, the water clock should
be the means of computing it . . . [further details are
given] Establish the length of the year and complete its
intercalation. Pay attention and be not careless! [A
helpful good and bad dates' table concludes.]

This testimony, deriving from an expert in the hot seat, shows
us explicitly several realities. On some level, ominous events
mirror one another in heaven and earth. Several factors can have
the effect of discounting an omen. Those that must be faced are
dealt with, but the date is of extreme importance, and establishing
the date in time of uncertainty crucial. There is here a great
impression of very serious activity; it is full, however, of shifting
criteria that allow, one might imagine, that many occurrences
brought to the attention of the authorities could be safely ignored
if need be.

I have the idea that the great lexical texts and sign lists between them were supposed to include every word in Sumerian and Akkadian and every cuneiform sign, so that they were meant to be encyclopaedic and comprehensive, in the same way that omens were meant to cover all eventualities. The idea of *mūdû kalāma*, 'knowing everything', is commonly mentioned. People often quibble as to whether, for example, the laborious amassing and cataloguing of systematic, logical and retrievable omen data over centuries in ancient Mesopotamia represents Science or not. Mixed up in this, I suppose, is the question of whether any of it 'worked'. For the ancient Mesopotamian diviner there was a theoretical cosmic structure and endless methodical observational data to support it and that sounds a lot like science to me.

After-words

A handful of cuneiform tablets give us the highly unexpected. Among these are solitary political satire, or the bawdy text of a street-theatre portrayal of the god Marduk reviling his mother-in-law, as well as a smattering of precious 'How-to' instructions, such as the way to stain stones to look expensive, dye wool to undercut foreign imports, build a water clock for the diviners, or even play a board game.

And that *reminds* me. Odd things can happen in a museum. The Sumerians did have a board game, the so-called Royal Game of Ur, for which Woolley had found the type series of boards and equipment from about 2600 BC in his Ur cemetery. This classic board game lasted in the ancient Middle East for a good three thousand years, but in 177 BC, just before it went out of fashion, a well-known Babylonian astronomer wrote down the rules. His tablet had arrived in the British Museum in 1879, and for years lived in its box on a shelf in a tablet cupboard virtually opposite my desk. No one had ever deciphered the inscription, which made it first interesting, and after a while utterly compelling. I discovered (a '99 per cent perspiration' job) that the game behind the rules was this old Sumerian game: the scribe likened the twelve playing squares up the middle of the board to the signs of the zodiac and the pieces to the planets moving through them.

I started hunting through the literature to find all the known archaeological examples, but in the heady first days after this breakthrough my colleague Dominique Collon came into my room one morning and said she had 'discovered the Royal Game of Ur downstairs in one of our galleries'. Naturally I put this down to defensive satire, but she took me by the ear lobe and frogmarched me down the staircase to the pair of giant, human-headed bulls from Khorsabad, Sargon II's royal capital, on the ground floor. She pointed triumphantly at the left bull and switched on the torch (which, oddly, she seemed to be carrying) and played the light across the worn marble plinth on which the bull was standing. The angle threw into sharp relief the scratched grid for the Royal Game of Ur which no one had ever noticed since the arrival of the sculptures in the 1850s. The grid had been recut with a dagger point several times, but the twenty-square design was unmistakable. A technical enquiry had come in from America, she said, about how Assyrian craftsmen carved the feet of the bulls and how broad the toenails were, so she had come down to check with ruler and torch, for that gallery was always in shadowy half-light. In so doing, she became the first ever person to spot the graffiti game board, which she could hardly fail to do after all my *Look at this!* droning on about the subject. The sculptures had originally been set up in a major public gateway with a great arch vaulting between them; it is not hard to imagine eighth-century-BC guards, uncomfortable on the plinth, whiling away point-duty out of the eye of the sergeant-at-arms with pebbles and dice which could be swept away at a moment's notice, like fly gamblers surprised by a police constable in a modern street market. Our second Assyrian bull, directly opposite, showed a much more worn board of the same type. Then Julian Reade, on a flying visit to the Louvre the following weekend, found a grid for the game on one of *their* Khorsabad bulls, and, eventually, an Iraqi colleague reported in that a re-excavated bull in Iraq also had a scratched game board in the equivalent spot. This is wonderful new evidence for everyday life and behaviour, and also proves that pure archaeological discovery can take place in a museum as well as in the ground!

Many other things happened when I started investigating that game, but that is for another book. (And there have been other discoveries like that inside the walls of the British Musuem, now and again . . .)

What, then, is *lacking* in Mesopotamian cuneiform? Truly personal, spontaneous writing of any kind is exceptionally rare, acknowledged authorship of even the famous, classic composi-tions likewise. Complex and evolving history meant that many voices and hands contributed to the literature we have, their names vanished for ever. Ironically it is mostly mundane admin-istrative tablets that name their scribes, although many of those who copied and transmitted literary or library texts – as opposed to authoring them – included their own name in a colophon. On top of that, the teaching of tablet craft seems to have instilled a clear sense of what could be done on clay, and what not. Cuneiform scribbles, jottings, drafts or other informal materials are rare beyond marginal calculations in administrative texts; even drawings on clay are rare, despite the fact that the few which have come down to us betray very considerable mastery.

Did any outsiders learn cuneiform in antiquity? In the second millennium BC trained scribes sometimes departed from the Mesopotamian heartland with expertise in their head and libraries in a bag to seek, as it were, their fortune abroad. The work of some of these individuals is known to us; for instance, at the Syrian site of Meskene, exporting cuneiform know-how so that schoolboys from a different world would find themselves carefully copying lexical texts with ancient words or names that could never have meaning for them. At the same time, as Akkadian cuneiform swelled out to become the international means of communication across the Middle East, all petty kings would want a cuneiformist on their staff to handle their international correspondence, even if that meant laboriously dictating in native Mitannian to one's Babylonian staff writer, the tablet then to be run to Egypt, where some other ex-pat Babylonian text-reader would read it and translate into Egyptian, perhaps adding a diplomatic touch, for the Pharaoh.

The widespread dissemination of cuneiform had other unanticipated consequences. At Ugarit in the fifteenth century BC new forces were at play in the history of writing. These led to the development of the first version of what is effectively an alphabet, in which thirty-one signs (including a *word divider*! *Sissies*!) sufficed to spell and record the Semitic Ugaritic language. The odd thing is that the signs in this new alphabet were also cuneiform, wedge-shapes written on clay in traditional fashion, but as simple as possible and quite unconnected with the Mesopotamian sign forms that had inspired them. It is as if the concept that writing had to be wedges on clay was too strong to allow a completely independent start. This Ugaritic script flourished in a context of a busy Bronze Age Mediterranean port, where the resident merchants no doubt spoke an abundance of languages and never lost a chance to do a bit of business, but it fell out of use after the city was destroyed in the early twelfth century BC, and the alphabet had to be invented all over again two hundred or so years later.

The invention of the alphabet with all its practical advantages did not directly affect the status of cuneiform writing for many centuries, and writing ink on parchment or leather with twenty-two letters was slow to displace wedge-writing altogether, although our picture of the use of Aramaic writing in the second half of the first millennium BC is hampered by the probability that it was extensively written on such perishable materials. The two systems certainly long overlapped, while the vastness of the resources in cuneiform coupled with the Mesopotamian sense of tradition and a very human reluctance to change meant that cuneiform was continuously kept alive in certain quarters long after Aramaic alphabetic script and language was in widespread use. The last users were, as far as we can see, astronomers and record keepers, who continued patiently doing what they had always done until the last heroic exponent laid down his stylus one day in the second century AD and expired.

Babylonian into Greek

How hard was it for motivated foreigners encountering cuneiform when it was still in use to make headway with it? Specifically, how could astronomical, mathematical and medical knowledge cross the immense divide from cuneiform Babylonian into alphabetic Greek, as we know it did from the use of sexigesimal calculations at the beginning of this chapter?

An astonishing fragment of Greek papyrus dated to the first century AD contains in one column a sequence of inked numbers that occur in a standard work of Late Babylonian astronomy referred to by scholars today as 'System B'. The identification was made on the spot by Otto Neugebauer when the papyrus was shown to him, somewhat bashfully, by its present owner, who had purchased it as a schoolboy many decades earlier from a second-hand bookshop that always had a tantalising box of 'old bits of writing' on the counter.

Babylonian System B numbers:
tabulated records of astronomical observations.

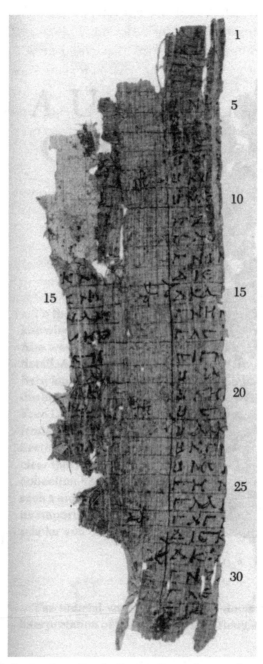

*Babylonian into Greek: System B numbers understood
and copied in inked Greek script.*

Babylonian System B is an astronomical table (or ephemeris) that records the movements of the moon for 104–102 BC. As is evident from the photograph – even to the would-be Assyriologist – it consists exclusively of *columns of cuneiform numbers*. Cuneiform numbers from 1 to 60 work very simply, in fact any child could understand them and an interested, numerate Greek would have them down in about four minutes. What is more interesting is that to read this and most of the many other astronomical tablets found in the classic work *Late Babylonian Astronomical Tablets* from top to bottom, to control their contents and do it all into Greek, it is only necessary to master the following groups of signs:

Task 1. The numbers 1–60:

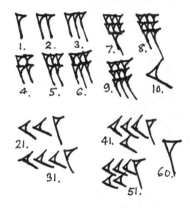

Task 2. The twelve month names:

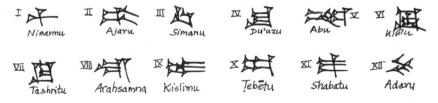

Task 3. Twelve signs of the zodiac:

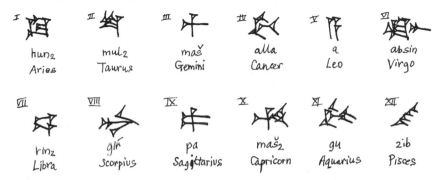

hun₂	mul₂	maš
Aries	Taurus	Gemini

alla
Cancer

a
Leo

absin
Virgo

rin₂
Libra

gir
Scorpius

pa
Sagittarius

maš₂
Capricorn

gu
Aquarius

zib
Pisces

Task 4. The names of the planets:

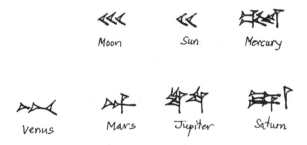

Moon

Sun

Mercury

Venus

Mars

Jupiter

Saturn

In addition, a handful of simple ideograms such as 'to be bright' or 'to be dark'.

Any Greek who was sufficiently motivated to get himself from Athens to Babylon, lured by the fabled shelves of astronomical observations and armed with relatively minimal starting knowledge, would be able to unlock cuneiform treasure in abundance. With this approach, learning bit by bit what common signs were and what they meant, texts with much more than numbers could be accessed. Astronomical, mathematical or medical texts are increasingly more complicated, but in fact these too could become accessible by learning limited numbers of new signs or sign sequences, mostly Sumerian ideograms. This smattering would give any medic a head start:

DIŠ NA	*If a man*
Ú	plant name follows
GIŠ	wood name follows
NA$_4$	stone name follows
ina-eš	*he should recover*
TI	*he should recover*

KI.MIN ditto
(Some verbs)
(Some nouns)

ÉN   spell

Babylonian doctors had descriptive lists of plants and fresh or dried specimens to hand: a lot of mutually profitable ground could be covered.

There was no necessity with all this to think of learning language or script proper, for no one was going to expect the visitors to read *Atrahasis*, or explain the complications of Sumerian on the basis of Akkadian lexicography. A few extra-ordinary tablets survive from this late period with Babylonian school cuneiform exercises on one side and the cuneiform signs transliterated into Greek letters on the other. It seems to me that these can only be the product of Greeks learning Babylonian beyond the level of numbers, and it is tempting to see reflected in them a kind of beginner's desperation as to whether it will *ever be possible to remember the damned signs*.

It is not trite to point out that this was a world altogether different before modern commerce, copyright and licences, and it is probable that there was warm collaboration within a small MIT-type group of talented Graeco-Babylonian individuals; I cannot see but that the Babylonians would be stimulated by the contact with new thinkers and keen to communicate. In this basic way a huge tranche of empirical knowledge, mathematical, astronomical, astrological and even medical, could pass with relative simplicity from complex cuneiform to graceful Greek: the inherited intellectual product of ancient Mesopotamian culture could be shipped out wholesale in a carpet-bag full of papyri.

Such a process is crucial to the humanities as a whole. There are many pointers that Babylonian ideas and data found their way into Greek learning, but the *mechanism* that enabled this has remained undiscussed and unexplained. In all likelihood it was simple. Intrinsic to it is that it was a two-way process. Most important is the realisation that essential intellectual achievement can be transmitted from a great but dying culture to renaissance within a younger and expanding culture, thanks to no more than a handful of intrepid and curious border-crossing individuals.

There is no reason either to assume that incoming Greek ideas fell on deaf ears. Two outstanding documents suggest this, one a medical text from the city of Uruk that attributes human diseases to one of four seats in the body – a wholly un-Babylonian proposition – the other the tablet of game rules already mentioned, again unlikely to be a wholly Babylonian conceit. It is probable, too, that the Greeks were bemused by the characteristic anonymity of Babylonian scholarship. Later, many Greeks put their names to inventions which had long been familiar to the old cuneiformists between the rivers and I have an idea that the Hellenes have got away with quite a lot in that direction.

Finally, let us return to the idea about the Babylonians (and all the others) being like us: easy to propose, complex to demonstrate, impossible to prove; and what exactly does 'like' mean, and what are 'we' like anyway . . . ?

If this supposition were to be argued from a lecture platform it is not unlikely that someone would shout out, 'Well what about the bodies in the <u>Royal Graves at Ur</u>? No one could say *them Sumerians* were like us!'

Around 2600 BC, several top-notch individuals at Ur went to their eternal rest accompanied not only by all the precious property they could want, but also by their faithful retainers. There were three or four such graves, of which the <u>Great Death Pit,</u> with about seventy-two neatly laid out bodies, was the most spectacular. The concept that dead royalty must be accompanied to their graves by their former retainers is shocking and essentially deeply primitive. In Egypt the Egyptians did flirt with this idea in predynastic times, but soon came up with *ushabti figures* instead, boxes of small faience workmen who would accompany the dead and do their work when needed. Explanatory theories about the Ur finds fizzed madly; were they all drugged? Prisoners of war? Already dead? Alongside such questions comes the broader issue, for burying crowds of young and beautiful court personnel on the assumption that they would be needed in the next world is certainly hard to digest. Sensibly, the practice disappears completely with the end of the dynasty; once rejected it was never to be reintroduced. That development is not at all hard to understand, but how retainer-sacrifice ever came to take hold within Ur society in the first place *is*. There are only two explanations: either it was an age-old practice for which there just happens to be no other real evidence from the ancient Middle East, or the idea finds it origin in circumstances surrounding a specific historic personage. In Mesopotamia the only real candidate for such a figure is Gilgamesh.

Gilgamesh, we can be sure, was a real man. He was an early king of Uruk who founded a short-lived dynasty at the beginning of the historical period. All the surviving literary traditions about Gilgamesh point to a figure of power and charisma that long-outlasted his own lifetime. The cycle of stories that came to circulate about his name testify to this, and give the impression that he was a man out of the same box as Alexander the Great, the impact of whose death led to narratives far beyond the sober scope of the historians who first tackled his life and times. In view of this, it seems a credible idea that the death of Gilgamesh himself could have seen the instigation of such a rite, where loyal retainers, à la Laertes, leapt into the grave, unable to face the future. A Sumerian literary text that describes the death of Gilgamesh has often been compared with the death scene as reconstructed at Ur. I would like to suggest that this primitive custom literally originated with the death of Gilgamesh, and was part of Uruk tradition long after. Perhaps a dynastic marriage between Uruk and Ur saw the custom imported to Ur, where it held sway for a while, and was then rejected for ever. This was not the typical Sumerian view in practice. But a restorative dip into Sumerian proverb and wisdom literature is very reassuring, as the real, everyday voices come out of the darkness: philosophical, puzzled, ironic, resigned, or sniggering. I see no reason at all to exclude the Sumerians from our brotherhood circle.

Babylon of the later time of Nebuchadnezzar, that of the Babylonian Exile, is certainly a familiar world. We have the huge public buildings: sky-scraper temples and far-famed palaces; we can gape at the wondrous walls and gates and marvel at the blue, swimming-pool tiles that lined the Ishtar Gate and Processional Way. We know most, however, from their magical writing that speaks of the many corners of life that buzzed and fretted there: rich bankers and speculators waxing fat, doctors and diviners with their cosmic operations, stall-keepers in the sūq selling fish and vegetables, myopic seal carvers and mutilated metalsmiths, and a bustling frenzy of peoples from around the Empire, their assorted gabbled languages lending reality to the image of Babel. We meet mercenaries, fortune-tellers, priests and prostitutes; cut-throats, mendicants, money-lenders and water-sellers. The great vanished metropolis with its noises and smells, garden luxury at one end and slum shacks at the other, must have been timeless in its daily life and thereby, thanks to its ancient words, almost within our grasp.

And those ancient people, writing their tablets, looking at their world, crawling between heaven and earth . . . *like us*.

4

Recounting the Flood

Thou too, sail on, O Ship of State!
Sail on, O Union, strong and great!
Humanity with all its fears,
With all the hopes of future years,
Is hanging breathless on thy fate!
Henry Wadsworth Longfellow

The story of a flood that destroyed the world in which human and animal life was saved from extinction by a hero with a boat is almost universal in the world's treasury of traditional literature. The (global) flood story, whose central preoccupation is the frailty of the human condition and the uncertainty of divine plans, would certainly feature as a thought-provoking entry in any Martian Encyclopaedia of the Human World. Its rich theme has inspired many thinkers, writers and painters, the topic moving far beyond the borders of scripture and the sacred to become an inspiration for modern opera and film, in addition to literature.

Many scholars have tried to collect all the specimens in a butterfly net, to pin them out and docket them for family, genus and species. Flood Stories in the broadest sense (which are sometimes booked under Catastrophe Stories, for not all possible disasters are floods) have been documented in Mesopotamia, Egypt, Greece, Syria, Europe, India, East Asia, New Guinea, Central America, North America, Melanesia, Micronesia, Australia and South America. The scholars who have contributed most to this endeavour have produced varying totals, somewhere around three hundred all told, and a range of publications will enable the devotee to sample them in abundance. Some of these narratives reduce everything to a couple of sentences, others blossom into powerful and dramatic literature, and looking them over reinforces the impression that any culture that cannot muster some form of flood story is in the minority.

The collection and comparison of traditions is always fascinating, and creating and pruning a family tree of flood narratives is probably as enticing as any other such project. It is the breadth and overall variety, however, that is more significant than any fundamental similarity. After all, the forces of nature, including rivers, rain and sea (alongside earthquakes, whirlwinds, fire and volcanoes), are irresistible by man when they are roused and are likely to underpin much traditional narrative, while in any flood, however disastrous, certain individuals always survive, *usually those with boats.* There is no need to strive for a complex web of origin, dissemination and interrelations on the broadest scale. One must always reckon, too, with the 'natural' flow of uncontaminated narrative being interrupted or influenced in a specific way at a specific moment, such as through Bible teaching by missionaries.

The central example from the collector's standpoint represents a unique case, however, where influence and dissemination are undeniable and have been of the greatest global significance. The story of Noah, iconic in the Book of Genesis, and as a consequence, a central motif in Judaism, Christianity and Islam, invites the comparative mythologer's greatest attention. In all three scriptures the Flood comes as punishment for wrongdoing by man, part of a 'give-up-on-this-lot-and-start-over' resolution governing divine relations with the human world. There is a direct and undoubted Flood continuum from the Hebrew Old Testament to the Greek New Testament on the one hand and the Arabic Koran on the other. Since the Victorian-period discoveries of George Smith it has been understood that the Hebrew account derives, in its turn, from that in Babylonian cuneiform, much older, substantially longer, and surely the original that launched the story on its timeless journey. This book focuses on the first stage of this process, looking at the various Mesopotamian stories that survive on cuneiform tablets, and investigating how it came about that the story came into our own world so effectively.

Such an approach entitles the researcher to avoid entirely the question as to whether there ever 'really was a Flood'. People have, however, long been concerned with that very question, and been on the lookout for evidence to support the story, and I imagine all good Mesopotamian archaeologists have kept the Flood at the back of their mind, just in case. In the years 1928 and 1929 important discoveries were made on sites in Iraq that were taken to be evidence of the biblical Flood itself. At Ur, for example, deep excavation beneath the Royal Cemetery disclosed more than ten feet of empty mud, below which earlier settlement material came to light. A similar, nearly contemporaneous, discovery was made by Langdon and Watelin at the site of Kish in southern Iraq. To both teams it seemed inescapable that here was evidence of more than ancient flooding, but of the biblical Flood itself, and Sir Leonard Woolley's fluent lectures round about the country, backed up by his versatile pen, certainly came to promote the idea that at Ur they had found proof that Noah's Flood had really taken place.

Similar deposits were identified at other archaeological sites, but in due course doubts were raised whether all such empty layers were really archaeologically contemporary, or indeed whether they were all water-deposited. In recent times this sort of would-be tangible evidence has fallen out of consideration. Certainly strata of empty mud confirm that human habitation in ancient Iraq was subject to disastrous and destructive flooding, and in general background terms such discoveries do much to enhance our appreciation of the extent to which ancient Mesopotamia was, in fact, vulnerable in this way, but few today would claim such discoveries concern the Flood described in the Book of Genesis. Sir Leonard, apparently, could hardly be surpassed as a persuasive speaker once he got going on the subject of Ur; Lambert told me in a rare confessional moment that it was as a schoolboy on the edge of his seat in a Birmingham cinema, listening to Woolley lecturing about discoveries, that he determined on his own life's work as an Assyriologist.

In recent times the hunt for archaeological flood-levels for their own sake has rather fallen out of fashion, while further such discoveries depend on evidence that can only come from very deep and extensive excavations which are hardly practical today. In more recent times scholars have turned to geological rather than archaeological investigation, pursuing data about earthquakes, tidal waves or melting glaciers in the hunt for the Flood at a dizzying pace, but it is far beyond the scope of this book to follow in their footsteps.

THE FLOOD STORY IN MESOPOTAMIA

Psychologically it is not surprising that a flood myth should be deeply embedded in the Mesopotamian psyche, for it derived from and reflected the very landscape in which they found themselves. Their dependence on the Tigris and Euphrates waters was absolute and inescapable, but the awe-inspiring emptiness of the deep sky above them, the suddenness of storm and the tangible powers of the ancient gods like the Sun, the Moon and the god of the Storm meant that even the most sophisticated individuals were never far from the reality of nature's forces. The flood, an ungoverned power that could sweep civilisation before it like a modern tsunami, was for sure no safe and comfortable bogeyman with which to frighten children but something that enshrined remote memory of a real disaster or disasters. Probably some version of the story had been told for millennia.

Culturally the Flood functioned as a horizon in time, according to which crucial events preceded it or followed it. Great Sages lived 'before the Deluge', and all the elements of civilisation were bestowed on mankind thereafter. Very occasionally in cuneiform literature the use of the phrase, 'Before the Flood', which acquires the ring of cliché, reminds one ever so slightly of the expression 'Before the Great War . . .'

The universal flood was intended as an efficient kind of 'new broom' approach that would allow the gods to start recreating more appropriate forms of life afterwards in a clean and empty world. The god Enki (clever, humorous, rebellious) is appalled at the proposal and seemingly alone in anticipating the consequences, so he picks out one suitable human being to rescue human and other life. The Flood Story was thus the very stuff of oral literature. Its central theme affected everybody and all listeners. All men and women knew that, if the gods so wished it, they were doomed; and that stoppage of the very life-giving water of the Euphrates and Tigris rivers would be their undoing if that happened, or if it swelled into a monstrous, all-encompassing water of chaos. The Flood Story is full of fearful drama, human struggle and, at the last minute, Hollywood-like, escape.

Many Mesopotamian stories, in Sumerian or Akkadian, bear indications that they derive from an older time before such compositions were written down. Repetition of key passages, for example, makes a long story easier to remember and promotes familiarity in listeners who might well come to 'join in' at certain parts, as small children do when a favourite book is read and re-read. Quite soon after writing had reached the point of recording language in full, at the beginning of the third millennium BC, we see that narrative concerning the gods came to be written down.

Very early clay tablets from southern Iraq contain narrative literature in which the gods feature, although to a large extent these first examples still defy translation. The Flood Story, in contrast, does not seem to have made it 'into print' at such an early date. The earliest tablets with any part of the story appear in the second millennium BC, a thousand years or more after the first experiments with writing on clay. We can only imagine how Sumerian and Babylonian storytellers might have spun tales of the Great Flood in the meanwhile, for it must long have been a staple of their craft. By the early second millennium, however, when it does start to appear in written form, we do not have just one

Mesopotamian Flood Story, but separate compositions in which the Flood is a central component. This in itself is an indication of the antiquity of the subject, for the power and drama of the flood narrative was unending, preoccupying poets and storytellers as long as the cultures of Mesopotamia endured, if not beyond.

The Mesopotamian Flood Story surfaces in three distinct cuneiform incarnations, one in Sumerian, two in Akkadian. These are the *Sumerian Flood Story*, and major narrative episodes within the *Atrahasis Epic* and the *Epic of Gilgamesh* respectively. Each incarnation has its own flood hero. This means that it is only partly appropriate to speak of a 'Mesopotamian Flood Story' as such, for there are important differences between them, although the essence of the story is common to all three. Within these three traditions, different versions of the flood story text were in circulation, some substantially different, where format, number of writing columns or even plot elements could vary as well as language. What we call the *Atrahasis Epic* was undoubtedly popular, appearing in many formats, never to be fully 'canonised', whereas the *Epic of Gilgamesh*, did eventually become fixed into an agreed literary format. First-millennium *Gilgamesh* tablets with the Flood Story from the Royal Library at Nineveh are true duplicates of one another that literally tell one and the same story. There are no *Atrahasis* versions of the Mesopotamian Flood Story so far from the first millennium BC. We need some.

Flood Story tablets distribute themselves over the following broad time periods:

Old Babylonian	1900–1600 BC
Middle Babylonian	1600–1200 BC
Late Assyrian	800–600 BC
Late Babylonian	600–500 BC

Here are the nine known tablets which contribute to our picture of the Mesopotamian story of the Flood and aid us in understanding and appreciating the newly found *Ark Tablet*.

The Sumerian Flood Story

'OLD BABYLONIAN SUMERIAN'

The Sumerian account of the Flood is found on a justly famous cuneiform tablet in the University Museum in Philadelphia. Once it had three columns of writing on each side, but approximately two-thirds is missing altogether so our grasp of the whole remains shaky. It was written down in about 1600 BC at the Sumerian city of Nippur, an important religious and cultural centre where many literary tablets have been excavated.

The Sumerian Flood Story *tablet from Philadelphia.*

Although this story comes to us in the Sumerian language there are features about the wording – such as odd verb forms – that led its translator, Miguel Civil, to conclude that the theme of the Flood which destroys mankind probably does not belong within the main body of Sumerian literary traditions. While it does look as if this *Sumerian Flood Story* account derives from a Babylonian account, its source must have been a version that we have never seen, and it is worth pointing out that separate Sumerian versions of the story, unknown to us, might have been in circulation too.

In this tablet, the great gods, long after the founding of the cities, decide on the destruction of the human race (although we don't know why), despite the pleas of the creator-goddess, Nintur. It fell to King Ziusudra to build the boat and rescue life, which he did successfully, deservedly becoming immortal:

> *Then, because King Ziusudra*
> *Had safeguarded the animals and the seed of mankind,*
> *They settled him in a land overseas, in the land of Dilmun,*
> *where the sun rises.*
>
> Sumerian Flood Story: 258–60

'SCHØYEN SUMERIAN'

For a long time the *Sumerian Flood Story* tablet was unique, but a second fragment has been found in the Schøyen Collection in Norway. This tells us that King Ziusudra, whom it prefers to call 'Sudra', was a gudu-priest of the god Enki. The hero Ziusudra was thus king and priest together, a joint appointment that was probably often the case in early times. The *Instructions of Shuruppak*, already mentioned in Chapter 3, considered Ziusudra's father to be a character called Shuruppak, providing a convincing-looking lineage:

> *Shuruppak, son of Ubar-Tutu*
> *Gave advice to Ziusudra, his son.*

Shuruppak was in fact a Sumerian city. The indispensable *Sumerian King List*, which records kings and reign-lengths before and after the Flood, tells us that Ubar-Tutu was king in the city of Shuruppak for 18,600 years and the last to rule before the Flood, but mentions neither Shuruppak – otherwise known to be a wise man and sometimes called the 'Man from Shuruppak' – nor Ziusudra! In another document called the *Dynastic Chronicle*, however, Ubar-Tutu is succeeded at Shuruppak before the Flood by his son Ziusudra, thus confirming that he was the hero who underwent the Great Deluge. This is a sizeable can of worms, but I think we can excuse our valiant chroniclers for getting confused about dates and lineage for kings who lived before the Flood, even though, according to Greek testimony, important cuneiform texts had been buried before the Flood for safekeeping.

The name Ziusudra is very suitable for an immortal flood hero, since in Sumerian it means something like *He-of-Long-Life*. The name of the corresponding flood hero in the *Gilgamesh Epic* is Utnapishti, of roughly similar meaning. In fact, we are not sure whether the Babylonian name is a translation of the Sumerian or vice versa.

The Akkadian Atrahasis Epic

'OLD BABYLONIAN ATRAHASIS'

The *Atrahasis Epic* is a three-tablet literary production of which no one should speak slightingly, for it is among the most significant works of Mesopotamian literature and wrestles with timeless human issues. The story of the Flood and the Ark for which it is best known is only part of a much wider narrative. The whole would make, I dare say, a corking opera.

The curtain rises on a very strange world. Man has not yet been created, and the junior gods are obliged to do all the necessary work. They mutter and rebel, finally burning their tools. Their complaint is not without justification; the senior gods will see to it that man, *Lullû*, is created instead to do the work. The birth goddess Mami, also known as Nintu and Bēlet-ilī, is called in, but she declares that she cannot create this being alone, so the god Enki announces to all that their fellow god We-ilu will be slaughtered and man created (see the quotations in Appendix 1). Mankind has now been doing the work for the gods, but, at the same time, reproducing itself enthusiastically without being subject to death. In their profusion mankind is extremely noisy. As Enlil puts it to his fellow gods,

> *"The noise of mankind has become too intense for me,*
> *With their uproar I am deprived of sleep."*

The dreadful racket warrants a plague to wipe out mankind altogether. Ea (Sumerian Enki), one of the senior gods responsible for the creation of man, thwarts this plan. Enlil's frustration increases and this time he resolves to wipe out human beings by starvation, so he withholds the rain. Again it is Ea who intervenes and reinstates the rain and restores life. Enlil's third plan is to send an annihilating flood once and for all, and it is to circumnavigate this disaster that Ea instructs Atra-hasīs to build his ark and save human and animal life. The gods, ultimately, are pleased at Ea's intervention. The Atra-hasīs family members are made immortal and human life is allowed to go on, although death is now added to the mixture, and barrenness, celibate priestesses and childbirth mortality are instituted for the first time to keep a cap on numbers.

To our minds, *noise abatement* as justification for the total annihilation of life looks a bit over the top. There can be no doubt, however, that this was the reason: seething human clamour had reached an intolerable point. Enlil's irritation in *Atrahasis* always makes me think of old people in deckchairs after lunch on the beach annoyed by other peoples' children and radios; it is a far cry from the moral standpoint of the Old Testament. Some Assyriologists have argued, unconvincingly, that the key Babylonian word, *rigmu*, 'noise', might here be a euphemism for bad behaviour but the real issue at stake is *overpopulation*. The noise is due to excessive numbers of persons and the Flood is a remedy for an antediluvian world situation in which none of the population ever actually had to die. Enlil meant what he said, though: there are cuneiform spells to quieten a single fractious baby whose *rigmu*, 'noise', disturbs important gods in heaven to the point of ungovernable annoyance all over again. The Flood Story is, therefore, woven into *Atrahasis* as one episode in a structured sequence. The hero of the day is Atra-hasīs himself, whose name means *Exceedingly-wise*.

Flood Story Tablets of the Atrahasis Epic

The most famous copy of the whole Atrahasis epic in Akkadian was written by a scribe called Ipiq-Aya, who lived and worked in the southern Mesopotamian city of Sippar in the seventeenth century BC. The Assyriologist Frans van Koppen has not only settled the long-running problem of how to read this great man's name but has investigated his biography too. As a young man he wrote out the whole of the *Atrahasis* story on three large cuneiform tablets between 1636 and 1635 BC, carefully recording the date and his own name. Ipiq-Aya would be put out to learn that the results of his labours are scattered today between the museums of London, New Haven, New York and Geneva. Together the three tablets originally contained 1,245 lines of text, of which we have all or part of about 60 per cent.

The crucial episode about the Ark and the Flood occurs in Ipiq-Aya's Tablet III, referred to regularly in this book as *Old Babylonian Atrahasis*. This tablet is now in two pieces. The larger, known as C1, might just possibly join C2 if they could ever be manoeuvred into the same room, but the former is in the British Museum and the latter in the Musée d'Art et d'Histoire in Geneva. One day I will try out the join . . .

There are six further tablets or pieces of the Akkadian *Atrahasis Epic* that survive from the Old Babylonian period, which, though obviously the 'same story', reveal four distinct versions. Only one of these tablets happens to contain Flood narrative.

'OLD BABYLONIAN SCHØYEN'

This recently published tablet, also in the Schøyen Collection, is textually strongly independent of those previously known, and earlier in date than *Old Babylonian Atrahasis* by about a hundred years. This is the passage in this tablet that is relevant here:

> "Now, let them not listen to the word that you [say],
>   The gods commanded an annihilation,
>   A wicked thing that Enlil will do to the people.
>   In the assembly they commanded the Deluge, (saying):
>   'By the day of the new moon we shall do the task.'"
> Atra-hasīs, as he was kneeling there,
> In the presence of Ea his tears were flowing.
> Ea opened his mouth,
> And said to his servant:
>   "For one thing you are weeping for the people,
>   for another you are kneeling (as) one who fears me.
>   There is a task to be done,
>   But you, you know not how to accomplish it."
>
> *Old Babylonian Schøyen*: iv 1–16

And that, tantalisingly, is the final line of *Old Babylonian Schøyen*. Judging by the well-known continuation of the story, the subsequent tablet written by this scribe – if we had it – would have begun with the same lines that open the *Ark Tablet*.

'MIDDLE BABYLONIAN UGARIT'

This important tablet fragment was excavated at the site of Ugarit (Ras Shamra) in modern Syria, and is still the only piece of the Flood Story to have come to light at a site outside of Iraqi Mesopotamia itself. Its presence there is a good example of how literature and learning was exported from the centre of the cunei-form world to important cities of the Middle East where Babylonian was not the predominant local language. It has been suggested that *Middle Babylonian Ugarit*, in contrast to the other

Atrahasis accounts, is written in the first person, but the lines that seem to suggest this are in direct speech and the narration is in the third person. The text as far as we have it is also quite distinct from other versions.

'MIDDLE BABYLONIAN NIPPUR'
This tablet fragment, like *Old Babylonian Sumerian*, was also excavated at the city of Nippur, southern Iraq, and is now kept in the University Museum, Philadelphia.

'ASSYRIAN RECENSION'
This first-millennium text in Assyrian script gives us a glimpse of a different and abbreviated recounting of the story. It also has the peculiarity of having been copied from a tablet that was damaged in one or two places, marked as such by the scribe (as described in Chapter 3).

'ASSYRIAN SMITH'
This is the historic flood fragment excavated at Nineveh by George Smith and understandably taken by him to be part of the Gilgamesh story. The abbreviation by which it is classified in the British Museum, DT 42, commemorates the generosity of his sponsor, the *Daily Telegraph* newspaper.

Flood Story tablets of the Gilgamesh Epic

The second Akkadian incarnation of the Flood Story is at once the most famous and the least ancient. It occurs in the *Epic of Gilgamesh*, so far the only Babylonian composition to make it as a Penguin Classic and unquestionably the crown jewel of Akkadian literature. In this very polished work the story of the Flood and the Ark is incorporated as a single episode in Tablet XI within a much longer literary achievement, which in its completed form ran to twelve separate tablets. From our perspective the Flood narrative originally formed part of a completely

independent story that was central not to the life and times of
Gilgamesh, king of Uruk, but rather to the behaviour and near-
destruction of the human race at large, not to mention the
animals. Within the *Gilgamesh Epic* as a whole the recycled story
has felt to many readers today to be something of an afterthought.

Tablet XI of the Gilgamesh Epic *in which George Smith read the Flood Story
for the first time in 1872; a reproduction of the first published photograph.*

While it is certain that the Late Assyrian Gilgamesh Ark-cum-
Flood narrative derives from earlier accounts written in the second
millennium BC, there is no known example of an Old Babylonian

97

Gilgamesh story that deals with these iconic events. All our Flood Story sources from that time belong to *Atrahasis*. We will consider in Chapters 7 and 8 the extent to which our earlier second-millennium *Ark Tablet*, likewise an example of *Atrahasis*, stands behind the latter first-millennium account in *Gilgamesh XI*.

In the Assyrian Gilgamesh story the hero of the Flood is called Utnapishti. This name means *I-found-life* (or *He-found-life*), and was directly inspired by, if not meant to be a translation of, the Sumerian name Ziusudra. When he appears in the Gilgamesh story he is called either *Utnapishti, son of Ubar-Tutu,* or *the Shuruppakean, son of Ubar-Tutu.*

In none of the surviving copies of *Atrahasis* (as far as I can see) is the hero ever referred to as a king. Utnapishti, too, is never referred to as a king, and there is no real reason to think he was one, except for one point in the *Flood Tablet* where a palace is suddenly mentioned (discussed later on), but this, in my view, has been stuck into the text, reflecting contamination from the historical chronicle tradition where Ziusudra – with whom Utnapishti is identified – really was a king.

The relationship between Enki and **Atra-hasīs** or Ea and Utnapishti is conventionally portrayed as that between master and servant. If neither **Atra-hasīs** nor Utnapishti was a king but, so-to-speak, a private citizen, this does raise the question of the grounds on which these 'proto-Noahs' were selected from among their peers to fulfil their great task. It is not evident that either was an obvious choice as, say, a famous boat-builder. There is some indication of temple connections, but nothing to indicate that the hero was actually a member of the priesthood. Perhaps the selection was on the grounds that what was needed was a fine, upright individual who would listen to divine orders and carry them out to the full whatever his private misgivings, but we are not told.

As investigation goes forward in this book now we will pursue what happened to the Flood Story as it translated itself beyond the cuneiform world into the Hebrew of the Book of Genesis and the Arabic of the Koran. In addition, there is the testimony of the excellent Berossus to round out the picture.

The Flood Story in Berossus

Just when the old cuneiform world was on the wane and rule over ancient Mesopotamia was in the hands of Aramaic and Greek speakers, a Babylonian priest known to us as Berossus compiled a work about everything Babylonian known to him which he called *Babyloniaka* (Babylonian things). His name is the Greek version (Βήρωσσος) of a proper Babylonian proper name, very likely to be reconstructed as Bel-re'ushu, 'The Lord – or Bel – is his shepherd'. Berossus lived in the ancient Iraq of the third century BC, spoke Babylonian (as well as Aramaic and Greek) and could no doubt read cuneiform fluently. Since he was employed in the Marduk Temple at Babylon he had access to all the cuneiform tablets he could possibly want (on top of which they were probably all perfectly complete, too). With their aid he compiled his great work, which he dedicated to the king, Antiochus I Soter (280–261 BC).

Berossus recounts the Flood Story in very recognisable terms in his Book 2, after a list of ten kings and their sages. Unfortunately, his writings (possibly also including those of a pseudo-Berossus) have only survived in quotations by later authors, and the chain of transmission is rather a tortuous one. What we have today are twenty-two quotations or paraphrases of his output, known as the *Fragmenta*, and eleven statements about the man himself, called *Testimonia*. These are the work of classical, Jewish and Christian writers, few of whom are household names today. It is interesting that good Mesopotamian details are preserved in Berossus's account of the flood that do not appear in the Genesis account version, such as the dream motif – or in either earlier tradition – such as the name of the month, or the burying of the inscriptions, an idea which actually does appear in a different cuneiform text altogether.

Berossus writes according to Polyhistor (as preserved by Eusebius):

After the death of Ardates (variant Otiartes: this is Ubar-Tutu!) his son Xisuthros ruled for eighteen sars and in his time a great flood occurred, of which this account is on record:

Kronos appeared to him in the course of a dream and said that on the fifteenth day of the month Daisos mankind would be destroyed by a flood. So he ordered him to dig a hole and to bury the beginnings, middles, and ends of all writings in Sippar, the city of the Sun(-god); and after building a boat, to embark with his kinsfolk and close friends. He was to stow food and drink and put both birds and animals on board and then sail away when he had got everything ready, If asked where he was sailing, he was to reply, 'To the gods, to pray for blessings on men.'

He did not disobey, but got a boat built, five stades long and two stades wide, and when everything was properly arranged he sent his wife and children and closest friend on board. When the flood had occurred and as soon as it had subsided, Xisuthros let out some of the birds, which, finding no food or place to rest, came back to the vessel. After a few days Xisuthros again let out the birds, and they again returned to the ship, this time with their feet covered in mud. When they were let out for the third time they failed to return to the boat, and Xisuthros inferred that land had appeared. Thereupon he prised open a portion of the seams of the boat, and seeing that it had run aground on some mountain, he disembarked with his wife, his daughter, and his pilot, prostrated himself to the ground, set up an altar and sacrificed to the gods, and then disappeared along with those who had disembarked with him. When Xisuthros and his party did not come back, those who had stayed in the boat disembarked and looked for him, calling him by name. Xisuthros himself did not appear to them any more, but there was a voice out of the air instructing them on the need to worship the gods, seeing that he was going to dwell with the gods because of his piety, and that his wife, daughter and pilot shared in the same honour. He told them to return to Babylon, and, as was destined for them, to rescue the writings from Sippar and disseminate them to mankind. Also he told them that they were in the country of Armenia. They heard this, sacrificed to the gods, and journeyed on foot to Babylon. A part of the boat, which came to rest in the Gordyaean mountains of Armenia, still remains, and some people scrape pitch off the boat and use it as charms. So when they came to Babylon they dug up the writings from Sippar, and, after founding many cities and setting up shrines, they once more established Babylon.

Berossus writes according to Abydenus:

After whom others ruled, and Sisithros, to whom Kronos revealed that there would be a deluge on the fifteenth day of Daisios, and ordered him to conceal in Sippar, the city of the Sun(-god), every available writing. Sisithros accomplished all these things, immediately sailed to Armenia, and thereupon what the god had announced happened. On the third day, after the rain abated, he let loose birds in the attempt to ascertain if they would see land not covered with water. Not knowing where to alight, being confronted with a boundless sea, they returned to Sisithros. And similarly with others. When he succeeded with a third group – they returned with muddy feathers – the gods took him away from mankind. However, the boat in Armenia supplied the local inhabitants with wooden amulets as charms.

Keep the excellent Berossus in mind; we will call upon him later.

The Koran

The life of Nuh (Noah) before the Flood is described in Sura 71 of the Koran. He was the son of Lamech, one of the patriarchs from the generations of Adam. Nuh was a prophet, called to warn mankind and encourage the people to change their ways. The following quotations collect what we learn about Nuh and his ark from the Koran (the translation uses Noah throughout):

We saved him and those with him on the Ark and let them survive.

Sura 10:73

It was revealed to Noah, 'None of your people will believe, other than those who have already done so, so do not be distressed by what they do. Build the Ark under Our [watchful] eyes and with Our inspiration. Do not plead with Me for those who have done evil – they will be drowned.' So he began to build the Ark, and whenever leaders of his people passed by, they laughed at him. He said, 'You may scorn us now, but we will come to scorn you: you will find out who will receive a humiliating punishment, and on whom a lasting suffering will descend.' When Our command came, and water gushed up out of the earth, We said, 'Place on board this Ark a pair of each species, and your own family – except those against whom the sentence has already been passed – and those who have believed,' though only a few believed with him. He said, 'Board the Ark. In the name of God it shall sail and anchor. My God is most forgiving and merciful.' It sailed with them on waves like mountains, and Noah called out to his son, who stayed behind, 'Come aboard with us, my son, do not stay with the disbelievers.' But he replied, 'I will seek refuge on a mountain to save me from the water.' Noah said, 'Today there is no refuge from God's command, except for those on whom He has mercy.' The waves cut them off from each other and he was among the drowned. Then it was said, 'Earth, swallow up your water, and sky, hold back,' and the water subsided, the command was fulfilled. The Ark settled on Mount Judi, and it was said, 'Gone are those evildoing people!' Noah called out to his Lord, saying, 'My

Lord, my son was one of my family, though Your promise is true, and You are the most just of all judges.' God said, 'Noah, he was not one of your family. What he did was not right. Do not ask Me for things you know nothing about. I am warning you not to be foolish.' He said, 'My Lord, I take refuge with You from asking for things I know nothing about. If You do not forgive me, and have mercy on me, I shall be one of the losers.' And it was said, 'Noah, descend in peace from Us, with blessings on you and on some of the communities that will spring from those who are with you.'

Sura 11:36–48

Noah said, 'My Lord, help me! They call me a liar,' and so We revealed to him: 'Build the Ark under Our watchful eye and according to Our revelation. When Our command comes and water gushes up out of the earth, take pairs of every species on board, and your family, except for those on whom the sentence has already been passed – do not plead with me for the evildoers: they will be drowned – and when you and your companions are settled on the Ark, say, "Praise be to God, who delivered us from the wicked people," and say, "My Lord, let me land with Your blessing: it is You who provide the best landings."' There are signs in all this: We have always put [people] to the test.

Sura 23:26–30

He said, 'My Lord, my people have rejected me, so make a firm judgement between me and them, and save me and my believing followers.' So We saved him and his followers in the fully laden ship, and drowned the rest.

Sura 26:117–20

We sent Noah out to his people. He lived among them for fifty years short of a thousand but when the Flood overwhelmed them they were still doing evil. We saved him and those with him on the Ark (safina). We made this a sign for all people.

Sura 29:14–15

> *So We opened the gates of the sky with torrential water, burst the earth with gushing springs: the waters met for a preordained purpose. We carried him along on a vessel of planks and nails that floated under Our watchful eye, a reward for the one who had been rejected.*
>
> Sura 54:11–14

> *But when the Flood rose high, We saved you in the floating ship, making that event a reminder for you: attentive ears may take heed.*
>
> Sura 69:10–12

The Ark Tablet

It is an exciting matter to compare the new *Ark Tablet* – dating to the Old Babylonian Period, probably about 1750 BC – with all these familiar and less familiar accounts. There are sixty new lines of literary Babylonian to occupy us, and poking about among the words certainly uncovers interesting things concerning the Flood Story as it developed within ancient Mesopotamian literature and beyond. The *Ark Tablet* packs in crucial and dramatic sections of the broader story which we will investigate in the following chapters, at the same time comparing what we have already known from these versions in Sumerian, Babylonian, Hebrew, Greek and Arabic.

Our task now is to see what evidence can be wrung out of each new line of cuneiform writing. Many new ideas come and some old ones will have to be upset, not least the shape of the famous Ark in the *Epic of Gilgamesh*, as we will see.

5

The Ark Tablet

And Noah he often said to his wife
When he sat down to dine,
"I don't care where the water goes
If it doesn't get into the wine."
G.K. Chesterton

Some wonderful cuneiform tablets have come to light for the Mesopotamian Flood detective since George Smith's day. Everyone is interested in them and all Assyriologists keep their eye out for pieces of cuneiform that might start off '*Wall! Wall . . . !*'. Texts of this exalted literary quality, either excavated on archaeological sites or identified in museum collections, have usually been quickly published and translated into one or more modern languages; the interested reader has always been able to find them and see what they have to offer. Such documents are of concern to the widest possible readership: culturally their content belongs to the world at large.

We come now to the Flood Story tablet that has led to the writing of this book and which it has been my good fortune to publish here for the first time. The tablet, like many documents of its period, is designed to fit comfortably in the reader's hand; it is much the same size and weight as a contemporary mobile phone.

Let us recap the important details.

The *Ark Tablet* was written during the Old Babylonian period, broadly 1900–1700 BC. The document was not dated by the scribe, but from the shape and appearance of the tablet itself, the character and composition of the cuneiform signs and the grammatical forms and usages, we can be sure that this is the period in which it was written. It was composed in Semitic Babylonian, that is Akkadian, in a literary style. The hand is smallish and neat and that of a fully trained cuneiform scribe whose name, unfortunately, is not recorded on the tablet. The text has been written out very ably without error and for a specific purpose; it is certainly not a school practice tablet from a beginner, or anything of that kind. It measures 11.5 x 6.0 cm and contains exactly sixty lines.

The front (or obverse) is in fine condition and virtually everything can be read and translated. The back (or reverse) is damaged in the middle of most lines, with the result that not everything there can be read now, although much of substantial importance can be deciphered; some parts are simply missing altogether and other parts are very badly worn. The tablet has at some time been fragmented in several pieces and has evidently been fired and assembled in modern times by a competent ceramic conservator. The *Ark Tablet* arrived in Great Britain in 1948 in the possession of Mr Leonard Simmonds and was given to his son Mr Douglas Simmonds in 1974. Throughout the time of writing it has been resident in the author's desk at the British Museum, which has allowed repeated checking of the signs and renewed attempts at incomplete words and signs.

The *Ark Tablet* is of colossal importance for the history of the Flood Story both in cuneiform and biblical Hebrew, and is among the most significant inscriptions ever to come to light on a clay tablet, for the reasons discussed in the following chapters. The narrative quotes verbatim speeches by the god Ea and the man Atra-hasīs, the heroic Babylonian equivalent of Noah, concerning what is about to happen and what he must do. It concludes at the point when Atra-hasīs's shipwright seals the door behind him before the waters come. We proceed with a straightforward translation of the original Babylonian text of the *Ark Tablet* into English.

The Ark Tablet, *front view: how to build an ark, hands on.*

On the front of the tablet we read:

"Wall, wall! Reed wall, reed wall!
Atra-hasīs, pay heed to my advice,
That you may live for ever!
Destroy your house, build a boat;
Spurn property and save life!
Draw out the boat that you will make
On a circular plan;
Let her length and breadth be equal,

Let her floor area be one field, let her sides be one nindan
    high.
You saw kannu *ropes and* ašlu *ropes/rushes for [a coracle before!]*
Let someone (else) twist the fronds and palm-fibre for you!
It will surely consume 14,430 (sūtu)!"
"I set in place thirty ribs
Which were one parsiktu-*vessel thick, ten* nindan *long;*
I set up 3,600 stanchions within her
Which were half (a parsiktu-*vessel) thick, half a* nindan *high;*
I constructed her cabins above and below."
"I apportioned one finger of bitumen for her outsides;
I apportioned one finger of bitumen for her interior;
*I had (already) poured out one finger of bitumen onto her
    cabins;*
I caused the kilns to be loaded with 28,800 (sūtu) of kupru-
    bitumen
And I poured 3,600 (sūtu) of ittû-*bitumen within.*
The bitumen did not come to the surface [lit. up to me];
    (so) I added five fingers of lard,
I ordered the kilns to be loaded . . . in equal measure;
(With) tamarisk wood (?) (and) stalks (?)
. . . (= I completed the mixture).

On the lower edge, only parts of two of the four lines can be
deciphered:

. . .
Going between her ribs;
. . .
. . . the ittû-*bitumen . . .*

On the other side we read:

"I applied (?) the outside kupru-*bitumen from the kilns,*
*Out of the 120 gur-measures, which the workmen had put to
    one side."*

The Ark Tablet, *back view, showing the kind of damage that can happen to the best of tablets.*

"I lay myself down (?) . . . of rejoicing
My kith and kin [went into] the boat . . . ;
Joyful . . . of my in-laws,
And the porter with . . . and . . .
They ate and drank their fill."
"As for me there was no word in my heart, and
. . . my heart
. . . my . . .
. . . of my . . .
. . . of my lips
. . . I slept with difficulty;
I went up on the roof [and prayed] to the moon god Sin, my
 lord:
'Let my heartbreak (?) be extinguished! [Do you not disap]pear!'
 . . . darkness;
 Into my . . .'
Sin, from his throne, swore as to annihilation
And desolation on (the) darkened [day (to come)]."
"But the wild animals from the steppe [(. . .)]
Two by two the boat did [they enter] . . ."
"I had . . . five of beer . . .
They were transporting eleven or twelve . . .
Three measures of šiqbum . . . ;
One-third (measure) of fodder . . . and **kurdinnu** plant (?)."
"I ordered several times (?) a one-finger (layer) of lard for the
 girmadû roller,
Out of the thirty gur which the workmen had put to one
 side."
"When I shall have gone into the boat,
Caulk the frame of her door!"

A very dramatic moment to stop!

6

Flood Warning

If the centre of the gall bladder is inflated with water a flood will come.

Babylonian liver omen

The *Ark Tablet* starts with no preamble: the Flood warning speech is delivered just like that, and it is only by investigating the other cuneiform accounts that we can understand the background and realise that it is the god Enki who is speaking and that he has to make two attempts, using distinct devices, to get the urgent message across.

First, then, we turn to the classic *Old Babylonian Atrahasis* version:

Atra-hasīs opened his mouth
And addressed his lord . . .

Just when the narrative is satisfactorily under way, as often happens with cuneiform stories, there are nine lines completely missing. Then the tablet resumes the narrative, from which it can be surmised that the missing lines contained some explanation of a worrisome dream:

Atra-hasīs opened his mouth
And addressed his lord,
*   "Teach me the meaning [of the dream]*
*   . . . that I may look out for its conclusion."*
[Enki] opened his mouth
And addressed his slave:

> *"You say, 'What am I to seek?'*
> *Take note of the message I am going to send you:*
> 20 *Wall, listen to me!*
> *Reed wall, observe all my words!*
> *Destroy your house, build a boat,*
> *Spurn property and save life . . ."*
> *Old Babylonian Atrahasis: iii* 1–2, 11–23

Enki thus has a very urgent set of instructions – such as no human had ever heard before – for the unwitting hero-to-be: many details would have to be got right. Enki's message-dream attempt was unsuccessful. It was probably too obscure or complicated, and no Frances Danby vision of a Deluge sweeping away the world with **Atra-hasīs** the only man who could save it. Mesopotamian dreams were an important means of communication from god to man and, like omens, could arrive spontaneously or be induced by ritual. (There is a manual of procedure, dating from around 450 BC, for this sort of thing in the British Museum: it explains how to procure a personal message dream, which is brought up from the underworld by Wind Messengers, with the help of a Dream Ladder, to the client waiting on the roof, stupefied with incense.) Either way dream messages often needed unravelling, and a specialist class of interpreters was to hand; message-laden dreams requiring exposition are a classic device in Mesopotamian stories.

The other Flood Story versions back up this dream-boat picture. *Middle Babylonian Nippur* is very damaged but one revealing word survives. Enki says, in the Akkadian, *apaššar*, '. . . I will explain . . .', using the verb that is always employed for expounding dreams (*pašāru*). From *Middle Babylonian Ugarit* we learn more: that **Atra-hasīs** is in Ea's temple:

> *When the gods took counsel concerning the lands*
> *They brought about a flood in the world regions.*

5   . . . hears . . .
     . . . Ea in his heart.

"I am Atra-hasīs,
I have been staying in the temple of Ea, my master,
And I know all.

     I know of the counsel of the great gods,
10   I know of their oath, although they should not have
         revealed it to me."

Line 7 in the version from Ugarit suggests that Atra-hasīs had stayed overnight in the temple hoping for a message dream, which was evidently successful and the dream informative. If so, some anxiety must have prompted his enquiry originally. (This procedure was favoured by rulers, and known rather curiously to Assyriology as *incubation*. King Kurigalzu tried it once at the great temple at Babylon in about 1400 BC, anxious to know whether his anorexic wife Qatantum was ever going to get pregnant, and the gods looked her entry up in the Tablet of Sins, but we never find out what happened.) Line 7 can equally well be translated 'I lived' or 'I was living in the temple of Ea', and some scholars have thought that Atra-hasīs must have been a priest, like Ziusudra in the Sumerian version. The *Assyrian Recension* shows Atra-hasīs waiting in the temple for Ea to tell him in some way of the gods' decision. (The scribe dutifully informs us in line 11 that some signs were broken in the text he was copying.):

"Ea, master, [I heard] your entry,
[I] noticed steps like [your] footsteps."

     [Atra-hasīs] bowed down, he prostrated up . . . himself,
     he stood.
He opened [his mouth], saying,

5   "[*Master*], *I heard your entry,*
         [*I noticed*] *steps like your footsteps.*
         [*Ea, master*], *I heard your entry,*
         [*I noticed*] *steps like your footsteps.*"

         "*. . . like seven years,*
10   *. . . your . . . has made the weak thirsty,*

     . . . (new it-was-broken) *. . . I have seen your face*
     . . . tell me your (pl.) decision(?).

In the *Sumerian Flood Story*, however, Ziusudra's message came to him in some other way:

> *Day by day, standing constantly at the . . . of Enki, the wise lord.*
> It was no dream, *coming out and speaking . . .*

Our slightly scrappy tablets, taken together, present a convincing picture of Enki's first attempt to warn **Atra-hasīs** through a dream, but there is unexpected confirmation from the very latest Mesopotamian witness, the Greek *Babyloniaka* of Berossus. In this, the dream tradition was a crucial part of the story, and proved to be the only message conduit needed. Cronus, the father of Zeus, is to be equated with the Babylonian god Marduk, according to Berossus. So Cronus corresponds to Ea, Marduk's father:

> *Cronus appeared to Xisuthros in a dream and revealed that on the fifteenth day of the month Daisios mankind would be destroyed by a flood.*

The important thing from the Babylonian story point of view is that the dream technique was ineffective in getting the message clearly across to **Atra-hasīs**. This is hardly surprising: it was a heavy matter and there were many details that would have to be got right. Ea, therefore, had to try another form of undercover speech.

Talking to the Wall

It is at this point that the text of the *Ark Tablet* (with which this book is so concerned) actually begins:

> *"Wall, wall! Reed wall, reed wall!*
> *Atra-hasīs, pay heed to my advice,*
> *That you may live for ever!*
> *Destroy your house, build a boat;*
> 5   *Spurn possessions and save life!"*

From the moment when George Smith stepped into the limelight in the London of 1872 to declaim 'Wall, wall! Reed fence, reed fence!' these dramatic words, god speaking to man, have been perhaps the most famous in cuneiform. Five flood-story versions, including our own *Ark Tablet*, preserve this speech or part of it. Enki gets the message to his servant this time by talking to the wall, by which means Atra-hasīs learns what will happen.

In the *Sumerian Flood Story* Ziusudra actually overhears the god Enki talking to the wall:

> 153 *"Side-wall, standing at the left side . . . ;*
> 154 *Side-wall, I want to talk to you; [heed] my words,*
> 155 *[Pay attention to] my instructions . . . "*

The speech in *Old Babylonian Atrahasis*:

> *Pay attention to the message that I will speak to you:*
> 20 *"Wall, listen to me!*
> *Reed wall, observe all my words!*
> *Destroy your house, build a boat,*
> *Spurn property and save life."*

And in *Middle Babylonian Ugarit*:

12   *"Wall, hear . . . "*

And in *Assyrian Recension*:

15   *". . . ! Reed hut! Reed-hut!*
        . . . pay attention to me!
        . . . make a boat (?) . . . "

And in *Gilgamesh XI*:

> *"Reed fence, reed fence! Brick wall, brick wall!*
> *Listen, O reed fence! Pay heed, O brick wall!*
> *O man of Shuruppak, son of Ubar-Tutu,*
> *Demolish the house, build a boat!*
> 25   *Abandon riches and seek survival!*
> *Spurn property and save life!*
> *Put on board the boat the seed of all living creatures!"*

Recruiting Atra-hasīs's reed walls and fences as a kind of jungle telegraph enables Ea to persist with the claim that he *didn't actually tell Atra-hasīs himself* what was going to happen. He just happened to murmur it out loud near the great reed walls, and it is not really his fault if some echo reached Atra-hasīs. How is this image to be understood?

The answer comes from the injunction to pull down the house in order to build the boat from the raw materials. As Lambert put it, and I entirely agree with him,

> *We are to conceive Atra-hasīs as living in a reed house such as are still found in southern Mesopotamia where reeds grow to an enormous height. No doubt the wind might whistle through the reed walls, and Enki seems to have whispered to his devotee in the same way, since it was no longer himself but the wall*

that transmitted the message. Since reed boats were as common as reed houses, the obvious course was to pull up the bundles of reeds which composed the walls of the house and to fasten them to a wooden framework as a boat.

Reed architecture: a mid-twentieth century mudhif of Abdullah of the Al-Essa tribe, in the marshes of S. Iraq.

Reed boats: the characteristic fishing boat of the marshes that dates back to the time before the Flood.

For the original readers of *Atrahasis* the events of the story were of course unfolding in the remotest antediluvian past, and this reed-and-water landscape of the southern marshes with its characteristic houses and boats would be how urban Babylonians of the second millennium BC imagined their own aboriginal world to have been in its entirety. For them this was the ultimate backdrop to the story of *Atrahasis* and Enki's inspiring speech. What is extraordinary is that we can still look in on this life in the wetland marshes of southern Iraq, for it survived more or less unchanged from primeval times right down until the murderous interference of Saddam Hussein twenty years ago. Many authors have written on the Iraqi marshes and their people and have drawn attention to what has happened there. Recently, the return of surviving families, who had fled east for their lives, offered the first sign that the original environment might one day be restored. Perhaps in no other area of Mesopotamian studies has it been possible for the modern world to bring things to life by virtue of an almost unchanging ancient landscape; many photographs show traditional reed houses, floating as though comprising a small island, with livestock happily milling about inside the fence roundabout. The same skilful use of plaited reeds can engender cathedral-like buildings of extraordinary beauty, as well as slim, almond-shaped boats high in prow and stern, which navigate the shallows like minnows to allow the leisured spearing of fish.

Atra-hasīs in this incarnation does not live in a mud-brick house in a city with temples and palaces; his house is made of reeds, strong and willowy, that can easily be recycled to plait a lifeboat if that is what is needed. By the time the story surfaces in first-millennium Gilgamesh the house is of mud-brick with a reed fence; the old resonant wording endures.

The elegant shape of the marsh boat is very ancient. There are examples pictured on seals; one of Woolley's graves at Ur included a model of one in bitumen. Two of the known Flood Story tablets enshrine a reed 'ark' constructed in the tradition of this antediluvian long marsh boat. It is old-fashioned, dysfunctional and, to be frank, of little more use than a prototype, but we had better have a look at it.

A bitumen boat model of the mid-third millennium BC from a Sumerian grave in the city of Ur.

The Prototype Ark

Two later second-millennium Flood versions from the old Sumerian city of Nippur (in southern Iraq) espouse this basic prototype form: the *Sumerian Flood Story* and *Middle Babylonian Nippur*. That both these tablets originated at Nippur does not force us to conclude that there was a strong-minded boat club there with its own ideas of what constituted a proper ark, but it is intriguing that the tradition only survives in Nippur sources.

In the *Sumerian Flood Story* the Ark is called a giš.má-gur₄-gur₄, which Miguel Civil, the Sumerologist whom I would follow anywhere, translated simply as 'huge boat'. It occurs three times within four lines, so we can be in no doubt as to the reading:

> *After the flood had swept over the land for seven days and*
>   *seven nights*
> *And the destructive wind had rocked the huge boat*
> *(giš-má-gur₄-gur₄) in the high water*
> *The Sun god came out, illuminating heaven and earth.*
> *Ziusudra made an opening in the huge boat*
> *And the Sun god with his rays entered the huge boat.*
>
> *Sumerian Flood Story*: 204–8

The Sumerian word for boat is giš.má, where giš shows that it is made of wood, and má means boat. In Akkadian the corresponding word is *eleppu*, like its English equivalent a feminine noun.

There is a common, everyday kind of Sumerian river boat called a má-gur, which gave rise to the Akkadian loanword *makurru*. The name literally means a 'boat that gurs'. Unfortunately, no one is absolutely sure what this verb 'gur' means, or how a má-gur differs from a plain má. We can say, if it is helpful, that any *makurru* is an *eleppu* but not every *eleppu* is a *makurru*. Whatever technically distinguishes a *makurru* from *eleppus* in general, the two words are often regarded as synonymous in literature; in *Old Babylonian Atrahasis* the Ark is referred to both as an *eleppu* and as a *makurru*, much as we might say 'ark' and 'boat' of the same vessel in English.

The *Sumerian Flood Story* mentions a super version of the giš-má-gur called the giš.má-gur₄-gur₄, evidently a special, outsized form of the same. This giant *makurru*-boat does not seem to be mentioned in any of the numerous documents from daily life concerned with boats, and perhaps it only took to the water in the world of mythology. Nevertheless it did warrant inclusion as line 291 of the cuneiform boat list, part of the ancient dictionary list-of-words project upon which we so often depend, in which old Sumerian words for boats and their parts are matched with their more modern equivalents in Akkadian. Line 291 records for us that the Sumerian word giš.má-gur-gur, like the giš.má-gur, also gave rise to a Babylonian loanword, *makurkurru*. It is this loanword *makurkurru* that is the type of ark in *Middle Babylonian Nippur*, and we are expressly told that it is made of reeds:

> "[*Fine reeds*], *as many as possible, should be woven (?),*
>   *should be gathered (?) for it;*
>   *. . . build a big boat (eleppam rabītam)*
>   *Let its structure be [interwoven (?)] entirely of fine reed.*
>   *. . . let it be a makurkurru-boat with the name Life-*
>   *Saver.*
>   *. . . roof it over with a strong covering.*
>   Middle Babylonian Nippur: 5–9

This 'big boat' of *makurkurru* type could be roofed over. I particularly like the fact that the *makurkurru* in *Middle Babylonian Nippur* has the name 'Lifesaver', *Nāṣirat Napištim*. It should have been painted on the prow in 3D luminous cuneiform signs, even if they skipped the champagne at the launch.

WHAT SHAPE WAS THIS KIND OF BOAT THEN?
We can identify the characteristic shape of the *makurru* with the help of a geometrical diagram from the world of cuneiform educational mathematics, much like that illustrated in the following chapter. This shows two circles, drawn with one overlapping the other. Here a Babylonian teacher is expounding the mathematical properties of the pointed almond or biconvex shape generated by such intimate circles. We learn from him at the same time that this shape is called *makurru*, which will therefore evoke or correspond to the outline of a contemporary *makurru* boat, seen from above.

makurru-shape

This is a boat that is, broadly speaking, in the same family as the traditional ancient craft from the marshes. I think it is fair to conclude that this is what the Nippur boat-builders had in mind, and that these mid-second-millennium accounts preserve a narrow almond-shaped reed-boat tradition that has been associated with the Flood Story from the moment it came into being. Enlil's speech is the hallmark of the *Atrahasis* story, probably honed to a pithy brevity and dramatic effectiveness through a long oral history, refined even into a kind of Mesopotamian mantra. The flood hero has been informed by Enki, in traditional terms, that a horrible watery end is nigh. He must encapsulate and safeguard the very germ of life, animal and human, so that the familiar planet can be revivified when it is all over. He must build a lifeboat. Perhaps, with the passage of time, or even the odd outbreak of uncomfortable flooding, people began to think that a *makurru*, however large, might not hack it when it came to saving the whole world. It is under those circumstances – in my view – that the prototype came to be replaced by a model that was superior in every way, ideal for world conservation purposes, namely the biggest rope and bitumen coracle the world had ever seen.

7

The Question of Shape

And when the Sieve turned round and round,
And every one cried, 'You'll all be drowned!'
They called aloud, 'Our Sieve ain't big,
But we don't care a button! we don't care a fig!
In a Sieve we'll go to sea!'

Edward Lear

The most remarkable feature provided by the *Ark Tablet* is that Atra-hasīs's lifeboat was definitely, unambiguously *round*.

No one had ever thought of that possibility. Confronting the fact comes, initially, as a shock. For everyone knows what Noah's Ark, the *real* Ark, looks like. A squat wooden affair with prow and stern and a little house in the middle, not to mention a gangplank and several windows. No respectable child's nursery at one time was ever without one, with its chewed pairs of lead or wooden animals.

A classic example of a toy Noah's Ark and animals in painted wood; from about 1825 and probably German.

123

Sunday entertainment.

The tenacity of the conventional Western vision of the Ark is remarkable, and remains, at least to me, inexplicable, for where did it come from in the first place? The only 'evidence' that artists or toymakers had before them was the description in the Old Testament where, as we will see, Noah's Ark is altogether a different proposition.

Whatever the pattern was before, we can now see that the Mesopotamian ark from Old Babylonian times was unquestionably round. We learn this fact from the new *Ark Tablet*, the remarkable and unexpected contents of which will now hold our attention for many pages to come. For this tablet, with its sixty lines, has more to offer than any other cuneiform tablet I have ever encountered, and it is the duty of any self-respecting Assyriologist to give such a document the full *squeeze* treatment and ensure that no possible item of information inside it is left unextracted.

We have seen that the tablet begins with a classic ancient speech advocating a boat of recycled reeds. Without pause Enki lays out unambiguously for Atra-hasīs what he is to do, which is to build something altogether different:

> *Draw out the boat that you will make*
> *On a circular plan;*
> *Let her length and breadth be equal,*
> *Let her floor area be one field, let her sides be one* nindan
> *(high).*
> 10. *You saw* kannu *ropes and* ašlu *ropes/rushes for* |*a coracle*
> *before!*|
> *Let someone (else) twist the fronds and palm-fibre for*
> *you!*
> *It will surely need 14,430 (sūtu)!*

Reading lines 6–7 for the first time was certainly an adrenalin-stirring moment, and my first reaction – as anybody's would have been – was *can this be right? A circular* plan . . . ?

But then, thinking it over, staring into space with the tablet precariously poised over the desk, the idea began to make sense. A truly round boat would be a *coracle*, and they certainly had coracles in ancient Mesopotamia and when you thought about it a coracle is exceptionally buoyant and would never sink and if it happened to be difficult to steer or stop from going round and round that would not matter, because all it had to do was keep its precious contents safe and dry until the waters receded. So, no need to gasp and stretch one's eyes. On the contrary, it made a lot of sense, and what was going on here was something serious and valid and highly interesting . . .

The Akkadian word for the Ark is, here too, *eleppu*, 'boat'. The phrase 'circular plan' in Akkadian is *eṣerti kippati*, in which *eṣertu* means 'plan', and *kippatu* 'circle'. The *Ark Tablet* does not use a special word for coracle, although there was one in Akkadian, *quppu*, as we will see.

Enki tells Atra-hasīs in a very practical way how to get his boat started; he is to draw out a field-sized plan of the round boat on the ground. The simplest way to do this would have been with a peg and a long string; the peg is stuck in what becomes the middle of the circle, the boat-builder walks the taut string round to mark the circumference, much as described later in this chapter by Colonel Chesney in laying out a differently shaped boat. The stage is thus set for building the world's largest coracle, with a base area of 3,600 m², with a diameter of, near enough, 70m. Atra-hasīs actually probably did not need to be told such elementary stuff. There is good background from other cuneiform texts where the word *uṣurtu*, the more common form of *eṣertu*, is used of the plan of a building detectable on the ground.

Then comes Enki's remark, 'let her length and breadth be equal', at first sight disconcerting because everyone knows what a circle looks like and therefore what a circular boat would look like. This is a god speaking, however, who is not concerned with the theoretical nature of circles but with reinforcing the image of a round boat; unlike any other boat, it has neither prow nor stern but is the same width – or as we would say, diameter – in all directions. Enki's instructions to be build a coracle were very specific, given the plan he had in mind, and his servant Atra-hasīs had to be clear on this.

A circle within a square forming part of an exercise in Sumerian geometry; this large tablet is the teacher's reference copy with all the answers.

Atra-hasīs in the *Ark Tablet*, one senses, knew as much about boats as the next man, although Enki did have to encourage him about details, suggesting that he could get help (lines 10–12) as he began to contemplate just what lay ahead of him in building the world's first Super Coracle.

It was obviously a sound idea to tackle the first reading of this new inscription with the familiar Flood Story texts close at hand, and there were further surprises to come. I discovered before long that two of the tablets, both conveniently in the collection of the British Museum and easily consulted, *also proved on reinvestigation to feature an ark that was round*. The crucial cuneiform signs were in one case damaged and in the other without good context, but in both the key word *kippatu*, 'circle', was there in the clay.

Old Babylonian Atrahasis

In *Old Babylonian Atrahasis* the section which describes the Ark is closely related to the wording of the *Ark Tablet* but is incomplete. In line 28 we can now recognise the partly preserved word *kippatu*:

> "*The boat which you are to build*
> *[Let its . . .] be equal [(. . .)] [. . .]*
> 28 *[. . .] circle . . . [. . .]*
> *Roof it over like the* Apsû."

The cuneiform signs readable in line 28 are: [. . .] ˹ki-ip-pa-ti˺ x x [x (x)].

Assyrian Smith

Lines 1–2 of *Assyrian Smith*, close enough in date to the first-millennium *Gilgamesh XI* tablets, contain the same important matter, but although the word has long been correctly read its significance could never be appreciated, and even now it is still not quite clear how this passage should be understood because it is incomplete.

> "[. . .] . . . *let [its . . . be . . .]*
> 2 *[. . .] . . . like a circle . . . [. . .]*"

The cuneiform signs in line 2 are: [. . .] x ki-ma ˹kip-pa-tim˺ x [. . .]

There is a crucial difference in the second case, one thousand years on, in that the boat, or some characteristic of it, is now '*like* a circle', which of course is not the same thing as *being* a circle, but it would be a stern sceptic who insisted that this was unconnected with the shape of the vessel itself, in view of the other two accounts. It is evident that Enki's description befuddled Atra-hasīs, who in this later Assyrian version of the story emerges as much more self-effacing than his Old Babylonian counterpart and asks for a guide drawing; one imagines a hand reaching down with Rembrandt's pointed finger to trace the explicit shape on the ground:

> Atra-hasīs opened his mouth to speak,
> And said to Ea, [his] master,
>   "I have never built a boat . . .
>   Draw the design on the ground
>   That I may see [the design] and [build] the boat."
> Ea drew [the design] on the ground.
>
> Assyrian Smith: 11–16

Here, in a flash of cross-millennial understanding, we encounter a recognisable human being. Atra-hasīs, going about his daily life and far from thinking about saving the planet, has been charged all of a sudden – by Enki himself – with an impossible responsibility for which he is perhaps Mesopotamia's least suitable candidate. He has never built a boat, and for him verbal descriptions are not enough: if he is going to have to do this he wants a clear plan. This professed reluctance or lack of skill to undertake an enormous task suddenly thrust upon him has parallels with Moses in the Book of Exodus, who cries 'Who am I that I should go . . . ?' or with the prophet Jeremiah who, taken aback when called by God to be a prophet, initially protests that he is too young and inexperienced to speak in public.

We now have *three* cuneiform flood tablets in which the Mesopotamian Ark's shape is given as (or in one case, *likened* to) a circle.

Could a round ark, therefore, be the Mesopotamian norm? Emboldened by this giddy progress – and it must be stressed that such an undertaking was courageous in the extreme – I decided to have another look at *Gilgamesh XI*: 48–80, which promotes that hugely famous – but very strange – *cuboid* ark. I say emboldened because this particular passage is one of the most celebrated in cuneiform with a classical status verging on that of Homer. To tamper with the text of *Gilgamesh XI* is probably to invite arrows and hot pitch.

Assyriologists have long known that Old Babylonian manuscripts like the *Ark Tablet* or *Old Babylonian Atrahasis* lie behind the Assyrian version of the whole Gilgamesh story that we know today from the Nineveh library; Jeffrey Tigay gave an enlightening examination of this matter in 1982. Such ancestor tablets were by then already a millennium or more old. Their texts, as we can see from what survives today, were not always identical; words could change their meanings or become obscure, cuneiform signs tend to get damaged, and the finished literature that the ancient editor-scribes who produced Assurbanipal's beautiful library manuscripts finally bequeathed us had run through many hands. Deliberate changes and interpolations were also made along the way, and signs of editorial work – sometimes over hasty – are occasionally still perceptible. With the help of the newly arrived *Ark Tablet* the parallel description of the boat and its building in *Gilgamesh XI* turns out to be a fertile and revealing case study. We can see that an Old Babylonian account of building a round ark, closely related to that of the *Ark Tablet*, lies right under the surface in *Gilgamesh XI*, and we can understand how in the interim its message has become heavily disguised. No one who pored over this story in Assurbanipal's reading room would ever have guessed that Utnapishti's gargantuan Ark was also once a giant coracle made of bituminised rope.

This is a big and bold claim which must be substantiated forthwith. To undertake tilting at this windmill requires another *sprinkling* of cuneiform philology – which will, I hope, suffice to prove the point.

Information about the shape of Utnapishti's Ark as we receive it in *Gilgamesh XI* is split into two sections; first as instructions from Ea; second in Utnapishti's account of the construction.

The instructions from Ea:

> *The boat that you are going to build,*
> 29 *Her dimensions should all correspond:*
> 30 *Her breadth and length should be the same.*
> *Cover her with a roof, like the Apsû.*
>
> *Gilgamesh XI: 28–31*

Next come twenty-six lines of quite separate narrative explaining what Utnapishti was to say to the elders and giving ominous warnings as to what he was to look out for, with no ark information. Then Utnapishti records:

> *On the fifth day I set in place her (outer) surface:*
> 58 *One "acre" was her area, ten rods each her sides stood high,*
> *Ten rods each, the edges of her top were equal.*
> *I set in place her body, I drew up her design.*
> *I gave her six decks,*
> *I divided her into seven parts.*
> *I divided her interior into nine . . .*
>
> *Gilgamesh XI: 57–63*

This is some boat! Square in cross-section, six decks, multiple rooms . . .

However, in *Gilgamesh XI* line 58 the highly significant ark word *kippatu*, = 'circle', is also found. Here, let us beware, it is not spelled in simple signs, but is written with the Sumerian ideogram GÚR. In his great Gilgamesh publication Andrew George took this word as 'area' (George 2003, Vol. 1: 707 fn. 5) and translated the first part of the line as 'one "acre" was her area'. With the benefit of the *Ark Tablet* we can retain the real meaning and take the word to refer to the Ark's *shape*, thus translating *kippatu* here as 'circle'.

Taking this step establishes that Utnapishti's Ark in the

Gilgamesh story was actually *circular* with a base area of one acre (*ikû*), exactly like the giant coracle of Atra-hasīs!

Ark Tablet 9:   Let her floor area be one 'acre', let her sides be one rod (high).

Gilgamesh XI 58:   One 'acre' was her circle, ten rods each her sides stood high . . .

In *Gilgamesh XI* the statement in lines 29–30 that the boat's *dimensions should all correspond* and her *length and breadth should be the same* have become divorced from the crucial issue of her *roundness*, for this is only referred to further on (and non-explicitly) in line 58. This separation within the text of features that belonged together imposed the unfounded idea of a 'square' boat, far from the original meaning. This had the effect of displacing the original circular ground plan idea, enabling the very improbable *cube* to come into existence.

Where does this leave us? Another round ark, but this time submerged and almost lost to view. Given that some Old Babylonian text of the same 'family' as the *Ark Tablet* underlies the classical text of *Gilgamesh XI*: 28–31 and 58–60, we can assume that originally there was one instruction speech by Ea, and that development of the text disrupted the original simple format. This simple 'proto-Gilgamesh' instruction speech probably originally read as follows:

*1   *The boat that you are going to build*
*2   *Draw up her design;*
*3   *Her dimensions should all correspond,*
*4   *Let her breadth and length be equal;*
*5   *Let one 'acre' be her circle, let her sides stand one rod high;*
*6   *The edge(s) of her top must be equal.*
*7   *Cover her with a roof, like the Apsû!*

The Ark as Coracle

Enki, looking down, knew all about coracles, and the reasons for his upgraded choice of ark model are, as already indicated, clear and intelligible. Atra-hasīs's Ark did not have to go anywhere; it just had to float and bob around, settling, when the waters subsided, wherever it had drifted or been carried. The coracle in question was to be traditionally built of coiled rope basketry coated with bitumen; it would be unimaginably huge, but a lot of room was going to be needed.

Coracles, in their unassuming way, have played a crucial and long-running role in man's relationship with rivers. They belong, like dugout canoes and rafts, to the most practical stratum of invention: natural resources giving rise to simple solutions that can hardly be improved upon. The reed coracle is effectively a large basket transferred to water, sealed with bitumen to prevent waterlogging, and its construction is somehow natural to riverine communities, so that coracles from India and Iraq, Tibet and Wales, are close cousins, if not easy-to-confuse twins.

Up until now no one seems to have afforded the ancient Mesopotamian coracle much attention, but with the arrival of the *Ark Tablet* on the Flood Story scene it suddenly becomes a very interesting creature indeed. There is hardly a mention of the coracle in standard works on ancient Mesopotamian boats, nor even the distinction of a specific word for coracle identified in the Akkadian language.

Or is there?

There is a cuneiform story known as the *Legend of Sargon* which is of huge significance within the pages of this book, and we will come back to it later in conjunction with the biblical story of Moses in the bulrushes. In the cuneiform version King Sargon of Akkad (2270–2215 BC) explains how his mother had deposited him, a new baby, on the River Euphrates in what is always translated as a 'basket', to go wherever the waters might take him:

I am Sargon, the great king, king of Akkad,
My mother was a high priestess but I do not know who my
*   father was,*
My uncle lives in the mountains.
My city is Azupirānu, which lies on the bank of the Euphrates.
My mother, a high priestess, conceived me, and bore me in
*   secret;*
She placed me in a reed quppu *and made its [lit. my] opening*
*   watertight with bitumen.*
She abandoned me to the river, from which I could not come
*   up;*
The river swept me along, and brought me to Aqqi, drawer
*   of water.*
Aqqi, drawer of water, lifted me up when he dipped his bucket,
Aqqi, water drawer, brought me up as his adopted son.
Aqqi, water drawer, set me to do his orchard work;
During my orchard work Goddess Ishtar loved me;
For fifty-four(?) years did I rule as king . . .

The Akkadian word *quppu* in line 6 of this composition has,
so far, only three meanings according to modern Assyriological
dictionaries: 'wicker basket', 'wooden chest' and 'box'. In modern
Arabic the word for 'coracle' is *quffa*, which also primarily means
'basket', since a coracle is nothing more than a large basket,
manufactured like a basket and waterproofed, and this is the
local word that has been heard up and down the bank of the
Euphrates in Iraq wherever coracles were in use. Akkadian and
Arabic are fellow members of the Semitic language family and
share many historical words in common. We can say, therefore,
that *quppu* and *quffa* are cognate words (for 'p' in Akkadian
comes out as 'f' in Arabic), and can see that the two words share
the same range of meanings, from basket to coracle. Given this
I think we can conclude therefore that Babylonian *quppu* also
had the specific meaning 'coracle', most especially with regard
to the experience of the baby Sargon.

We can say more. Sargon's autobiographical fragment undoubt-edly alludes directly to the national Mesopotamian Flood Story, exactly as the story of Moses refers back to Noah's Ark in the Book of Genesis. The baby was to be one of the greatest kings of Mesopotamia, his life saved at the outset against all odds by a bitumen-sealed, basket-like vessel launched on water into the unknown. The description of sealing the opening with bitumen is a direct textual parallel to the traditional Flood Story account.

There is an additional dimension to this. In the Gilgamesh account there is a striking poetic image at the end of the great storm on the seventh day:

The sea grew calm, that had fought like a woman in labour.
Gilgamesh XI: 131

It is easy to take this as a simple metaphor, but it would carry deeper meaning for a Mesopotamian. There is a cycle of magical spells to aid a woman in travail which share the image that the unborn child within the amniotic fluid is a boat in a stormy sea, moored in the darkness to the 'quay of death' by the umbilical cord and unable to break free to be washed out into the world. The round, nutshell Ark containing the whole seed of life, tossed on the waters before reaching anchorage, is undoubtedly likened to a storm-battered foetus, albeit obliquely; the voyage to eventual safety is re-enacted each time a baby is born.

According to F. R. Chesney, writing in the late nineteenth century, the smallest Iraqi coracle recorded was '3 feet 8 inches in diameter'. The chances are, then, that wee Sargon's coracle, woven of reeds and waterproofed, was the smallest specimen ever made. If so, we have the unique privilege here of simultaneously documenting at one blow the world's *smallest* and *largest* Iraqi coracles!

Now that we have the ancient name and two extremes in size we are entitled to look a little further into the question of *normal* coracles in ancient Mesopotamia. Where in fact are all the others? Since the *Ark Tablet* uses the general word *eleppu* for the round craft, it is natural to wonder whether other *eleppus* in cuneiform texts might not sometimes refer to a coracle, but only the odd example can be quoted as we proceed.

Although this humble riverine vessel has largely slipped by unnoticed under the radar, I maintain that skin-covered or bitumen-coated coracles must have crossed the Euphrates and Tigris waters, this way and that, more or less since the beginning of time. Pictorial evidence supports this. From the middle of the third millennium BC some of the hard stone cylinder seals that were used to ratify clay documents by rolling over the surface and leaving a customised imprint depict boats in their carved scenes. Most are evidently classic Mesopotamian reed boats with high prow and stern of the school that we have branded (from the Ark point of view) 'prototype', but we can distinguish at least one with the characteristic rounded profile, or rather cross-section, of a coracle. This seal is from the Iraqi site of Khafajeh on the Diyala River, seven miles west of Baghdad, and it appears to depict a genuine coracle in about 2500 BC.

*

Nearly *two thousand years later* we see the Assyrian army, nothing if not practical, making excellent use of campaign coracles, and fortunately for us these were depicted in accurate detail by the court sculptors within the daily-life and military scenes of the famous palace wall-sculptures.

The Assyrian King Shalmaneser III (859–824 BC) left us a graphic account of a military campaign in Mazamua (an Assyrian province on the northwestern slopes of the Zagros Mountains, modern Suleimaniyah), during which he was forced to use 'reed boats' and 'skin-covered boats' to pursue the enemy:

> *They became frightened in the face of the flash of my mighty weapons and my tumultuous onslaught and they swarmed into reed boats on the sea. I went after them in skin-covered coracles (and) waged a mighty battle in the midst of the sea. I defeated them (and) dyed the sea red like red wool with their blood.*

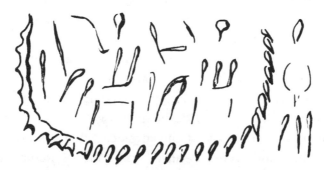

The earliest coracle from the Khafajeh seal.

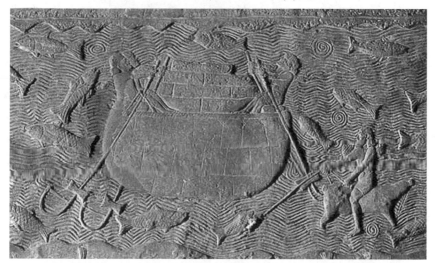

King Sennacherib's ancient four-man, heavy-duty coracle at work.

Ship-to-shore: a heavily laden 20th century coracle approaches the bank.

In a sculpture from the palace of King Sennacherib (705–681 BC) at Nineveh (see previous page), two sturdy pairs of Assyrian oarsmen negotiate the fast river currents in a heavy-duty coracle laden with bricks. Their long steering poles end in a curved hook and are apparently weighted at the lower end, perhaps with lead ingots. A fellow Assyrian astride an inflated animal-skin lilo on either side is spearing fish for their lunch. The men are seated on top of the coracle, which is loaded to the full and more, and seems to have some kind of bench running around the top. The oars are secured in a rowlock device. The coracle sides are marked with horizontal and vertical lines, which do not represent the lower layers of bricks inside the vessel but rather some external characteristic of its finish, probably panels of skin stitched together. The top rim or gunwale is clearly shown as a tightly bound and distinct reinforcing element although the binding is not shown at the right-hand edge.

These sepia snapshots in stone of ancient coracles in use are invaluable to us in demonstrating the existence and practical utility of the vessel in the ninth to eighth centuries BC. No doubt, as was certainly the case later, coracles were made in a range of sizes, from the two-person 'water-taxi' to a substantial craft capable of transporting, à la Noah, serious numbers of livestock.

Further south, a little later, we get hard information on Babylonian coracles in Greek, from the redoubtable Herodotus, writing his *Histories* in the second half of the fifth century BC when cuneiform writers were very alive and fertile; his book is one of the world's ultimate bestsellers. An ongoing dispute persists about whether or not Herodotus actually went to Babylon himself, or about how reliable his statements are, and so forth, but when it came to facts about coracles he knew which way was up:

They have boats plying the river down to Babylon which are completely round and are made of leather. In Armenia, which is upstream from Assyria, they cut branches of willow and make them up into a frame, around the outside of which they stretch watertight skins to act as a hull; they do not broaden the sides of the boat to form a stern or narrow them into a prow, but they make it round, like a shield. Then they line the whole boat with straw and send it off down the river laden with goods. Their cargo is most commonly palm-wood casks filled with wine. The boats are steered by two men, who stand upright and wield a paddle each; one of them pulls the paddle towards his body and the other pushes the paddle away from his body. These boats vary in size from very large downwards; the largest of them can manage cargo weighing five thousand talents. Each boat carries a live donkey – or, in the case of larger boats, several donkeys. At the end of their voyage to Babylon, when they have sold their cargo, they sell off the frame of the boat and all the straw, load up the donkeys with the skins, and drive them back to Armenia. They do this because the current of the river is too strong for boats to sail up it, and that is why they make these boats out of skin rather than wood. Once they have got back to Armenia with their donkeys, they make themselves more boats in the usual way.

Herodotus, *Histories* Bk 1

Tigris coracles in the hands of professionals later caught the fancy of the Romans in the fourth century AD, who, with an eye to stowage and manoeuvrability, brought Tigris *barcarii* all the way from Arbela on the Tigris to South Shields in Tyneside to build coracles and run their river transports there, perhaps thereby introducing the first coracles to the British Isles. The Latin *barca* is a small boat carried on a ship and convenient for shipping cargo to shore, a common use of the coracle. Interestingly, an existing Latin term was applied instead of adapting the contemporary local Tigris word, which at that time was surely a form of *quppu/guffa*.

THE CORACLE, B.C. 100.

On account of the almost impenetrable forests which extended inland, the Ancient Britons lived mostly near the coast, and, when not engaged in fighting, spent their time in fishing. Their boats were made of wicker, in the form of a shallow basket, carrying one passenger and sometimes not that. They were called Coracles.

Early evidence for the British coracle.

It is this practical background that makes sense of the *Ark Tablet* coracle. Some remote poet once asked himself or was enquired of by a listener – given that the Flood had *really happened*, and the Ark had *really been built* – what did the thing actually *look like*? What kind of vessel would be spacious enough, unsinkable yet buildable? Not a pointed *magurgurru*, by any means. Looking out over the river, rapt in a daydream, one can readily imagine that the solution would present itself in a lightning bolt of understanding: a *coracle*, a round coracle, on a – how you say? – *cosmic* scale . . .

We are entitled to focus in on an ancient river scene thronged with coracles because these traditional craft remained in use unchanged on the rivers of Mesopotamia right down into the first half of the last century, although in today's Iraq they are, sadly, extinct. Coracles in general are a much studied and understood phenomenon, and the coracles of Iraq hold a more than respectable position among them. Many nineteenth- and early twentieth-century photographs taken there show coracles, portrayed either as specific studies or as part of the inevitable river background to daily life. E. S. Stevens, whose useful 1920s coracle-construction photographs are reproduced here, wrote evocatively:

*. . . we rattled over devious ways, splashing through the flood
when we came to it, until the four lean horses came to a stop
where a* gufa *was drawn up onto the bank. A* gufa *is a large
bowl-shaped basket, made water-tight by a coating of bitumen.
Some of these round craft are huge; ours would have held
thirty people easily. We got in, and the* gufachi *slung a towing
rope over his body, and waded upstream . . . When we had
reached the actual river-bed, he jumped in with his helpers
and began to paddle the boat across at an angle; for Samarra,
on the high opposite bank, was by this time a good distance
down-stream. The current was so swift and strong that it took
only a few minutes before he landed us at the landing-stage
below the city.*

Stevens 1923: 50

Then there is the enigmatic E. A. Wallis Budge, later Keeper
in the British Museum, an old coracle hand himself who knew
them to be useful even in battle. At Baghdad in 1878 (he
confesses) there was a little trouble over a tin of important clay
tablets which had been mistaken by customs for a case of whisky
and which needed to be deftly manoeuvred onto a British
gunboat:

*This procedure did not please the Customs' officials, several of
whom leaped into* kuffahs *and followed us as fast as their men
could row. They overtook us at the gangway ladder, and tried
to cut me off from the ship by thrusting their* kuffahs *in the
way; and as some of them jumped on to the rounded edge of
my* kuffah, *and tried to drag out of it my trunks and the box
of Tall Al-'Amarnah Tablets, I became anxious lest the box of
tablets be lost in the Tigris.*

*The "*kuffah*" [Budge added] . . . is a large basket made of
willows and coated with bitumen inside and out. It is perfectly
circular, and resembles a large bowl floating on the stream; it is*

THREE STAGES OF A GUFA.

(1).   Weaving the basket foundation.

(2).   Adding the "ribs."

(3).   The finished gufa, daubed with bitumen to make it watertight.

Three stages in building a coracle as recorded by E. S. Drower (née Stevens).

Walking the plank coracle-style.

*made in all sizes, and some are large enough to hold three horses
and several men. The small ones are uncomfortable, but I have
journeyed for days in large ones, over the flood waters of the
Euphrates around about Babylon, and on the Hindiyah Canal,
and slept in them at nights.*

Budge 1920: 183

I am only sorry he didn't bring one back for the British Museum.

This is as far as I think we can go in investigating Mesopotamian
ark shapes on the basis of the known cuneiform Flood Story
tablets. We know that tradition varied between the long and
pointed °*makurru* (antiquated, unsuitable and unseaworthy) or
the round and hospitable *quppu* (modern, practical and preferred).
Later processes of textual accretion 'developed' the latter model
into a tall, multi-floored tower of a cruise ship that was apparently endorsed by Gilgamesh himself (utterly unusable).

The next old photograph shows a cluster of traditional Tigris
riverboats at the end of the nineteenth century. Side by side with
plentiful round coracles are boats called *taradas*, whose characteristic

143

outline, viewed from above, corresponds closely to the biconvex *makurru* shape in the Old Babylonian diagram. The *tarada* is made of wood, with mast and sails, but in *shape* such boats are descendants of the ancient *makurru*. Looking at the two possibilities I think we can agree that Enki chose his round coracle Ark wisely.

J. P. Peters described his photograph of 1899 as 'A Scene on the Tigris at Baghdad, showing characteristic native boats, the long taradas, *and the round, pitch-smeared* kufas, *with bridge of boats beyond.'*

Noah's Ark in Genesis

From here, as good investigators, we must follow the Ark trail where it naturally leads, which is to the Hebrew Bible and beyond.

Make yourself an ark (tēvāh) of gopher wood [came the instruction]; *make rooms (qinnîm) in the ark, and cover it (kāpar) inside and out with pitch (kopher). This is how you are to make it: the length of the ark three hundred cubits, its width fifty cubits, and its height thirty cubits. Make a roof for the ark, and finish it to a cubit above; and put the door of the ark in its side; make it with lower, second, and third decks.*

Genesis 6:14–16

Noah's Ark as illustrated in Martin Luther's bible, reflecting the Hebrew description.

Such was the order to Noah, facing in his turn the awful task of saving the world more or less single-handedly with the help of a custom-order boat. This is the breakdown of the specs:

Ark:	*tēvāh* (unknown word for rectangular boat)
Material:	*gopher*-wood (unknown species)
Rooms:	*qinnîm* (cells; the basic word means 'bird's nest')
Waterproofing:	pitch or bitumen (*kopher*), smeared on (*kāphar*), inside and out
Length:	300 cubits (*ammah*) = 450 ft = 137.2 m

Width:	50 cubits = 75 ft = 22.8 m
Height:	30 cubits = 45 ft = 13.7 m
Roof:	1 cubit high(?)
Door:	1
Decks:	3

Compare the sparser data for Moses' 'arklet' in Exodus 2:2–6:

Ark:	*tēvāh* (unknown word for rectangular boat)
Material:	*gomeh*, bulrushes; rush/reed/papyrus; wicker
Waterproofing:	*hamār*, slime; bitumen/asphalt; bitumen; *zefeth*, pitch.

The biblical word *tēvāh*, which is used for the arks of Noah and Moses, occurs nowhere else in the Hebrew Bible. The flood and baby episodes are thus deliberately associated and linked in Hebrew just as the *Atrahasis* and Sargon Arks are linked associatively in Babylonia.

Now for something extraordinary: no one knows what language *tēvāh* is or what it means. The word for the wood, *gopher*, is likewise used nowhere else in the Hebrew Bible and no one knows what language or what kind of wood it is. This is a peculiar state of affairs for one of the most famous and influential paragraphs in all of the world's writing!

The associated words *kopher*, 'bitumen', and *kāphar*, 'to smear on', are also to be found nowhere else in the Hebrew Bible, but, significantly, they came from Babylonia with the narrative itself, deriving from Akkadian *kupru*, 'bitumen', and *kapāru*, 'to smear on'. In view of this it is logical to expect that *tēvāh* and *gopher* are similarly loanwords from Babylonian Akkadian into Hebrew, but there has been no convincing candidate for either word. Suggestions have been made for gopher-wood, but the identification, or the non-Hebrew word that lies behind it, remains open. Ideas have also been put forward over the centuries concerning the word *tēvāh*, some linking it – because Moses was in Egypt

– with the ancient Egyptian word *thebet*, meaning 'box' or 'coffin', but these have ended nowhere. The most likely explanation is that *tēvāh*, like other ark words, reflects a Babylonian word.

I have a new suggestion.

A cuneiform tablet dealing with boats from around 500 BC, now in the British Museum, mentions a kind of boat called a *ṭubbû* which is found at a river crossing, apparently as part of a vessel swap among boatmen:

> . . . a boat (*eleppu*) which is six cubits wide at the beam, a *ṭubbû* which is at the crossing, and a boat (*eleppu*) five and a half (cubits) wide at the beam which is at the bridge, they exchanged for (?) one boat which is five cubits wide at the beam.
>
> BM 32873: 2

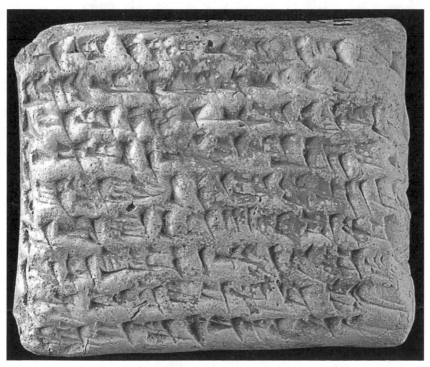

The Babylonian ṭubbû tablet, front.

The Babylonian ṭubbû tablet, back.

The consonants t (in *tēvāh*) and ṭ (in *ṭubbû*) are distinct from one another, so it is impossible that *ṭubbû*, a masculine noun of unknown etymology, and *tēvāh*, a feminine noun of unknown etymology, represent the same word etymologically. I think that the Judaeans encountered the Akkadian boat word *ṭubbû* used for the Ark in the story along with the other Akkadian ark words and Hebraised it as *tēvāh*. In this case the original consonants are less important; the idea was to render the foreign word, for it was only to be used twice in the whole Bible, once for Noah, once for Moses. The relationship between the words is thus that they are neither cognate nor loaned: the Babylonian was given a Hebrew 'shape'. It is much the same as the way in which Nebuchadnezzar's eunuch Nabu-sharrussu-ukin became *Nebu-sarsekim* in the Book of Jeremiah. This would perforce mean that the word *ṭubbû* must have occurred in place of *eleppu*, 'boat', for Utnapishti's Ark, in some first-millennium BC Babylonian source for the Flood Story that we do not have now.

An alternative possibility is that the Hebrew word *tēvāh* is a so-called *Wanderwort*, one of those basic words that spread across numerous languages and cultures, sometimes as a consequence of trade, whose original etymology or language becomes obscured (a good example is *chai* and *tea*), lasting for ever. We would have then an old, non-Semitic word for a very simple kind of river boat – conceivably even ultimately ancestral to the English *tub* – which appears as *ṭubbû* in Babylonian, *tēvāh* in Hebrew. One could imagine readily enough that such a simple word for a simple boat might survive along the waterways of the world for endless centuries. Turned upside down these boats produce a dull 'dub' sort of thumpy thud. It is curious that tub, like ark, can mean box, chest and boat. Ironically this Babylonian word *ṭubbû*, like *tēvāh*, is rare too: it occurs twice in the tablet just quoted and nowhere else!

Either proposal would account for the biblical name for the Ark: either the Judaeans encountered the ark word *ṭubbû* and Hebraised it to *tēvāh*, or they called the Ark *tēvāh* because it corresponded to the shape characteristic of that kind of old boat which was known to them as a *tēvāh* and to the Babylonians as a *ṭubbû*.

But, again, what about the shape?

The traditional river craft of Iraq once included a type of boat which in shape and proportions closely resembles the Ark as described in Genesis. Lieut.-Col. Chesney, compiling a government survey, himself witnessed such boats being made and used in the 1850s:

A remarkable kind of boat is constructed at Tekrít and in the marshes of Lamlúm, but more commonly near the bituminous fountains of Hít. At these places the operation of boat building is an every-day occurrence, and extremely simple. The self-taught shipwrights have not, it is true, the advantage of docks, basins or even slips; yet they can construct a vessel in a very short time, and without employing any other tools than a few axes and saws, with the addition of a large metallic ladle to pour out the melted pitch, and a wooden roller to assist in smoothing it. The first step in this primitive mode of ship-building is to choose a level piece of ground of suitable size, and sufficiently near the edge of the water; on this the builders trace out the size of the vessel's bottom, not with mathematical precision it is true, still a line is used, and a certain system followed, the floor or bottom of the boat being the first object.

This procedure is exactly similar to that in the *Ark Tablet* when Enki instructs Atra-hasīs on how to lay out the plan for the boat described above. Chesney continues:

In the space marked out a number of rough branches are placed in parallel lines, at about a foot distance; other branches are places across them at similar distances, and interlaced. These, with the addition of a sort of basket-work of reeds and straw, to fill up the interstices, form a kind of rough platform, across which, to give the necessary stability, stronger branches are laid transversely from side to side, at distances of about eight or twelve inches. The bottom being in this state, the work proceeds to the second stage, by building up the sides. This is done by driving through the edge of the former, upright posts, about a foot apart, of the requisite height; these are filled up in the same way, and the whole is, as it were, consolidated by means of rough pieces of timber, which are placed at intervals of about four feet from gunwale to gunwale.

Having completed detailing the structural aspects of the boat, Chesney goes on to describe the next stage of waterproofing, again parallel to the *Ark Tablet*:

All parts are then coated with hot bitumen, which is melted in a hole close to the work, and reduced to a proper consistency

The author aged 9, in Exeter Museum, talking for the first time about becoming a British Museum curator.

The Arched Room library in the Middle East Department of the British Museum, where 130,000 cuneiform tablets are housed.

Professor W. G. Lambert, as encountered by the author in September 1969.

Leonard Simmons in Egypt, at the time he was collecting curios, among which this Christmas card can be included.

With very best wishes for a Merry Christmas and a Happy New Year

Douglas Simmonds as a boy with the cast of *Here Come the Double Deckers*.

Douglas Simmonds with a Mesopotamian hero in the Louvre.

The Ark Tablet, front view.   *The Ark Tablet*, back view.

A Sumerian reed hut, or *mudhif*, as depicted on
a stone trough of about 3000 BC.

The characteristic and timeless landscape of the
southern marshes in modern Iraq.

Reeds, water, man and livestock in harmony in a 1974
photograph taken in the southern Iraqi marshes.

Coracles in use,
Iraq, 1920s.

The coracle to capture the
imagination of boys as
part of the Churchman
cigarette card set entitled
Story of Navigation.

CHURCHMAN'S CIGARETTES

A "GUFFA" ON THE TIGRIS

LA VIE ASSYRIENNE. — 14. *Le Commerce*. Les Marchands du Tigre.
Fernand Nathan, Editeur, Paris. — 3014

An artist's
impression of
ancient Assyrian
riverside life.

A model of a traditional coracle from Iraq;
the bead and shells are to promote good luck and
are also found on full-size coracles.

A seventeenth-century view of the animals waiting patiently to embark,
by the Flemish painter Jacob Savery.

This sixteenth-century drawing by Hermann tom Ring gives a good idea of the practicalities involved when it actually came to boarding.

The flood as depicted by Frances Danby, first exhibited in 1840, and a striking canvas.

by a mixture of sand or earth. This bituminous cement being spread over the frame-work, the application of a wooden roller gives the whole a smooth surface, both within and without, which after a brief space becomes not only quite hard and durable, but impervious to water, and well suited for navigation. The usual shape of the boats thus constructed is much like that of a coffin, the broadest end representing the bow; but others are of a neater shape. Such a boat, 44 feet long, 11 feet 6 inches broad, and 4 feet deep, drawing 1 foot 10 inches of water when laden, and only 6 inches when empty, can be constructed at Hít in the course of one day . . .

Chesney saw at once that the shape and proportions of such vessels strongly recalled the biblical Ark, arguing rather plausibly that Noah could have produced a boat of this type without much trouble:

The ark, as we are all aware, was three hundred cubits in length, fifty cubits in breadth, and thirty cubits in height, finished in a cubit, or sloping roof. These dimensions, presuming the smallest cubit to have been in use, would give 450 feet for the length, 75 feet for the breadth, and 45 feet for the depth of this enormous structure, whose burthen, making an allowance for the cross-beams with which it was braced and the supports, would be upwards of 40,000 tons. From the description just given of the Hít boats, it will be seen that there is not anything to prevent the people of that town, or of the neighbouring country, from constructing such a vessel, a larger scantling only being necessary for the frame-work. The lower story being intended for quadrupeds, must necessarily have been divided into compartments; and these divisions, as a matter of course, would support the second floor, which was appropriated for the people, whose apartments, again, supported the upper story, or that allotted for the birds. As this arrangement required three floors and a roof, the divisions and the necessary supports would have given sufficient stability to the whole structure; therefore the objections raised on account of the supposed difficulty of the work, may be considered as obviated, more particularly as the ark was destined to remain and be floated on the same spot . . .

Thanks to the archaeologist John Punnett Peters we have a photograph of several boats of this kind, in construction or finished, taken in 1888. Judging by his caption he, too, was irresistibly reminded of Noah's Ark.

The second of J. P. Peters' photographs, which he described as 'A Noachian Boatyard at Hit on the Euphrates.'

So now we have a real, functional boat-style candidate that is neither long and thin (Sumerian-type), round (**Atra-hasīs**-type) or square (Utnapishti-type), but which matches the oblong Genesis ark description to a disconcerting degree. It is reasonable, I suggest, to assume that the Hebrew description in the Bible reflects an oblong boat of this pattern, which, like the coracle, was surely commonly seen on the rivers of Mesopotamia in antiquity, and was encountered there by the Hebrew poets. Unfortunately neither Chesney nor Peters records the nineteenth-century Arabic name, but all things considered it seems not unlikely that this type of boat was called *ṭubbû* in Akkadian, *tēvāh* in Hebrew.

The existence of such boats contributes an important element to our assessment of the Hebrew encounter with the Babylonian story. If the oblong shape of the Hebrew ark reflects an existing type of Babylonian boat easily seen 'out of the window', this has direct implications for the transmission of the story.

It is conceivable that, while Utnapishti at Nineveh ended up tweaking a square ark out of a circular one, another and unknown cuneiform edition tweaked this a little further into an oblong, convinced that a cubic boat would never work and swayed by the existence of the oblong barge-type called a *ṭubbû*. While retaining virtually the same base area (15,000 cubits^2 as against 14,400 cubits^2), the length and width of the Ark were adjusted to round numbers reflecting the relative proportions of such a barge.

The importance and brevity of the biblical description of Noah's Ark meant that successions of scholars, religious and otherwise, have pored over these lines of Noah text. The rabbis have left us many details to amplify the simple narrative.

Noah, for example, is supposed to have planted cedar trees one hundred and twenty years in advance with the double advantage that the population would have time to turn away from sin, and the trees could grow tall enough. The ark is variously attributed three hundred and sixty cells, or chambers, ten by ten yards, and nine hundred cells, six by six yards. Some authorities saw the top floor for the unclean beasts, the middle for the humans and clean beasts, and the bottom for refuse, while others favoured the reverse, while there was a trapdoor to allow waste disposal into the sea. Atra-hasīs, emptying pans, must have often mused rancorously over this supposedly humorous Akkadian fable:

> *An elephant spoke to himself and said, 'Among the wild creatures of the god Shakkan there is no one who can defecate like me.' The sipidiqar-bird answered, 'And yet, I, in my own proportion, I can defecate like you.'*

Since the sky was sealed off from the Ark's inhabitants day and night there would have been darkness but the Rabbis explained that Noah hung up precious stones which shone like the noonday sun. The rounding up of all the animals, with their fodder, had been handled by a team of angels, while the hand-picked animals behaved in an exemplary manner and did not go in for reproduction while on board. Noah never slept for he was up the whole time feeding the inmates. Another thing: while the loading was going on, imposing lions guarded the gangplank to prevent the wicked from sneaking on board, which reminds me of the lions at the back door of the British Museum, which, however, are there to discourage visitors from *leaving*.

The Berossus Ark

Berossus, as we have seen in Chapter 5, gives no description of the boat beyond its dimensions:

> He (Xisuthros) did not disobey, but got a boat built, five stades long and two stades wide . . .

Patai writes that its length was 'five stadia or furlongs – about 1,000 yards – and its breadth was two stadia – about 400 yards'. In the Armenian version of Eusebius's *Chronicles*, which is based on Berossus, the length of the ship is given as fifteen furlongs, that is, nearly two miles.

The Ark in the Koran

Nuh's [Noah] lifeboat Ark had no special name, but is referred to as *safina*, the common word for boat, Sura 54:3 describing it as 'a thing of boards and nails'. There is no Koranic counterpart to the details of building the Ark or its appearance, although Abd Allah ibn Abbas, a contemporary of Muhammad, wrote that when Noah was in doubt as to what shape to make the Ark

Allah revealed to him that it was to be shaped like a bird's belly and fashioned of teak wood. In Islam, too, there was much later discussion and analysis of the story and its implications by the religious authorities. Abdallah ibn Umar al-Baidawi, writing in the thirteenth century, explains that in the first of its three levels wild and domesticated animals were lodged, in the second the human beings, and in the third the birds. On every plank was the name of a prophet. Three missing planks, symbolising three prophets, were brought from Egypt by Og, son of Anak, the only one of the giants permitted to survive the Flood, and the body of Adam was carried in the middle to divide the men from the women. There was a tradition that Noah had to say, *In the Name of Allah!* when he wished the Ark to move, and the same when he wished it to stand still.

An abundance of shapes, then. But we must return to the primary model. First, we must build our coracle.

English ladies on tour by coracle in the 1880s, but not entirely relaxed.

8

Building the Arks

There's nothing . . . absolutely nothing . . .
half so much worth doing
as simply messing around in boats.
Kenneth Grahame

1. Building Atra-hasīs's Ark in the Ark Tablet

Building Noah's Ark as depicted by a 17th century Flemish painter

The life-preserving ark is central to the story of the Flood in any
telling and we have established that what the hero Atra-hasīs had

to build was a giant coracle. Before the arrival of the *Ark Tablet* all we really knew about constructing an ark in ancient Mesopotamia came from the famous description in the eleventh tablet of the *Gilgamesh Epic*. Hard facts for the boat-builder have accordingly been all too sparse and we have had to wait until now for the vital statistics of shape, size and dimensions, as well as everything to do with the crucial matter of water-proofing. The information that has now become available could be turned into a printed set of specifications sufficient for any would-be ark-builder today.

It has been an adventure, struggling forward within the forest of wedges in this precious document, especially where the tablet is sorely damaged on the reverse, but it is remarkable how so much can be extracted from Atra-hasīs's laconic accounts. Businesslike data comes in lines 6–33 and 57–8, which cover the various stages of the work in the order in which they were carried out. The information comes as a series of 'reports' from Atra-hasīs, submitted to Enki as the work progressed; it is now our chance to look over his shoulder.

Requirements, Enki to Atra-hasīs:

6–9:   Overall design and size
10–12: Materials and their quantities for the hull

Progress reports, Atra-hasīs to Enki:

13–14: Fitting the internal framework
15–17: Setting up the deck and building the cabins
18–20: Calculating the bitumen needed for waterproofing
21–5:   Loading the kilns and preparing the bitumen
26–7:   Adding the temper to the mix
28–9:   Bituminising of the interior
30–33: Caulking the exterior
57–8:   Exterior finishing – sealing the outer coat

The cuneiform content we have to work with, leaving aside the difficulty of reading the broken lines, is put across in a very compact fashion and does not quite emerge as an easy 'user's manual'. We have to interpret each line as if we were coracle-builders ourselves, an approach thankfully made easier by the traditional method of building a Mesopotamian coracle having not changed since antiquity. We can see this from an informative description of constructing a contemporary Iraqi *quffa* published in the 1930s by the boat historian and expert James Hornell. Today such information would be irretrievable: the Iraqi coracle is extinct and the riverside makers and boatmen who once proliferated have vanished. Side by side with this precious account come late nineteenth- and early twentieth-century photographs of Tigris coracle-builders at work employing the same techniques, which can also help the enquirer today.

Hornell's coracle testimony has been utterly indispensable for this book; in fact it is hard to convey without headline phraseology exactly what it has contributed. There are several stages involved in coracle production and our boat historian has recorded these in full. With them as a guide it has been possible not just to read and translate the Akkadian description – as one would normally do – but to grasp what the cuneiform really means in terms of building a functional coracle. What is more, the content and measures of the cuneiform specifications are, *amazingly*, demonstrably based on realistic and practical data. Hornell's description has both facilitated and confirmed interpretation of the construction technique, dimensions and order of procedure set out in the *Ark Tablet*.

The *Ark Tablet*, remember, with all this accumulated boat-building experience wrapped up in clay – was written the best part of *four thousand years before Hornell recorded his own account.*

The very oldest coracle-makers perfected a technique that was passed on for uncounted generations to follow, using the same locally available raw materials. Such a long history is inspiring, but not surprising, for there is every reason that the coracle – which can hardly be improved on as a practical design – should have remained unchanged in structure and use. But it is one thing to claim the likelihood of such longevity and quite another to be able to demonstrate it and, on top of that, benefit from it directly.

Writing this chapter, I might add, has been an assault course challenge for me. I have found it perfectly possible to get through life as a wedge-reader without being a boat person or functionally numerate, but both shortcomings were soon highlighted by having to deal with **Atra-hasīs**'s work problems. My one personal experience with boats occurred on holiday when I was about twelve, on a canal at Hythe, canoeing with my sister Angela. She was at the front; I had power and steering responsibilities from the back. Finding that we were dangerously close to the bank I swung my paddle up and over my sister's head in order to correct our course, but, miscalculating substantially, thwacked her on the side of the head with the flat of the blade. This immediately knocked her unconscious; she slid down into the bottom of the canoe, understandably relinquishing her own paddle, which promptly drifted off behind us, while we somehow spurted forward out into mid-stream, later to be ignominiously rescued and resuscitated by adults in a passing rowing-boat. For me that was enough. As for mathematics, successive teachers suggested in school reports that I be sedated into oblivion before lessons. Until I learned about counting, right up to sixty, in cuneiform I always found this working horizon from Mary Norton comforting:

> '*Your grandfather could count and write down the numbers up to – what was it, Pod?*'
> '*Fifty-seven,*' *said Pod.*
> '*There,*' *said Homily,* '*fifty-seven! And your father can count, as you know, Arrietty; he can count and write down the numbers, on and on, as far as it goes. How far does it go, Pod?*'
> '*Close on a thousand,*' *said Pod.*
>
> *The Borrowers*, Vol. I

This Ark-building chapter is divided into two sections. The first explains the stages of the *Ark Tablet*'s building instructions in the light of the Hornell report, and makes full use of the results of the calculations, which are given in Appendix 3. The second investigates and compares the much less detailed account of the same activity in the eleventh tablet of the *Gilgamesh Epic*, with specific attention to disinterring the Old Babylonian tradition that lies behind it to throw light on how the present 'classic' text evolved. Appendix 3 thus covers all the technical matter, mensuration, procedures and calculations that are raised by this remarkable cuneiform document and that lead to the results presented in the first section. I could say that this section has been worked out and presented in partnership with my friend Mark Wilson but actually I just asked him a few stupid questions and this is the result. To admit that the methods were beyond me is unnecessary.

Building Atra-hasīs's Ark

> "*Let her floor area be one 'field'* [continued Enki],
> "*let her sides be one* nindan *(high).*"
>
> *Ark Tablet*: 9

In the *Ark Tablet*, we see that Enki has placed an order for a truly giant coracle. It works out to be the size of a Babylonian 'field', what we would call an acre, surrounded by high walls. In our terms, utilising all the evidence from Mesopotamian mathematical sources and terms of measurement, the coracle's floor-area comes out at 3,600 m². This is about half the size of a soccer pitch (roughly 7,000 m²), while the walls, at about six metres, would effectively inhibit an upright male giraffe from looking over at us.

ARK TABLET: ROPE

Atra-hasīs's coracle was to be made of rope, coiled into a gigantic basket. This rope was made of palm fibre, and vast quantities of it were going to be needed, as reflected in Enki's mollifying remarks:

> "You saw kannu *ropes and* ašlu *ropes/rushes for* [*a coracle before!*]
> *Let someone (else) twist the fronds and palm-fibre for you!*
> *It will surely need 14,430 (*sūtu*)!*"
>
> Ark Tablet: 10–12

Here we turn without delay to James Hornell:

Hornell's Section 1
In construction a quffa is just a huge lidless basket, strength-ened within by innumerable ribs radiating from around the centre of the floor. The type of basketry employed is of that widely distributed kind termed coiled basketry. In this system the arrangement is that of a continuous and flattened spiral. Formed of a stout cylindrical core of parallel lengths of some fibrous material – grass or straw generally – bound by parcelling or whipping into a rope-like cylinder. By concentric coiling of this 'filled rope', the shape required is gradually built up. The parcelling consists of a narrow ribbon of strips split off from date-palm leaflets, wound in an open spiral around the core filling. As this proceeds the upper part of the coil immediately below is caught in by the lacing material being threaded through a hole made by a stout needle or other piercing instrument; this securely ties together the successive coils. The method is similar to that in use throughout Africa in the making of innumerable varieties of baskets and mats. The gunwale consists of a bundle of numerous withies, usually of willow, forming a stout cylin-drical hoop attached to the uppermost and last-formed coil by closely set series of coir lashings.

Atra-hasīs's *kannu* and *ašlu* in the *Ark Tablet* line 10 correspond to Hornell's beaten palm-fibre and date-palm parcelling.

Consider the god Enki's remarks, 'developed' a little:

You know about these coracles, surely, they're everywhere . . .
Let someone else do the work; I know you have other things
    to do . . .
Why don't I just tell you how much you are going to need
    and save you the trouble of working it out . . . ?

The raw material from which the rope is to be twisted and wrapped is palm fronds, for the Akkadian verb *patālu* means 'to twist', 'to plait', and the derived noun *pitiltu* denotes 'palm fibre'. An unrelated Old Babylonian tablet from the city of Ur mentions no fewer than 186 labourers employed to make this kind of rope out of palm-fibre and palm-leaf. A century or so earlier a harassed bookkeeper totted up in another text 'no less than 276 talents (8.28 tons) of palm-fibre rope . . . and 34 talents (1.02 tons) of palm-leaf rope', raising the question as to *what a shipyard would do with almost 10 tons of palm-fibre and palm-leaf rope of cord,* as Dan Potts put it. To me this can only mean mass coracle production.

By Enki's calculations they were going to need 14,430 *sūtu* measures of rope to coil the body of the Ark. This statement proves to be quite remarkable for two reasons. One is the actual way in which the total is recorded, the other the calculation that produces the total.

To me at least, 14,430 is a big number. It is written '4 x 3,600 + 30' = 14,400 + 30. In other words four '3,600' signs are used to make up the main total, followed by the sign for 30 and the same '3,600' system quantifies the wooden stanchions in line 15 and the waterproofing bitumen in lines 21–2.

The number 3,600 is written with the old Sumerian ŠÁR sign and, as a number word, borrowed into Babylonian and pronounced *šar*. This ŠÁR is an important cuneiform sign. In shape and meaning it conveys enclosure and completeness, for originally it was a circle, so it was used to express ideas like 'totality' or the 'entire inhabited world' as well as the large number 3,600.

When it occurs in literary texts *šár* = 3,600 is conventionally understood as no more than a conveniently large round number. This is evident when a well-wisher writes in a letter, 'may the Sun God for my sake keep you well for 3,600 years', or a battle-flushed Assyrian king claims to have 'blinded 4 x 3,600 survivors'. Assyriologists therefore often translate *šár* as 'myriad', as conveying the right sort of mythological size and feel, although of course the Greek decimal *myriad* literally means '10,000', whereas Mesopotamians naturally thought in sixties, one ŠÁR being 60 x 60. What is truly surprising in the *Ark Tablet* calculations is that this sign 3,600 does not function just as a large round number but *is to be taken literally*.

To anyone familiar with Seven League Boots or the Hundred Acre Wood this statement, especially in a literary composition, will cause surprise, while any Assyriologist who knows the sign in texts such as the *Sumerian King List* or *Gilgamesh XI* will raise more than one quizzical eyebrow. Indeed, the conclusion takes a bit of swallowing, and it took a bit of swallowing for me too. All I can say is that, having finally deciphered Atra-hasīs's big cuneiform numbers in the *Ark Tablet*, I had a strong hunch that they were *not* just fantasy totals and should at least be afforded the opportunity to speak for themselves. The principal reason for this was the added '+ 30' after the 14,400. What was that? A joke? Enki putting over the equivalent of 'a million and four?' That interpretation, in context, seemed out of the question, leaving no other plausible conclusion than that the extra 30 was needed to reach a real total, meaning that the number totals had to be taken seriously. It was at that moment that things got alarming: a *mathematician* was needed, happily forthcoming in the person of Mark Wilson. The consequence was to establish and confirm that the numbers in Atra-hasīs's work reports have to be taken seriously: real data and proper calculation have been injected into the Atra-hasīs story. Furthermore, the underlying

Babylonian measurement, which is not mentioned in the text, has to be the *sūtu*, which we need to know in order to understand the numbers.

We can support this clearly with Enki's calculation of the volume of necessary rope, having established:

1. Total surface area = coracle base + coracle walls + coracle roof. To sort this out, as I need hardly mention, requires a spot of *Pappas's Centroid Theorem*, closely followed by a dose of *Ramanujan's Approximation*.
2. The thickness of the rope. In the *Ark Tablet* we are not told about rope thickness, which suggests that it must be of a standard width for making coracles. A handful of old black and white photographs of Iraqi coracles are sufficiently in focus to suggest that traditional coracle rope was approximately of one finger thickness. As one *ubānu*, 'finger', was a standard Babylonian measure, we take this to be the thickness of Atra-hasīs's rope. This choice will be confirmed in a later calculation concerning the thickness of the coracle's bitumen coating.

The display of mathematical liveliness in Appendix 3 shows what has to be assayed to reach the result. Here we only need the *answer*, expressed in Babylonian *sūtū* measures:

Enki's rope volume estimate: 14,430 *sūtu*.
Our rope volume calculation: 14,624 *sūtu*.

Enki's calculation differs from ours by a smidgeon over 1 per cent. This is no accident or coincidence.

Just to be clear:

1. What might look like 'myriad' in the *Ark Tablet*, ŠÁR, means literally 3,600.
2. Enki is certainly thinking in terms of Babylonian *sūtus*.

3. The total length of one-finger-thickness rope needed to make Atra-hasīs's Super Coracle works out at 527km. I repeat, *five hundred and twenty-seven kilometres*. A good way to think of that? It is approximately the distance from London to Edinburgh.

Enki imparts no further dimensions in the *Ark Tablet*. After his initial speech the narrative changes tack: it becomes an account by Atra-hasīs of what he himself has done, written in the first person.

ARK TABLET: RIBS

Coiling the rope and weaving between the rows eventually produces a giant round floppy basket. The next job is to provide the whole with a stiffening framework of ribs. Hornell's coracle building description continues:

> The inner framework, giving strength and rigidity to the coiled walls of the quffa, is formed of a multitude of curved ribs, closely set; usually split branches of willow, poplar, tamarisk, juniper or pomegranate are employed; when these are not available the midribs of date-palm trees are used, but these are less esteemed. According to the size of the craft to be built, 8, 12 or 16 of these split branches are chosen of a length sufficient both to extend across the floor at its centre and also to pass up one side as a rib. These principal 'frames' are disposed in two series, one at right angles to the other. As half of those in each series pass down the side and across the bottom from opposite sides, their lower sections overlap and interdigitate, forming a strong double band across the floor; an equal number are similarly disposed at right angles to the first series, thereby giving two series of flooring or burden bands crossing one another on the floor. The quadrant spaces between these series of frames or main timbers are filled with very closely set ribs, bent, after soaking in warm water, to fit the concavely curved form of the

walls of the quffa on the inside; sometimes the sharpness of the bend causes a splintering at the point where the side begins to turn inwards towards the gunwale. As the width of the quadrants bounded by the four series of frames widens with distance from the centre, the first-placed ribs are slightly longer than those on each side of them and those intercalated later are progressively slightly shorter, pair by pair. The lower ends are pointed in order to fit close together at the centre.

As each of these ribs and frames is placed in position, it is sewn with coir cord to the basketry walls. Two men are necessary for this operation, one inside the quffa to pass the cord through the wall of the basketry to his companion on the outside, who, in turn, threads it back to the inside, after hauling it taut. On the exterior the cord is seen passing obliquely upward from one seam to another; on the inside it passes horizontally over the rib from side to side and then emerges on the outside to repeat the oblique stitch to the seam above. On the inner side of the quffa the regularity of the series of horizontal stitches imparts an appearance of annulated ribbing that is characteristic and pleasing in its symmetry.

Atra-hasīs summarises this very succinctly.

> "*I set in place thirty ribs*
> *Which were one* parsiktu-*vessel thick, ten rods long* . . .
> *Ark Tablet*: 13–14

The Babylonian word for rib is *ṣēlu*, and there are nice cases of it applied to boats, such as the entry in the bilingual dictionary which explains that Sumerian giš-ti-má = Babylonian *ṣēl eleppi*, 'rib of a boat', or the exorcistic incantation in which a demon 'wrecks the ribs of the patient as if they were those of an old boat'. There must have always been old vessels beyond repair or waterproofing rotting in the mud by the rivers, not to mention carcasses of water buffalo or camels with their ribs exposed, white and gleaming. In the cuneiform the word is spelled *ṣe-ri*, with 'r' for 'l', but this does sometimes happen in Babylonian.

His ark-quality ribs, Atra-hasīs tells us, are as thick as a *parsiktu* and ten nindan long. This word *parsiktu* is not actually spelt out on the tablet but, as occurs in other tablets from southern Iraq, is written with an abbreviation, the sign PI. As one might say, 'PI' for *parsiktu*. In line 16 the whole word *parsiktu*, applied to the stanchions, has to be supplied by the reader, for the scribe abbreviates even further, writing '½', to stand for '½ PI'.

The *parsiktu* is both a measuring vessel – a scoop – and a capacity measure. This is not surprising as many Mesopotamian metrological terms derive from vessel names. What is surprising is that a volume measure should be used to convey thickness. The vessel, we know, had a capacity of about sixty litres. Assuming it to be a box-shaped scoop with robust walls of about two fingers thickness we therefore arrive, as demonstrated in Appendix 3, at a *parsiktu* with an overall 'thickness' (width) of approximately one cubit or fifty centimetres.

Atra-hasīs, in response to Enki, is speaking colloquially and expressively. He declares that the boat ribs he produced were 'as thick as a *parsiktu*', much as we might say that something is 'as thick as two short planks' without knowing exactly how thick or short a plank might be, or whether there is even such a thing as uniformity in plank dimensions: *everyone knows what you mean*. At fifty centimetres across a *parsiktu* was close to a cubit thick, but Atra-hasīs avoids the word cubit for thickness even though he uses the nindan to define length. The point he wanted to put across was that these ribs were thicker than coracle ribs had ever been before. He was not a man, one might say, to be content with spare ribs.

Nota Bene: The expression 'as thick as a *parsiktu*' has no parallel in cuneiform literature beyond *one perfectly extraordinary, extremely important and directly related case*, which is discussed later in Chapter 12.

Each of Atra-hasīs's coracle ribs is ten *nindan* long, which comes out at sixty metres, and about fifty centimetres thick. Once installed, each J-shaped rib ran down from the top of the coracle to the flat floor and out across the floor where, as Hornell describes, the ends form a kind of lattice, over and under. Once the main series of ribs is in place the remainder can be fitted in so that their ends will all lie interlocked together (or, as Hornell put it so magnificently, they will *interdigitate*), forming the floor itself, which achieves mat-like strength and solidity. Bitumen is then poured all over it.

Hornell mentions up to sixteen ribs for the normal coracle; the thirty set in by Atra-hasīs is modest for such a giant vessel and one can imagine that the framework would need to be supplemented by cross-bracing and other precautions.

Hornell lists the species of tree used by the Iraqi coracle-makers for these ribs, and they are all in fact attested in cuneiform inscriptions:

Willow:	*ḫilēpu* – used for door panels and furniture; grows along rivers and canals.
Euphrates poplar:	*ṣarbatu* – the most common tree of lower Mesopotamia, wood cheap; used for inexpensive furniture and often as fuel; can however furnish logs (a letter request: 'eleven times sixty poplars suitable for roofing').
Tamarisk:	*bīnu* – a native and ubiquitous small tree or shrub; wood only for small objects (literary context: 'You, Tamarisk, have a wood which is not in demand').
Juniper:	*burāšu* – juniper proper used for wooden objects and furniture.
Pomegranate:	*nurmû* – there is no evidence for the use of pomegranate tree wood.

Annoyingly, these types of wood do not seem to turn up in cuneiform boat texts, at least so far.

ARK TABLET: STANCHIONS

I set up 3,600 stanchions within her
Which were half (a parsiktu-*vessel) thick, half a* nindan *high*
(lit. long)

Ark Tablet: 15–16

Here Atra-hasīs follows Enki in reckoning with the ŠÁR = 3,600. Stanchions at half a *parsiktu* by half a *nindan* were a crucial element in the Ark's construction and an innovation in response to Atra-hasīs's special requirements, for they allow the introduction of an upper deck. Very probably they were intended to be square in cross-section, with an area of about 15 x 15 fingers =225 fingers^2. Assuming that Atra-hasīs's ŠÁR, like Enki's, meant that there were literally 3,600 stanchions, their combined area massed together would represent only about 6 per cent of the total 3,600 m^2 floor space, a load-bearing distribution which is, so to speak, not unrealistic (see Appendix 3).

There is no need to visualise these stanchions in serried rows; on the contrary they could be placed in diverse arrangements, while, set flat on the interlocked square ends of the ribs, they would facilitate subdivision of the lower floor space into suitable 'cabins' and areas for bulky or fatally incompatible animals.

One striking peculiarity of Atra-hasīs's reports is that he doesn't mention either the deck or the roof explicitly, but within the specifications both deck and roof are implicit.

ARK TABLET: THE DECK

With regard to the deck, we can hardly doubt the implications of Atra-hasīs's stanchions. This deck would come halfway up the sides, and, attached to the walls, would undoubtedly greatly strengthen the whole craft as well as enabling the fitting of the upper cabins. No conventional Iraqi coracle ever had a deck at all, needless to say, but, on the other hand, no other coracle had such a job to do.

ARK TABLET: CABINS

Accommodation was needed for Atra-hasīs, his wife and immediate family, not to mention the other humans (discussed in the next chapter). There would be plenty of room upstairs for other life forms too; two conversational Babylonian parrots might cheer things up, for example.

Atra-hasīs says:

> "*I constructed her* ḫinnu *cabins above and below.*"
>
> Ark Tablet: 17

Although 'cabin' sounds anachronistic and cruise-like, the rare word *ḫinnu* means just that, as we are again informed by our ancient lexicographer:

> giš.é-má = *bīt eleppi*, 'wooden house on a boat'
> giš.é-má-gur₈, 'wooden house on a *makurru*'.

(The same word occurs in a sophisticated symbolic dream described on a tablet from the time of Alexander the Great, in which the barque of the god Nabu is in a cult procession winding down a thoroughfare in Babylon and his cabin, *ḫinnu*, is quite clearly described.)

Captain A. Hasīs speaks of cabins in the plural, and the verb applied is *rakāsu*, 'to tie', or 'to plait', suggesting that they were at least partly made of reeds rather than wood. Atra-hasīs tells us that he installed them above and below, that is on the upper and lower decks. We might not stray far from the mark if we understand these cabins to resemble the small tied-reed houses in the southern marshes discussed in Chapter 6, especially those that are located within a round fence with animals mooching round about, floating gently.

ARK TABLET: THE ROOF

We can be equally sure that the Ark had a roof. In line 45 Atra-hasīs goes up there to pray to the Moon God, and we know from the instructions in three parallel Flood accounts quoted in Chapter 7 that arks were to be roofed like the Apsû, suggesting a black circular shape consistent with Mesopotamian models of the cosmic Apsû, the waters under the earth. (Anyway, on a different level, without a roof the rain and sea would get in.) For the implications as to structure and material see Appendix 3.

ARK TABLET: BITUMEN

The next stage is crucial: the application of bitumen for waterproofing, inside and out, a job to be taken very seriously considering the load and the likely weather conditions. The primary Akkadian word for bitumen is *iṭṭû*, which still survives in the modern name of Hít, the most famous of the natural sources of bitumen in Iraq now as then; it was known to Herodotus as *Is*. The old Sumerian name is ESIR. Bitumen comes bubbling out of the Mesopotamian ground for *myriad* uses as an unending, benevolent supply. For waterproofing a *guffa* it is unsurpassable, as we see in Hornell's description.

> After the structure of the quffa is complete, the outside is coated thickly with hot bitumen brought either from Hit on the Euphrates or from Imam Ali. This forms an efficient waterproofing. In addition, a thick layer of bitumen is spread over the floor to level it and to protect the floor lashings from damage. The inner surface of the sides is left bare. If the boatman or *quffāji* be superstitious, as often is the case, he will embed a few money cowries (Cypraea moneta) and some blue button beads in the bitumen on the outer side in the hope of thereby averting the evil eye . . . The life of a well-made quffa is long, for bitumen is an ideal preservative against rot, and when the coating cracks and begins to flake off, a fresh application makes the craft nearly as good as new.

There are in fact two Babylonian words for bitumen, *iṭṭû*, as mentioned, and *kupru*, both of which types are used by

172

Atra-hasīs. The great bulk is *kupru*-bitumen, which is written with the Sumerian sign ESIR followed by the signs UD.DU.A (there are traces of signs left which I have restored in line 22, given the spacing in the gap), which mean something like 'dried'. This is supplemented by a quantity of *ittû*, written simply ESIR.

Atra-hasīs devotes twenty of his sixty lines to precise details about waterproofing his boat. It is just one of the many remarkable aspects of the *Ark Tablet* that we are thereby given the most complete account of caulking a boat to have come down to us from antiquity. The technical details behind these lines are to be considered carefully:

> I apportioned one finger of bitumen for her outsides;
> I apportioned one finger of bitumen for her interior;
> I had (already) poured out one finger of bitumen for her
>   cabins;
> I caused the kilns to be loaded with 28,800 (sūtu) of kupru-
>   bitumen
> And I poured 3,600 (sūtu) of ittû-bitumen within.
> The ittû-bitumen was not coming up to the surface (lit. to
>   me);
> (So) I added five fingers of lard,
> I ordered the kilns to be loaded . . . in equal measure.
> (With) tamarisk wood (?) (and) stalks (?)
> I . . . (= completed the mixture(?)).

Ark Tablet: 18–27

First he works out the quantities of bitumen needed to waterproof all exterior and interior surfaces – including the cabins which he seems to have treated already – to a depth of one finger. Having calculated the amount required for the whole vast operation he is then seen doctoring the mixture in the kilns until it reaches the correct consistency for application. He tests it, perhaps with a dip-stick to gauge flow or viscosity, and finds that it is not yet perfect (line 23); he then adds equal quantities of lard and fresh bitumen to loosen it up. Eventually it is ready.

Fingers of bitumen

Here we have to understand the measure as the Sumerian ideogram ŠU.ŠI (usually written ŠU.SI), standing for the Babylonian *ubānu*, 'finger', one of which comes out at about 1.66 centimetres. Bitumen is thus applied to all ark surfaces to a depth of one finger.

Loading the kiln

The word *kīru*, 'kiln', occurs here in the plural but we do not know how many there were. Although bitumen as a staple commodity is often mentioned in cuneiform texts there is surprisingly little information about technical matters to help us. The Babylonian verb in line 21 is very often used of loading boats, but the bitumen here is not to be loaded aboard but put into the kilns to be heated up, so, 'I ordered to be loaded', refers in the *Ark Tablet* to the process of shovelling the raw material into the waiting kilns.

Quantities of bitumen

Atra-hasīs also tells us the quantity of bitumen that the waterproofing would involve, again expressed by the *šár* or 3,600 sign. The quantity of *kupru*-bitumen is 28,800 *sūtu*, written 8 x 3,600, which works out at 241.92 cubic metres. To this is added 3,600 *sūtu*, 30.24 cubic metres, of *ittû*, 'crude bitumen', and five finger-thicknesses each of lard and fresh bitumen, whose volume cannot be worked out; the quantity of the latter two components need not have been considerable to make a difference to the whole. Nor do we know how many bitumen kilns there were running, or what their capacity was. We are told that a finger thickness of bitumen is needed inside and out. Our calculation involving the quantity of rope puts that bitumen total at eight *šár*, and the tablet confirms that we need eight *šár* of *kupru* plus a small amount of a more mastic quality applied separately for an external coat.

We get a glimpse of these operations in some scrappy records from a bitumen-supplier in the city of Larsa in about 1800 BC. The different types of boat-making bitumen shipped include: over fifteen gur of *kupru* for a 100-gur boat belonging to Ṣilli-Ishtar; two *sūtu* of *iṭṭû* for the kiln; *iṭṭû* for '*talpittu*' of a wooden cabin; *iṭṭû* which has been poured into *kupru*; *iṭṭû* which has been poured into boat hulls; these and other supplies had been loaded onto a twenty-gur boat for delivery.

Some of this might have gone to coracle-builders. The little-known boat word *talpittu*, 'smearing', is used twice in this Larsa archive of a bitumen layer for wooden cabins. It derives from the Babylonian verb *lapātu*, 'to touch', and probably reflects the idea that bitumen was applied to a thickness of one finger (*ubānu*), as with the cabins that Atra-hasīs had to fit in his own giant model in line 20: 'I had (already) poured out one finger of bitumen onto her cabins.'

We can assume that the bitumen layers were applied to the Ark long before everything and everybody was loaded on board. No one would be painting zoo cages with Babylonian creosote when all the livestock was in residence. If any part of that huge undertaking was described within the Flood Story we can learn nothing from the *Ark Tablet*, which is very badly damaged after the clear bitumen lines. The same is true of the corresponding part of *Old Babylonian Atrahasis*, while *Gilgamesh XI* dispenses with any description of such detail.

We learn from the *Ark Tablet*, however, that when everything was ready, and just before Atra-hasīs came aboard himself, another practical operation took place:

> "I ordered several times (?) a one-finger (layer) of lard for the girmadû-*roller,*
> *Out of the thirty gur which the workmen had put to one side."*
>
> Ark Tablet: 57–8

Nine cubic metres of lard in the hands of workmen is no simple matter of bread and dripping and this material can only be destined for physical application to the outer surface on a large scale. Such a large quantity will also have been prepared in advance, probably alongside the bitumen operation. Atra-hasīs tells us that a one-finger layer out of that supply must now be applied, using a roller called a *girmadû* (on which, see presently). Lard or oil applied as a final coating to a bitumen surface has a softening effect which enhances the level of water-proofing and this is undoubtedly what is going on here. It would only be necessary to oil the outside of the boat, of course, and so the process could be carried out at the last minute.

The remainder of the *Ark Tablet* concerns the continuation of the Flood Story plot: people and animals going aboard, last-minute deliveries and Atra-hasīs's agony of mind, all of which we will look at in Chapter 10. Only selected parts of this great boat-building operation, described in such detail, were taken up into *Gilgamesh XI*, to which august narrative we now turn.

2. Building Utnapishti's Ark in the Gilgamesh Story

Work began on Utnapishti's Ark as early as possible, and there was a good turnout:

> At the very first light of dawn,
> The population began assembling at Atra-hasīs's gate.
>> *Gilgamesh XI*: 48–9

Immediately we perceive imported Old Babylonian narrative under this much later text. Utnapishti is reminiscing in the first person, so he ought to say 'at *my* gate'. The Old Babylonian name of Atra-hasīs was there in the original but does not belong in the new text; it should have been edited out but has sneaked in under the wire. This single line is also a very important indication that the Old Babylonian text in the background was in the third person and not the first person, exactly as we can see it in *Old Babylonian Atrahasis*:

> Atra-hasīs received the command,
> He assembled the elders to his gate.
>
> *Old Babylonian Atrahasis*: 38–9

It took five days before the 'outer shape' was ready. Unlike the *Ark Tablet*, which bypasses the episode, *Old Babylonian Atrahasis* (not much left) and *Gilgamesh XI* both list the workers who came to help with Atra-hasīs's great project. We can see how well this labour force reflected the building of the giant coracle that we have been discussing:

Worker	Project
The carpenter carrying his axe	Ribs, stanchions, plugs
The reed worker carrying his stone	Cabins
The young men bearing . . .	. .
The old men bearing rope of palm-fibre	Boat structure
Rich man carrying bitumen	Waterproofing
Poor man carrying . . . 'tackle'	'Tackle'

One ancient contributor to the text added a specialist with an *agasilikku* axe, probably also for woodworking. The presence of 'palm-fibre rope', Akkadian *pitiltu*, is especially significant in view of what the god Ea says about the same fundamental material in *Ark Tablet* line 11 above.

The poor man's 'tackle' (the word means 'the needful things') is a bit of a mystery. Utnapishti explains:

> I struck the water pegs into her belly.
> I found a punting-pole and put the tackle in place.
>
> *Gilgamesh XI*: 64–5

Its safety importance had been stressed by the god Ea a millennium before:

> *The tackle should be very strong;*
> *Let the bitumen be tough and so give (the boat) strength.*
>
> Old Babylonian Atrahasis: 32–3

The 'punting pole' in the Gilgamesh description, Akkadian *parrisu*, is essential for coracle navigation and its inclusion here is another pointer to the authentic riverine Old Babylonian background to the passage. The traditional Iraqi coracle made specific journeys to set destinations and required a paddle:

> *When small or moderate in size, the* quffāji, *leaning over one side (the functional fore end for the time being) propels his craft with a paddle. The usual system is to make several strokes first on one side and then on the other, changing over as necessary to keep a straight course. In medium-sized quffas two men paddle standing on opposite sides; the largest requires a crew of four paddlers . . . The paddle used to-day has a loom 5–6 feet in length, with a short blade, round or oblong, nailed to the outer end. It bears no resemblance to the 'oars' working on thole pins shown in Assyrian bas-reliefs of the quffas of Sennacherib's period* [see Pl. . . .].
>
> Hornell 1946: 104

Under flood conditions Atra-hasīs's Ark had one job only: to stay afloat and safeguard its contents, but perhaps any giant coracle had to have its giant punting pole. The 'tackle' could therefore be the matching rowlock to keep the thing in place and stop it drifting away (as I know paddles are apt to do). The pole, if not for steering, might also help to prevent the vessel from spinning round and round, and we know from *Tablet X* that a character like Gilgamesh could handle thirty-metre *parrisu* poles by the three hundred when it came to it. The water pegs are also mentioned in *Ark Tablet* 47, and are sometimes thought to be bilge plugs.

The process of roofing the Round Ark with all its implications and associations reminded some early poet of the Apsû, the water under the world, and the idea is made explicit:

> *Cover her with a roof, like the Apsû.*
> > Old Babylonian Atrahasis: 29; Gilgamesh XI: 705

Middle Babylonian Nippur, in contrast, says, '... roof it over with a strong covering', for talk there is of the non-round *makurkurru* ark, and the cosmic Apsû metaphor does not apply. Mention of the roof was not integral to every Old Babylonian version, however, for, as we have seen, the author behind the *Ark Tablet* omits the topic entirely, just as he makes no mention of installing a deck (although we can be sure there was one for reasons given above). A round Babylonian ark, then, had a lower deck or base and a deck above that, with cabins on both decks and a roof whose profile mirrored the base.

Utnapishti's internal arrangements put this modest one-up, one-down structure to shame!

> *I gave her six decks*
> *I divided her into seven parts*
> *I divided her interior into nine.*
> > Gilgamesh XI: 61–3

This is a flamboyant achievement, especially if, like so much else in this tablet, it ultimately derives from a far simpler Old Babylonian model.

When this narrative section is compared to the *Ark Tablet* (our only other source of information on these highly interesting matters), it is noticeable that the long and sticky bitumen passage with which we have just engaged is whittled down in *Gilgamesh XI* to two lines. Perhaps Assurbanipal's editors experienced technical overload, and in any case the right way to bituminise a coracle didn't have much to do with their narrative (which was really focused on *Gilgamesh* and what happened to *him*), and the symbolic nature of the structure far exceeded interest in how it was actually made.

While the matter of bitumen was substantially reduced in the Gilgamesh version, it is the same two principal types of bitumen that went into Utnapishti's kiln. For these, and the oil that comes next, we are given the only *Gilgamesh XI* quantity measurements on offer, preserved partly in a tablet from Babylon as well as in the Nineveh copies:

> *I poured* 3 x 3,600 [Nineveh, source W], *or* 6 x 3,600 [Babylon, source j] *(sūtu) of* kupru-*bitumen into the kiln;* [*I poured*] *in* 3 x 3,600 [Nineveh and Babylon](sūtu) *of* iṭṭû-*bitumen* . . .
>
> *Gilgamesh XI*: 61–3

If we choose the 6 x 3,600 of the Babylon tradition over the Ninevite Assyrian 3 x 3,600 (as I much prefer to do) we find that Utnapishti put a total of nine *šár* of mixed bitumen into his kiln, with the idea of waterproofing – be it remembered – what was originally a round coracle boat of one-*ikû* area with one-nindan walls. This makes a suggestive point of comparison with the Old Babylonian *Ark Tablet,* which prepares a total of nine *šár* of bitumen for the identical purpose. This shows that the original bitumen number came through the process of textual transmission undistorted or unaltered, and that the quantity of bitumen was not altered to match the increased size. On the contrary, those responsible for the finished text of *Gilgamesh XI* reveal themselves to be aware that the original quantity of bitumen would only suffice to cover the lower two-thirds of the outside of the Ark in its Gilgamesh form (see below, and Appendix 3).

Utnapishti itemises his oil quantities as if accounting to someone rather defensively for expenses:

The workforce of porters was bringing over 3 x 3,600 (sūtu)
  of oil;
Apart from 3,600 (sūtu) of oil that niqqu *used up*
There were 3,600 x 2 (sūtu) that the shipwright stashed away.
Gilgamesh XI: 68–70

His oil came in three lots of 3,600; one was used for *niqqu* (the meaning of which is uncertain) and the remaining two went to Puzur-Enlil, shipwright and man-in-charge, who was to keep it until needed. No one is quite sure what *niqqu* means, although 'libation' has been suggested. The 'apart from . . .' idea derives from the *Ark Tablet* tradition, with a slight change from the original Babylonian meaning 'out of'. Finally, we know that *Ark Tablet* 57 refers in this oily context to a tool called *girmadû*, here clearly spelled *gi-ri-ma-de-e*. This important term has also survived in *Gilgamesh XI*: 79, but scholars have usually thrown it out, emending the text. This rejection is now seen to be unjustified. Here is the crucial passage:

At sun-[rise to] I set my hand to oiling;
[Before] sundown the boat was finished.
[...] were very difficult.
We kept moving the girmadû *from back to front*
[Until] two-thirds of it [were mar]ked off.
Gilgamesh XI: 76–80

The term 'oiling' in line 76 confirms the nature of the activity to which these five lines are devoted: it took all day and it wasn't easy. Applying bitumen all over, inside and out, was a bigger job, but this final waterproofing attracted greater interest in the Gilgamesh version. Perhaps it was accompanied by some concluding ceremony. Puzur-Enlil's supply of oil was applied with the *girmadû*, presumably by him. This word must mean 'wooden roller', exactly as described above by Chesney, for smoothing over the surface of the bitumen on a new boat once it was applied.

The same roller would be used both for the bitumen, and then for the oily layer. Puzur-Enlil must have supervised both bitumen and oil sealing operations to have received such a handsome reward as this:

> To *the man who sealed the boat, the shipwright*
> *Puzur-Enlil — said Utnapishti —*
> (variant: To *the shipwright Puzur-Enlil in return for sealing*
> *the boat*)
> I gave the Palace with all its goods.
>
> Gilgamesh XI: 95–6

This, to me, is an unforgettable, cinematographic image. Here the word 'Palace' is inserted, rather late in the proceedings, to show that Atra-hasīs has been king all along. At the last minute we meet Puzur-Enlil, who, one imagines, had been humouring Atra-hasīs and building his mad I-have-to-get-away-from-it-all boat without a murmur (but no doubt discussing it sardonically over a beer with his fellow workers). Now, as the hatch closes tight, momentous news! One pictures him running hysterically up the road to the Palace, bursting through the front door, ordering a banquet, half the cellar and as many of the harem as he could possibly manage. Later, sprawling and sated on the royal cushions, unable to move, he hears the first ping of raindrops on the roof over his head . . .

If *Gilgamesh* line 80 is correctly restored as '*until two-thirds of it were marked off*', this means that the oil layer was only applied to the lower two-thirds of the boat's exterior, which would correlate perfectly with the Nineveh issue of bitumen, for this only sufficed to coat the bottom two-thirds of Utnapishti's Ark. They clearly anticipated little danger from leaks. Interestingly, modern coracles are often not bituminised up to the rim.

Up until now, it must be said, lines 76–80 in the *Gilgamesh* passage have been understood to describe the *launching* of Utnapishti's Ark. Launching could hardly precede the loading of everything on board, and the apparently supportive interpretation, 'poles for the slipway we kept moving back to front', has depended on the unwarranted throwing out of the reading *girmadû*, which is now confirmed as a real word by the spelling in the *Ark Tablet*.

A launch with a bottle of fizz across the bows was never an option for the Babylonian flood hero or for his ark. The vast coracle would be 'launched' of its own accord as the waters arrived, like an abandoned lilo on the beach gradually taken up by an incoming tide.

TEXT-FIG. 10. Method of transporting a large new *quffa* to the river Euphrates at Hit. (*After Vernon C. Boyle.*)

How to launch a large coracle (if you have to).

9

Life on Board

The animals went in two by two, Hurrah! Hurrah!
The elephant and the kangaroo, Hurrah! Hurrah!
The animals went in two by two,
The elephant and the kangaroo,
And they all went in-to the Ark for to get out of the
  rain

Anon

The Ark in the storm as portrayed by Dutch artist Reinier Zeeman.

We left the completed ark at the end of the last chapter, water-proofed, anointed and ready, its occupants surely apprehensive as to what could possibly await them. The Flood Story versions that build up to this dramatic moment differ in their accounts of who and what came to be on board at Atra-hasīs's side in his great vessel and it is to these intriguing questions that we now turn our attention. Most important, of course, are the *animals*, and then the *people*.

'Spurn property and save life!' said the god Enki to Atra-hasīs, and the essence of the task that lay ahead of him, one can only reflect, remains a valid proposition for our own modern world. The same injunction appears in our three chief flood tablets, *Old Babylonian Atrahasis*, the *Ark Tablet* and *Gilgamesh XI*, 'save life' in line 26 of the latter being amplified for emphasis by 'Put on board the seed of all living creatures.'

Boat-building notwithstanding, one cannot help but worry about the various Noahs, Babylonian and otherwise, and all their animals. The thought of rounding them up, getting them in line, marching them up the gangplank like a schoolteacher on an outing and ensuring good behaviour all round for a voyage of unknown length . . .

Atra-hasīs's Animals

The animal boarders divide fundamentally into domestic and wild, and to convey this the Babylonian poets who write of **Atra-hasīs** use three Akkadian words: *būl sēri, umām sēri* and *nammaššû*. The word *ṣēru* means 'hinterland, back country, open country, fields, plain and steppe land', the broad countryside that outlies a village or town, uncultivated and more often than not the haunt of demons. The word *būlu* can mean on the one hand 'herd of cattle, sheep or horses', on the other 'wild animals, as a collective, referring mainly to herds of quadrupeds'. Finally, *umāmu* means 'animal, beast', often but not necessarily wild, and *nammaššû*, 'herds of (wild) animals'.

This breakdown makes it look as if words in Akkadian can mean whatever you want them to mean, but that is not the case. These are literary words whose full range of possible meanings seems too all encompassing to be much help when it comes to the Great Natural History Project, but, in context, the appropriate meaning – domestic or wild, one or many – is usually clear. I think that we cannot go far wrong with understanding *būl ṣēri* in the Ark situation as referring to 'domesticated animals' and *nammaššû* as meaning 'wild animals'. We can comfortably translate *umām ṣēri* with our expression 'beast of the field', which can be either domestic or wild.

With these translations in mind, it becomes apparent that *Old Babylonian Atrahasis* has normal livestock, domesticated animals and wild animals being taken on board:

> *Whatever he [had . . .]*
> *Whatever he had [. . .]*
> *Clean (animals) . . . [. . .]*
> *Fat (animals) [. . .]*
> *He caught [and put on board]*
> *The winged [birds of] the heavens.*
> *The cattle (*būl šakkan*)[. . .]*
> *The wild [animals of the steppe (*nammaššû ṣēri*)]*
> *[. . .] he put on board.*
>
> Old Babylonian Atrahasis: 30–38

It is a pity that such timeless lines are broken in what is our best-preserved account of the cuneiform story. 'Clean' and 'fat' animals are separated here from the other categories, probably referring to domestic sheep and goats. In prime condition they would be brought on board not only with the survival of species in mind, but also to provide milk, cheese and meat. The distinction between *būl šakkan* and *nammaššû ṣēri* is essentially that between domesticated and wild animals, but it is worth pointing out there is no indication in *Old Babylonian Atrahasis* (in the surviving lines) that species *completeness* was conceived as part of the deal, or indeed that there were Male and Female of each. The category of 'clean', too, cannot pass without comment, for the notion of clean and unclean animals did not exist in ancient Mesopotamia as it does in the Bible. While the pig was certainly typecast as unclean there is no occurrence of, or antecedent to, the Hebrew dietary conception: it is certainly more than curious that it should occur here, of all places, in the clearest parallel of all, parallel to the text of Genesis, where the issue is important.

Middle Babylonian Nippur mentions wild animals and birds but is fragmentary:

> [Into the boat which] you will make
> [Bring aboard] wild beasts of the steppe (umām ṣēri), birds of
> heaven.
> Heap up . . .
>
> Middle Babylonian Nippur: 10–12

Assyrian Smith specifies domestic animals and non-carnivorous wild animals as part of the initial building instructions. Atra-hasīs is off the hook, though, as regards herding and rounding-up:

> [Send up into] it . . .
> Domestic [animals] (būl ṣēri), all the wild beasts
> (umām ṣēri) that eat grass,
> [I] will send to you and they will wait at your door."
>
> Assyrian Smith: 8–10

At first sight, the very broken lines 51–2 of the *Ark Tablet* look very unpromising. The surface, if not completely lost, is badly abraded in this part of the tablet. I needed, then, to bring every sophisticated technique of decipherment into play: polishing the magnifying glass, holding it steady, repeatedly moving the tablet under the light to get the slightest shadow of a worn-out wedge or two, and, of course, trying a hundred times. Eventually the sign traces in line 51 could be seen to be 'and the wild animal[s of the st]ep[pe]'.

What gave me the biggest shock in 44 years of grappling with difficult lines in cuneiform tablets was, however, what came next . . . My best shot at the first two signs beginning line 52 came up with *ša* and *na*, both incompletely preserved. On looking unhopefully for words beginning *šana*- . . . in the *Chicago Assyrian Dictionary* Š PART 1 ŠA-ŠAP, I found the following entry and nearly fell off my chair as a result of the words: '*šana* (or *šanā*) adv. Two each, two by two; OA*; cf. *šina*'.

In plain English, there is an Akkadian word *šana*, or possibly *šanā*, an adverb derived from the numeral two, *šina*, which has the specific meaning 'two each, two by two'. It is a very rare word among all our texts – in fact when the dictionary was published there had only been two occurrences (as is indicated by the asterisk that follows 'OA', which stands for Old Assyrian Period, about 1900–1700 BC). A merchant wrote using this word, 'I will set aside one or two garments apiece (*šana*) and send them to you.'

The world's most beautiful dictionary definition.

For the first time we learn that the Babylonian animals, like those of Noah, *went in two by two*, a completely unsuspected Babylonian tradition that draws us ever closer to the familiar narrative of the Bible. So, we can read in the *Ark Tablet*:

> *But the wild animals* (namaštu) *from the steppe* (ṣēru) [. . .]...
> *Two by two . . . did* [*they enter the ark.*]
>
> Ark Tablet: 51–2

The Ark tablet, back view, with close-up to show the signs for 'two-by-two'.

This discovery meant that a fresh look had to be taken at the corresponding cuneiform in *Old Babylonian Atrahasis*, for there

is a broken line in *exactly this spot* where only the traces of the
first sign survive: '*x* [. . .]... *he put on board*', and previously
there had been no way of identifying this sign for certain.

This innocuous-looking 'x' sign proves to be highly important.
Consulting the original tablet in the British Museum shows that
this sign, of which only the front wedges are preserved, can now
be positively identified as *š*[*a-*.

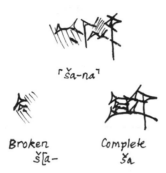

⸢*ša-na*⸣

Broken
š[*a–*

Complete
ša

This is clear from my sketches, which show both the *š*[*a-* as it is
preserved and a complete ŠA sign from the same tablet for comparison. (The large upper horizontal wedge over two smaller hori-
zontals tucked underneath are characteristic of the beginning of
this sign.) This, then, is the remains of *ša-*[*na*. We can see, therefore, that *Old Babylonian Atrahasis* included the same two-by-two
idea found in the *Ark Tablet* and, furthermore, the discovery
reinforces the reading of the crucial signs in the *Ark Tablet*, which
are, as I already stated, very worn. We can thus restore the crucial
words in *Old Babylonian Atrahasis* col. Ii line 38 as:

> *š*[*a-na i-na e-le-ep-pi-im uš*]*-te-ri-ib*
> *Two by two he brought on board the boat,*

and *Ark Tablet* 52 as:

> ⸢*ša-na* MÁ! *lu-ú x x x x x x x* [*x x x x*]
> *Two by two the boat did* [*they enter* . . . . . .] . . . [. . . . . . .]. . . . . .

There is a further consideration raised by these two lines in the *Ark Tablet*: they only mention *wild* animals. Given the fuller spectrum covered by the other manuscript traditions I think we have to assume that taking domestic livestock in this telling was plainly understood, rather than imagine that a line of narrative has fallen out (especially given the line total of sixty). Domestic livestock might well be taken for granted, especially if some of the animals were going to be part of their own food chain. Line 51 begins with the word 'and', as if following on directly from the preceding line, which has nothing to do with quadrupeds, feral or otherwise, and for that reason is better translated 'but'.

The following materials listed in the *Ark Tablet* are surprisingly difficult to make out; the lines are broken and the measurement system behind the numbers is not given.

> *Five (measures) of beer (?) I . . . [. . .]*
> *They were transporting eleven or twelve [. . . . . .]*
> *Three (measures) of* šiqbum(?) *I [. . .] . . . . . . ,*
> *One third (measure) of fodder, . . . and* kurdinnu *plant (?)*
> > *Ark Tablet: 53–6*

Probably all this was for the animals; diluted beer might have had its uses in husbandry, and one of the lines, probably line 54, might refer to straw or bedding.

Gilgamesh XI takes a very different stance on these issues. Once the boat was ready and the moment had arrived, Utnapishti loaded aboard a good deal more than the 'seed of all living creatures' that had earlier been specified.

> *[Everything I had] I loaded aboard it.*
> *I loaded aboard it whatever silver I had,*
> *I loaded aboard it whatever gold I had,*
> *I loaded aboard it whatever seed I had of living things, each*
> > *and every one.*

All my kith and kin I sent aboard the boat,
I sent aboard domestic quadrupeds (būl ṣēri), *wild beasts of*
  the steppe (umām ṣēri), *persons of every skill and craft . . .*

Gilgamesh XI: 81–7

The first three of these items are really surprising when one recalls the pure injunction, 'Despise property and save life!' Who needs silver and gold on board an ark? If such items were so important couldn't they just find more later? Rescue of living things, it seems, now plays second fiddle. Note, too, the reduction in scale of the operation, from the ideal 'seed of *all* living things,' which Ea commanded in line 26 to 'whatever seed I had'. What does the text mean by 'seed?' Breedable animals that carry seed? *All* the animals, plants and birds?

This is the only animal line anywhere in cuneiform in which the word 'all' appears. It looks as if someone had said to Utnapishti, 'We couldn't take *all* living things, how on earth would we collect them? And think of *ants* together with *elephants*, or those *giant baby-eating lizards* we saw in Syria,' and the story, to its disadvantage, is reinterpreted to mean *living things within Utnapishti's reach*.

The wild animals in Utnapishti's line 84, moreover, look like an afterthought to me, for they should have come under the umbrella of *all* living things above; again this looks like careless editing. If the two lines were meant together to cover all living things, domestic and wild, they should have formed a couplet. Utanapishti's speech has been elaborated beyond the rational necessities that were quite sufficient according to the contemporary *Assyrian Smith* fragment quoted above.

Based on this evidence, one could say, on balance, that whereas the Old Babylonian narrative is concerned with the preservation of *life*, the Late Assyrian tradition is thinking more in terms of the preservation of *civilisation* . . .

To summarise all this succinctly:

Old Babylonian Atrahasis:	normal livestock; birds; domesticated animals; wild animals; ⌜2⌝ [x2]
Middle Babylonian Nippur:	wild animals and birds (as preserved)
Assyrian Smith:	domestic animals and non-carnivorous wild animals
Ark Tablet:	2 x 2 wild animals

Probably the underlying Babylonian conception is 'all animals, domestic and wild' but this is not articulated as such. Only *Gilgamesh XI* uses the word 'all'. Only *Old Babylonian Atrahasis* mentions birds on board although *Middle Babylonian* does include them in Ea's plan. There are three categories of animals involved between the versions: domestic, wild and non-predatory wild. Avoiding predators would certainly be a sensible Ark policy.

The *Ark Tablet*, with its two-by-two, even without any domestic species, remains a miraculous discovery!

Noah's Animals

There is something about Noah and his queue of ark animals that inspires cartoonists. One of my favourites shows Noah remarking ruefully to his wife, three days out, that perhaps they should have made an exception in the case of Mr and Mrs Woodworm. There is another fine drawing of two Diplodoci on a beach, the Ark meanwhile disappearing over the horizon, where one says to the other, 'I *told* you it departed on Thursday!'

Noah, of course, could manage. He too had Instructions. In fact there were two slightly conflicting versions:

1: Genesis 6:19–22
> *And of every living thing, of all flesh, you shall bring two of every kind into the ark, to keep them alive with you; they shall be male and female. Of the birds according to their kinds, and of the animals according to their kinds, of every creeping thing*

of the ground according to its kind, two of every kind shall come in to you, to keep them alive. Also take with you every kind of food that is eaten, and store it up; and it shall serve as food for you and for them.

The first stipulates one male and one female of every species together with food for one and all, thus encapsulating the essence of what we might call the Ark Project. If hand-picked pairs were destined to guarantee survival of their species, none could themselves be eaten. The tooth-and-claw Laws of Nature would thus need to be suspended for the duration, with every link in the normally voracious food chain agreeing to hold off. However you look at it, umpiring life on board was going to be a matter of considerable finesse for the Captain. This simple instruction is not, however, the whole story.

2: Genesis 7:2–3

Then the Lord said to Noah, "Go into the ark, you and all your household, for I have seen that you alone are righteous before me in this generation. Take with you seven pairs of all clean animals, the male and its mate; and a pair of the animals that are not clean, the male and its mate; and seven pairs of the birds of the air also, male and female, to keep their kind alive on the face of all the earth."

Here, a follow-up suggestion, with an extra six male and female pairs for every clean species, while birds are itemised separately from the animals, with seven pairs of each for every type. The amendment reads almost as if a disadvantage had been spotted in the first plan. Since Noah's first post-diluvial deed on dry land was to offer grateful sacrifices of clean animals and birds, perhaps anticipation of this led to the amendment. A cartoonist might attribute the suggestion to Mrs Noah, responsible for the cooking and trying to plan ahead for an unknown number of meals. In the end, though, as we again see from the two following accounts,

Noah took on board one male and one female of absolutely every living species and rejected the sevens options.

Account 1: Genesis 7:8–9

There went in two of clean animals, and of animals that are not clean, and of birds, and of everything that creeps on the ground, two and two, male and female, went into the ark with Noah, as God had commanded Noah.

Account 2: Genesis 7: 13–16

On the very same day Noah with his sons, Shem and Ham and Japheth, and Noah's wife and the three wives of his sons, entered the ark, they and every wild animal of every kind, and all domestic animals of every kind, and every creeping thing that creeps on the earth, and every bird of every kind—every bird, every winged creature. They went into the ark with Noah, two and two of all flesh in which there was the breath of life. And those that entered, male and female of all flesh, went in as God had commanded him; and the Lord shut him in.

Reading this over, I find it remarkable in such a consequential matter as the future survival of the entire life of the world that the long-suffering Noah should be confronted by conflicting instructions. What was he supposed to do? Can this vacillation perhaps be explained?

In fact, the feature of two distinct instructions can be understood from the inside history of the Hebrew text itself. As is the case with many passages in the Old Testament, a close look at the received Hebrew wording makes it clear that certain paragraphs or even sentences have been woven together out of more than one strand of underlying text. This approach to the Hebrew text of Scripture depends on a long-established and largely noncontentious branch of biblical scholarship known as the Documentary Hypothesis. This distinguishes four principal sources as lying behind the text of the Hebrew Bible on the basis of, primarily, which name was used for God. These sources are referred to by the theologians who work on such matters as J (Yahwist source), E (Elohist source), D (Deuteronomist source) and P (Priestly source). It occurred to me to separate out the sources behind the Flood Story, and the animals section in particular as an experiment. The wording of Genesis 6–8 is constructed out of two sources, J and P, of which the former is considerably the shorter:

Genesis J first paragraph: *¹Then the LORD said to Noah, 'Go into the ark, you and all your household, for I have seen that you alone are righteous before me in this generation. ²Take with you seven pairs of all clean animals, the male and its mate; and a pair of the animals that are not clean, the male and its mate; ³and seven pairs of the birds of the air also, male and female, to keep their kind alive on the face of all the earth . . .'*

Genesis J second paragraph: *⁷And Noah with his sons and his wife and his sons' wives went into the ark to escape the waters of the flood. ⁸Of clean animals, and of animals that are not clean, and of birds, and of everything that creeps on the ground, ⁹two and two, male and female, went into the ark with Noah, as God had commanded Noah.*

Genesis P first paragraph: *'You shall come into the ark, you, your sons, your wife, and your sons' wives with you. ¹⁹And of every living thing, of all flesh, you shall bring two of every kind into the ark, to keep them alive with you; they shall be male and female. ²⁰Of the birds according to their kinds, and of the animals according to their kinds, of every creeping thing of the ground according to its kind, two of every kind shall come in to you, to keep them alive. ²¹Also take with you every kind of food that is eaten, and store it up; and it shall serve as food for you and for them.' ²²Noah did this; he did all that God commanded him . . .*

Genesis P second paragraph:*¹³On the very same day Noah with his sons, Shem and Ham and Japheth, and Noah's wife and the three wives of his sons, entered the ark, ¹⁴they and every wild animal of every kind, and all domestic animals of every kind, and every creeping thing that creeps on the earth, and every bird of every kind – every bird, every winged creature. ¹⁵They went into the ark with Noah, two and two of all flesh in which there was the breath of life. ¹⁶And those that entered, male and female of all flesh, went in as God had commanded him . . .*

So, the input of the seven pairs motif comes only from the source J first paragraph; it was already rejected in J second paragraph and did not occur at all in P. (This question recurs in Chapter 10 when we have to compare the Genesis Flood Story as a whole with the cuneiform tradition.) Here we can visualise unmistakably the hand of a human editor, attempting to amalgamate traditions distinct in their content and wording. Faced with divergent traditions about the numbers of animals, he felt unable to decide on such a serious point and so *included both*.

In Koranic tradition Noah took one pair of each species on board, as is clear from Suras 11:40 and 23:27: '*Place on board this Ark a pair of each species . . .*'

Noah in biblical and Koranic traditions, thus found himself

charged with collecting two specimens of *all* birds, animals and insects, one of each gender. This sounds like a very tall order, for the terms 'every' or 'all' add up rapidly, and thanks to Sir David Attenborough everyone today has an inkling of just what that 'all' might entail. The statistics, in fact, are staggering. Apparently there are about 1,250,000 identified species of animal. This includes 1,190,200 invertebrates, among them 950,000 insects, 70,000 molluscs, 40,000 crustaceans, and 130,200 others. There are about 58,800 identified vertebrates, including 29,300 fish, 5,743 amphibians, 8,240 reptiles, 9,800 birds, and 5,416 mammals. As a comparison, almost 300,000 plant species are known.

It is no great feat of imagination to see the problems, then, with Noah's agenda. Nothing aboard would be able to breathe, the big would squash the small, it would surely be impossible to control the carnivores for long, especially in the dark, and the vessel would sink anyway under the weight. Anything like all the world's life forms together would be impossible, but there is one reassuring let-out factor to be considered: the Hebrew flood tradition – like the Sumerian and Babylonian that preceded it – could only have in mind the range of species that *prevailed locally*. All the animals, birds and insects, in other words, meant only *all that they were familiar with*. This means that many of the world's bulkiest, most dangerous or least cooperative animal varieties (rhino, polar bear, giraffe), were unheard of and didn't come into the picture, as well as uncountable myriads of lesser creatures. Bird, insect, mammal and reptile species in the Middle East did not – and do not – exist in unimaginable numbers. There was no need, either, to worry about accommodating fish or whales: they would all be in their element. From this perspective, the Ark idea begins to look more or less feasible after all.

It is time, therefore, to think about all these animals, Babylonian and biblical, and see what we can provide in the way of a checklist for ourselves at the top of the gangplank.

Atra-hasīs's Animals

To get a handle on Atra-hasīs's animal carnival we find ourselves remarkably well served, thanks to our indispensable ancient cuneiform dictionaries, one of which has chapters actually listing the words for all living things. The dreary-sounding ancient name by which cuneiform librarians referred to this Super Dictionary is 'Urra = *hubullu*', the Sumerian and Babylonian respectively for 'interest-bearing loan', because the first line of the first chapter deals with bilingual legal and business terminology. There are chapters for all known domestic creatures (*Urra Tablet XIII*), birds and fish (*Urra Tablet XIV*), and wild animals (*Urra Tablet XVIII*). Impressively large, heavy tablets can contain a complete chapter, but many school exercise tablets – of the kind familiar to the *Ark Tablet* scribe as a schoolboy – show that a few excerpted lines of natural history could be scribbled as a daily chore. Old lists, going back at least to the period of our *Ark Tablet*, provided first of all the words in Sumerian. One thousand years later King Ashurbanipal's librarians at Nineveh had bilingual versions of all the Urra = *hubullu* chapters in near-perfect calligraphy, with everything translated into Akkadian. The result is that today we know the names of all the birds, animals and creeping things of ancient Mesopotamia, in two dead languages. If our venerable Babylonian Noah ever had to tick off names on a register, in other words, we have an idea of what the entries would have been.

Urra Tablet XIII lists basic domestic animals, sheep, goats and so forth, of which particular twos or sevens could easily be selected. The Old Babylonian sheep section, for example, contains eighty-four entries, and is the last word on the subject:

> *Fattened sheep; good quality, fattened sheep; knife-shorn, fattened sheep; male sheep; male breeder sheep; grass-fed sheep . . . sheep with a collapsed lung; sheep with mange; sheep with arthritic hips; sheep with diarrhoea; sheep given to butting . . .*

Urra Tablet XIV lists all the other animals, big and small. The structure is consistent: a head section word, on the basis of Sumerian, acts like a dictionary *hyperlink*. Sumerian UR = Akkadian, *kalbu*, 'dog,' for example, meaning dog, heads up a long run of words that are dog or dog-like that all begin with ur-.

I think, for fun, we should list them. That these entries can be translated today reflects selfless decades and mountains of philology by many valiant cuneiformists, in the forefront of whom was the Chicago Assyriologist Benno Landsberger, who pulled all the ancient dictionaries into shape for incorporation within the modern *Chicago Assyrian Dictionary*. Some identifications are more or less certain, others are conventional, but viewed as a whole we have a reliable impression of what the ancient list of animals was intended to achieve.

ATRA-HASĪS'S ANIMALS

The animal names given below are more or less in the order in which they occur in *Urra* Chapter XIV, except that, with Atra-hasīs's responsibilities in mind, I have in each case put male and female together and collated scattered entries for the same name. 'Types' include Sumerian names, habitats, colours and even temperament; mythological animals find their way in, too, but in and among the lexical distinctions are what we call distinct species.

Snake (*ṣēru*: forty-four types)
Turtle (*šeleppû*: three types) and young
Eel (*kuppû*)
Rodent (*asqūdu*)
Wild bull (*rīmu*: two types) and wild cow (*rīmtu*: two types)
Elephant (*pīlu*: two types)
Camel, dromedary (*ibilu*: two types)
Cow (*littu*: two types)
Dog (*kalbu*: nineteen types) and bitch (*kalbatu*)

Lion (*nēšu, labbu, girru*: twenty types) and lioness (*nēštu*: seven
   types)
Wolf (*barbaru; parrisu*)
Tiger or cheetah (*mindinu*)
Leopard (*dumāmu*)
Badger (*kalab urṣi*)
Hyena (*būṣu*: two types)
Fox (*šēlebu*)
Cat (*šurānu*)
Wild cat (*murašû*)
Caracal (*zirqatu*)
Lynx (*azaru*)
Zebu(?) (*apsasû*) and female zebu(?) (*apsasītu*)
Ape (*pagû*) and female ape (*pagītu*)
Bear (*asu*)
Bull (*lī'û*)
Leopard (*nimru*)
Eagle (*erû*: five types)
Jackal (*zību*: three types)
Wild sheep (*bibbu; atūdu*)
Wild ram (*sappāru*)
Bison (*ditānu; kusarikku*: two types)
Red deer (*lulīmu*)
Stag (*ayyālu*: two types)
Mountain goat (*turāḫu*)
Roe deer (*nayyālu*: two types)
Gazelle (*ṣabītu*: two types and kid *ḫuzālu*)
Buck (*daššu*)
Hare (*arnabu*) and female hare (*arnabtu*)
Bear (*dabû*) and female bear (*dabītu*)
Pig (*šaḫû*: twenty-three types)
sow (*šaḫītu*: five types) and piglet (*kurkizannu*)
Wild boar (*šaḫ api*)
burmāmu (unidentified: three types)
Doormouse (*arrabu; ušummu*)

piazu (small rodent: three types)

Mongoose (*šikkû*: two types; *puṣuddu*; *kāṣiru*)

Mouse (*humṣīru*; *pērūrūtu*)

Doormouse (*arrabu*) *iškarissu* (rodent)

kurusissu (rodent)

Vole (*harriru*) *aštakissu* (rodent)

Shrew (*ḫulû*: two types)

Jerboa (*akbaru*)

asqudu (rodent: three types)

Otter (*tarpašu*)

Marten (*šakadirru*)

Chameleon (*ḫurbabillu*; *ayyar-ili*: four types)

Lizard (*anduḫallatu*: two types; *ṣurārû*: five types)

Tortoise (*raqqu, usābu*)

Crab (*kušû*: two types; *alluttu*: two types)

Locust or grasshopper (*erbu*: three types; *irgilum*; *irgizum*; large:
    ṣinnarabu; medium: *ḫilammu*; small: *zīru*; tiny: *zerzerru*)

Cricket (*ṣāṣiru*: three types; *ṣarṣaru*)

Praying mantis (*ša'llu*: two types; *sıkdu*; *adudillu*)

lullurtu (insect: three types) *ısıd-bukannu* (insect)

Head louse (*uplu*)

Louse (*nābu*)

kalmatu insect (thirteen types)

šīḫu (insect)

Flea (*perša'u*)

Weevil (*tal'ašu*)

Termite (*bušṭītu*: five types)

Moth (*ašāšu*; *sāsu*: seven types; *miqqānu*: three types; *mēqiqānu*)

Bug (*ibḫu*)

Worm (*tūltu*: four types; *urbatu*: four types)

Earthworm (*išqippu*)

Grub (*mubattiru*)

Caterpillar or larva (*munu*: eight types; *nappilu*: five types; *ākilu*:
    five types; *upinzir*: three types; *nāpû*)

šassūru (insect: three types)

Butterfly (*kurṣiptu*: three types; *kurmittu*: three types; *turzu*)
Nit (*nēbu*)
Fly (*zumbu*: nine types)
Horse fly (*lamṣatu*)
Small fly (*baqqu*: three types)
Mosquito (*zaqqītu*)
Gnat (*ašturru*: two types)
Wasp (*kuzāzu* 'the buzzer'; *ḫāmītu* 'the hummer'; *nambubtu*)
Water boatman (*ēṣid pān mê*)
Centipede (*ḫallulāya*: two types)
Spider (*ettūtu*: four types; *anzūzu*; *lummû*)
Jellyfish (*ḫammu*: four types)
mūr mê (insect)
ummi mê (water insect)
Dragonfly (*kulilītu*; *kallat-Shamash*: four types)
Ant (*kulbabu*: eight types)
Scorpion (*zuqaqīpu*: eleven types)
Gecko (*pizalluru*: three types)
Lizard (*humbibittu*)
Frog (*muṣa''irānu*)
Toad or frog (*kitturu*: seven types)

Atra-hasīs would probably identify with the common insect, the water boatman, *ēṣid pān mê* (whose elegant name means 'reaper-of-the-water-surface'). Perhaps, in his place, we might have thought twice about booking seats for the eight types of annoying flies who, according to the lexicographers, specialise in biting people, lionesses, wolves, oxen, water, stone, honey, butter and cucumber, while, if he had any sense at all, he would have left out the *zaqqītu*, or mosquito, altogether.

Noah's Animals

Today the question of Noah's animals is no longer a preoccupation of scientific enquiry, but there was a time when serious scholars like Justus Lipsius (1547–1606) and especially the great polymath Athanasius Kircher (*c*.1601–80), thought a good deal about them, just when knowledge of natural history was on the increase. I fancy Kircher would have approved of the *Ark Tablet* and its implications, for his religious convictions in no way inhibited his burning scientific curiosity, and exposition of its content would have found a place in his wonderful *Arca Noe*, published in 1675. Kircher was renowned in his day as 'master of a hundred arts', and his great illustrated work on Noah's Ark is stunning, with full plates to show the Ark under construction in Noah's workshop and the animals, tidily accommodated in their quarters, in a cross-section view of the finished boat.

The great Athanasius Kircher himself.

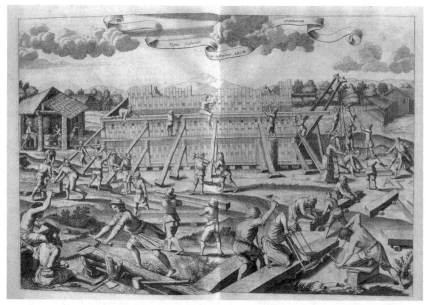

Kircher's view of Noah's Ark under construction.

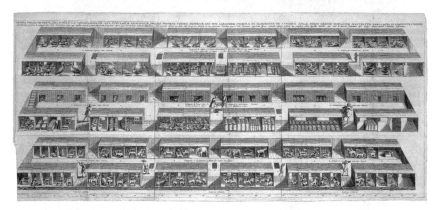

Kircher's understanding of how the animals were accommodated.

Kircher's Ark taxonomy ran to only about fifty pairs of animals, leaving him to conclude that space inside was not such a difficulty. He developed the interesting explanation that Noah had rescued all the animals that then existed, and that the subsequent profusion of different species in the world resulted from post-diluvian adaptation, or interbreeding among the core Ark species; so that giraffes, for example, were produced after the

Flood by camel and leopard parents. Kircher even had a serious try at deciphering Egyptian hieroglyphs, and although no one relies on his voluminous three-tome work today he learned Coptic in 1633 and was the first to argue – correctly – that living Coptic was the last stage of the ancient Egyptian language. Kircher would have had fun with cuneiform, especially as another of his works, the wonderful *Turris Babel*, represents an early outbreak of Assyriology, and is a volume that is hard to put down.

For Noah all we can do is collect the Hebrew words for animals that appear in the Old Testament and see what sort of bulk they make. This procedure is little easier than with the ancient Akkadian tablets, for identifying many nouns depends either on old translations into different languages, or on etymology, for words certainly change their meaning over time, and lots of animal words are rare in the Hebrew text. Since we are only seeking a glimpse of Noah's register, we need not dwell on such problems. The creatures we find are as follows:

Domestic: horse, ass, mule; swine; one humped camel; cattle, buffalo, goat, sheep; dog, cat.

Wild: bat; hedgehog(?); jackal and fox; bear; hyena; lion; leopard; coney; onager; wild boar; red deer, fallow deer, roe deer; wild ox; gazelle; ibex; antelope; hare; mole rat; mouse; elephant (import!); apes; peacock or parrot.

Birds: eagle, vulture, hawk; various owls; ostrich (?); swallow or sparrow; heron, stork, cormorant, crane; rock pigeon, turtle-dove; goose; domestic fowl; partridge; quail.

Reptiles: various lizards; frog (and several irrelevant monsters and dragons).

Invertebrates: viper, adder, (and others); scorpion, leech.

Insects: lice; grasshopper and locust; ants; wasp; bee; moth; flea; fly; gnat; spiders.

For Noah, then, this is maybe not such a bad proposition: a few ropes, some strong nets, some honey perhaps and a lot of patience . . .

The Bible has accustomed us to think of the Flood lasting for forty days and nights although the Babylonian tradition is for seven days and nights, which would be sufficient time to annihilate life on earth very efficiently. Did the god Enki actually mention to Atra-hasīs how long the Deluge would last? There is no clue from the cuneiform.

As the work reaches completion and the Ark is ready for loading Atra-hasīs declares himself exhausted but, at first, joyful, according to the *Ark Tablet*:

> *I lay myself down (?) . . . [. . .] . . . of rejoicing*
> *My kith and kin [went into] the boat . . . ;*
> *Joyful . . . [. . . . . .] . . . . . . of my in-laws,*
> *and the porter with . . . . . .*
> *They ate and drank their fill.*
>
> *Ark Tablet*: 34–8

Who actually did go on board then? Kith and kin (in Babylonian *kimtu* and *salātu*), means the immediate family – the nuclear Mr and Mrs A. H., their unnamed sons and daughters-in-law – and kin by marriage ('in-laws'), that is, the families of their daughters-in-law. We do not know in this case what this meant in terms of total numbers. In *Old Babylonian Atrahasis* there is a clear distinction between the workers who had built the boat and the family (*kimtu*) who were to go on board:

> *. . .] he invited his people*
> *. . .] to a banquet.*
> *. . .] . . . he sent his family on board, They ate and drank*
> *their fill.*
>
> *Old Babylonian Atrahasis*: 40–43

This phrase 'They ate and drank their fill', occurs word for word in both Old Babylonian accounts. Literally it translates, 'The eater eats, the drinker drinks', and it is difficult to capture the right nuance. There is a similar Babylonian expression used by diviners, 'the seer sees, the hearer hears'; both have the ring of a folk proverb or saying.

In *Gilgamesh XI* the workmen had already been well treated throughout the work, right up until the day before the oiling, so there was no need for another celebration:

> *For the workmen I butchered oxen.*
> *Every day I slaughtered sheep.*
> *Beer, ale, oil and wine.*
> *[I gave my] workforce [to drink], like the waters of a very*
> *   river!*
> *They were celebrating as on the feast-days of the New Year*
> *   itself!*
>
> > *Gilgamesh XI: 71–5*

The on-board humans get their mention later. There is no partying for them, and the on deck quarters will need to accommodate more than just Utnapishti's nearest and dearest:

> *All my kith and kin I sent aboard the boat,*
> *I sent aboard . . . persons of every skill and craft.*
>
> > *Gilgamesh XI: 85–6*

First-millennium Utnapishti is planning ahead with no wish to find himself and his family in a post-Deluge world uncomfortably devoid of expertise. The same point is made in *Assyrian Smith*:

> *[Send up into] it . . .*
> *[Your wife], your kith, your kin, and the skilled workers.*

It is interesting, considering what was afoot, that Puzur-Enlil the shipwright was not numbered among these indispensable on-board experts, to deal with leaks. All of them, one presumes, were accustomed to animals and at least one (it is to be hoped) was a vet.

In Hebrew tradition it was just the nucleus of the family taken on board:

> *But I will establish my covenant with you; and you shall come into the ark, you, your sons, your wife, and your sons' wives with you.*

This meant Mr and Mrs Noah, Shem, Ham and Japheth and their respective wives, and that was that. Eight people, in other words.

In the Koran not even Nuh's own son came aboard to join the few believers:

> *We said, 'Place on board this Ark (. . .) your own family – except those against whom the sentence has already been passed – and those who have believed,' though only a few believed with him. He said, 'Board the Ark. In the name of God it shall sail and anchor. My God is most forgiving and merciful.' It sailed with them on waves like mountains, and Noah called out to his son, who stayed behind, 'Come aboard with us, my son, do not stay with the disbelievers.' But he replied, 'I will seek refuge on a mountain to save me from the water.'*
>
> Sura 11:40–43

In the Old Babylonian narrative, thanks to previously unknown lines from the *Ark Tablet*, we are confronted with Atra-hasīs the man, the Suffering Servant. The daily distraction of shipbuilding was over and he must face reality; he sees his family in innocent party mood, possibly even construing the imminent voyage as a treat or an adventure and oblivious to the imminent fate – known to him alone – that was to overwhelm all their friends and neighbours together with every other living thing. He gives a banquet for his 'people', those who had worked on the project for him, knowing that each would soon be drowned. The burden on his mind became intolerable. Consider the picture in *Old Babylonian Atrahasis* once everyone was aboard; the moon had already disappeared, and Atra-hasīs knew what that meant. As for the hero himself,

> *he was in and out: he could not sit, could not crouch*
> *For his heart was broken and he was vomiting gall.*
>
> Old Babylonian Atrahasis: 45–7

The *Ark Tablet* develops this image at greater length in a poetic but sadly damaged section of text. Atra-hasīs tries to avert the catastrophe and prays to the Moon God for intercession before it is too late.

> *As for me, there was no word in my heart, and*
> *. . . my heart;*
> *. . . my [. . .]*
> *. . . of my . . .*
> *. . . of my lips*
> *. . . , I slept with difficulty;*
> *I went up on the roof and pr[ayed] to my lord Sin:*
> *"Let my heartbreak (?) be extinguished! [Do you not*
>   *disap]pear!"*
> *. . . darkness*
> *Into my . . .*
> *Sin, from his thr[one, swo]re as to annihiliation*
> *And desola[tion on (the)] darkened [day (to come)]*
>
> Ark Tablet: 39–50

The background to this is explicit in the *Old Babylonian Schøyen* tablet where it is recorded that the Flood will begin at the *new moon*:

> *The gods commanded an annihilation,*
> *A wicked thing that Enlil will do to the people.*
> *In the assembly they commanded the Deluge, (saying): "By*
> *the day of the new moon we shall do the task."*
>
> Old Babylonian Schøyen: 21–2

Atra-hasīs's reasoning was evidently that, if the Moon God proved sympathetic and just didn't disappear as usual, there would be no new moon and the fateful day would never actually come.

In *Old Babylonian Atrahasis* Enki had been very clear about the timetable:

> *He opened the water-clock and filled it;*
> *He announced to him the coming of the flood for the seventh*
> *night.*
>
> Old Babylonian Atrahasis: 36–7

If the anguished Atra-hasīs was praying with this stratagem in mind at very much the last minute, the date will have been the evening of the 28th since the moon would normally disappear on the 29th or 30th; the conversation about building the rescue boat will therefore have taken place during the day on the 22nd or 23rd of the month and Atra-hasīs had his six days to build the Ark. In *Gilgamesh XI* the timetable is the same: the great boat has taken shape by Day 5; oiling and so forth is done on Day 6; the Flood comes on Day 7. In the *Assyrian Smith* Atra-hasīs is simply told, '[*observe*] *the appointed time of which I will inform you*'.

In *Gilgamesh XI*, in comparison, Atra-hasīs's counterpart Utnapishti is faceless. He receives his instructions and the god Ea gives him a cover story for the Babylonians; he will be descending to the subterranean waters of the Apsû to live with his master. The sign will be a symbolic rain of plenty including birds, fishes, bread-cakes and wheat. Once the work is over and everything is loaded on board, Utnapishti reveals that Shamash, the Sun God, had set a deadline, and the day on which that very downpour is seen will be the day of the Flood. There is no room here for any sympathising with Atra-hasīs, or any visualising of his personal predicament. This literary episode with the symbolic rain has evolved – laden with ripe meanings for a Babylonian – out of a much simpler passage in *Old Babylonian Atrahasis*, which promises simply,

> *'I will rain down upon you here*
> *An abundance of birds, a profusion of fishes.'*
> *Old Babylonian Atrahasis*: iii 34–5

There is no reference to this topic in the *Ark Tablet*.

The word for water-clock in *Old Babylonian Atrahasis*, incidentally, is *maltaktu*, from the verb *latāku*, 'to test'. One cannot help thinking that for Atra-hasīs the relentless *drip-drip-drip* of the water measure must have seemed quite unnecessarily stressful considering what lay ahead.

10

Babylon and Bible Floods

The human species,
according to the best theory I can form of it,
is composed of two distinct races,
the men who borrow, and the men who lend.
Charles Lamb

Since the wonderful moment when my life as a British Museum cuneiformist began (2 September 1979), I have given innumerable public gallery talks about clay tablets and what is written on them, and very often found myself in front of George Smith's *Flood Tablet* stressing its remarkable closeness to the Genesis Account. Each time I have exhorted tolerant listeners to go home and compare the two together by *reading* them one after the other. Whether any of these victims ever did this I do not know, but no reader of this book should need such encouragement, for it has now become a pressing – if not unavoidable – matter to clarify what results from such a comparison.

So far we have examined the literary evidence for the Flood Story in ancient Mesopotamia over two millennia, and established that it is an ancient story deeply set within Mesopotamian culture. Since George Smith's brilliant discovery in the nineteenth century it has been widely known that there are strong links between the Genesis narrative and the seventh-century BC text of *Gilgamesh XI*. At the same time it has been widely acknowledged that the cuneiform tradition as known in the case of Atra-hasīs at least is of greater antiquity than the biblical, for the earliest cuneiform flood stories that we have go back at least to the eighteenth century BC. Two tasks now lie ahead of us. The first is to demonstrate the literary dependence of the Hebrew text on cuneiform flood tradition; the second – assuming that demonstration to be convincing – is to explain how it was that materials from Babylonian cuneiform could have passed into biblical Hebrew.

The *Ark Tablet*, being new and full of surprises, has so far acted as the springboard for this investigation, but it does not support us all the way, for its sixty lines end just before the waters come, and we need to look at the Flood Story from start to finish in order to evaluate the relationship between Cuneiform and Hebrew. Also, the other pre-*Gilgamesh* flood sources at our disposal, all of which have made regular appearances in previous chapters, do not cover anything like the whole story or this crucial part, but only the announcement of the Flood, and in part, the building of the Ark. Thus comparison of the Babylon and Hebrew traditions relies almost as heavily on *Gilgamesh XI* now as in Smith's day, when the issue of such a connection first came to attention.

Here, then, the Flood Story in *Gilgamesh* (*Tablet XI: 8–167*), bolstered where possible from our other cuneiform flood tablets, is summarised to see how it really overlaps with Genesis. The argument, therefore, is not that the Genesis narrative is translated from, or directly derived from, the Assyrian version of *Gilgamesh* that we now have. The comparison illustrates strong connections between the traditions in topic and ideas, and establishes that the Hebrew text reflects an antecedent version or versions of the Flood Story in cuneiform that must itself have been strongly related to *Gilgamesh XI*, while not being identical.

As we have already seen in Chapter 10 with regard to the birds and animals, the Hebrew text of Genesis can be seen to have been forged out of separate literary strands according to the Documentary Hypothesis, and this line of approach is again useful in any assessment of the relationship between the cuneiform and Hebrew texts. In quoting Genesis passages here we can consider separately the traditions represented by the background biblical sources known as J and P.

This is not the first time that such a comparison has been made, but the new material presented here calls for a fresh look. Within the context of this book the following nine sections seem to me to address the salient issues regarding the connection between cuneiform and Hebrew tradition:

1. Why the Flood and Who the Hero?

Gilgamesh XI gives no reason for the Flood. Utnapishti simply explains to Gilgamesh what the important gods have decided but their motive – of paramount interest to us – was evidently irrelevant. Utnapishti, though traditionally a king, does not seem like one to me. We have no insight into his moral or personal qualities (*Gilgamesh XI*: 8–18). Similarly, in the *Atrahasis* tradition we know virtually nothing of the hero's qualifications or qualities, though we do see that the flood was the gods' third attempt to destroy Man, a noisy, over-abundant and expendable irritant.

In Genesis 6, in contrast, the Flood is explicitly punishment for sinful behaviour, with Noah, son of Lamech, selected for the role of saviour because he was a just and perfect man. The theme is clear in both sources J and P.

This encapsulates a significant contrast between the Babylonian plot and its Judaean recycling, underpinning the importation of Babylonian narrative into the Hebrew Bible. The cuneiform version is vested only in the convenience of the gods, the biblical is preoccupied with human morality; man, the highest creation, had disgusted his creator by his wicked behaviour. In *Gilgamesh*, the most significant narrative of Mesopotamian literature, it is striking that no reason for the destruction is given at all.

2. Breaking the News

In *Gilgamesh XI*, the god Ea, although sworn to secrecy, divulges to Utnapishti what is going to happen and what he must do, by whispering the famous Flood Story speech through the reeds. He thus dispenses with the dream-message approach that is an important feature in the *Atrahasis* story (although, intriguingly, the dream is acknowledged as having played its part later in the Gilgamesh story).

In *Atrahasis* much more is made of the messages, to good narrative and dramatic effect, but the *Gilgamesh* version, preserving the famous speech, pares it down to advance the plot.

There is no counterpart to this very Mesopotamian motif in the Judean text. In Genesis 6, God, not having to disguise or account for his actions to anyone, just *tells* Noah.

3. Ark-building

Once Utnapishti's Ark, thanks to Smith's discovery, floated onto the scene, its odd cubic shape and marvellous indoor facilities provided a strong contrast to what was at Noah's disposal, and to some writers the very difference indicates that this comparison reveals little more than that 'people in floods have boats'. These are the two received *Gilgamesh* descriptions:

> The boat that you are going to build,
> Her dimensions should all correspond;
> Her breadth and length should be the same;
> Cover her with a roof like the Apsû.
>
> *Gilgamesh XI: 28–31*

> Ten nindan *each her sides stood high.*
> Ten rods each, the edges of her top were equal
> I gave her six decks
> I divided her into seven parts
> I divided her interior into nine.
>
> *Gilgamesh XI: 59–63*

Genesis 6, source P, gives all the details within one brief – but memorable – section:

> ¹⁴*Make yourself an ark of gopher wood; make rooms in the ark, and cover it inside and out with pitch.* ¹⁵*This is how you are to make it: the length of the ark three hundred cubits, its width fifty cubits, and its height thirty cubits.* ¹⁶*Make a roof for the ark, and finish it to a cubit above; and put the door of the ark in its side; make it with lower, second, and third decks.*

Genesis source J omits this.

As shown in Chapter 8 (summarised in Chapter 14, with the textual evidence in Appendix 2), the apparently asymmetrical procession from circle to square in these two passages represents a single line of transmission: the *Gilgamesh* cubic Ark is a distortion of the original round coracle, and the Judaean oblong version an adapation of that. What is important for the appraisal of textual connection is that a case which seems to mitigate against a shared origin does the opposite.

4. *Utnapishti's Cover Story and the Omens*

Utnapishti accepts his building instructions but, apprehensive about 'the city, the crowd and elders', needs a cover story to explain to everybody why he is building the boat. Ominous bizarre rainfalls of birds, fishes and bread-cakes will be the sign that the Flood is about to come (*Gilgamesh XI*: 32–47). Later in *Gilgamesh* the Sun God warns that the ominous rain is imminent. *Atrahasis* contains the anxieties and the same ominous motif. Later this 'cover story' motif is preserved in the Greek of Berossus (see Chapter 5).

In the Bible there is no counterpart to either plot component, especially 'Babylonian' in the emphasis on omens, and an important element within the cuneiform build-up to the climax of the Flood. The passage was doubtless included in the compilers' sources for Genesis and understandably expunged.

5. The Ark is Stocked

The details of what went on board the Arks – and their differences – has been taken up in Chapter 10, and the troubling disparity between the animal requirements imposed on Noah in Genesis 6 is shown to reflect differences between Hebrew sources J and P. Most important for the present discussion is the new contribution from the *Ark Tablet*, in which lines 51–2, written over a thousand years before the text of Genesis, speak of the wild animals going up into the boat 'two by two'. This small two-by-two speck of gold indicates how, when you are dealing with cuneiform matters, a bombshell with new implications can go off at any moment.

6. The Flood Cometh

At this juncture, by the way, the *Gilgamesh Epic* gives us some of the most powerful writing in cuneiform. Utnapishti's deluge saw a catastrophic storm, rain and waters sweeping over everything; it lasted for six days and seven nights. Everything died ('turned to clay'). Calm returned on the seventh day (*Gilgamesh XI: 97–135*).

Genesis sources J and P are surprisingly individual in the information they give us:

J: time only vague: after seven days, forty days of rain; everything dies.

P: gives exact date in terms of Noah's life: 2/17/600; all fountains of the great deep burst forth, and windows of the heavens were opened. Flood rose for 150 days; all mountains covered. Everything dies. Fountains and windows closed; waters take 150 days to go down. Flood ends 1/1/601.

7. The Ark Landeth

Mesopotamian and biblical traditions about the landing of the Ark are compared in detail below in Chapter 12.

8. Test Flights

The shared occurrence of birds released to seek land has been consistently viewed since George Smith as one of the most compelling pieces of evidence to link the Babylonian and Hebrew narratives. Here is the passage from *Gilgamesh*:

> I brought out a dove, setting it free;
> Off went the dove but then it returned;
> No perch was available for it and it came back to me.
> I brought out a swallow, setting it free;
> Off went the swallow but then it returned;
> No perch was available for it and it came back to me.
> I brought out a raven, setting it free;
> Off went the raven and it saw the waters receding;
> It was eating, bobbing up and down; it did not come back
>   to me.
>
>

Gilgamesh XI: 148–56
>

The Hebrew equivalent, which corresponds so closely to the *Gilgamesh* passage, is found only in Genesis source J:

> *. . . sent out the raven; and it went to and fro until the waters were dried up from the earth. ⁸Then he sent out the dove from him, to see if the waters had subsided from the face of the ground; ⁹but the dove found no place to set its foot, and it returned to him to the ark, for the waters were still on the face of the whole earth. So he put out his hand and took it and brought it into the ark with him. ¹⁰He waited another seven days, and again he sent out the dove from the ark; ¹¹and the*

dove came back to him in the evening, and there in its beak was a freshly plucked olive leaf; so Noah knew that the waters had subsided from the earth. ¹²Then he waited another seven days, and sent out the dove; and it did not return to him any more.

Here particularly, it seems to me, the parallels between the two traditions are overwhelming, and can only be explained by literary borrowing. Differences in detail – such as the species or order of the birds – are of an altogether different order: it is the whole literary episode which is so telling.

In the Koran Nuh spent five or six months aboard the Ark, at the end of which he sent out a raven. But the raven stopped to feast on carrion, and so Noah cursed it and sent out the dove, which has been known ever since as the friend of mankind.

9. Sacrifices and Promises

Utnapishti – moved, shaken and relieved – did the right thing straightaway:

> *I brought out an offering and sacrificed to the four corners of*
>   *the earth,*
> *I strewed incense on the ziggurat of the mountain;*
> *Seven flasks and seven I set in position,*
> *Below them I heaped up (sweet) reed, cedar and myrtle.*
> *The gods smelled the savour,*
> *The gods smelled the sweet savour,*
> *The gods gathered like flies around him making the sacrifice.*
> *As soon as Belet-ili arrived,*
> *She lifted aloft the great flies that Anu had made when he*
>   *wooed (her):*
> *'O gods, let these be lapis lazuli (beads) around my neck,*
>   *so that I remember these days and never forget them!'*
>   *Gilgamesh XI: 157–67*

In Genesis Noah, too, responds thankfully with sacrifice, but both J and P are more concerned with the divine promise that destruction will never be inflicted on the human race, and it is only source P that tells us of the great rainbow sign that everyone has known of since childhood:

> [12]God said, 'This is the sign of the covenant that I make between me and you and every living creature that is with you, for all future generations: [13]I have set my bow in the clouds, and it shall be a sign of the covenant between me and the earth. [14]When I bring clouds over the earth and the bow is seen in the clouds, [15]I will remember my covenant that is between me and you and every living creature of all flesh; and the waters shall never again become a flood to destroy all flesh. [16]When the bow is in the clouds, I will see it and remember the everlasting covenant between God and every living creature of all flesh that is on the earth.' [17]God said to Noah, 'This is the sign of the covenant that I have established between me and all flesh that is on the earth.'
>
> Source P

An articulated, reassuring promise does not come to Utnapishti, but the Metropolitan Museum in New York has a Late Babylonian cuneiform tablet with a version of a non-flood part of the *Atrahasis* story (in which the flood hero is mentioned by his original Sumerian name, Ziusudra), which does articulate the same sort of idea:

> Henceforth let no flood be brought about,
> But let the people last forever.
>
> Spar and Lambert 2005: 199

Implications

The implications of comparing Babylonian and biblical flood accounts here are clear; the unfolded parallels between the stories demonstrate that they are closely connected textually and sequentially; the finished Hebrew is assuredly dependent on pre-existing Mesopotamian Flood Story literature. To what extent can we focus closer on this relationship?

We know from the texts investigated in this book that different versions of the Flood Story circulated on clay tablets in ancient Babylonia at different periods. We also know that the Flood-and-Ark Story was central to two long-running and quite distinct compositions: the *Atrahasis* story (circulating with free variations) and the *Epic of Gilgamesh* (apparently in more stable form). We can suspect, too, that there were many more cuneiform flood accounts to be found in the first millennium BC than are now available to us.

The separated-out contributions from sources J and P reflect more than disentangled fragments trickling down from earlier traditions: as received, each represents a structured text with its own traditions *but with large and significant omissions*:

Genesis source J (short version)

1. No ark description
2. J$_1$ seven pairs of clean; one pair of unclean; seven pairs of birds
   J$_2$ one pair of clean; one pair of unclean; one pair of birds; one pair of creepers
3. Rain only
4. Flight tests: raven, dove, dove, dove
5. *No landing spot mentioned*

Genesis source P (long version)

1. Ark description
2. One pair of every kind of living thing
3. Fountains of deep and rain
4. *No flight tests*

5. Landing spot: mountains of Ararat
6. Sacrifices; promise; rainbow

The fact that J contributes nothing at all about the Ark itself must mean that the Ark coverage was somehow 'better' or more appropriate in P's version, and taken over completely; it cannot be taken that J omitted the principal component of the story, but merely that nothing on that subject was taken from J. Perhaps J's source included more technical details about boat-building than suited the biblical narrative, much as the abundant coracle hard data in the *Ark Tablet* over which we have been labouring was reduced to a succinct line or two in first-millennium BC *Gilgamesh*. The reverse situation applies with the equally crucial flight tests, apparently omitted by P, probably due to J's having a fuller or more suitable version that was taken up *en bloc*.

Source J is itself an amalgam of two quite separate animal number traditions, as we have seen in the previous chapter. The 'original' idea was surely one male and one female of every species, as found in P. J is closer to *Old Babylonian Atrahasis* in including birds which (as far as we can see) do not occur in the other cunei-form sources. Only the *Ark Tablet* attests to the two-by-two tradition in cuneiform, but now we know it was there in Babylon.

J mentions only rain but P, closer to *Gilgamesh XI*, describes flood and rain, and here again it is likely that two background traditions are involved. J's source, rather than having no moun-tain landing at all, more likely presented an unfamiliar Babylonian name, while the resonance of mountainous Ararat in the far north offered by P made its choice obvious to a Judaean. We can go no further here.

The Hebrew text as we have it is a highly moulded literary production formed out of parts of two primary and different strands of Hebrew flood literature. These two sources, having been woven together, are no longer complete, but can be compre-hended as distinct once they are 'resuscitated'. Omissions and editorial processes do not disguise that J and P were not identical.

In my view these very differences are likely to reflect distinct cuneiform versions of the Flood Story. These varying background tablet versions almost certainly recounted the Babylonian *Atrahasis* story rather than that of *Gilgamesh*. The classic biblical story of Noah and the Flood in Hebrew thus preserves for us the shadowy ghosts of what we can think of as 'Cuneiform Tradition J' and 'Cuneiform Tradition P'.

How it was possible for Hebrew redactors to convert those tricky impressed wedges to elegant inked Hebrew is the subject of the following chapter.

11

The Judaean Experience

'The horror of that moment,' the King went on,
'I shall never, never forget!'
'You will though,' the Queen said,
'If you don't make a memorandum of it.'

Lewis Carroll

The previous chapter has, I hope, demonstrated that the story of the Flood in the Bible came into Hebrew from an older story in Babylonian cuneiform. We have seen, too, that the stories of the infants Moses and Sargon in their respective coracles reflect a similar borrowing, and that there are other elements in the Book of Genesis in particular (the Great Ages of Man) that suggest the same process. How was it, then, that the ancient story of the Flood and the Ark could pass from Babylonian cuneiform into biblical Hebrew?

On the whole, people have run away from this question. The pith of the problem concerns the transmission of written text from one 'difficult' type of script to another, that is, Babylonian cuneiform to alphabetic Hebrew, and to answer it we need to establish plausible circumstances in time and place, an explanation of why it happened at all, and a convincing mechanism to allow it. In as much as these problems have been faced at all with regard to the Flood Story there have been, broadly speaking, two approaches.

The first approach sees the Flood Story as having survived independently from the second millennium BC onwards both in Babylon and among the Hebrews, deriving from a shared ancestor. In other words, Abraham at Ur will have known the Flood story, and the narrative will have been passed down from that time as part of Hebrew oral, and ultimately written, tradition. In my opinion the textual parallels between *Gilgamesh XI* and the Genesis account are too close to represent the fruit of two long, independent streams. We can see, for one thing, that the Babylonian story in cuneiform circulated in different forms and with considerable variation over that interval (more than one thousand years) and was not itself an unchanging single tradition. Given this background, and the span of time involved, I think that the Hebrew account would have ended up as a very different construction, telling the same basic story with similar components, perhaps, but recognisibly the outcome of a separate history.

The other approach has been to assume that the Exile in Babylon exposed the Judaeans to stories current among the home populations. Here some kind of literary osmosis is apparently thought to have operated whereby people who are in the same place as people who know a story – in this case downtown Babylon – somehow 'pick it up'. According to this theory, Babylonians simply liked telling foreigners the story – or, perhaps, it got into the drinking water! Leaving aside the intrinsic improbability, such undemonstrable processes likewise would not produce Hebrew narrative that would parallel the carefully structured literary account that we know from *Gilgamesh XI*.

The two-part solution proposed here came into the writer's head in the middle of a crowded public lecture entitled 'New Light on the Jewish Exile' given in the British Museum on the evening of Thursday 26 February 2009. It was the consequence of my having spent the preceding two years or more thinking and writing about Babylon in preparation for the exhibition 'Babylon: Myth and Reality', which ran in the British Museum from 13 November 2008 to 15 March 2009. Round and round went the materials, ancient voices in Babylonian, Aramaic and Hebrew, like spun clothes in a washing machine. It was not until the exhibition was almost over and the lecture programme that accompanied it nearly completed, that the simple idea presented here articulated itself.

The *place* and *time* for the encounter with the cuneiform tradition must be at Babylon during the period of the Babylonian Exile, when the Judaeans were actually there. This basic idea has been proposed by many people and thus is nothing astonishing, although there are certainly new considerations to be clarified.

The *explanation* must be that the borrowing took place when the Hebrew Bible, created out of existing Judaean documents, was first being put together, and narratives about very early times were needed. This is, as far as I know, a new idea.

The *mechanism* was that certain crucially placed Judaeans learned to read and write cuneiform, and so became *directly familiar* with the Babylonian stories for themselves, which they recycled for their own purposes with new messages. This too, as far as I know, is a new idea.

Can the validity and cohesion of this four-part argument be convincingly demonstrated?

To do so we need briefly to look at how the Judaeans ended up in Nebuchadnezzar's capital in the first place, to try to imagine the effect that this experience had on them, and see how and why the Great Ages of Man, the Flood Story and the Baby in the Boat were absorbed at that time into their own literary tradition. There are some really wonderful cuneiform tablets to help us with this plan, mostly in the British Museum.

Why were the Judaeans in Babylon?

On the morning of 16 March 597 BC, Jehoiachin, the eighteen-year-old king of Judah, woke in Jerusalem to find the army of Nebuchadnezzar II, king of Babylon, encamped round his city. According to the Bible:

> *Jehoiachin was eighteen years old when he became king, and he reigned in Jerusalem three months. His mother's name was*

Nehushta daughter of Elnathan; she was from Jerusalem. He did evil in the eyes of the Lord, just as his father had done. At that time the officers of Nebuchadnezzar king of Babylon advanced on Jerusalem and laid siege to it, and Nebuchadnezzar himself came up to the city while his officers were besieging it. Jehoiachin king of Judah, his mother, his attendants, his nobles and his officials all surrendered to him. In the eighth year of the reign of the king of Babylon, he took Jehoiachin prisoner . . . He carried all Jerusalem into exile: all the officers and fighting men, and all the skilled workers and artisans – a total of ten thousand. Only the poorest people of the land were left. Nebuchadnezzar took Jehoiachin captive to Babylon. He also took from Jerusalem to Babylon the king's mother, his wives, his officials and the prominent people of the land. The king of Babylon also deported to Babylon the entire force of seven thousand fighting men, strong and fit for war, and a thousand skilled workers and artisans. He made Mattaniah, Jehoiachin's uncle, king in his place and changed his name to Zedekiah.

2 Kings 24:8–17; see also 2 Chronicles 36:9–10

Judaea was strategically placed on a much broader stage – sandwiched between the superpowers of Babylon and Egypt – and Nebuchadnezzar's military behaviour was concerned with far wider issues than come across in the biblical record.

The surrender of young Jehoiachin meant the first stage of the beginning of the Babylonian Exile. The consequences were thus incalculable. It is no exaggeration to say it was to affect the history and progress of the world from that moment onward.

Uncle Zedekiah, whom the Babylonians installed in his stead, flirted disloyally with the Egyptians, and the second campaign meant punitive destruction in full by Nebuchadnezzar's storm troopers under no-nonsense Nabuzaradan a decade later in 587/6 BC. The temple was robbed of all its venerated contents and destroyed, the city was laid waste, and the story ended in the wholesale deportation of the royal Judaean family, the government and administration, the greater part of the military, and all useful craftsmen, artisans and other personnel to Babylon. The lifeblood of the country in terms of intellect, intelligence and ability was snatched away.

For the Babylonians this operation was standard military procedure. It swelled the royal coffers, put a permanent stop to difficulties with a troublesome native dynasty, and meant extensive human resources were incorporated into their kingdom, strengthening the army, helping with building and construction, and producing high-class goods. The deportees, after the most formidable journey, came face to face in two big waves with the ancient, superpower culture of their conquerors. The impact of this experience must have affected all aspects of their lives. It was during the traditional seventy years of exile that followed – (in fact it was fifty-eight calendar years, from 597–539 BC) – that the Judaeans were directly exposed to a new world, new beliefs and *cuneiform writing and literature*. It was also at this crucial time that they became familiar with the Babylonian story of the Flood, the boat-builder and his Ark.

In addition to the passage above from the Hebrew Bible, we have Nebuchadnezzar's own account of the first Jerusalem campaign in the form of the standard Babylonian court chronicle, which records occurrences throughout a reign by day, month and year. This particular tablet runs from Nebuchadnezzar's accession until his eleventh regnal year, giving therefore the Babylonian view of the first Jerusalem campaign described in the biblical Books of Kings and Chronicles, which took place in his seventh year (597 BC).

> *The seventh year: in the month Kislev the king of Akkad* [i.e. Babylon] *mustered his army and marched to Hattu* [i.e. Syria]. *He encamped against the city of Judah and on the second day of the month Adar he captured the city (and) seized its king* [Jehoiachin]. *A king of his own choice* [Zedekiah] *he appointed in the city (and) taking the vast tribute he brought it into Babylon.*
> Nebuchadnezzar's Chronicle, rev.: 11–13

*Nebuchadnezzar's Court Chronicle, the back view which
describes the capture of Jerusalem.*

Nebuchadnezzar's Chronicle for the second campaign has not
come to light but we hear all about what happened from the
prophet Jeremiah:

> *In the ninth year of Zedekiah king of Judah, in the tenth month,*
> *Nebuchadnezzar king of Babylon marched against Jerusalem*
> *with his whole army and laid siege to it. And on the ninth day*

*of the fourth month of Zedekiah's eleventh year, the city wall
was broken through. Then all the officials of the king of Babylon
came and took seats in the Middle Gate: Nergal-Sharezer of
Samgar, Nebo-Sarsekim a chief officer, Nergal-Sharezer a high
official and all the other officials of the king of Babylon . . .*

*So Nebuzaradan the commander of the guard, Nebushazban
a chief officer, Nergal-Sharezer a high official and all the other
officers of the king of Babylon sent and had Jeremiah taken
out of the courtyard of the guard . . .*

Jeremiah 39:1–14; see also Jeremiah 52:3–23

In 2007 Michael Jursa, an Assyriologist from the University of
Vienna, made a stunning new discovery in the British Museum
among trayfuls of unexciting-looking and (to tell the truth)
slightly soporific business documents of the Nebuchadnezzar
period.

Nabu-šarrussu-ukin deposits his gold.

This is how this particular tablet reads in English:

Regarding 1.5 minas (0.75 kg) of gold, the property of Nabu-
šarrussu-ukin, the Chief Eunuch, which is entrusted to Arad-
Banitu the eunuch, which he sent to [the temple] Esagil:
Arad-Banitu has delivered [it] to Esagil. In the presence of
Bel-usat, son of Aplaya, the royal bodyguard, [and of] Nadin,
son of Marduk-zer ibni.

Month XI, day 18, year 10 [of] Nebuchadnezzar, king of
Babylon.

There were many eunuchs in the Neo-Babylonian court but only one Chief Eunuch at a time, so we know that Nabu-šarrussu-ukin who served under Nebuchadnezzar must be the same person as Jeremiah's 'Nebo-Sarsekim'. We can be sure that the biblical title conventionally translated 'chief officer' literally means Chief Eunuch, for *rab-sarīs* is the Hebraised form of Babylonian *rab ša-rēši*, 'chief eunuch'.

The tablet came to public attention quietly. Having been a colleague and friend of Jursa for many years it is my habit to stroll past his desk when he is on a visit in our Students' Room – the magnificent Victorian library where we house all our tablets – and ask patronisingly whether he has managed to find anything *at all interesting* over the last week, or whether he has encountered any difficult cuneiform signs with which a *more experienced colleague* might be able to help. Usually this sort of enquiry provokes little more than a sigh, but on this occasion he mentioned that he had found a tablet mentioning Nebo-Sarsekim, *rab sarīs*, one of Nebuchadnezzar's chiefs of staff named by Jeremiah as being at Jerusalem. This was not in the least bit soporific, and off I rushed to muster all the forces in the kingdom to make sure somehow or other that anyone who had ever read the Bible knew that an individual mentioned in the text had been found on a clay tablet in the British Museum inscribed in cuneiform writing. Before long it was Michael who had to face the camera.

What is *extraordinary* about this tablet is that one previously unnoticed individual recorded among other names in the Old Testament (and not a king) should suddenly emerge as a real person; we see him going about his business, sending underlings to pay gold into the temple in 595 BC, fourteen years before the second Jerusalem campaign, when – because of his high political office – he no doubt came face to face with troublesome Jeremiah himself.

Putting together the cuneiform evidence, by the way, including an extraordinary document in Istanbul called Nebuchadnezzar's *Court Calendar*, we can actually draw up – with apologies – a more accurate list of Nebuchadnezzar's five highest-ranking officers than Jeremiah could manage, for we know of these people Assyriologically:

Nergal-šar-usur
Nabu-zakir
Nabu-šarrussu-ukin
Nabu-zer-iddin
Nabu-šuzibanni.

The names and titles, perhaps alien-sounding, suffered understandably in transmission. What is interesting is the Judaean urge to record by name for posterity the specific individuals who were responsible for the destruction of their temple and city.

State Records in Hebrew

The Books of Kings and Chronicles give good historical material in chronological order, but what is really of concern to them is whether a given king was god-fearing, idol-rejecting and, generally, a 'Good Thing', or the opposite. Diagnostic data to this end are excerpted from longer accounts which were available to the compilers at that time and incorporated into the Bible. The Old Testament not infrequently names the source from which information has been derived. There are two versions of the *curriculum vitae* of 'Good King' Jehoshaphat, for example. The first concludes:

> *As for the other events of Jehoshaphat's reign, the things he achieved and his military exploits, are they not written in the Book of the Annals of the Kings of Judah?*
>
> 1 Kings 22:45

The parallel reads:

> *The other events of Jehoshaphat's reign, from beginning to end, are written in the Annals of Jehu son of Hanani, which are recorded in the Book of the Kings of Israel.*
>
> 2 Chronicles 20:34

The reader is thus referred to source accounts rather in the manner of a modern footnote with references; i.e.:

' For fuller details on this period see the *Book of the Annals of the Kings of Judah*; cf., with additional material, the *Annals of Jehu son of Hanani*, in the *Book of the Kings of Israel*.

The Israelite source was evidently more detailed than the Judaean. Both must have been court chronicles of the type produced for the kings of Babylon, recording political deeds, religious activities and military accomplishments by day, month and year, and, like the Babylonian examples, free of any assessment of the king's morals or behaviour. That was for the Bible to provide. The sources excerpted for the biblical histories will have been written in Hebrew script on leather or parchment scrolls and safeguarded in the royal chanceries of the houses of Israel and Judah.

This acknowledgement of manuscript sources anticipates a literate readership that – theoretically at least – could follow them up, and seriously reinforces the authority and historical reliability of the 'published' account. There are many of these umbral works, which also seem to include poetry. Here are some of their titles: *The Book of Jasher, The Book of Songs, The Book of the Wars of the Lord, The Chronicles of the Kings of Israel, The Chronicles of the Kings of Judah, The Book of Shemaiah the Prophet, The Visions of Iddo the Seer, The Manner of the Kingdom, The Book of Samuel the Seer, The Acts of Solomon, The Annals of King David, The Book of Nathan the Prophet, The Book of Gad the Seer, The Prophecy of Ahijah, The Acts of Uzziah, The Acts and Prayers of Manasseh, The Sayings of the Seers, The Laments for Josiah* and *The Chronicles of King Ahasuerus.*

This makes quite a bookshelf. Its importance in the context of *Arks* and *Floods* is this: we can see explicitly that at least part of the biblical text was distilled out of existing written sources, and extracts were put to new purposes within the context of the biblical message. This compositional process underlies the creation of the biblical text as a whole: the narrative incorporates very diverse types of records, oral and written, that were available to the compilers for the Great Work. The same principle will operate for the Flood Story.

What written resources were likely to have been available in Jerusalem prior to the arrival of the Babylonians in 597 BC? Scrolls will have existed with, *at a minimum*, the following contents:

Shelf 1. Court chronicles from Israel and Judah
Shelf 2. Royal correspondence
Shelf 3. Political writings; treaties; trade matters; censuses
Shelf 4. Court poetry; songs; proverbs
Shelf 5. Cultic protocols; sacrifices; temple administration
Shelf 6. Prophetic writings
Shelf 7. Any other business . . .

Material of all these kinds is incorporated into the historical books of the Old Testament. The probability is that writing proliferated at the court of Judah as it does everywhere, and the singular preoccupations of biblical authorship preserve only parts of a far bigger whole. Certain royal privileges might have been accorded to King Jehoiachin on the wearisome road from Jerusalem to Babylon; what we can be sure of is that the heritage Hebrew scrolls cannot have been torched by Nabuzaradan's men but must have been taken with them too. Otherwise there would be no Old Testament.

Israelite refugees being deported on the road from Lachish after the city was sacked by Sennacherib's army in 701 BC, long before the Babylonians did the same to the Judaeans at Jerusalem.

Judaeans Encountering Babylon: The Tower of Babel

The Judaean exiles approaching the city in 597 BC, and again those in 587 BC, will have glimpsed the Tower of Babel from a long way off, for the great stepped temple tower or ziggurat that reposed in the centre of Nebuchadnezzar's capital attained a height of well over seventy metres, its base measuring ninety-one square metres. The ever-growing profile against the horizon must have struck awe into all those who approached the city. It is perhaps hard to imagine the impact of that skyscraper on outsiders who saw it for the first time; there was no building in Jerusalem that could have prepared them for the sight.

And ẏ whole earth was of one language, v. 1. etc. And they said one to another, let us make brick v 3 And let us build us a City, & a tower, whose top may reach unto heaven et, v. 4 Therfore is the name of it called Babel, etc. Verse. 9.

Building the Tower of Babel in about AD 1754, showing the making of bricks. Artist unidentified.

The Tower of Babel in the Book of Genesis is no literary conceit invented for didactic purposes. The great building was slap bang in front of them, built as high as possible to facilitate contact between the king of Babylon – favourite of the god Marduk – and Marduk himself. The ziggurat was a ladder to heaven to allow the king's voice, confident, intercessional or pleading, the best chance of being heard. We are not well informed about the exact use of the building or of the small temple that reposed on top, but its function as a royal 'hot line' to heaven is beyond dispute.

The story of the Tower of Babel in Genesis is one brief, nine-verse episode but the tower has in some measure loomed over human society with its sombre message ever since.

Now the whole earth had one language and the same words. And as people migrated from the east, they found a plain in the land of Shinar and settled there. And they said to one another, 'Come, let us make bricks, and burn them thoroughly.' And they had brick for stone, and bitumen for mortar. Then they said, 'Come, let us build ourselves a city and a tower with its top in the heavens, and let us make a name for ourselves, lest we be dispersed over the face of the whole earth.' And the Lord came down to see the city and the tower, which the children of man had built. And the Lord said, 'Behold, they are one people, and they have all one language, and this is only the beginning of what they will do. And nothing that they propose to do will now be impossible for them. Come, let us go down and there confuse their language, so that they may not understand one another's speech.' So the Lord dispersed them from there over the face of all the earth, and they left off building the city. Therefore its name was called Babel, because there the Lord confused the language of all the earth. And from there the Lord dispersed them over the face of all the earth.

Genesis 11:1–9

There can be no doubt that the composition of this passage was the consequence of the physical presence of the Judaeans in Babylon. The 'land of Shinar' referred to reflects the old Sumerian name for southern Mesopotamia, Sumer. The over-weening ziggurat *was*, as described, built of brick and mortar. The whole city in fact was built of clay bricks, thousands upon endless thousands of them, some glazed, many stamped in cunei-form with Nebuchadnezzar's name and titles. Unimaginable numbers had been used to build the ziggurat itself, intended by

Nebuchadnezzar's architects in every way to surpass what any predecessor had ever achieved.

In the context of Genesis we can discern two distinct components in this story. One, since the principal phenomena of the world are being explained, answers the question, *Why are there so many languages in the world?* Many children, bewildered by unfamiliar tongues in the street or on the bus, ask the same natural question today. The explanation is that the superabundance of mutually unintelligible languages is punishment by God: men should have understood what they could and couldn't do. The intrusion of humans into the kingdom of heaven like so many intrepid firemen clambering up the steps would be intolerable. To Hebrew sensibilities the urge in any man for physical proximity to heaven was blasphemous. The moral lesson is strict and unforgiving, and is a direct illustration of the Hebrew mind at work. The child's naive question is turned round, and used to underwrite a deeper message.

There is, moreover, disdain and reserve running under this text for the 'them', who are the Babylonians. For the construction of the arrogant building was an alien episode in earlier times that was none of the Hebrews' doing but which was seen as responsible for how things had become in the world. The Judaean view is that the Babylonian tower, what it stood for and the religious ideal it embodied was *sinful*. The Hebrew text thus embodies detachment from, if not hostility towards, the state cult of Marduk.

There is a further point. The Hebrew term for the 'tower' in the expression Tower of Babel is *migdal*. This word is certainly correctly translated as 'tower', but in the usual meaning of the word a tower is – more or less – straight-sided, even if its base is wider for stability, as in a lighthouse. The profile of the Babylonian ziggurat, however, is opposite. It seems quite probable to me that the building's very profile will have suggested to the Judaeans that the ziggurat was unfinished. If the building was really meant to be a tower that would reach from earth to heaven, it would have looked as if the work (or the funding!) had run out in the early stages. The top was nowhere near the clouds and the whole operation hardly got off the ground. To the Hebrew mind the Babylonians' tower work must have been brought to a halt by a divine hand. This brief passage, so familiar and often so swiftly read over, can thus be seen, in the context of the first unwilling Judaean presence in the city, to be pregnant with highly intelligible meaning.

Nebuchadnezzar's capital was then the world's greatest city. The king was all-powerful, his empire was huge, his riches inexhaustible and on the whole life was stable. The city itself was the jewel in the crown; it was dedicated to and under the protective eye of Marduk, the greatest of the gods of Babylon, who had vanquished the forces of darkness as described in the *Epic of Creation*, establishing the world as it should be and setting up Babylon for ever as his cult home. The king was his agent on earth.

Judaeans Encountering Babylon: Immigration, Culture and Writing

To understand the incorporation and presence of Babylonian traditions within the Bible we must consider the religious and psychological state of the Judaeans who first encountered the towering capital that was to be their home. They were an entire community of, so-to-speak, enforced refugees, bodily transported from a ruined capital into that of an alien and vastly superior country. Berated by their prophets for their sacrilegious behaviour, reeling from long-threatened and unimaginable punishment, and carrying but a fraction of their wealth and possessions, they finally arrived at the gates of Babylon as *displaced persons*.

We still know next to nothing of what happened to this incoming population. We know that the more skilled found places at the capital, while great swathes of immigrants were no doubt relocated outside the main cities to wherever they were most needed. One group of Judaeans in particular can be followed through Nebuchadnezzar's city gate with the help of the so-called Palace Archive tablets. These itemise prosaic items like oil, barley and other commestibles for the support of people brought from across the Babylonian Empire, including the young king Jehoiachin from Jerusalem and his entourage, who were thus 'guests of the state':

> *30 litres (of oil) for Ja'ukin, king of Judah*
> *2½ litres for the five sons of the king of Judah*
> *4 litres for the eight Jahudeans, ½ litre for each.*

Royal provisions: Babylonian ration list mentioning Jehoiachin by name.

Also included in these records are Judaean carpenters and boatmen, just as are described by Jeremiah as being among the deportees. Later, things improved a bit for Jehoiachin:

And in the thirty-seventh year of the exile of Jehoiachin king of Judah, in the twelfth month, on the twenty-seventh day of the month, Evil-Merodach [Amel-Marduk] king of Babylon, in the year that he began to reign, graciously freed Jehoiachin king of Judah from prison. And he spoke kindly to him and gave him a seat above the seats of the kings who were with him in Babylon. So Jehoiachin put off his prison garments. And every day of his life he dined regularly at the king's table, and for his allowance, a regular allowance was given him by the king, according to his daily needs, as long as he lived.

2 Kings 25:27–30

This Amel-Marduk was Nebuchadnezzar's crown prince and unenviable successor, who managed to rule for only two years, 562–560 BC, before he was assassinated. According to the *Chronicle of Jerachmeel*, compiled by a French rabbi in the twelfth century AD from sources unknown to us, the prince, then called Nabū-šuma-ukīn, was thrown into Jehoiachin's prison by his father because of a court conspiracy. (This episode is not recorded in the Bible, but a cuneiform tablet from Babylon exists with Nabū-šuma-ukīn's poetic appeal to the god Marduk written in that prison; later he took what was to be his throne name, Amel-Marduk, 'man of Marduk', in gratitude for his rescue.)

Following the Judaeans further is impossible, given our present archaeological and written resources. Some personal names in the records appear to be Judaean, or Hebrew, but this can be uncertain evidence.

We can make certain observations on another level, however. Given the Babylonians' utter destruction of the Jerusalem Temple and city in 587 BC the Judaean deportees must have found themselves with nothing substantive at all to define their culture or hold their identity together. They had lost their political and religious capital, spelling the end of their ancient line of kingship, descended from David. In addition, they now had no cult centre to provide the focus of their religious life, which meant no cult practice; the complex round of worship, sacrifice and liturgy that had been practised in the Temple for endless generations was brought to an abrupt end.

In principle the Judaeans' religious life was supposed to sustain itself without images of their god to provide a physical focus of worship. Their religion, at least as it is transmitted to us, when free of the adulterations so bemoaned by its prophets, was essentially monotheistic, vested in a single omnipotent god who could never be seen. The second Commandment – *Thou shalt have no other gods before me* – is no flat statement that there *are* no other gods; if anything, the language can be taken to reflect that there may well be other gods but they are for other nations. Theirs was a male god with no name, no wife and no children. The religion of the Judaeans, therefore, especially out of its normal context, was purely conceptual, dealing in the intangible and unsupported by comforting likenesses and paraphernalia. Unlike the Babylonians all around them the Judaeans had no divine statue resident on a divine throne who would accept their offerings and hear their exhortations, staring down from above with the assurance of a wise parent. The religion of the Old Testament Hebrews from its inception differed crucially from that of all its predecessors and contemporaries, in the abstraction of the Hebrews' god to a concept, remote and invisible, with no graven image, and no surrounding family. No other religion of antiquity could have survived focused exclusively on one god who could never be seen. Once they arrived in Babylon the Judaeans had little beyond this highly elusive abstraction to exemplify their belief or give structure to their displaced identity.

If we imagine a Babylonian and a Judaean immigrant in friendly conversation in that market, in other words, the latter would have no answers at all to perfectly natural questions such as: *What is your god called? What does he look like? Where does he live? Who is his wife? How many children does he have?* At the same time, there were significant religious changes under way in Babylon throughout the period of the Judaean Exile. There had been an evolving idea that the Babylonian state god Marduk was not so much king of the gods – his traditional status – but rather the one single god who mattered. For the best part of three millennia the cultures of ancient Mesopotamia had served a profusion of gods great and small, but in the period of these Neo-Babylonian kings we can see a new monotheistic framework evolving out of this rich pantheistic background. Consider the message of this innocent-looking little theological text:

Urash	is	Marduk	of planting
Lugalakia	is	Marduk	of ground water
Ninurta	is	Marduk	of the hoe
Nergal	is	Marduk	of war
Zababa	is	Marduk	of battle
Enlil	is	Marduk	of lordship and deliberation
Nabu	is	Marduk	of accounting
Sin	is	Marduk	as illuminator of the night
Shamash	is	Marduk	of justice
Adad	is	Marduk	of rain
Tishpak	is	Marduk	of hosts
Ishtaran	is	Marduk	of . . .
Shuqamunu	is	Marduk	of the trough
Mami	is	Marduk	of potter's clay . . .

Monotheism in the making: structuring Marduk theology.

This is a truly remarkable document, for in it we witness theological innovation in process, fixed in time. A theologian is speculating that Marduk is 'really' the only god, expressing this by the proposition that fourteen major and ancient gods, independent deities with their own temples, cult and followers, are but aspects of Marduk, his offices, so to speak. This text does not stand in isolation. There are similar 'syncretisms' laid out for Zarpanitu, Marduk's wife, and their son Nabu, making what in other contexts might be called a divine trinity, and there are longer theological disquisitions in the same vein.

Marduk's unique status as *the* god under Nebuchadnezzar undoubtedly paved the way later for a similar development with the Moon God, Sin, under Nabonidus, the last king of Babylon before the Persian period, who had been brought up by his rather formidable mother as a hardcore Moon God devotee. There was tension aplenty between the Marduk priesthood and the devotees of Sin, sufficient for Cyrus, the incoming conqueror, to take advantage of it. Prior to this period it is hard to point to any sign of religious hostility or prejudice in Mesopotamian society that has found its way into written expression. Foreigners were foreigners; one kept on one's guard and probably despised their ways, but no one ever declared hostility to a person of 'another religion' on those grounds. Everyone knew of and believed in many gods, and divine newcomers were welcome; statues of foreign gods were imported after successful warmongering as a matter of course, to be installed in the temples of Assyria or Babylonia. Gods from outside, like foreign magic, could be powerful, especially if they had belonged to powerful enemies, and with a new seat and cycle of sacrifices they would hopefully transfer their loyalties. In due course their names were even entered, barbaric sounding though they might be, in official god lists. It is only with the promotion of exclusive monotheism that religious intolerance can be the consequence, and Babylon in this very period saw the emergence of such monotheism for the very first time in Mesopotamian culture.

The Judaeans were thus to encounter a native religious system more akin to their own than would have been the case at an earlier date. Babylonian monotheism, whether a matter of wider state policy or closed theology within the colleges (let alone debated loose on the streets), must have offered a threatening backdrop to Judaeans with their own belief in a single god and responsibility to preserve that belief from contamination. It is also worth pointing out that the epithets of praise that were heaped on Marduk (shepherd, champion of the poor and weak, protector of widows and children, fighter for justice and truth) would not have sounded strange to Judaean ears brought up in their own tradition.

For a variety of reasons the passing of the Judaean population into the cosmopolitan mass of sixth century Babylon might be expected to have seen its complete absorption and the ultimate disappearence of its religion within a relatively short time. This is especially the case since both communities, incoming minority and resident majority, shared the Aramaic language in common on top of their own substrate: Hebrew in the former case, Babylonian in the latter.

A Babylonian schoolroom challenge: Who can write the Aramaic alphabet in cuneiform signs?
Answer: a bi gi da e u za he tu ia ka la me nu ṣa a-a-nu pe ṣu qu ri shi ta.

In addition, although such an issue is hard to calibrate, the populations were on some level 'cousins' in terms of Semitic-speaking Semitic stock. Under predictable conditions, without intervention, the Judaeans and their elusive, non-idolatrous faith would have surely disappeared from view. Support for this argument comes from the fate of the Israelites a century earlier, who were transported to Assyria and beyond by the Assyrians in military campaigns, and who are – more or less – entirely lost sight of as a result. Given this situation, it is thus intelligible that those who felt themselves responsible for the Judaean populations – both from a social and religious point of view – should have considered that preventative action should be taken to bind them together.

It is these very circumstances, in the present writer's view, that provided the first stimulus for the drawing up of the Hebrew Bible as a full work. The need was pressing from the outset, not at some point during the Persian or Hellenistic period (as is usually suggested), but from the inception of the Exile. It was necessary to provide a satisfactory explanation for the Judaeans of just how they could all come to be in Babylon in their present state, with their home country and all it meant to them in ruins.

The whole had to be a long and convincing story, commencing with the very creation of the world, and proceeding down through the Patriarchs and the Monarchy and what came after, coming right up to date. The backbone of the whole would be the historical continuum through all its vagaries and disputes and confusions. The rounded text, along the way, would incorporate a rich collection of cultic traditions, poetry and wisdom, but its essential function would be to provide a lucid explanation for what had happened from the beginning of time and to demonstrate explicitly that the whole historical process from the inception of the world had been the unfolding of a divine plan of which they – the chosen people – were the central concern. The resulting compilation with its skilfully blended narratives emerged as a virtual handbook for ex-patriot Judaeans.

In the light of this argument the constituent parts of the Old Testament all fulfil a transparent role. The great emphasis on family trees and genealogy throughout constitute the very materials on which threatened Judaean identity was predicated. Due to this collecting and listing of all the tribal descent information that survived, no one could remain in doubt as to who belonged and who didn't. The first volume of Chronicles emerges as a sort of telephone book in which all the names were to be found, indispensable when it came to dealing with suitors for daughters.

The *written text* of the Hebrew bible (whatever inspiration might have engendered it or arisen from it) is the work of human hands. Reading through it with this principle in mind shows this truth to be everywhere apparent. A basic list of features includes, for example, unnecessary repetitions and inappropriate insertions on the one hand, conflicting and overlapping accounts, and, as we have seen, specific acknowledgement of utilised writings on the other. Granted this, certain rational conclusions about the processes which produced the biblical text can be drawn, analogous to the production of any large-scale and complex literary compilation, such as a multi-volume encyclopaedia.

The Hebrew text is infinitely more than could have been accomplished by any single individual; many were therefore involved, with a few in charge of the project. The production was – in large part – dependent on diverse pre-existing materials that could be reworked or streamlined into a whole. From this, certain points emerge:

1. There must have been both some specific event or need to trigger such an undertaking, and a chronological moment when the work actually began.
2. There must have been a clear vision that endured throughout the labour and resulted in internal consistency.
3. Eventually there must have been a consensus as to the point when the primary work, at least, was finished.

In my view, therefore, the Bible first developed into the work that we have today in the period, location and circumstances of the Babylonian Exile, as a direct response to that Exile.

This broad principle does not conflict with the long-running internal analysis of the received biblical text that distinguishes separate authorship (such as J, P and E) on a line-by-line basis, for I assume that all available sources would be utilised, some coming with a history of internal editing; further moulding, interweaving and editing would be a long and ongoing process.

That such a complex production could be so effectively engendered out of such diverse sources has several implications. The work of compilation must have been carried out by a group of specific individuals who had access to all existing records, under an agreed editorial authority. One must envisage a Bureau of Judaean History. That the whole, or almost the whole, was written in Hebrew and not Aramaic gives, I think, a clue to the agenda of political identity. It was for one readership only.

It is against this backdrop that the incorporation of particular Babylonian traditions becomes intelligible. Perhaps there was a shortfall of native ideas among the Hebrew thinkers about the beginning of the world and civilisation. Whatever the case, certain powerful Babylonian narratives were taken up but, crucially, not adopted wholesale. The beginning of the Book of Genesis especially would be unrecognisable without the cuneiform substratum, but the stories were given *a unique Judaean twist that allowed them to function in a wholly new context*. There are three unambiguous cases that we can consider here.

THE GREAT AGES OF MAN BEFORE THE FLOOD
The Book of Genesis attributes superhuman longevity to Adam and his descendants all the way down to Lamech, the father of Noah, all of whom lived before the Flood. The champion, of course, is Methuselah:

Adam: 930 years
Seth: 912 years
Enosh: 905 years
Kenan: 910 years
Mahalaleel: 895 years
Jared: 962 years
Enoch: 365 years
Methuselah: 969 years
Lamech: 595 years.

The Babylonians earlier had a similar tradition in cuneiform, for the earliest kings in the *Sumerian King List* had hugely long reigns expressed in the same ŠÁR units of 3,600 that we encountered in Chapter 8 in the *Ark Tablet*'s specifications:

When kingship was lowered from heaven
The kingship was in Eridu.
In Eridu Alulim became king
and reigned 28,800 years;
Alalgar reigned 36,000 years.
*   2 kings reigned 64,800 years;*
Things changed
Kingship went to Bad-Tibira
In Bad-Tibira Enmenluanna
Reigned 43,200 years;
Enmengalanna
Reigned 28,800 years
Divine Dumuzi, the shepherd, reigned 36,000 years
*   3 kings*
reigned 108,000 years.

Sumerian King List: 1–17

The Judaeans, anxious to establish lineage, undoubtedly took over this grand-scale idea, but they concluded that these early rulers with such long lives must have been giants, although the idea does not appear in the cuneiform tradition. The attempt by some scholars to treat the Genesis Great Ages tradition as if it had nothing to do with the cuneiform world seems to me utterly absurd.

WHY THE FLOOD?

Universal destruction by water is imposed on mankind in the *Atrahasis* story because humans were so *noisy*, and we are left uninformed as to what qualified the Babylonian hero for selection as saviour. The flood in the Bible, and the Koran after it, was punishment for *wickedness*. Noah was chosen explicitly because of his upright character and behaviour.

THE SARGON LEGEND

Sargon's mother (*Legend of Sargon*, Chapter 8, p. 16) was a priestess who had no business having a baby in the first place and nobody was quite sure who the father was. His origins were thus murky, even a trifle sordid, and he grew up watering tomatoes in the country. Moses in the Book of Exodus was rescued by none other than the Pharaoh's daughter. Unwittingly, they paid his own mother to suckle him, and the boy grew up with every possible advantage in the fat of the palace. It was necessary for such an iconic personage as Moses to have romantic or miraculous beginnings, but when the Babylonian story is given its new Judaean colouring the whole episode carries a different message. I think the milk-money episode must have induced *roars of laughter* at the *stupid Egyptians*.

How then did these specific cuneiform materials find their way, reworked with moral flavour, into the biblical narrative?

JUDAEANS LEARN CUNEIFORM

The Hebrew Bible tells us in so many words that a hand-picked group of Judaean intelligentsia were inducted into the mysteries of cuneiform at the capital, and I see absolutely no reason not to take this statement at face value:

³Then the king commanded his palace master Ashpenaz to bring some of the Israelites of the royal family and of the nobility, ⁴young men without physical defect and handsome, versed in every branch of wisdom, endowed with knowledge and insight, and competent to serve in the king's palace; they were to be taught the literature and language of the Chaldeans. ⁵The king assigned them a daily portion of the royal rations of food and wine. They were to be educated for three years, so that at the end of that time they could be stationed in the king's court.

Daniel 1: 3–5

The Book of Daniel is composed of tales about the Babylonian court interspersed with great visions, set in the time of the Exile, under the Neo-Babylonian kings and their Persian successors. Whereas it was once believed that the book dated to the sixth century BC, scholars now consider the editing of the whole, which incorporates older, traditional material, to date to the second century BC, just four hundred years after the Exile. This verdict may be true in general but to my mind the opening chapters of the book give, just for a moment, an oddly convincing flavour of Nebuchadnezzar's court, and with regard to particularly the reference to learning the literature and language of the Chaldeans cuneiform classes, which are given such pointed attention right at the beginning of the book, I follow the text resolutely.

There can be no doubt that what is meant, by this, is instruction in the cuneiform writing system and the Babylonian language. The Judaeans spoke Hebrew; the educated among them knew Aramaic. The programme was evidently part of Babylonian state policy to avoid long-term difficulty with imported populations: the cream would be acculturated to Babylonian life and ways, and the most effective and lasting way to achieve this was through reading and writing. We are told that Daniel and his intimates went on to become judges: all legal matters were conducted in Babylonian and recorded in cuneiform for a long time to come.

As far as I know, my idea that this three-year teaching programme must refer to cuneiform has neither been proposed nor defended before, largely due perhaps to the absurd dismissal of the Book of Daniel as a reputable witness, but it is easy to show that, from the point of view of the humanities, this is one of the most significant passages in the Hebrew Bible. It allows us to make sense of many matters that are both unexplained and often left unconnected with one another.

Curricular exercise no. 1: The Great Ages of Man. This tablet is inscribed with an interlinear Babylonian translation of the traditional Sumerian preamble to their list of antediluvian kings, with their great reign lengths, for study in school. This composition is known today as the Dynastic Chronicle; *it derives directly from the* Sumerian King List.

We know from very abundant numbers of curricular tablets what went on in Babylonian schools of the Nebuchadnezzar period. The young candidates will have had the best of teachers.

Hebrew and Aramaic were sisters to Babylonian, so mastery of the tongue for bright young persons was nothing. There were established ways to learn scribal technique, and before long they would be writing lists of signs and numbers, followed by words and formulae, names and a great variety of literary passages.

What is so compelling for my argument is that we actually have cuneiform school tablets from Babylon of this period with study of and extracts from the Great Ages of Man, the *Sargon Legend* story, and the Epic of Gilgamesh, showing that the three works that best exemplify the process of borrowing were *on the school curriculum*. The trainee Judaeans would have encountered these very texts in their palace classroom.

Curricular exercise no. 2: The Baby Sargon in his Coracle. *A quotation appears in the second column, between other literary extracts and lists of signs. It covers lines 1–6.*

The existence of these three tablets suffices to identify the conduit that has previously eluded us. What is more, it is very straightforward. Judaeans learned to read cuneiform tablets.

Curricular exercise no. 3: a classroom extract from Tablet III of the Epic of Gilgamesh.

For the sharpest Judaean brains, encountering the vastness of the cuneiform heritage at the beginning of the sixth century BC must have been electrifying in its effect and must undoubtedly have launched certain individuals on long-term study and into participation in many kinds of work in which mastery of cuneiform was essential.

In the years before Cyrus the Great conquered Babylon in 539 BC the Judaeans certainly did more than sit about and weep. They adjusted and settled. In time they became Mesopotamian citizens. By the time Cyrus arrived, by no means all of Nebuchadnezzar's displaced persons wanted to go 'home' to Jerusalem. However, the Judaeans' ancient and somewhat ramshackle religious identity had meanwhile been crystallising into permanence due to their encyclopaedia of history, custom, instruction and wisdom. They became literally the people of the book. From this angle it can be argued that the Babylonian Exile, far from being the disaster it is usually judged, was ultimately the process that forged what became modern Judaism.

The development of the Hebrew Bible introduced something new into the world. For the first time *scripture* came into existence, a finite text corpus with beginning and end on which religious identity was predicated. Prior to this the world had only known religious texts. A pattern was established which has endured also through Christianity and Islam; a monotheistic religion with scripture at its core, which, being finite, generates commentary, explanation and interpretation, and often has to deal with apocrypha.

Afterword

The behaviour mechanics of the Judaean exiles once settled within Babylonia probably conformed to patterns discernible in the modern world among displaced and incoming large communities, whether compulsory immigrants or political and religious refugees. A mass of individuals, initially close together, in time fans out, ultimately around the country, if not already settled in areas by authority. In the case of the Judaeans, in particular, much as with the Jewish population that ended up in London or Manhattan after the Second World War, social or national identity and religious identity were simultaneously powerful factors. The consequent evolution of this complex identity within Babylonia over time would result in three broad categories among the Judaeans that operated on a level separate from traditional tribal allegiance:

1. those who were strongly aware of their history and
   culture, determined to continue as before and, while

adjusting to the reality of the destruction of the Temple, were waiting to return to Jerusalem as soon as possible to rebuild it;

2. those whose cultural allegiance and personal religious adherence was to traditional Judaean practice but without embracing a fully exclusive lifestyle;

3. those who simply immersed themselves in Babylonian life in every way and to all intents and purposes became fully assimilated.

To individuals in the third group, and possibly the second, the distinction between Marduk and their own Judaean god would come to seem far from clear. If both were, so to speak, the one god, then Marduk might well triumph as the visible counterpart of the other, and it seems probable that to many individuals, especially those of the second or third generation after the arrival, there might not have seemed much to choose between the two. Possibly both groups would have been quite content to give their children Babylonian names formed with those of Marduk, or his son Nabu, or Bel. Group 1 would avoid such names and use . . . -*yahu* names or names without any divine element. To the first group the separation of Marduk from the god of the Hebrews would remain an essential and cohesive preoccupation.

Later documents from after the arrival of Cyrus the Great in 539 BC give us a fragmentary glimpse of these Judaean communities living together in Iraq after the departure of the others to Jerusalem. One of these places was called Jahudu, 'Judaean Town'. The communities were well settled and organised, answerable to central authority, but still preserved the customs and practices they had brought with them, and they were certainly not 'slaves in bondage'. Furthermore, their documents were written in Babylonian cuneiform.

A cuneiform tablet from Jahudu, a marriage contract including individual Judaean names.

Ultimately it was descendants of these Judaean settlers in Babylonia who generated the Babylonian Talmud in their academies between the second and fourth century AD, writing in several Aramaic dialects mixed with biblical and later Hebrew. The Talmud is made up of the Mishnah ('case histories') and the Gomorrah (principles). The essential preoccupation is to facilitate the clarification of exact meaning in a given textual passage. This is achieved by a variety of learned approaches, in which different views are very often attributed by name to those revered teachers and individuals who thought of them, built up from insights and interpretations that developed in the academies over many generations. At the heart of all the ordered discussion is, of course, the Bible.

The Talmud is the latest corpus of writings in which the direct influence of earlier Babylonian tradition and learning is discernible. Such influences can take the form of loanwords from Babylonian into Aramaic, or the survival of Babylonian ideas and practices (medicine, magic and divination or the playing of the Royal Game of Ur, for example). Particularly revealing in this regard are Talmudic word play and interpretation which parallel those long established in the native Babylonian academies, such as in the commentaries quoted in Appendix 1. These devices are ultimately due to the multivalent characteristics of cuneiform signs and their presence in rabbinic learning written in alphabetic Aramaic undoubtedly reflects the consequence of that first Judaean acquaintance with cuneiform scholarship. The influences of the specifically cuneiform world on the Judaean exiles and their successors have often remained unexplored, but they were certainly far-reaching and long-lasting. One eloquent measure of permanent Babylonian influence is the fact that the month names used today in the Modern Hebrew calendar preserve the ancient names as used in Nebuchadnezzar's capital:

Babylonian:	Hebrew:
Nisannu	*Nisan*
Ayaru	*Iyar*
Simanu	*Sivan*
Du'ūzu	*Tammuz*
Abu	*Av*
Ulūlu	*Elul*
Tashrītu	*Tishrei*
Arahsamna	*Marcheshvan*

Kislimu	*Kislev*
Ṭebetu	*Ṭebet*
Shabatu	*Shevat*
Adaru	*Adar*

In contrast we know the names of only four native ancient Hebrew month names: *Aviv* (which in modern Hebrew is the word for spring, but which was previously used for the month *Nisan*), *Ziv* (*Iyar*), *Ethanim* (*Tishrei*) and *Bul* (*Marcheshvan*). Living in Babylon the Judaeans naturally adopted the prevailing calendar. The old names fell out of use, but the Babylonian words live on and are heard in daily conversations all over the world today.

12

What Happened to the Ark?

The map of the world ceases to be a blank;
It becomes a picture
Full of the most varied and animated figures.
Each part assumes its proper dimensions.

Charles Darwin

In all the stories, as the floodwaters subsided, the Ark with its precious cargo landed safely on top of a mountain. Life on earth escaped by the skin of its teeth so the human and animal world could regroup and carry on as before with renewed vigour. Where the great craft actually landed, and what happened to it, only became important afterwards.

Different traditions grew up about the identity of the mountain, for the ancient Babylonian story always retained its importance within Judaism, Christianity and Islam. Earlier, in the cuneiform world, there had also been more than one tradition about it. As we have seen, our oldest versions of the Flood Story, including the *Ark Tablet*, come from the second millennium BC, but, most unhelpfully, no tablet from that period tells us anything about the Ark landing. To push things further we really need a contemporary Babylonian map.

Fortunately we have one.

The Babylonian Map of the World

The map in question is nothing less than a map of the whole world. It is one of the most remarkable cuneiform tablets ever discovered, so smart that it has its own Latin nickname – in the

world of Assyriology at least – the *mappa mundi*, notwithstanding other claimants for the title. It is, in addition, the *earliest
known map of the world*, drawn on a tablet of clay.

The Babylonian Map of the World, front view.

The most important element is the drawing, which takes up
the lower two-thirds of the obverse. It is a brilliantly accomplished
piece of work. The known world is depicted from far above as

a disc surrounded by a ring of water called *marratu* in Akkadian. Two concentric circles were drawn in with some cuneiform precursor of a pair of compasses whose point was actually inserted south of Babylon, perhaps at the city of Nippur, the 'Bond of Heaven and Earth'. Within the circle the heartland of Mesopotamia is depicted in schematic form. The broad Euphrates River runs from top to bottom, originating in the northern mountainous areas and losing itself in canals and marshes in the south. The great river is straddled by Babylon, awesomely vast in comparison with other cities on the map, which are represented by circles, some inscribed in small cuneiform signs with their names. The locations of cities and tribal conglomerations are partly 'accurate' but by no means always so. The crucial components of the heartland are assembled within the circle, but this is no AA map for planning a motoring trip: the relative geographical proportions and relationships of the encircled features are far less important than the great ring of water that surrounds everything, while even further beyond is a ring of vast mountains that marks the rim of the world. These mountains are depicted as flat, projecting triangles; each is called a *nagû*. Originally they numbered eight.

The Babylonian Map of the World is justly famous and always on exhibition in the British Museum, but the surface of the clay is so delicate that it is has never been kiln-fired by the Museum's Conservation Department, as is usually recommended to safeguard the long-term survival of cuneiform tablets. Now it is never even moved from its case or given on loan for exhibition. The reason for this is that when the tablet was on loan somewhere many years ago the *nagû* triangle in the lower left corner somehow became detached and, disastrously, lost.

When the *mappa mundi* was acquired by the British Museum in 1882 there were four triangles preserved, two complete and two with only the bottom section surviving. The tablet was first published in a sober German journal in 1889 and we have several other ink drawings and photographs that show the map at different times with the SW triangle still in position there, and these can be relied on as giving a faithful picture.

It must be said that damage or loss of this kind to our cuneiform tablets happens exceedingly rarely, and it is doubly unfortunate that it should have happened to a Map-of-the-World 'triangle', but it so turned out that I was able in a strange way to make up for this accident, with consequences for this book that I could never have anticipated. The British Museum excavations conducted in the Mesopotamian sites of Sippar and Babylon by the archaeologist Hormuzd Rassam in the later decades of the nineteenth century uncovered cuneiform inscriptions in quite staggering numbers. When they arrived in the Museum they were all registered by a cuneiform curator, who recorded basic details, allotted each a running number within its group, and housed each in a glass-topped box on the collection shelves. There was such a waterfall of incoming clay documents that the largest in a given consignment were naturally attended to at once, then all the good-sized pieces and so on. The tablets and fragments in each packing case often arrived wrapped in a twist of paper. Each consignment also included large quantities of small fragments – for Rassam's workmen were, thank goodness, careful to collect every scrap of writing – but it often turned out that the curator in London had no chance to finish dealing with all the tiny pieces, some of which might contain only two or three signs of writing, before a fresh and important packing case arrived to claim his attention. The consequence was that over time a huge accumulation of small tablet fragments built up that would one day need to be dealt with. These fragments were often only a corner of a business document ('Witnesses: Mr . . . ; Mr . . . ; Mr . . .') or a flake from the surface ('Day 1, Month 4, Darius year . . .'), which of themselves might not seem to hold much promise, but they are all treasure, for they all belong to and will ultimately join other pieces in the collection; in the end (probably after centuries of labour!) most of the cuneiform tablets in the British Museum will be completed and their inscriptions become fully readable. This entails a jigsaw puzzle of ungovernable proportions; all Assyriologists who work on our collection play this game and dream that one day the tantalising missing piece that they need so badly will turn up to be glued into place by a patient conservator. Sometimes it happens. Sometimes a mere scrap can turn out to be of the greatest significance.

For many years (as already confessed) I ran an evening class in cuneiform after hours in the British Museum. Once a week a loyal troupe of die-hards turned up to be initiated into the mystery of the wedges; we read all sorts of texts together and sometimes they even did a little homework. The class carried on for several years and by the time it reluctantly wound down one of the students, Miss Edith Horsley, had become a convinced cuneiform devotee and was anxious to continue as a volunteer in our Department. This seemed a good opportunity to have a crack at some of the long-ignored fragment collections. Miss Horsley was to unwrap and lightly clean the fragments from one of the chests, sort them as best she could and re-box them. After all those classes she certainly knew what a cuneiform business document looked like, so we agreed that she would distinguish corners, edges and body sherds, while anything that looked odd, or non business-like, should go in a special pile to be examined by me every Friday afternoon. On the whole these oddments turned out to be either pieces of school text in untidy writing or tabular lists of astronomical numbers, but one week on top of the pile was a scrap of inscribed clay with a *triangle*.

I have tried already to convey how life as a cuneiformist is full of adrenalin moments, but this was an extreme case. For I knew instantly, as any tablet person would, that this fragment with a triangle must join the *mappa mundi*. It had to. With trembling hands I picked up the fragment, put it in a little box, and rushed off to collect my keys to open the case in Room 51 and try it. But when I got downstairs the Map of the World tablet was, unbelievably, not in its place. I had forgotten in all the excitement that it was on exhibition elsewhere in the building as part of a historical display of maps put together by the British Library (who were then still on the Bloomsbury premises). It was an abominable wait until Monday morning. Then, at last, a librarian turnkey met me, a museum assistant and Miss Horsley to give us access so that we could test the join. Finally the locks opened. The triangle fragment fitted so snugly in the gap that it would not come out again.

This, however, is but the tip of the iceberg. The triangular *nagû* belonged right next to the long-known cuneiform label on the tablet that read: 'Six Leagues in between where the sun is not seen.' The new *nagû* was itself inscribed 'Great Wall'. It could not be the Great Wall of China, of course, but an earlier big wall that was already known from cuneiform stories.

Making a join to the Map of the World was really something. I was perhaps a little preoccupied with this achievement and fell naturally into telling everybody within earshot about it, whether or not they were interested. A day or so later, queuing in the Museum Staff Canteen, I mentioned it to Patricia Morison, then editor of the *British Museum Magazine*, who immediately talked me into writing something. I had remarked to her blithely that this was just the sort of snippet that would come over well at the end of a day's television news, when the broadcaster, struggling to dispel the gloom caused by the day's events, likes to finish with such news as a pregnant cat being safely rescued from the top of a lighthouse by helicopter. It was nevertheless a very considerable shock the following morning to receive a telephone call from the front hall to say that Nick Glass and the Channel 4 news team had arrived to see me and Miss Horsley and the *fragment*. The magazine editor and he were neighbours, and she had apparently mentioned all this over the garden fence to him . . .

'Have you ever lost a piece of a jigsaw puzzle down the back of the sofa?' asked Trevor McDonald, wrapping up the 7 o'clock news the following evening. 'Well, today in the British Museum . . .'

So, there was the whole story in full Technicolor, featuring our Mesopotamian Galleries, our Tablet Collection, our students at work in the Students' Room, Miss Horsley surrounded by all her dusty fragments of tablet and, to top it all, *wizard* computer graphics (this was 1995) that showed the triangle fragment in blue jumping of its own accord into the empty space on the tablet. The whole report lasted four minutes and forty-two seconds. It was pure Andy Warhol. And it was my birthday. Little did I know it then, but that *nagû* join would have the most remarkable consequences for my subsequent Ark investigation . . .

The cuneiform handwriting dates the map to, most probably, the sixth century BC. The map's content undoubtedly reflects Babylon as the centre of the world; the dot that can be seen in the middle of the oblong that is the capital city probably represents Nebuchadnezzar's ziggurat. The tablet contains three distinct sections: a twelve-line description concerning creation of the world by Marduk, god of Babylon; the map drawing itself; and twenty-six lines of description that elucidate certain geographic features shown on the map.

These first twelve lines differ from the text on the reverse in spelling many words with Sumerian ideograms, and we can deduce that the scribe himself viewed this section as distinct from the map and its description from the double ruling across the width of the tablet that follows line 12. This ideographic style of spelling is fully in keeping with the first millennium BC date of the tablet itself, which is established by topographical terms in the map, in addition to the word *marratu*, as already mentioned. There were certainly eight *nagûs* originally. All are of the same size and shape, and where the tablet is still preserved we can see that the distance between them, travelling round parallel to the circular rim, varies between six and eight *bēru* or double hours, a measurement conventionally translated as 'Leagues'.

The Babylonian Map of the World, back view.

The whole of the reverse is given over to a description of these eight *nagû*s, stating that in each case it is the same seven-League distance across the water to reach them, and describing what is to be found on arrival. It is heart-breaking that such an interesting text is so broken, but as seasoned Assyriologists we are now resigned to the rule that the choicer the context the harder it will be to decipher.

While it has been argued that the map in its present form cannot be older than the ninth century BC – for this is the time when the word *marratu* is first used for sea, for example – in my opinion the conceptions behind the map and the description of the eight *nagûs* are much older, originating in the second millennium BC; in fact dating back to the Old Babylonian period in which the *Ark Tablet* was written. This can be concluded from the description's very spellings, for the words are written in plain syllables in a style abhorred in first-millennium literary manuscripts, where ideograms, as found in the first twelve lines of this same tablet, are usually favoured. With this in mind we find ourselves with a cosmological system and tradition that is much older than the document on which it is written. The nature of the Map of the World tablet falls thereby into sharper focus: it represents an old tradition partly overlaid with later data or speculative ideas. The scribe at any rate tells us that his production is a copy from an older manuscript.

The world in the map is portrayed as a disc, and we can therefore assume that the world itself was generally visualised in the same way at the time when the map originated. The circular waterway *marratu*, which is written with the determinative for river, derives from the verb *marāru*, 'to be bitter'. Since this word, although marked with the river sign, certainly means sea in other texts, we translate it here as 'Ocean', although 'Bitter Sea' or 'Bitter River' are equally possible. In eight directions, beyond that water, lie the *nagûs*. In the first millennium BC this word has a very practical meaning, used of regions or districts that are politically or geographically definable and literally within normal reach. In the *mappa mundi*, however, the meaning is quite different. These eight *nagûs* are giant mountains beyond the rim of the world which are unimaginably remote. Although necessarily depicted as triangles they must be understood as mountains whose tips would gradually appear above the horizon as they were approached across the Great Ocean.

In placing the mountainous *nagûs* in this position the cosmologists were answering with simplicity an unanswerable question: what lies beyond the horizon? It is rational to assume that there would eventually always be water, for all land known to man is fringed with water, but once across the *marratu*, what then? According to this system the world is hedged around by eight immense and unreachable mountains, which enclose the world like a fortress. Beyond that was the sky, or nothing, however you liked to look at it.

This geographical actuality is explicit in the tag at the end of the document, which refers to the Four Quarters of the World as the stage on which the eight-fold triangle descriptions play out. This grand expression, in Sumerian or Babylonian, had been favoured by the kings of Mesopotamia to express the breathtaking reach of their kingdoms since time immemorial. The understanding of the map in its original incarnation therefore is that all outlying geography is situated on the flat; travel outwards across the ocean ring and there the traveller will find these remote mountain land masses waiting with their curious occupants or larger-than-life features. On the other hand the triangles that ring the circular world could also be conceived to point up into the heavens, so that the map, drawn on the flat, represents a world like an eight-pointed crown.

In as much as they are decipherable the eight descriptions that accompany the *nagûs* read as if presented by a very bold traveller returned, passing on his discoveries and explaining as best he could what marvels could be expected by anyone who followed in his footsteps. The tone feels like a digest of heroic journeys and exotic traditions, reduced to a formula. Who might such a traveller be? Some Babylonian proto-Argonaut, sailing fearlessly across horizons in search of adventure and the unknown? A highly intrepid merchant, returning home full of wonderful tales and dining off them ever since? Or, might it not rather be some observer who could fly over the world beyond the ends of the earth? After all, the whole map is a bird's-eye view, and the original compiler of this account, whoever he was, did have a dad called *Bird*, as we can see from the last line of the tablet.

Flying over the whole in English translation, *nagû* by *nagû*, we can encounter just a glimpse of the miraculous features far below.

Nagû I
   Traces of an introductory line in very small writing
   [*To the first, to which you must travel seven*
      Leagues, . . .]
   . . . they carry (?) . . .
   . . . great . . .
   . . . within it . . .

Nagû II
   [*To the second*], *to which you must travel seven*
      Leagu[*es, ...*]
   . . .

Nagû III
   [*To the third*], *to which you must travel seven*
      Leagu[*es, . . .*]
   . . . [*where*] *wingéd* [*bi*]*rds cannot fla*[*p their own*
      wings . . .]

Nagû IV
   [*To the fo*]*urth, to which you must travel seven*
      Lea[*gues, . . .*]
   [*The . . .*] *. . . are as thick as a* parsiktu-*vessel; 10*
      fingers [*thick its . . .*]

Nagû V

[*To the fift*]*h, to which you must travel seven Leagues,*
   [. . .].
[*The Great Wall,*] *its height is 840 cubits;* [. . .].
[. . .] . . . , *its trees up to 120 cubits;* [. . .].
[. . . *by da*]*y he cannot see in front of himself* [. . .].
[. . . *by night (?)*)] *lying in* . . . [. . .].
[. . . *you*] *must go another seven* [*Leagues* . . .].
[. . . *in the s*]*and (?) you must* . . . [. . .].
[. . .] . . . *he will* . . . [. . .].

Nagû VI

[*To the sixt*]*h, to which you must travel* [*seven*
   Leagues, . . .].
[. . .] . . . [. . .]

Nagû VII

[*To the sevent*]*h, to which you must travel* [*seven*
   Leagues, . . .].
. . . [. . .] *oxen with horns* . . .];
They can run fast enough to catch wild [*animals* . . .].

Nagû VIII

To the [*eight*]*h, to which you must travel seven*
   Leagu[*es,* . . .];
[. . .] . . . *the Very Hairy One comes out of his gate*
   (?).

Summary:

[*These are the* . . .] . . . *of the Four Quarters, in*
   every . . .
[. . .] . . . *whose mystery no one can understand.*

Scribal family:
[. . .] . . . *written and checked against the original,*
[*The scribe* . . .], *son of Bird, descendant of Ea-bel-ili.*

The mountainous *nagûs*, as far as we can judge from the broken text, are thus each home to remarkable things; the third has (giant?) flightless birds; the fifth the 420-metre-high Great Wall which is labelled on the map itself, with forests of giant 60-metre trees; the sixth (giant?) oxen that can outrun and devour the wild beasts themselves. Unfortunately, due to damage the first, second and sixth *nagûs* can now tell us almost nothing.

Close-up of Babylonian Map of the World, front view, showing Urartu, the Ocean and Nagû *IV, the original home of the Ark.*

It is the *fourth nagû*, however, which houses the greatest discovery. We can now understand, thanks to the *Ark Tablet*, that it is on that particular mountain, remote beyond the rim of the world, that the round Babylonian ark came to rest. These lines, compellingly, have to be read in the original:

> [*a-na re*]-*bi-i na-gu-ú a-šar tal-la-ku* 7 KASKAL.GÍ[D
> . . .]
> [*To the fo*]*urth* nagû, *to which you must travel seven
> Leag*[*ues*, . . .]
> [*šá* GIŠ *ku*]*d-du ik-bi-ru ma-la par-sik-tu*₁ 10 ŠU.S[I
> . . .]
> [*Whose lo*]*gs* (?) *are as thick as a* parsiktu-*vessel; ten
> fingers* [*thick its* . . .].

The first broken word in the second line, must, I think, be the
uncommon Akkadian noun *kuddu*, 'a piece of wood or reed, a
log'. This is described as being 'as thick as a *parsiktu*-vessel', the
same curious phrase that is applied to the giant coracle ribs in
the *Ark Tablet*: 'I set in place in thirty ribs, that were one *parsiktu*-
vessel thick, ten *nindan* long.' As discussed in Chapter 8, the
comparison 'thick as a *parsiktu*-vessel', which expresses thickness
in terms of volume, does not occur in other texts, and corresponds
to our own 'thick as two short planks'. The image must have
remained permanently tied to Atra-hasīs's Ark and have always
been associated with it, and it here surfaces in the Map of the
World in what is, to all intents and purposes, a quotation from
the Old Babylonian story.

In the map inscription the equivalent 'logs' or 'woodblocks'
is used, referring to the 'ribs'. Each of Atra-hasīs's coracle ribs
is ten *nindan* long, which comes out at sixty metres, and about
fifty centimetres thick. Where was Atra-hasīs's carpenter to
procure wood of this size in southern Babylonia? It might well
be that the Map of the World answers this question too, for it
tells us that trees of exactly the desired sixty-metre length grew
in the adjacent *Nagû* V. Gilgamesh's punting poles mentioned
in Chapter 8 were a mere thirty metres in comparison. It looks
as if '*ten fingers* [*thick its* . . .]', takes the place of '*ten* nindan
long', and probably refers to the thickness of the bitumen coating
(measured in fingers in *Ark Tablet* 18–22), with the number
'bumped up' as we have seen happen with other Ark numbers,

for great lumps of bitumen might well have been scattered over a wide area.

As I understand it, the description of *Nagû* IV in the Map of the World describes the giant ancient ribs of the Ark. We can imagine Atra-hasīs's great craft askew on top of that craggy peak, the bitumen peeling, the rope fabric long ago rotted away or eaten, and the arched wooden ribcage stark against the sky like a whitened, scavenged whale. The rare adventurer who makes it to the fourth *nagû* will see for himself the historic remains of the world's most important boat.

This, then, is really something new. The oldest map in the world, safe and mute behind its museum wall of glass, tells us now where the Ark landed after the Flood! After 130 years of silence this crumbly, famous, much-discussed lump of clay divulges an item of information that has been sought after for millennia and still is!

But, there is more to be said. If it is established that the fourth *nagû* is the landing spot, can we identify on the map which of the eight *nagûs* is in fact number IV? The answer to this is, thankfully, in the affirmative.

The newly adhered *nagû* with the Great Wall as advertised on television allows us to do what has previously been impossible, namely to relate the eight mountains on the map to the eight descriptions on the back. The Horsley Triangle simply has to be the fifth *nagû*. How does it work? Observe the following 'points':

New readings coaxed out of the fragmentary description of *Nagû* V mean that this can now be safely identified with the 'Great Wall' *nagû* shown on the map. This is the one at the top pointing more or less north when the tablet is held in the normal reading position, and is the *nagû* shrouded in darkness.

From this fixture we can deduce that *Nagû* I is the completely lost *nagû* which once pointed due south.

We now have to decide whether the sequence I–VIII runs clockwise or anticlockwise in order to locate the other six *nagûs* correctly.

The triangle annotations in cuneiform were probably inscribed by the scribe on the tablet in an *anticlockwise* sequence. The legends will naturally have begun with the left *nagû*s, probably with west, because cuneiform writing runs from left to right, and proceeded triangle by triangle downwards, again because writing proceeds from top to bottom. The tablet will have been slightly rotated in a clockwise direction for each *nagû* so that the legend could be comfortably inscribed below the lower arm of each triangle. This process was followed throughout the eight, since the writing for the northeast *nagû* is upside-down for the reader.

I read the sequence therefore, *anticlockwise*, following the order of physical writing. This is not problematical; there are other Babylonian sky diagrams on tablets that run anticlockwise too. Given that, we conclude that *Nagû* IV, the *Home for Lost Arks*, is that which still survives on the map to the immediate right of the Great Wall *Nagû* V. With the help of the map we can now see how to get there.

The ark *nagû* can be reached most conveniently by travelling straight through the place called Urartu in the northeast of the Mesopotamian heartland – as it is depicted and named (Uraštu, in fact) on the map – and onwards in the same direction, crossing the *marratu* that encircled the world to the mountain that lay directly beyond at the very end of the world. This was the original conception of what happened to Atra-hasīs's Ark. It had been carried by the floodwaters beyond the rim of the world, across the enclosing Ocean which must itself at that moment have been overwhelmed by the onrush, coming to rest on the fourth of the eight remote *nagû*s which were the furthest outposts of human imagination. And, except for heroes, unreachable. And anyone interested had first to get to Urartu.

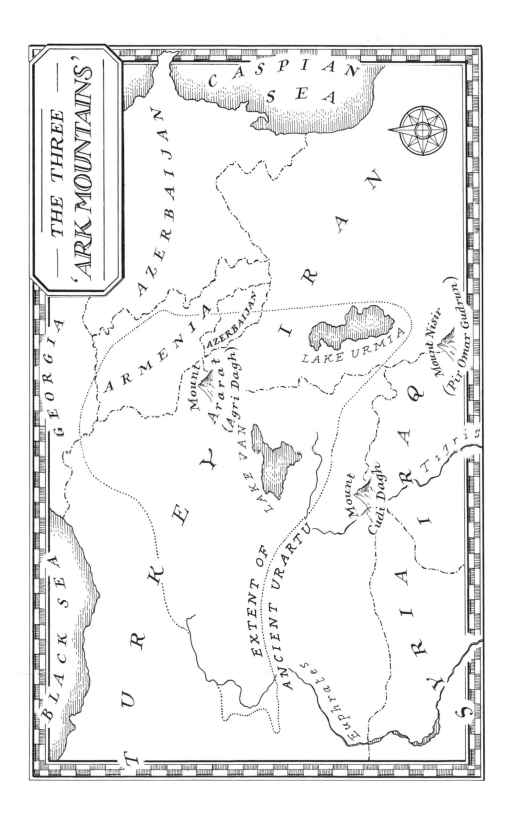

THE THREE
'ARK MOUNTAINS'

CASPIAN SEA

GEORGIA

AZERBAIJAN

ARMENIA

AZERBAIJAN

IRAN

TURKEY

BLACK SEA

Mount Ararat (Agri Dagh)

LAKE URMIA

LAKE VAN

Mount Nisir (Pir Omar Gudrun)

IRAQ

Tigris

Mount Cudi Dagh

EXTENT OF ANCIENT URARTU

Euphrates

SYRIA

Biblical Mount Ararat

In a world where quiz shows love to provoke people into giving a knee-jerk answer that is then triumphantly condemned as wrong I suspect that Mount Ararat might often feature. It is a widespread belief that Noah's Ark came to rest on 'Mount Ararat', the defence of the proposition being that it 'says so in the Bible'. In a way it does, but with one important rider:

> *At the end of 150 days the waters had abated, and in the seventh month, on the seventeenth day of the month, the Ark came to rest on the mountains of Ararat. And the waters continued to abate until the tenth month; in the tenth month, on the first day of the month, the tops of the mountains were seen.*
>
> Genesis 8:3–5

The Hebrew text speaks of 'mountains' in the *plural*, so the key passage means 'in the mountains of Ararat', much as we would say, 'in the Alps'. We cannot therefore really translate this as if it meant one particular mountain called 'Mount Ararat', but this understanding is very ancient and, as it turns out, represents a respectable tradition of its own. (Mt. Ararat is, incidentally, only the modern name. The venerable Armenian name is Massis; the equivalent Turkish name is Agri Dagh.)

The account in Genesis about the fate of the Ark came along, as discussed in the previous chapter, as part and parcel of the whole Flood Story, and there is every reason to assume that this matter too reflects Babylonian tradition. We can now see that, in broad terms, this is in fact the case. Biblical Ararat corresponds to the ancient name Urartu, which was the ancient political and geographical entity due north of the Mesopotamian heartland included in the Map of the World.

Judaeo-Christian tradition, following the Genesis passage, always identified Noah's mountain with what is now called Mount Ararat, on the basis that it was a 'huge mountain somewhere to

An Ottoman
Turkish miniature
with the prophet
Nuh in his Ark.

Noah sends out his
raven and his first
dove in a mosaic from
St Mark's Basilica,
Venice, eleventh-century.

The Tower of Nebuchadnezzar's Babylon, as visualised by an unknown
sixteenth-century Flemish painter.

The Babylonian *mušhuššu* dragon, sacred to the God Marduk, that bedecked King Nebuchadnezzar's royal walls at Babylon, probably modelled on a giant and carnivorous monitor lizard.

The traditional view of the Judaeans grieving at Babylon, as described in Psalm 137. But, as shown in this book, much happened after the first tears dried…

The Babylonian Map of the World, front view:
the world's oldest usable map.

The Babylonian Map of the World, back view:
an old photograph of the hard-to-read triangle descriptions.

The profile of Mount Pir Omar Gudrun, near Kirkuk, northern Iraq.

An eternal icon: a rainbow over Mt. Ararat hidden by storm clouds; seen from Dogubeyazit, Turkey.

Gertrude Bell's view from Mt. Cudi Dagh.

The twin peaks of Mt. Ararat,
irresistible to romantic painters.

The author battling with broken *Ark Tablet* signs in the British Museum.

the north', in the area they knew to be called Ararat. Mount Ararat, located in northeastern Turkey near the borders with Iran and Armenia between the Aras and Murat rivers, is by far the highest mountain in the whole area. The mountain is a dormant volcano with two snowy peaks (the Greater Ararat and the Lesser Ararat). Mt. Ararat is, however, only the modern name. The venerable Armenian name is Massis; the equivalent Turkish name is Agri Dagh. To anyone who knew the story it would be the unmistakable location, easily the first that would have appeared above the waters, with ice-pack resources that could easily accommodate and preserve an ark. Everybody knew that the further north you went the more mountains there were, even if they had never been anywhere near them.

Assyrian Mount Niṣir

The Ark mountain denoted in the *mappa mundi* was not, however, the only Ark mountain that existed in the Mesopotamian world. An alternative comes with the classical authority of the seventh-century BC Assyrian Gilgamesh story, the only surviving cuneiform flood account that refers to the manner in which Utnapishti's Ark came to rest. I translate these lines as follows:

> *The flood plain was as flat as my roof;*
> *I opened a vent and the sunlight fell on the side of my face;*
> *I squatted down and stayed there, weeping;*
> *Tears pouring down the side of my face.*
> *I scanned the horizon in every direction:*
> *In twelve [var. fourteen] places emerged a* nagû.
> *On Mount Niṣir the boat ran aground.*
> *Mount Niṣir held the boat fast and did not let it move.*
> *One day, a second day, Mount Niṣir held the boat fast and did not let it move.*
> *A third day, a fourth day, Mount Niṣir held the boat fast and did not let it move.*

279

> *A fifth, a sixth, Mount Niṣir held the boat fast and did not*
>   *let it move.*
> *When the seventh day arrived . . .*
>
> *Gilgamesh XI: 136–47*

As the waters receded at least twelve, possibly fourteen *nagûs* became visible. This is the same specific term that we have encountered in the Map of the World, and here we are informed that they became visible as the floodwaters subsided. One particular *nagû*, at any rate, was called **Mount Niṣir**, and it was on this spot that Utnapishti's Ark came securely to rest. The other eleven (or thirteen) are unnamed. The information here is given in the reverse order to the biblical tradition. Utnapishti sees and counts the mountain tops before his Ark comes to rest on one of them. When the bottom of Noah's Ark caught fast (October 17th), the tips of no other mountains were yet visible and it took a further three months before the slowly descending waters could reveal them (January 1st).

The Gilgamesh *nagû* was originally called 'Mount Nizir' by George Smith in 1875, and this version of the name, or the form Niṣir, is still the one often encountered in books. The uncertainty as to the correct reading arises because the second cuneiform sign in the writing of the name (with which it is always spelt) can be read both -*ṣir* and -*muš*. It was not until 1986 that the alternative reading 'Nimuš' was seriously proposed, although I still prefer **Mount Niṣir** because this is the Mesopotamian name for the mountain and the Babylonian root behind it, *naṣāru*, 'to guard, protect', makes very good sense given the emphasis in this very *Gilgamesh* passage on how the mountain holds the Ark fast and will not let it move.

Mount Niṣir is an altogether different proposition to the Old Babylonian mountain of the *mappa mundi*. It was no remote, mythological conceit confined to the world of the poet or the wanderer, for the Assyrians knew exactly where it was, and so do we. **Mount Niṣir** is part of the Zagros mountain range, located

280

in what is today Iraqi Kurdistan, near Suleimaniyah. An Assyrian exorcistic spell explicitly describes Mount Niṣir as 'the mountain of Gutium', the latter an old geographical term for the Zagros range. The mountain is mentioned by name in a very matter of fact manner as a landmark in the military annals of the Assyrian king Ashurnasirpal II (883–859 BC) recounting a punitive campaign in the ancient kingdom of Zamua, formerly Lullubi. To an Assyrian, in other words, Mount Niṣir was *just over the border.*

This means that when Utnapishti looked out from his window and saw a dozen or more *nagûs*, of which Mount Niṣir was one, they were all inside the circle of the known world. The territory on which all those mountains stood to peek above the water lay within familiar, earthly geography. Here, accordingly, we witness at first-hand a drawing-in mechanism whereby the fabled, formerly unreachable icon is wound in like a fish until it is within desired range. The new location deprives the story of almost all of its 'somewhere far beyond the most distant north' quality. I cannot help but think that this prosaic attitude to the whole story correlates directly with the image of Utnapishti himself in *Gilgamesh XI,* careful to load his boat with gold and silver and a group of experts and only those animals that could be rounded up with the minimum of effort. We see here the Old Babylonian narrative diminished on all fronts.

Topographical evidence makes it certain that Mount Niṣir is to be identified with Pir Omar Gudrun, as has been shown especially by the scholar Ephraim Speiser, wandering through the terrain himself:

Ashurnasirpal starts from Kalzu early in the fall of 881 and, having passed Babite, directs his troops towards the Niṣir mountain. That mountain, 'which the Lullu call Kinipa', is the famous mount of the Deluge Tablet (141) on which the Flood-ship finds a resting place. The identification of Niṣir with Pir Omar Gudrun may be considered as absolutely certain. I have tried to indicate above how impressive the peak appears at close range. But its remarkably-shaped top, especially when snow-capped, also attracts the eye from a great distance. Often visible for more than a hundred miles, it was to the Babylonians the most natural place to perch their ark upon; the hub of the Universe has been placed at times in far less unusual spots.

Here is King Ashurnasirpal's official ninth-century-BC account, translated out of his cuneiform annals:

On the fifteenth day of the month Tishri I moved on from the city Kalzi (and) entered the pass of the city Babitu. Moving on from the city Babitu I approached Mount Niṣir, which the Lullu call Mount Kiniba. I conquered the city Bunāši, their fortified city which (was ruled by) Muṣaṣina, (and) 30 cities in its environs. The troops were frightened (and) took to a rugged mountain. Ashurnasirpal, the hero, flew after them like a bird (and) piled up their corpses in Mount Niṣir. He slew 326 of their men-at-arms. He deprived him (Muṣaṣina) of his horses. The rest of them the ravines (and) torrents of the mountain swallowed. I conquered seven cities within Mount Niṣir, which they had established as their strongholds. I massacred them, carried off captives, possessions, oxen (and) sheep from them, (and) burnt the cities. I returned to my camp (and) spent the night. Moving on from this camp I marched to the cities in the plain of Mount Niṣir, which no one had ever seen. I conquered the city Larbusa, the fortified city which (was ruled by) Kirteara, (and) eight other cities in its environs. The troops were frightened (and) took to a difficult mountain. The mountain was as jagged as the point of a dagger. The king with his troops climbed up after them.

I threw down their corpses in the mountain, massacred 172 of their fighting men, (and) piled up many troops on the precipices of the mountain. I brought back captives, possessions, oxen, (and) sheep from them (and) burnt their cities. I hung their heads on trees of the mountain (and) and burnt their adolescent boys and girls. I returned to my camp (and) spent the night.

> *I tarried in this camp. 150 cities belonging to the cities of the Larbusu, Dūr-Lullumu, Bunisu, (and) Bāra – I massacred them, carried off captives from them, (and) razed, destroyed, (and) burnt their cities. I defeated 50 troops of the Bāra in a skirmish in the plain. At that time awe of the radiance of Aššur, my lord, overwhelmed all the kings of the land Zamua (and) they submitted to me. I received horses, silver, (and) gold. I put all the land under one authority (and) imposed upon them (tribute of) horses, silver, gold, barley, straw, (and) corvée.*

In fact the literal Assyrian description of **Mount Niṣir** here is, *'the mountain presented a cutting edge like the blade of a dagger'*, which certainly matches the profile of Pir Omar Gudrun.

So what did those Assyrians think in the ninth century BC as they skirted the great mountain and gazed in awe at the jagged profile that hung remote above them? Had Gilgamesh and the Flood Story not been dinned into their youthful ears? Did not each man, from King Ashurnasirpal down, wonder whether the great boat was still there, and speculate on his chances of making it to the top to see? The king went up at least part of the way, but nothing is said anywhere about any arks.

In principle I find this strange, but perhaps they were all too busy, or maybe there had been Ark expeditions there long before. I do not believe that soldiers had no time for 'fairytales' or that the topic was simply never mentioned. If only one of them had written a letter home . . .

The appearance of **Mount Niṣir** in *Gilgamesh XI* exemplifies an important process within Ark history in general, for the Assyrian tradition must surely be a reaction against the much older Babylonian one, rejecting the 'far beyond Urartu' idea to reposition the Magic Mountain much nearer home. It is now in a far more convenient mountainous range, the Zagros. In the first millennium BC this area was usually under Assyrian control and thus safe and accessible, but at the same time conveniently 'other' to some extent. But the fact is, any Assyrian with a rope and a packet of sandwiches could go Ark-hunting in the secure knowledge that he had the right mountain.

The Assyrians certainly picked a very suitable-looking mountain for the purpose. What is beyond our knowing is when this revised tradition first took root, and, perhaps, what provoked the change. Ashurnasirpal gives both the Assyrian, Niṣir, and the local name, Kinipa, for the mountain in his account, possibly reflecting care to establish that **Mount Niṣir** was *the* mountain. In addition – although this is a bit of a long shot – the mention of **Mount Niṣir** *four* times in the *Gilgamesh XI* passage might also be significant. While the repetition might simply be a hangover from a rather heavy-handed oral technique, it seems equally possible on re-reading that it was designed to establish clearly which the mountain in question was – whatever other people might have said – and to use the authority of the classical text to guarantee its identification.

One day an Old Babylonian tablet with the Ark-landing episode will come to light. If that mountain turns out to be called **Mount Niṣir**, like in Assyria, I will need to buy an edible hat.

Islamic Cudi Dagh

While the story of Nuh and the Flood within Islam is strongly connected with the biblical tradition, there was a divergence in tradition with regard to the mountain.

> *Then it was said, 'Earth, swallow up your water, and sky, hold back,' and the water subsided, the command was fulfilled. The Ark settled on Mount Judi . . .*
>
> Sura 11:44

Cudi Dagh (pronounced Judi Dah) is located in southern Turkey near the Syrian and Iraqi borders at the headwaters of the River Tigris, just east of the present Turkish city of Cizre (Jazirat ibn Umar). It is a good two hundred miles south of Mt Ararat and represents in every way an alternative Ark Mountain.

Certain Islamic authorities fill out the picture of this mountain:

The ark stood on the mount el-Judi. El-Judi is a a mountain in the country Masur, and extends to Jezirah ibn 'Omar which belongs to the territory of el-Mausil. This mountain is eight farasangs from the Tigris. The place where the ship stopped, which is on top of this mountain, is still to be seen.

Al-Mas'udi (869–956)

Al-Mas'udi also says that the Ark began its voyage at Kufa in central Iraq and sailed to Mecca, circling the Kaaba before finally travelling to Mount Judi where it settled.

Ibn Haukal (travelling 943–69)

Joudi is a mountain near Nisibin. It is said that the Ark of Noah (to whom be peace!) rested on the summit of this mountain. At the foot of it there is a village called Themabin; and they say that the companions of Noah descended here from the ark, and built this village.

Ibn al-'Amid or Elmacin (1223–74)

Heraclius departed thence into the region of Themanin (which Noah – may God give him peace! – built after he came forth from the Ark). In order to see the place where the Ark landed, he climbed Mount Judi, which overlooks all the lands thereabout, for it is exceedingly high.

Zakariya al-Qazwini (1203–83)

This last writer records that there was still, at the time of the Abbasids, a temple on Mount Judi which was said to have been constructed by Noah and covered with the planks of the Ark.

Then Rabbi Benjamin of Tudela, who travelled extensively in the Middle East in the twelfth century, recorded this intriguing account:

> *Thence [from a place on the Khabur river] it is two days to*
> *Geziret Ibn Omar, which is surrounded by the river Hiddekel*
> *(Tigris), at the foot of the mountains of Ararat. It is a distance*
> *of four miles to the place where Noah's Ark rested, but Omar*
> *ben al Khataab took the ark from the two mountains and made*
> *it into a mosque for the Mohammedans. Near the Ark is the*
> *Synagogue of Ezra to this day.*
>
> Adler 1907: 33

Jezirat Ibn Omar is the village at the foot of Cudi Dagh where
Rabbi Benjamin undoubtedly saw the mosque for himself. What
is especially interesting about this is that the rabbi, who knew
as well as anyone the details of the antecedent Jewish tradition
and the real meaning of the mountains of Ararat in Genesis 8,
is evidently happy to accept the recycled Ark as the genuine item.
In describing Cudi Dagh as being 'at the foot of the mountains
of Ararat' it seems that he is attempting to reconcile the biblical
location with this one, confirming this in remarking that the
ancient synagogue is still there, 'near the Ark', and perhaps by
referring to the twin mountains. When his account was written,
therefore, it was clearly not only Moslems who believed that this
was the resting place. A similar view is propounded by Eutychius,
Patriarch of Alexandria in the ninth to tenth century: '*The Ark*
rested on the mountains of Ararat, that is Jabal Judi near Mosul'
– unless this means that the name Ararat was at times applied
to Cudi Dagh.

The same mountain played the same role in local Christian
tradition. Much earlier, there was an early Nestorian monastery
on top of Cudi Dagh, as the remarkable Gertrude Bell described
in 1911, although where she got the 'Babylonian' evidence to
which she refers so offhandedly defeats me entirely:

> *The Babylonians, and after them the Nestorians and the*
> *Moslems, held that the Ark of Noah, when the waters subsided,*
> *grounded not upon the mountain of Ararat but upon Jûdî Dâgh.*

To that school of thought I also belong, for I have made the pilgrimage and seen what I have seen . . . And so we came to Noah's Ark, which had run aground in a bed of scarlet tulips. There was once a famous Nestorian monastery, the Cloister of the Ark, upon the summit of Mount Jûdî, but it was destroyed by lightning in the year of Christ 766. Upon its ruins, said Kas Mattai, the Moslems had erected a shrine, and this too has fallen; but Christian, Moslem and Jew still visit the mount upon a certain day in the summer and offer their oblations to the prophet Noah. That which they actually see is a number of roofless chambers upon the extreme summit of the hill. They are roughly built of unsquared stones, piled together without mortar, and from wall to wall are laid tree-trunks and boughs, so disposed that they may support a roofing of cloths, which is thrown over them at the time of the annual festival. This is Sefinet Nebi Nuh, 'the ship of the Prophet Noah'.

The top of Mt. Cudi Dagh, as photographed by Gertrude Bell in 1909.

The enduring, cross-religion importance of Cudi Dagh as the Ark's landing site encourages me to ask whether its earliest association with the Ark did not precede the arrival of Christianity, but rather goes back to a Mesopotamian tradition.

In 697 BC, four years after his much discussed unsuccessful attempt to capture Jerusalem, Sennacherib, king of Assyria (705–681 BC), was on campaign again. (It would be another hundred years before Nebuchadnezzar's successful Judaean siege.) This fifth campaign took him northwards, over the border into the land of Urartu, to deal – as Assyrian kings so often had to do – with a conglomeration of local rulers who needed straightening out. They pitched camp, he tells us in his own account of the proceedings, at the foot of Mt Nipur. We know for certain that Nipur was the contemporary Assyrian name for Cudi Dagh because, at the successful conclusion of the campaign, Sennacherib had a whole row of panels with cuneiform inscriptions commemorating this campaign carved into the base of the mountain depicting himself and proclaiming the might of the Assyrian god Assur. They are still there.

> *On my fifth campaign: The population of the cities Tumurrum, Sharum, Ezama, Kibshu, Halbuda, Qua and Qana, whose dwellings are situated like the nests of eagles, foremost of birds, on the peak of Mount Nipur, a rugged mountain, and who had not bowed down to the yoke – I had my camp pitched at the foot of Mount Nipur.*

Sennacherib was not only present on campaign, like King Ashurnasirpal before him, but he was personally and actively involved. He wanted to get all the way to the top of the mountain, to the point that he was prepared to vacate his sedan chair and proceed painfully on foot to get there:

> *Like a fierce wild bull, with my select bodyguard and my merciless combat troops, I took the lead of them. I proceeded through the gorges of the streams, the outflows of the mountains, (and) rugged slopes in (my) chair. When it was too difficult for (my)*

chair, I leaped forward on my (own) two feet like a mountain goat. I ascended the highest peaks against them. Where my knees became tired, I sat down upon the mountain rock and drank cold water from a water skin to (quench) my thirst.

There is a fragment of sculpture in the British Museum which actually shows Sennacherib climbing a steep mountain path like this, steadied from behind by a sturdy officer. What was going through Sennacherib's mind as he climbed Mount Nipur?

Heaving King Sennacherib up the mountain, tactfully, in a fragment of palace sculpture from Nineveh.

It might have been nothing beyond the fervour of a general on campaign, but one cannot help but wonder if there was not more to it than that. If, for example, there was already some local rumour about the Ark and that particular mountain . . .

Sennacherib had *for certain* known the Flood Story since boyhood and presumably been brought up with the Assyrian idea that **Mount Niṣir** was the Ark Mountain. He must have mused more than once over the nature of Utnapishti's stock of pedigree animals, for we know of his fascination with animals from other countries; as a grown man and powerful king he had a park at Nineveh in which imported natural history specimens could disport themselves freely. More than one writer has pointed out that the number of carved relief panels at Cudi Dagh – eight or nine – was surprising in view of the army's relatively slight achievement there; conceivably the campaign had a deeper significance for Sennacherib than mere army manoeuvres. Perhaps locals at Cudi Dagh had been promoting the Ark idea for a long time – locals at iconic shrines are notoriously persuasive. If so, all the soldiers in the Nipur camp would have bought an amulet or two of the *Real Ark* to take home to their wives. We might imagine that Sennacherib might well think the thing worth checking out for himself while they were there.

Of course it can be replied that this is all supposition and that Sennacherib makes no more mention of Ark hunting than does his predecessor Ashurnasirpal at **Mount Niṣir**. If he found nothing, of course, there would be nothing in the official annals, but there are two slight items of evidence that we can bring before the jury.

EXHIBIT A: A SPOT OF MAGIC

A contemporary Assyrian cuneiform incantation text discloses to us a general awareness that arks were not always to be found on mountains. This spell, which, judging by the handwriting, dates to about 700 BC, is to drive out a *succubus*, a spectral seductress sent in the night to create a nightmare for the sufferer:

> *You are conjured away, Succubus, by the Broad Underworld!*
> *By the Seven, by God Ea who engendered you!*
> *I conjure you away by the wise and splendid God*
> *Shamash, lord of All:*
> *Just as a dead man forgot life,*
> *(Just as) the Tall Mountain forgot the Ark,*
> *(Just as) a foreigner's oven has forgotten its foreigner,*
> *So you, leave me alone, do not appear to me!*

The magical power lies in establishing examples of separation that are irreversible: life is forgotten by the dead; the transitory embers of a traveller are cold for ever. There are many Mesopotamian exorcistic spells that rely on this principle, but this allusion to the Ark (*eleppu*) is unique. To my mind it implies not only familiarity with the Ark-on-the-Mountain idea, but also that there was nothing to be seen of it by then on that mountain, and that, therefore, *someone had been looking for it*. I submit that the use of this motif in an incantation tablet is the consequence of widespread publicity and discussion and an echo of some unsuccessful royal Assyrian hunting expedition to that end. After all, if Sennacherib had really gone up Mount Nipur looking for the Ark, all his army would have known about it, and on their return everybody in the palace, the capital, the surrounding countryside and, before long, probably the entire empire would have known about it too.

EXHIBIT B: AN ENDURING REPUTATION

Sennacherib's wicked siege of Jerusalem in 701 BC and the punishment that followed earned him a good deal of posthumous attention in the rabbinical commentaries of the Babylonian Talmud of the early first millennium AD. One of these passages sees Sennacherib back home, in the temple, *worshipping a plank from Noah's Ark*:

> He then went away and found a plank of Noah's ark. 'This,' said he, 'must be the great God who saved Noah from the flood. If I go [to battle] and am successful, I will sacrifice my two sons to thee,' he vowed. But his sons heard this, so they killed him, as it is written, and it came to pass, as he was worshipping in the house of Nisroch, his god, that Adrammelech and Sharezer his sons smote him with the sword . . .
>
> Babylonian Talmud, *Tractate Sanhedrin 96a*

These sons, according to the underlying passage 2 Kings 19:36–37, murdered their father Sennacherib and fled to Ararat, and the murder is confirmed from contemporary Assyrian sources. That the reality of his murder should be a focus for stories against

Sennacherib is natural, but it is hard to credit that the Ark-plank story could be pure fabrication many hundreds of years later with no kernel of tradition inside it. Again, one wonders if this motif does not echo an Ark-hunting event – this time more successful in that Sennacherib did come home with a bit of wood – that became part of the story tradition around the great Assyrian king. All in all, Sennacherib should have stuck to what his governess taught him.

Cashing In

In comparing the details of the miscellaneous Flood stories it will be remembered that Berossus, the Babylonian priest writing in Babylon in the third century BC, had useful things to tell us. He was certainly a witness to what people were saying about the Ark Mountain in his day, as we know thanks to Polyhistor and Abydenus. For example, Berossus transmitted by Polyhistor:

> *Also he [Xisuthros] told them they were in the country of Armenia. They heard this, sacrificed to the gods, and journeyed on foot to Babylon. A part of the boat, which came to rest in the Gordyaean mountains of Armenia, still remains, and some people scrape pitch off the boat and use it as charms.*

Polyhistor's version sounds like an attempt to harmonise two diverse traditions; Armenia to the north – the survival of the Urartu-and-beyond idea – and the Kurdish (Gordyaean) mountains further south, perhaps by then already centred on Mount Cudi. Berossus as transmitted by Abydenus reads:

> *However, the boat in Armenia supplied the local inhabitants with wooden amulets as charms.*

Considering how little we are otherwise told about the Ark, it is extraordinary how much emphasis is put on the *commercial*

factor. There had obviously been a vigorous local trade in Ark
mementoes with amuletic powers since time immemorial. In these
remarks, in fact, we encounter an early example of the enduring
human hunger for relics, culminating in pieces of the true cross
and the finger bones of the holy. One thinks inevitably of booths
displaying scraps of wood or pitch lining the roads to the foot-
hills. One of their predecessors could easily have furnished
Sennacherib with a heavy-duty plank fit for a king. If this does
not illustrate the unchanging nature of human behaviour I know
not what does.

At this point on our journey we can conclude:

1. The Ark's resting place in Antiquity was a massive religious
   and cultural icon whose significance would be valued and
   appreciated universally; that is, *across borders and across
   religions*. We are operating in timeless terrain with modern
   analogies.
2. Such sites, then as now, were possessed of religious or
   magical power sometimes mixed with commercial
   implications.
3. They will always have attracted pilgrims, tourists and the
   sick.
4. There will always have been the inbuilt likelihood of
   contrast or conflict between the 'real' site and any number
   of rivals or alternatives.
5. The appearance of such rivals may or may not have
   provoked response from the 'first'.

Traditions about where Noah's Ark landed do not need to be
reconciled, therefore; merely understood for what they represent.

Conclusions

The written and illustrated tradition of the Babylonian Map of
the World is the oldest information we have; it encapsulates Old

Babylonian ideas of the early second millennium BC which are a thousand years older than the tablet on which it is preserved. According to this the Ark came to rest on a very remote, gigantic mountain, located far beyond Urartu on the other side of the world-encircling Ocean, far indeed beyond the ken of man. To find the Ark, in other words, would have meant travelling to and through Urartu and virtually into infinity beyond. This was the traditional view that prevailed from at least 1800 BC, and almost certainly we would find it made explicit had we access to the whole contemporary Flood Story narrative of which the *Ark Tablet* is only part.

Under these circumstances it is far from difficult to understand how Agri Dagh in northeast Turkey became identified as *the* mountain; it was located in the 'right' place and direction in northern Urartu, it had outstanding geological magnificence and plausibility for the role, and, unlike the ethereal mountain of the original conception, it was near and visible and visit-able. This process, if not originally due to the Bible, was certainly confirmed and reinforced by the biblical account, the potency and effect of which was far greater than any tradition that ran before. In response, the mountain actually came to be called Mount Ararat.

This tradition of the original 'somewhere *beyond* Urartu' drawing in closer to 'somewhere *in* Urartu' resulted in, as we may say, the version which has run uninterruptedly ever since; it was old and entrenched by the time of most of the writers who ever wrote about it, and to a large extent it still holds sway today.

By the first half of the first millennium BC the Assyrians, for reasons that are unclear, had instituted a deliberate Ark-mountain change and promoted **Mount Niṣir**. Perhaps the reasons were several.

In 697 BC, if slight clues have been correctly put together, Sennacherib, for whom **Mount Niṣir** was certainly the 'real' Ark Mountain, encounters a second, rival set-up flourishing already at Cudi Dagh. This would be the first evidence for what later became a very strong rival to Mount Ararat and easily outlived the Assyrian **Mount Niṣir**, which disappeared entirely from the field with the fall of Nineveh in 612 BC and was otherwise unheard of until George Smith read the Assyrian library copies in the 1870s, when the name experienced a new lease of life.

Cudi Dagh was successively embraced by Nestorian Christianity and, then, Islamic tradition as the landing place for Noah or Nuh's boat. In the course of time, other, less durable, Ark mountains made their appearance.

Ironically, whatever phenomena adventurers may claim to have found, it is Mount Ararat today that is closest in location and spirit to the original conception of the Babylonian poets.

The Babylonian Map of the World, by the way, is full of other secrets and to wander after them now would take us far beyond this book into cuneiform byways of astrology, astronomy, mythology, and cosmology (at least), brave journeys themselves that cannot be undertaken here. The map story is far from concluded. The map's uniqueness from our point of view, however, does not mean for a minute that it was such a rarity in its own day. On the contrary it is probable that many such maps existed, both on clay and on bronze, fulfilling different functions and even expressing different theories. One reason for this conclusion is that the Babylonian tradition exemplified by the Map of the World found its counterpart in the maps known to historical geographers as 'T-O' or 'O-T' maps, which survived from the Early Middle Ages until perhaps the fifteenth century AD. The origin of this name lies in the fact that these European maps show the world as a disc surrounded by the *mare oceanum*, with a T fixed in the middle that represents the three major waterworks that divide the three parts of the earth. These maps bear an uncanny – and usually unexplained – resemblance to the Babylonian Map of the World, with its N→S River Euphrates transversed by the waterway to the south. The resemblance is such that the European maps seem literally to be a reinterpretation of a Babylonian model.

*A so-called T and O map by Isidore of Seville dating to 1472.
Its antecedents are unmistakable.*

Computerised reconstruction of the Babylonian Map of the World; front view.

That the Babylonian design survived and could exert its influence so long after the event is surely a further demonstration of what followed when Greek mathematicians and astronomers came to investigate Babylonian cuneiform records. Surely they copied whatever they found interesting onto papyrus for consideration and development once they got home, and that would have included any maps and diagrams that they came across in the libraries.

Noah's Ark lands convincingly on the Mountain,
as painted by Aurelio Luini (1545–1593).

13

What is the Ark Tablet?

'We may as well imagine the scene.'
'No, my mind baulks at it.'
'Mine does worse. It constructs it.'

Ivy Compton-Burnett

In pursuit of the Flood Story in its cuneiform incarnations we have subjected the *Ark Tablet* to prolonged decipherment, dissection and discussion. The time has come to face another question: what, in fact, *is* the *Ark Tablet*?

When the text as a whole is read over with the other versions now in mind – *Atrahasis* on the one hand, *Gilgamesh* on the other – a remarkable phenomenon becomes apparent: the *Ark Tablet* contains absolutely no narrative.

On the contrary, a succession of nine speeches takes up the entire quota of sixty lines of text. The god Enki delivers his key speech verbatim to our hero, and the subsequent lines break down very naturally into eight separate report monologues by Atra-hasīs. Each marks an important stage in the unfolding of the plot, but none of those moments is otherwise described or built upon. This is what the *Ark Tablet* looks like when analysed from that perspective:

Speech 1. Enki to Atra-hasīs: 'Wall, wall . . . !' (Lines 1–12)
Speech 2. Atra-hasīs: 'I set in place . . .' (Lines 13–17)
Speech 3. Atra-hasīs: 'I apportioned one finger . . .' (Lines 18–33)
Speech 4. Atra-hasīs: 'I lay me down . . .' (Lines 33–8)
Section 5. Atra-hasīs: 'As for me . . .' (Lines 39–50)

298

Speech 6. Atra-hasīs: 'And the wild animals . . .' (Lines 51–2)

Speech 7. Atra-hasīs: 'I had . . .' (Lines 53–6)

Speech 8. Atra-hasīs: 'I ordered . . .' (Lines 57–8)

Speech 9. Atra-hasīs to the shipwright: 'When I shall have . . .'
        (Lines 59–60)

Substantial, if not vital, plot elements (such as Enki's telling Atra-hasīs what to say to the elders to explain his absence, *or* the strange and ominous rain that will be the sign of the Flood to come, *or* the rather important question of the boat-building time available, *or* the punctual arrival of the workmen with their various tools) are completely left out. All we have is Enki's famous address and Atra-hasīs telling him, and us, what he accomplished, step by step. What is more, Atra-hasīs speaks in the first person: *my* building (past tense); *my* waterproofing, *my* troubles (past tense); *my* order to the shipwright (present tense).

From several standpoints this is quite remarkable. In the more or less contemporary *Old Babylonian Atrahasis* the corresponding elements of the story are couched in the third person by an unseen narrator. It is only in *Gilgamesh XI* that we find this narrative reported in the first person, and here it is perfectly understandable since Utnapishti, who had built the Ark and endured the Flood himself, is reminiscing to Gilgamesh. While it has always been clear that in recycling the old story this shift from third to first person was necessary for Gilgamesh, it is significant to encounter an Old Babylonian Flood Story tradition in which it occurs.

Because of this close perspective, there is certainly more emphasis in the *Ark Tablet* on Atra-hasīs the man and his predicament than is perceptible in *Old Babylonian Atrahasis* (even though this is incomplete at important points), while *Gilgamesh XI* has no time for that side of things at all beyond a rush of tears on landing.

Enki's reassuring tone about boat-building, *You know what sort of stuff is needed for boats*, and *Someone else can do the work* (*Ark Tablet* 11–12), implies that **Atra-hasīs** had protested his inability to do what was wanted, as he does explicitly in *Assyrian Smith* 13–15 ('I have never built a boat . . . Draw the design on the ground that I may see the design and build the boat'). His suffering and address for mercy to the Moon cover the whole of lines 39–50, and when complete must have been a more affecting passage than we can now fully grasp. In *Old Babylonian Atrahasis* there are three terse lines in counterpart.

Side by side with the considerable detail about building and waterproofing there is clearly an attempt to develop the character of **Atra-hasīs** so that he emerges as a person, and to invite sympathy with his predicament.

Think again for a moment what this predicament was: the world and all its life forms were to be destroyed and **Atra-hasīs** alone had the task of ensuring the survival of all species for a post-Flood world. His instructions came from one god who had gone out on a limb to rescue life, while the gods as a body were intransigent and deaf to appeal. He has to get everyone on board, he has to get all living things up the gangplank and meanwhile the water clock is ticking. His boat springs a single leak and that's the end of everything. This is a role for a hero as nerve-racking as that in any contemporary Action Film, in which charismatic actors are usually responsible for saving the world against all odds and under ludicrous time-pressure from something utterly appalling.

There is a further and related oddity that must be registered. There is no indication in the *Ark Tablet* as to *who is speaking*. We have to know that it is the god Enki who speaks at the beginning. From line 13 onwards it is up to us to understand that the man **Atra-hasīs** is speaking since the change of speaker goes unmarked. But to whom is he talking, in recounting his achievements? And who would guess from the tablet alone that the last two lines are addressed to his (unmentioned) shipwright?

This unusual situation is due to the fact that the tablet omits all outbreaks of the conventional literary structure – *Anu opened his mouth to speak, saying to the lady Ishtar* . . . followed by *Ishtar opened her mouth to speak, saying to her father, Anu* . . .

Gilgamesh VI: 87–88; 92–93

– with which Babylonian narrative literature is, not to put too fine a point on it, slightly tiresomely littered. In fact, I cannot come up with another example of Babylonian mythological or epic literature that is devoid of this characteristic speech-linking device. Its repetitive nature at first sight looks like a remnant of oral literature, where things are repeated more than we would repeat them today, which the modern connoisseur of cuneiform literature just has to accept, or appreciate as atmospheric and authentic. On reflection, however, it is just the opposite. The characteristic dependence on this formula originates in the *very transition* from oral to written literature, for who is speaking at any one time will always be clear in a storyteller's presentation, but the process of writing down what has previously been spoken aloud creates ambiguity for the reader unless each speaker is clearly identified.

Assyriologists have long convinced themselves that the stories of which we have written versions circulated for a very long period as oral literature, enjoying a level of freedom and improv-isation that was shut off once the process of formally recording them swung into action, with its inevitable inhibition of literary creativity and variety. The arrival of the second millennium BC was probably the period when the writing down of stories got a substantial push. Before that major step, the story of the Flood was the province of storytellers, although we can feel confident that the arrival of written versions of the stories in urban contexts did not spell the end of storytelling as an art.

Let us imagine one of these Old Babylonian storytellers. Such people surely existed on many levels, from penniless itinerants who followed their muse from village to village, telling stories for a place by the fire and a mess of pottage, to plumper professionals, patronised by proper kings for when they had had enough of blind harpists, dancing girls and snake charmers or wanted to impress visitors.

Our storyteller is recounting the *Story of Atra-hasīs*, with the Ark, and the Flood. Probably everybody knew the rudiments, but in the hands of a skilled storyteller its power and magic would know no bounds. For he is dealing with the largest possible issues: the life and death of mankind, the narrowest of escapes, how all eggs were entrusted to one big basket, buffeted above heaving waters, all living things crying in terror (or because they were seasick or being squashed). The narrative could be supported with props; a small reed fence for Ea to whisper through, a horned head-dress for the speaking god, a toy coracle for **Atra-hasīs**, a stick to draw in the dust. A popular narrator might muster a simple drummer, a flautist, a boy assistant. With these tools he could transport his audience, telling a story that was always the same but always different; sometimes terrifying with the unsway-able cruelty of the gods and the onrush of deathly waters, some-times soothing with everything turning out all right, maybe sometimes even *funny*, when a dreamer who has never got his hands dirty is told by a god that he has to achieve the impossible *right now* and he doesn't want to. *Why pick on me, already?*

The *Ark Tablet*, however, did not belong to such a wanderer with a head full of narratives learned by heart. It begins at a very dramatic moment, 'Wall, wall! Reed fence, reed fence!' imparting the worst news in the world, and ends equally dramat-ically with everyone sealed in their capsule, waiting for the Deluge. Here we have the words extracted from a much broader sequence of high drama, packaged in such a way as to commence with and pivot on moments of maximum storytelling tension. This cannot be coincidence. On the contrary, it seems to me to under-line the use of this narrative in real storytelling circumstances, a sixty-line, pocket-sized episode that will leave the listeners, by the end, agog. The sound of the first raindrops would be like the closing theme tune for a television series, followed by the announcer's infuriating explanation that everyone will have to wait a whole week for more.

This is not to say that we have here the 'script' of a traditional storyteller, for such things are incompatible. It is rather a note of the essential spoken parts for the roles of Enki – one voice – and Atra-hasīs – the other – which, rationally speaking, can hardly derive from any other use than some kind of public performance. We know from cuneiform texts of street performers, clowns, wrestlers, musicians, people with monkeys; we know of formal cult processions with the boats of the gods in the street; and the public recitation of the Creation Epic at the New Year Festival. Perhaps, in between all these, we might sandwich the *Big Babylonian Atrahasis Show*. Can we not imagine some clear-voiced narrator, our hero swaying between fright, despair and confidence, declaiming his speeches, upright by the end of the story in his travelling boat, with his unspeaking, unnamed wife and sons and a quantity of tame livestock immune to stage-fright? What else, indeed, can our *Ark Tablet* be?

So I had concluded, with this chapter written and virtually ready to send off to my editor, when a colleague notified me of the existence of the following most helpful book:

Claus Wilcke, *The Sumerian Poem* Enmerkar and En-suḫkeš-ana: *Epic, Play, Or? Stage Craft at the Turn from the Third to the Second Millennium B.C. with a Score-edition and a Translation of the Text* (American Oriental Series Essay 12. Newhaven 2002).

The author, Claus Wilcke, has argued in this book that this early Sumerian composition, which reflects tension between the ancient precursors of Iraq and Iran, has a cast of gods and mortals and built-in stage directions. Action varies between Sumer, in the cities of Uruk and Kulaba – at a cattlepen and sheepfold near the city of Eresh, then a gate facing sunrise and on the banks of the Euphrates – after which at Aratta in mountainous Iran – in a priestly residence and at the so-called 'Sorcery

Tree'. The demonstrative role of the narrator can be seen in the grammar, which is full of elements called, in a self-explanatory way, 'demonstratives'. Wilcke derives the action from real events, locating court performance early in the reign of the Sumerian king at Ur, Amar-Sin (c.1981–1973 BC).

As Wilcke very reasonably put it, 'ancient Near Eastern theatre seems at first sight difficult to imagine', and this had troubled me, too, in proposing public performance behind the text of the *Ark Tablet*, but now each case – the one Sumerian, the other Babylonian – reinforces the plausibility of the other. With the *Ark Tablet*, in fact, I think there can be no other possible interpretation.

What can we deduce further? Even formally speaking, the *Ark Tablet* is unusual for a literary document; it looks more like a letter or business record. Literature usually comes larger, with more than one column of writing per side and more text. As literary compositions evolved, the component tablets became fixed in content, so that eventually everyone knew with *Gilgamesh I* how many lines there should be, and how much of the story it covered. With a large composition, tablets recorded as a catchline the first line of the subsequent tablet, assuring the reader of what came next. Tablet 1, line 1, also served as the name for the whole composition, so the *Epic of Gilgamesh* was known to librarians as *He Who Saw the Deep*.

The *Ark Tablet*, in comparison, is small, with one column of text per side, and its total of sixty lines of writing completely fill both obverse and reverse. This is no complete chapter from within a conventional tablet sequence but a very specific and unusual kind of extract, so it is important to try and establish where the underlying full narrative that must lie behind this fits within the tradition.

The tablet begins very abruptly with the celebrated 'Wall, wall! Reed fence, reed fence!' speech (*Old Babylonian Atrahasis* III, col. I 21–2, and *Gilgamesh XI*: 21–2). Behind it probably stands a 'Tablet no. III' of some edition of the full *Atrahasis* story.

(*Old Babylonian Schøyen in Chapter 5* has four columns of text and its content crosses over from *Old Babylonian Atrahasis* Tablet II to III, so it represents a really different structure. From its shape there might have been originally thirty lines per column, giving a rough line total of 120 lines. From several standpoints the *Schøyen* tablet is maybe a century or more older than the most well-known Sippar edition of *Old Babylonian Atrahasis* and can be regarded as the oldest version of the story we have had. For the same reasons it is probably also slightly older than the *Ark Tablet*, but while sign shapes, spelling and other details rule out their being contemporaneous or even the work of a single scribe, it is quite likely that the *Ark Tablet* represents the same Old Babylonian version of the Atra-hasīs story.)

The story of Atra-hasīs, the Ark and the Flood is, by any criteria, *literature*. It is mythological in nature and eventually epic in proportion, but certainly literature. From this standpoint the detailed practical boat-building data embedded in Atra-hasīs's *Ark Tablet* proclamations also comes as a surprise, all the more so given that the technical and practical specifications that we have disentangled in Chapter 8 are not arbitrary or 'mythological' but practical and realistic.

What are technical specs doing in the middle of an exciting story? For most listeners, *What was going to happen next?* was surely more pressing for the listener than do-it-yourself water-proofing!

Two factors could have contributed to the inclusion of the very technical boat-building material.

The primary factor could well be *audience demand*. Recounting the *Atrahasis* story to fisher- or river-folk who built and used boats for their livelihood is likely to have provoked questions from listeners such as, *What did the boat look like? How big was it? Where did all the animals sleep?* This seems to me inevitable, and would demand that any good storyteller had answers ready; a giant coracle would be best because they never sink, everybody would have been in one, animals often rode in them, and each listener could easily imagine 'the biggest coracle you ever saw', portrayed with outstretched arms and gaping eyes. There was no need for dimensions or detail: *The world's biggest coracle* which would need *buckets and buckets of bitumen . . .* The shape, size and interior construction of the vessel could be developed and exaggerated at will, depending on the audience.

Eventually, though, a second phase is reached, when a good deal more 'hard' information than is strictly needed for telling a good story is incorporated. How did this come about? Such material can only derive from *classroom investigation*.

It is of the deepest significance that the quoted 'specs' in this literary document are not only realistic but actually mathematically accurate. Transposed into a modern technical drawing as a model for a building programme the vessel that emerges is lifelike, in proportion to a real coracle, and capable of construction. Such a state of affairs cannot for a moment be accidental. If a story-teller were to improvise figures for the world's largest boat off the top of his head he would take recourse to fairytale measurements, as we have seen, like 'a hundred double-miles' or 'ten thousand leagues'. The input of 'exact' coracle-building and waterproofing data into the story not only inevitably reflects a schoolroom background, but of itself implies that the same issues had been sensibly worked out in the classroom.

Measurement of a practical nature – the number of bricks in a wall, the quantity of barley to feed a gang of workmen – was the bread and butter of the scribal schools once apprentices had learned to read and write to a basic level. It is natural, moreover, that a teacher, attempting to interest inattentive schoolboys in dry mensuration, should light on one novelty or another to secure their attention. Probably it was often necessary. In one contemporary school composition the boys are set to recite Sumerian verbal paradigms, using as a model the verb 'to fart', and it is not hard to imagine that a teacher who opened his lesson with the announcement that *Today we are going to learn 'to fart'* would certainly have commanded full attention for the morning.

So we might hear a teacher remark one morning: Given that the Ark – as every Babylonian knew since the cradle – was the world's largest coracle, if it measured such-and-such a size across and its walls were of such-and-such height to accommodate all the animals, let us ask ourselves, *What was its surface area? How many miles of ropes would you need to build it? How much bitumen would you need to waterproof its surfaces?* All much more fun to work out than prosaic equivalents about canal dykes and mountains of cereal.

It is here that the great ŠÁR or '3,600' measurements are so extraordinary, because, as was freely conceded earlier, any cuneiformist encountering such numerals in a literary context would immediately class them as huge round numbers and nothing more, whereas in the *Ark Tablet* each such numeral is to be taken absolutely at face value. Very large numbers written in bunched-up compounds of ŠÁR signs bring to mind the similar-looking numbers for the giant regnal years before the Flood recorded in the *Sumerian King List*. It is not unlikely that advanced Old Babylonian pupils will have looked at this text with their teacher and discussed such huge numerals, while at the same time it could easily be understood that they might think that Atra-hasīs, being an antediluvian himself, would naturally use antediluvian numbers of this kind in his own calculations. It is surely for this reason that they are used in the *Ark Tablet* to communicate the great measurements needed.

From the school mathematical tablet illustrated on p. 127 we can see that calculation of the area of circles or circles within squares was part of a well-ordered investigation of geometrical matters. We can assume, therefore, that whoever contributed this data to the flow of the *Atrahasis* story must have been put through this particular wringer himself, and that the circle-within-a-square image that underlies the passage in the story reflects his own classroom experience.

Despite the frequency with which boats and bitumen are mentioned in cuneiform texts there is no other text that even alludes to, let alone details, the way in which bitumen had to be applied to a completed boat. Such matters were second nature in the riverside boatyards where coracles were continuously in production and everybody knew inside out what to do, but the calculation of quantities here, crucially, is based on real facts.

Some specific need, or burst of inventiveness, must have led to the incorporation of hard data within this literature. Given our present knowledge, we cannot know whether it was taken up within *Atrahasis* in general, or whether a very human reluctance to cope with figures might not have meant that, for non-boatmen, these hard-won details were really otiose: the narrative of *Gilgamesh XI* at any rate was certainly happy to reduce them to a minimum.

From this standpoint the contrasting lack of detail about the animals that were supposed to be rescued is noticeable. In a different milieu one might have expected a full list, from cockroaches to camels, to assure listening farmers that no species was left behind. Perhaps we are to assume that if anyone called out *Which animals do you mean?* or *What about all the different kinds of snakes?* a good storyteller would have thought that through too and have the answers up their sleeve.

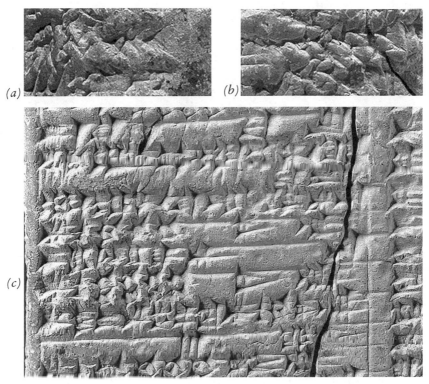

(a) Bunched-up šār signs in Ark Tablet *line 12. (b) More in* Ark Tablet *line 21. (c) The immaculate calligraphy of the šār signs in the Weld–Blundell copy of the* Sumerian King List.

14

Conclusions: Stories and Shapes

Quinquireme of Nineveh from distant Ophir,
Rowing home to haven in sunny Palestine,
With a cargo of ivory,
And apes and peacocks,
Sandalwood, cedarwood and sweet white wine.

John Masefield

I think it is only fair to offer anyone who has actually been reading this book a summary in one place of the conclusions I have reached about the transmission of the Flood Story and the evolving forms of the Ark as a result of these various investigations.

First, as has been widely accepted, the iconic story of the Flood, Noah and the Ark as we know it today certainly originated in the landscape of ancient Mesopotamia, modern Iraq. In a river-dependent land where flooding was a reality and disastrous destruction always remembered, the story was all too meaningful. Life, always at the mercy of the gods, surviving against all odds by means of a single vessel whose crew, human and animal, withstood the cataclysm to repopulate the world. The story in its earliest form must go back, far beyond any writing, into the very distant past, rooted in their circumstances and integral to their very basic existence.

In Mesopotamian terms, the remote world as it existed before the Flood was visualised as the unchanging landscape of the southern Iraqi marshes, where houses and boats were made of reed, and where, to build a lifeboat, the one could easily be recycled as the other. Here, as I see it, the boat type for the early story was naturally long and narrow, high in prow and stern, efficient in movement along the shallow waterways. Larger boats with that basic 'almond' shape were known in Sumerian as a *magur*; the huge version needed in flood circumstances had to be a super *magurgur*.

In the written accounts from the early second millennium BC we encounter two traditions about the shape of the Ark, which sprang from a common ancestor. At Nippur in southern Iraq the original reed *magurgur* tradition persisted unquestioned. Elsewhere, however, we see, starting with the clear description provided by the *Ark Tablet*, that the Ark was a much more practical and appropriate kind of boat, the round coracle. Coracles were not used in the marshes, but were very common on the heartland rivers, especially the Euphrates, as a water taxi that could transport people, livestock and materials from one side to the other with no fear of sinking. Boats of this kind were not made from reed but from coiled palm-rope, being effectively a great basket waterproofed all over. Coracles came in all manner of sizes; the one to do the job for Atra-hasīs would break all records.

I argue, therefore, that the traditional understanding of the boat plan changed from *magur* (long and thin) to coracle (big and round). Evidence is not plentiful, from the second millennium BC we only have two other cuneiform descriptions of the Ark beyond that in the *Ark Tablet*, but both of these – as we can now see – thought of the boat as round, and I see this process as representing an old-fashioned prototype superseded by modern improvement.

Transmission in the early second millennium BC was as much oral as written; in the hands of front-line performers or narrators, such a change in ark model would be natural: it produced better sense and a better story for their listeners. That this change from the ancient idea did come about does not surprise me at all; one relevant factor is that itinerant storytellers would probably usually work with riverside populations for whom the Ark had to be a credible and functional vessel, and a coracle would be just the job, as everyone knew.

Atra-hasīs's round Ark had a base area of 3,600 m² and one deck.

The only other description of a cuneiform ark available to us is the one in the classical Gilgamesh story. Here we are presented with an ark that embodies two important innovations: one, it is neither an almond-*magur* nor a round coracle but a cube with walls of equal length and height; two, this is an ark that to the practical Mesopotamian mind would never work adrift on the bosom of the floodwaters.

As already alluded to, and laid out below in Appendix 2, it is possible to understand how the underlying Old Babylonian coracle of circular plan in which 'length' and 'breadth' were equal could be interpreted in Late Assyrian Gilgamesh as a square plan, and how the Old Babylonian single deck could later develop into six decks, themselves divided into seven parts, sub-divided into nine. This double process is partly due to textual misunderstanding or adjustment, and partly to a kind of midrashic enthusiasm that had Utnapishti's own iconic vessel blossom into something virtually unrecognisable, magnificent-sounding and practically dysfunctional. Nevertheless, the textual clues show that the narrative behind Utnapishti's Ark in *Gilgamesh* certainly derived from the traditional Old Babylonian round coracle.

The next stage of the Flood and Ark story comes from the Book of Genesis. Comparison of the Hebrew text with *Gilgamesh XI* highlights such a close and multi-point relationship between the accounts that the dependence of one upon the other is unavoidable. I have thus maintained in this book what has often been proposed before: that the Hebrew text derives from and is predicated upon a cuneiform flood story forerunner or forerunners, but at the same time I have contributed the first explanation of the mechanisms that enabled that borrowing. In my view the Judaeans' need for their own written history led them to incorporate certain Babylonian stories of early times for which their own traditions were inadequate. These stories had become accessible through the induction of their youthful intelligentsia into cuneiform writing and literature, whereby they encountered and read these stories in the original, as part of the curriculum. The process of literary adoption by the Judaeans imbued already-striking narratives with a fresh and independent moral quality, so that the Great Ages of Man, the Baby in the Coracle and the Story of the Flood experienced a new lease of life far beyond the moment that saw the final extinction of the venerable parent cuneiform traditions.

As we have seen, internal evidence has long been taken to reflect different strands of Hebrew within the biblical text as being the work of authors such as 'J' and 'P', and I have argued that differences between them with regard to the Flood Story are to be explained by distinct traditions within the cuneiform sources from which they are drawn, as in the case of the numbers of animals and birds to be taken on board. Not to be forgotten is one huge new component in this link: the *Ark Tablet*'s revelation that the animals went on board two by two, previously unknown in any cuneiform version and therefore considered to be an innovation in Genesis.

Comparison of Noah's Ark with that of Utnapishti introduces the fourth shape, for Noah's famous Ark is an oblong, coffin-shaped vessel of wood. When arguing for the close dependence of the Genesis Flood Story on the cuneiform heritage the contrast between Utnapishti's cubic Ark (which is all we have for the first millennium BC), and Noah's oblong Ark has previously been problematical and unexplained. Real boats of the Noah kind (described and photographed in the nineteenth century) are also numbered among the traditional river craft of the Land Between the Rivers, and evidence has been offered to identify such oblong craft with the Babylonian boat name *ṭubbû*, which surfaces, reshaped as Hebrew, in the Ark name *tēvāh*, assuming that the same kind of boat is meant by both. In terms of transmission we postulate that a practical oblong *ṭubbû* craft had already found its way into some cuneiform Flood Story (after the Utnapishti-type boat had been contemplated in some scribal circles and found implausible), and that it was this tradition which passed into Hebrew.

Since the whole description of Noah's oblong Ark comes from Hebrew source J we cannot know whether the tradition about the shape in source P contained the same idea or something different. This would mean that the *ṭubbû*-barge was already a valid Babylonian tradition embedded in some version of the cuneiform Flood Story yet to be discovered and also that it was the one favoured by source J.

Most significant here is the fact that the area of the ground plan remained virtually unchanged despite the shifts in shape:

1. Atra-hasīs's round coracle: 14,400 cubits^2 (1 ikû).
2. Utnapishti's cube: 14,400 cubits^2 (120 cubits x 120 cubits = 1 ikû)
3. Noah's Ark: 15,000 cubits^2 (300 cubits by 50 cubits = 1.04 ikû).

The Utnapishti Ark, despite restructuring a circular plan as a square, retains the same 'starting' size of ground plan as originally communicated by Enki to Atra-hasīs, for this was no doubt constant in Old Babylonian texts, on one of which it drew. This shift of circle to square, at first reminiscent of an awkward peg in the hole and hard to dismiss, is after all not so drastic: given that the Old Babylonian 'length' and 'breadth' terms were disassociated from defining the original circle they led naturally to a square, while the identical ground area of 14,400 cubits^2 was retained.

What is more remarkable – and assuredly no coincidence – is that the base area of Noah's Ark is virtually identical to that inherited from cuneiform (within 4 per cent) at 15,000 cubits^2, revealing it unmistakably as a reworking of the same original Babylonian idea, to construct on the same basis a boat of another shape altogether, one typical of practical, heavy-duty, riverine cargo barges.

In this light, the procession from circle to square and square to oblong within a single continuum, at first indigestible and incompatible, becomes explicable, and to my mind reinforces the linear descent from cuneiform into Hebrew, the tracing of which represents the core of the present work.

Seldom has it been that a single cuneiform tablet could engender an entire book. The *Ark Tablet* is so extraordinary that it leads of its own accord to myriad enquiries to which new answers have to be supplied. I close these pages dedicated to decoding the immortal Story of the Flood in the hope that, in doing my best, I have at least launched an idea or two on a voyage of their own.

Appendix 1

Ghosts, the Soul and Reincarnation

Drawings of a male and female ghost for a ritual model. The female ghost is furnished with a male partner to keep her happy and distracted; he walks respectfully behind her with his hands tied.

The Akkadian word for ghost or spirit, the sometimes, somehow visible human form that survives death, is *eṭemmu*, which is a loanword from the older Sumerian word GEDIM with the same meaning. The latter is written with what looks like a particularly elaborate symbol but it actually consists of the cuneiform fraction '1/3' next to two other signs, IŠ and TAR, one written inside the other (which we can best write as IŠxTAR). Ancient Babylonian scholars interpreted the IŠ and TAR signs as the Sumerian words for 'dust,' and 'street,' either thinking of a ghost along the lines of our 'dust into dust,' or perhaps rather some evanescent phenomenon. Either idea makes sense, but no one seems to have explained what the '1/3' element is doing. There is also a second, closely similar sign to GEDIM, which consists of the fraction '2/3' placed next to IŠxTAR. This latter sign is pronounced UDUG in Sumerian, borrowed into Akkadian as *utukku*, and it is the name of a particular kind of troublesome evil demon. Two similar signs for two 'shady' entities, a ghost and a demon.

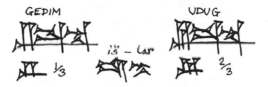

It has occurred to me that the signs IŠxTAR – notwithstanding the ancient interpretation above, can also be understood as a 'fancy' writing of the Akkadian noun *ištar*, 'goddess' (that is, a female divinity, not the famous goddess Ishtar). The sign as a whole could therefore mean that a ghost is either one-third goddess in make-up, or in itself constitutes one third of a goddess. Similarly an *utukku* demon is either two-thirds goddess in make-up or in itself represents two-thirds of a goddess.

Simple understanding comes if we conclude that the ghost or spirit represents one third of the make up of what was the living person, and that this is somehow equivalent to female divinity. The lost two-thirds is therefore flesh and blood.

With an *utukku* demon, which does not teeter on the live-and-die fulcrum, the proportion of feminine divinity is two-thirds. The remaining third, whatever that might be, cannot therefore be analogous to flesh and blood, but is alien and enduring.

Just from the cuneiform sign itself, therefore, we can infer the following suggestive equation:

$$\text{man} = \text{flesh and blood} + \text{divinity}$$

Tablet I of the Old Babylonian *Atrahasis Epic* describes the creation of man by the goddess Nintu out of the body of a slaughtered god. Here are the two passages in translation:

Let the one god be slaughtered
So that all the gods may be cleansed by immersion.
Let Nintu mix clay with his flesh and blood,
Let god and man be thoroughly mixed in the clay,
So that we may hear a heartbeat for the rest of time
Let there be spirit (eṭemmu) from the god's flesh.
Let it proclaim living (man) as its sign,
So that this not be forgotten let there be spirit (eṭcmmu).

Atrahasis I: 208–17

They slaughtered We-ilu, who had reason (ṭēmu),
in their assembly.
Nintu mixed clay with his flesh and blood;
For the rest [of time they heard a heartbeat],
From the flesh of the god [there was] spirit (eṭemmu).
It proclaimed living (man) as its sign,
And so that this was not forgotten [there was] spirit (eṭemmu)

Atrahasis I: 223–30

Mankind according to this account is composed of three divine constituents out of the sacrificed god We-ilu: flesh and blood and reason (*ṭēmu*). Clay, mixed with flesh and blood and animated by *ṭēmu*, generates the human spirit and institutes man's first and never-to-be-interrupted heartbeat. After death it is only the human spirit or *eṭemmu* that endures, while the body – the other two-thirds of 'clay' – returns to the earth.

The Atrahasis passage thus articulates the idea that *ṭēmu* (reason) is the crucial component of *eṭemmu* (human spirit) at the very birth of mankind. The strange name of the sacrificed god, We-ilu, clearly embodies this idea: it is the '*we-*' element (before *ilu*, 'god') that, added to *ṭēmu*, produces *eṭemmu*:

$$we + ṭēmu = eṭemmu$$

One of the known cuneiform source tablets for *Atrahasis* Tablet I actually writes *weṭemmu* instead of *eṭemmu* for spirit in this passage, which has usually been dismissed as an error, but I think it is deliberate and meaningful.

There is also interplay between the Sumerian and Akkadian words, for *ṭēmu* in Akkadian is connected with Sumerian DIMMA, and GEDIM with *eṭemmu*, although the linguistic affiliations are a conundrum. The words *ṭēmu* and *eṭemmu*, so crucially intertwined at creation, were ever after linked with one another. On such a fundamental matter there is, naturally, Babylonian textual speculation available. Let us investigate by looking over the shoulder of a learned *ummānu* (teacher) in about 300 BC. This is real cuneiform stuff, but nothing to be afraid of.

We find our teacher talking about the name of the disease called Hand of a Ghost, which is ŠU.GEDIM.MA in Sumerian, *qāt eṭemmi* in Akkadian, to a handful of advanced students. The teacher defines the nature of an *eṭemmu* from 'inside' its very name, but in a way quite different from what I have just been doing. To separate our words and ideas he uses two wedges one on top of the other exactly as we employ a colon, and adds explanations in tiny gloss script, here printed above the line. Sumerian words are in capital letters and Akkadian in italic, for it is important not to lose sight of which is which.

GEDIM is normally written with the complex sign drawn above. Here the scribe makes use of a second, much rarer sign for this word, which can be pronounced the same way, and which we differentiate as GEDIM₂: Although GEDIM₂ is actually one sign made up of three wedges the teacher for present purposes considers it formed of two parts, BAR (the 'cross' part) and U (the single diagonal).

Here is what he wrote on the tablet:

GI-DI-IM GEDIM₂ (BAR.U) : *eṭemmu*(GEDIM) : *pe-tu-u*
uznē(GEŠTUG^II) : BAR : *pe-tu-u*

U^{BU-UR} : *uz-nu* : *e-ṭem-me* : *qa-bu-ú ṭè-e-me*
E : *qa-bu-u* : KA$^{DE-EM_4-MA}$HI : *ṭè-e-me*

There are two beautiful techniques involved. The first extracts meaning in Akkadian by literally deconstructing a Sumerian sign. The second is more sophisticated: it extracts meaning in Akkadian out of the Sumerian meanings of the syllables used to spell an Akkadian word. Words in bold all occur in the commentary text; everything in brackets is me trying to make it clear for cuneiform apprentices.

TECHNIQUE 1
(The Sumerian sign) GEDIM$_2$ (pronounced) gi-di-im [consisting, as noted, of 'BAR' plus 'U'] is the same as (Sumerian) GEDIM (*eṭemmu*, Akkadian 'ghost' or 'spirit'). The latter means *pētū uznē* (Akkadian 'those that open ears') [in the explanation the word *uznē*, 'ears,' is written with the Sumerian ideogram] GEŠTUG^{II} (because the) BAR (part of GEDIM$_2$ in Sumerian) means *petū* (Akkadian 'to open,' and the) U (part of GEDIM$_2$, when pronounced) *bu-ur* [because U has *multiple* values] has the meaning *uznu* (Akkadian 'ear').

TECHNIQUE 2
e-ṭem-me (this simple, syllabic spelling of the Akkadian word *eṭemmu* can itself be 'interpreted' as Akkadian) meaning *qabû ṭēme* (Akkadian for anything from 'giving orders' to 'speaking with intelligence). This is possible because taking the first Akkadian syllable *e-* as Sumerian) gives us the capital E which equates with *qabû* (Akkadian 'to speak).' In Sumerian there is a word DIMMA written with two signs together as if a single sign, one KA, the other HI, together pronounced de-em$_4$-ma. (The Sumerian word DIMMA) means *ṭēme* (Akkadian 'order, information, mind, intelligence'). The words for ghost in the two languages can be shown to mean those that open the ear and speak with intelligence.

In this deft way, using associative meaning plucked out of the heart of the signs, a true scholar teaches how the troublesome *etemmu* spirit enters the patient's ear when he is asleep. This invasion can bring about the condition known as *šinīt ṭēmi*, lit. 'changing of reason,' which interferes with the normal pattern of a person's mind and behaviour, as shown by this description of the condition:

> *If šinīt ṭēmi affects a person and the balance of his reason is disturbed, his words are strange, his faculties fail him and he raves all the time . . .*

Having got so far we can consider another ancient exposition, this time interpreting a medical omen. This particular omen is the first line of a great, multi-tablet compilation:

> *If an exorcist sees a kiln-fired brick on the way to a sick person's house the sick person will die.*

The outcome of a patient's condition can thus be foretold from what he happens to pass by in the street before he even gets to the house! What he sees is not an obvious 'bad sign,' such as encountering a violent road accident on the way to an exam might appear to us. It is something very different and very Mesopotamian. Another brilliant Babylonian had the most interesting ideas about what it really meant. Here most words are Sumerian ideograms, so I have included the Akkadian readings in brackets:

The omen: *šumma* (DIŠ) *agurru* (SIG$_4$.AL.ÙR.RA) *īmur* (IGI) *murṣu* (GIG) *imāt* (UG$_7$)

There follow three separate explanations lines.

Explanation 1: *kayyān* (SAG.ÚS)
normal meaning (Akkadian *kayyān*)

The first interpretation is that the text means what it says: the exorcist sees a baked brick. Babylon was full of baked bricks and there must be some focal point here, such as the doctor treading on a sharp upturned fragment, which hurt him through his sandal, or seeing a brick dangerously dislodged from a wall. This would be discussed, but not recorded, for it is obvious.

Explanation 2:   *šá-niš amēlu* (LÚ) *šá ina hur-sa-an i-tu-ra*
                  A : *me-e* : GUR : *ta-a-ra*
                  Secondly it means a man who returned from the river-ordeal (Akkadian *amēlu šá ina hursān itūra*)

The second interpretation is deeper; the brick is interpreted as a man who has survived the water ordeal, a primitive legal device not unlike the medieval European stool, which establishes guilt or otherwise by dunking. This meaning is accomplished by a very sophisticated device. The Akkadian word for baked brick is *agurru*. This word is not written here syllabically but with the Sumerian ideogram with the same meaning, SIG$_4$.AL.ÙR.RA. The commentator supplies the Babylonian equivalent *agurru*, takes the syllables 'a' and 'gur' from it and uses their Sumerian meanings. Sumerian A is 'water,' and Sumerian GUR is 'to return,' thus allowing the Akkadian paraphrase, 'returned from the water.'

Explanation 3:   *šal-šiš arītu* (MUNUS.PEŠ$_4$) : A *ma-ru* :
                  $^{ki-ir}$*kìr* (GUR$_4$) : *ka-ra-ṣa*
                  Thirdly it means a pregnant woman (Akkadian *arītu*)

To show that the brick can mean a pregnant woman requires further mental dexterity. The teacher returns to the 'a' and 'gur' of *agurru*, 'brick,' and supplies different Sumerian meanings. Sumerian A, in addition to 'water,' can mean 'semen' and 'son.' Starting with GUR, the homophonic tendencies of cuneiform mean that there are several quite different-looking 'gur' signs, including GUR_4, which is the one he chooses. This sign GUR_4 can itself be pronounced in more than one way: when pronounced 'kir,' as shown by the gloss $^{ki-ir}$, it corresponds to the Akkadian verb *karāṣu*, 'to nip off a piece of clay,' a verb which tellingly is used of the creation of mankind in Akkadian mythological compositions. Thus we arrive at 'one who is making a son out of basic clay.'

The teacher who produced this deft display of cuneiform exegesis was of rare ability. There is, however, more to be explained. What should we take from his interpretations of the brick in the street as passers by? The hurrying doctor would be unaware that he had bypassed an ordeal survivor or a pregnant woman (for a pregnant woman who had to be publically outdoors would certainly dress modestly). The force of the explanation is that he saw a man who had *evaded death* – cheating the under-world assistants of a body who were waiting to claim him as he drowned – or a woman in the very process of engendering *new life*. Either means that the death of the patient is required in compensation. The clear implication, although this point too is apparently nowhere articulated in ancient Mesopotamian writ-ings, is that for a new life to come into the world someone first must die. There is a simple beauty about this idea, which, to me, is irresistible. I imagine that contemplation of it could be a great solace to many people who are aware that they are soon to die.

To me this discloses an unacknowledged Mesopotamian system of reincarnation. The bodiless, personality-bearing one-third matter that remains after death – equal in some way to female divinity – sustains the *eṭemmu* spirit in a recyclable state until needed for a new birth. It suggests the underlying conception of a finite number of human spirits in circulation, reflecting the idea that the material of life, like any other natural resource, and especially water, is not boundless. It does seem hard to divorce this spirit from what is usually referred to, in common under-standing, as a soul.

I cannot help but wonder if the netherworld depicted in the famous myth entitled the *Descent of Ishtar*, an ultra-depressing limbo, is not where the spirits all waited until, so to speak, there was a summons:

> *To the gloomy house, seat of the netherworld,*
> *To the house which none leaves who enters,*
> *To the road whose journey has no return,*
> *To the house whose entrances are bereft of light,*
> *Where dust is their sustenance and clay their food.*
> *They see no light but dwell in darkness,*
> *They are clothed like birds in wings for garments,*
> *And dust has gathered on the door and bolt.*
>   The Descent of Ishtar to the Netherworld: 4–11

Admittedly the poem tells us that no one can get out and there is certainly a very strict and overbearing gatekeeper always there, but perhaps the system was primarily organised to keep the great masses there until they were called for, to be let out one by one. Gates, after all, work in two directions.

Mesopotamian rituals concerned with the dead and indeed all texts to do with ghosts make it clear that they are supposed to stay quiet and peaceful in the Netherworld, but it is never explained what they are supposed to be doing there or what they are waiting for. There was no moral assessment of a person's life ahead of them, no punishment or reward, and certainly no choice between a heaven and a hell; the Mesopotamians never had that set of problems. But if there were no destination beyond the waiting, what were they waiting for, if not for the call to step back on the great cycle of birth and death, as and when there was a vacancy?

Ishtar, trying to get in to look for her dead lover, is refused entry by this gatekeeper so she shouts at him:

"Gatekeeper! Open your gate for me!
Open your gate that I may enter!
If you will not open the gate that I may enter,
I will break down the frame, I will topple the doors.
I will raise up the dead to devour the living,
The dead shall outnumber the living!"
The Descent of Ishtar to the Netherworld: 14–20

Normally one pictures this outcome as a sort of Hollywood zombie movie, but I wonder whether the real fear was not that if all the sojourners in the Land-of-No-Return were let out at once the delicate, calibrated balance between life and death would be irredeemably destroyed.

The one-third and two-third divine component of the spirit and the demon is reminiscent of the description of the heroic Gilgamesh and his personal genesis:

*Gilgamesh was his name from the day he was born
Two thirds of him a god but a third of him human.*
Gilgamesh I: 47–48

Gilgamesh = one-third humanity + two-thirds male divinity

While king lists are uncertain about the parentage of Gilgamesh, King of Uruk, the Old Babylonian version of his story gives his mother as the goddess Ninsun, while his father is sometimes recorded as Lugalbanda, a mortal who in time had to be elevated to divinity as Ninsun's husband. The divine-to-mortal balance of Gilgamesh's make-up is thus out of sync with mythological tradition; it is perhaps because he was alive and not dead that the divine element is male (*ilu* not *ištaru*). The tripartite division in Gilgamesh's case now makes sense if it is reckoned, as in the Atrahasis story, that he, too, is composed of flesh, blood and spirit, but it is back to front in that the god contributes flesh

325

and blood and man the spirit. At any rate this hybrid quality in Gilgamesh was obviously instantly apparent – almost like a smell – to beings who were themselves a mixture, such as the scorpion-folk (half-man, half-scorpion) on duty at **Mount Māšu**, the mountain of sunrise:

> *There were scorpion-men guarding the gate,*
> *Whose terror was dread and glance was death,*
> *Whose radiance was terrifying, enveloping the uplands –*
> *At both sunrise and sunset they guard the sun –*
> *Gilgamesh saw them and his face grew dark with fear and*
>   *dread,*
> *He collected his wits and drew near their presence.*
> *The scorpion-man called to his female:*
>   *"He who has come to us, flesh of the gods is his body."*
> *The scorpion-man's female answered him:*
>   *"Two-thirds of him are god but a third of him is human."*
>
> Gilgamesh IX: 42–51

One final point concerns the name of the boatman Ur-Shanabi, who ferried Gilgamesh across the cosmic ocean at the border of the world to meet Utnapishti, the Babylonian Noah. Ancient Babylonian scholars analysed this name as Man-of-God-Ea, because ur in Sumerian means 'man,' and shanabi is '40,' which is a mystic god number that can be used to write Ea's name. On the other hand shanabi also means 'two-thirds,' so the boatman's name could be equally well be understood as Two-Thirds-Man. Perhaps he too was a 'mixed-up' sort of chap, but it wouldn't do to argue with the heads of the Babylon Academy too often.

Appendix 2

Investigating the Text of Gilgamesh XI

1. The Shape

The argument that Utnapishti's Ark was originally a round coracle like that described in the *Ark Tablet* raises three problems that need to be addressed:

Problem (a):
How does a round boat turn into a square one?

Answer:
The *Ark Tablet* gives us explicitly the height of the sides of the boat, and this makes perfect sense of the boat's proportions:

9 *lū* 1 NINDAN *igāratuša*
   And let be one nindan (high) her sides.

Atrahasis Vocabulary Box:
Akkadian *lū*, 'let be'.
Sumerian NINDAN = Akkadian *nindānu*, 'nindan measure'.
Akkadian *igāru*, pl. *igārātu*, 'wall'.

Utnapishti's description of the finished sides of his boat in *Gilgamesh XI* runs over two lines and repeats the measurement:

58 10 NINDAN.TA.ÀM   *šaqqā igārātuša*
    Ten nindan each stood high her sides,
59 10 NINDAN.TA.ÀM
    Ten nindan each.

<u>*Gilgamesh* Vocabulary Box:</u>
Akkadian *šaqû*, 'to be high'.
Sumerian NINDAN = Akkadian *nindānu*, 'nindan measure'.
Akkadian *igāru*, pl. *igārātu*, 'wall'.
TA.ÀM just means 'each'.

This repetition of 'ten nindan each', acceptable enough in a
Romantic poem, reads very awkwardly in Akkadian. It could just
be an error, for this can easily happen when an editor is amal-
gamating separate written sources to produce one text. More
probably, though, the repetition of 'ten nindan each' was introduced by some *Gilgamesh* redactor to make sense of the text in
his hands, reasoning that if length and breadth were identical,
as it says in line 30, he should give each its height. Losing sight
of the circle at this point gave the old description – 'her breadth
and length should be the same' – which originally reinforced the
idea of the *circular* plan – a wholly different meaning, which led
to the permanent misunderstanding in *Gilgamesh XI* that
Utnapishti built himself a *square* ark. The original, simple round
vessel, subjected to subsequent textual elaboration, thus jelled
into an implausible cube, and the Assyrian text, vivid and meaningful enough in itself, left Utnapishti with a waterborne life
capsule that was utterly impractical. The Ark whose vital statistics are quoted in *Gilgamesh XI*: 61–3 has provoked a good deal
of discussion ever afterwards but it is, from a historical point of
view, a *phantom*.

Problem (b):
How can the wall height in Gilgamesh XI *be ten times higher
(ten* nindan = *sixty metres) than those in the parent text tradition
(one* nindan = *6 metres)?*

Answer:
The crucial point is that the measure of one nindan for the wall-
height in the *Ark Tablet* results, as we shall see, in a coracle of

normal proportions, so this has to be taken very seriously. In cuneiform writing, 10 is represented by a single diagonal cuneiform wedge and 1 by a single upright. The 10 now found in the *Gilgamesh XI* tablets could either be an ancient misreading of the original number '1' or could reflect a deliberate 'upgrading' of the numeral because of the idea that everything about the Ark was going to be big.

Problem (c):
Why, in the Gilgamesh story, does Utnapishti only draw up a work-plan after five days of hard labour when the basic shell of the craft is already finished?

Answer:
The explanation again comes from comparing the received text with the *Ark Tablet* version. The out-of-place verbal form in *Gilgamesh* line 60, 'I drew up her design', which has always been interpreted as a verb in the past tense, should really be understood as the imperative, 'draw up her design!' as Ea commands Atra-hasīs in *Ark Tablet* line 6. (The cuneiform spelling makes these two similar-sounding verbal forms confusable.) Originally this line belonged right after the contents of *Gilgamesh* line 31, when the hero was receiving his instructions, in parallel with the *Ark Tablet*.

2. The Interior

These are the Akkadian verbs for constructing the five-star floating hotel as the late poet described it:

> *urtaggibši ana 6-šu*, 'I gave her six decks' (verb: *ruggubu*)
> *aptarassu ana 7-šu*, 'I divided her into seven parts' (verb: *parāsu*)
> *qerbīssu aptaras ana 9-šu*, 'I divided her interior into nine' (verb: *parāsu*)
>
> *Gilgamesh XI: 61–3*

Proposition: It seems to me that these three lines derive ultimately from the very 'fingers of bitumen' passage that is missing in *Gilgamesh*, signifying a gross misinterpretation of the underlying text.

Defence: The verb *ruggubu* (from the root *RGB*), 'to roof', in the form *urtaggibši* occurs only in one passage, *Gilgamesh XI* according to the *Chicago Assyrian Dictionary*. There are admittedly not many contexts in life where deck-providing might be a central issue, and it is specious to argue that 'to roof' is not the same as 'to provide with decks', since the effect is the same. However, there is the very similar-sounding verb *rakābu, rukkubu, šurkubu* (root *RKB*) in the Old Babylonian account:

I caused the kilns to be loaded (uštarkib) *with 28,800* (sūtu)
    of bitumen into my kilns . . .
I ordered the kilns to be loaded (uštarkib) *with fresh bitumen*
    . . . in equal measure . . .

Ark Tablet: 21 and 25

Perhaps the later tablet-editors found the Old Babylonian verb *uštarkib,* 'I caused (the kilns) to be loaded', confusing when not applied to vehicles or boats, as it almost always is, and as I certainly first interpreted it when struggling to understand those lines in the *Ark Tablet*. Perhaps, too, in an effort to make sense of an unclear passage, they associated the underlying root *rkb* with the noun *rugbu*, 'loft' or 'upper room', and came up with a derivative verb – as one can in Semitic languages – *ruggubu*, meaning 'to fit with *rugbus*'. It is as if, in English, one were to say 'deckify' or 'loftisise'; terms not in the dictionary but transparent in meaning.

Let us continue a little further in this vein. In *Gilgamesh*, the verb *parāsu* appears twice in the form *aptaras*, 'I divided', once with reference to the Utnapishti boat's interior. This is an echo of the verb *aprus*, 'I divided', in the *Ark Tablet*, where the distinction between exterior and interior was the main point:

> *I apportioned (*aprus*) one finger of bitumen for her outsides.*
> *I apportioned (*aprus*) one finger of bitumen for her interior.*
>   *Ark Tablet*: 18–19

    Careless recycling of an Old Babylonian text like the *Ark Tablet* could also explain the oddity that feminine suffixes for the boat are not given in *Gilgamesh*: 61–3, although they do appear correctly from line 64 onwards.

    I suspect, too, that the Old Babylonian signs ŠU.ŠI standing for 'finger' in *Ark Tablet* 18–20, which include the cabins, were later interpreted as *šūši*, 60, and that the three 60s of the original became disassociated from bitumen-thicknesses. Instead they were thought to have something to do with the decks and chambers and evolved by distinct numerological activity and cosmological speculation into the sequence 6, 7 and 9, undoubtedly compounded by the conviction that the vessel itself was a giant, straight-sided cube. A sort of Babylonian midrashic development, subtle and full of allusion, then played long on Utnapishti's over-inflated time-capsule, the simple 1,000-year old text subjected to theological-cum-philosophical interpretation and symbolical elaboration, as has been discussed at length in George 2003, Vol. 1: 512–13. (The theoretical Assyriological idea advocated by several scholars that Utnapishti's Ark was connected with the multi-layered ziggurat temple at Babylon is rendered less innovative by the fact that *Gilgamesh XI*: 158 actually refers to the Ark, once landed on the mountain, as the ziggurat!)

    The growing number of floors and subdivisions is also a practical response, for not all species were equally compatible, and humans might want separate quarters. For these reasons, one can understand how the Ark blossomed into a five-star skyscraper hotel with certain cosmic resonances. My suspicion, however, is that the *Gilgamesh* Ark as it came to be launched from Nineveh is primarily the consequence of textual misunderstanding compounded by the insertion of narrative without care as to overall meaning coupled with interventive editing. I doubt that many people who knew or heard the story ever believed for a moment that the Ark was really a perfect cube.

Appendix 3

Building the Ark – Technical Report (with Mark Wilson)

> To safeguard the world's largest boat
> They smoothed on a bitumen coat
> They brought in the oracle
> Who said, of their coracle,
> 'Though dry I doubt it will float.'
>
> C. M. Patience

Atra-hasīs's Ark

The following notes on the text of the *Ark Tablet* look at each building section in turn, supporting what can be gleaned from the tablet and interpolating from construction accounts of other similar traditional vessels. For clarity, the calculations involved are carried out in Babylonian units. We take 'one finger' as our basic unit of length, after the Babylonian *ubānu* 'finger' measure which is used in the *Ark Tablet*. One Babylonian finger is approximately $1^2/_3$ cm and it is usual to take it as exactly that for ease of calculation.

MEASURES

Length:
1 *ubānu* = 1 *finger* ≡ 1.666 cm
1 *ammatu* (*cubit*) = 30 *fingers*
1 *nindanu* = 12 *ammatu* = 360 *fingers*

Area:
1 *ikû* = 100 (= 10 × 10) *nindanu*^{2} = 12,960,000 *fingers*^{2} = 3,600 m^2

Volume:

1 *qa* = 216 (= 6 × 6 × 6) *fingers*^{3} = 1 litre
10 *qa* = 1 *sūtu* = 2,160 *fingers*^{3}
1 *gur* = 300 *qa* = 64,800 *fingers*^{3}
1 *šar* = 3,600 (*sūtu*) = 7,776,000 *fingers*^{3}

'Floor area' is *qaqqaru*, 'ground', which also has the more specific meaning 'surface', or 'area'. Here it means the floor of the boat, as we are told in the technical dictionary:

Sumerian giš-ki-má = Babylonian *qaq-qar eleppi* (GIŠ-MÁ), 'wooden floor of a boat'
crib: giš = *īṣu*, 'wood'; ki = *qaqqaru*, ground'; má = *eleppu*, 'boat'

1. OVERALL DESIGN AND SIZE

The fundamental facts regarding the Ark are given in lines 6–9. The Ark has a circular design, and is to be built inside a circle drawn out on the ground. We are told that its base area is one *ikû*, and that its walls are one nindan high. That is (using Area = π × Radius^2), its diameter is 67.7 metres, its walls six metres tall. As it is essentially a giant coracle, its construction methods have been compared with those of the traditional Iraqi coracle, or *guffa*, as reported by Hornell.

This record-breaking *guffa* differs from its conventional relatives in several ways. Chief among these is the existence of a roof, obviously indispensable. Although the roof is not explicitly mentioned in the construction details, we are assured of its final presence by the fact that we are told that **Atra-hasīs** goes on to it to pray later on in the tablet.

2. MATERIALS AND THEIR QUANTITIES FOR THE HULL

Lines 10–12 give the materials for the hull of the boat, and these are described as the 'ropes and rushes of a boat'.

The ropes: *kannu*
This word, *kannu* 'A', means a fetter, band, rope, belt or even a wisp of straw. It can be tough enough to restrain a runaway slave or make a wrestler's belt, and slim enough to be a hair band. The verbal root from which it derives, *kanānu*, means 'to twist', or 'to coil', which is natural for a word meaning 'rope'.

The rushes: *ašlu*
There are two identical-looking words pronounced *ašlu*. 'A' means 'rope', 'tow rope', 'surveyor's measuring rope'; 'B' means a kind of rush which can be used to make matting for furniture but also, in narrow quantities, as a thread or twine. This is the *ašlu* we want. It is written with a complex cuneiform sign that also serves for other types of rush, and is thus distinct from *ašlu* A, which is a true rope.

The structure is thus made totally of plaited palm-fibre rope and rushes, whose intrinsic twisting and interlacing immediately suggests the process of basket weaving, and from this we conclude the form to be a giant coiled rope basket. That this is produced before any internal framework is consistent with Hornell's account of how a traditional Iraqi *guffa* is manufactured.

As well as the *material* for the basket – palm fibre – we are also told its required *volume*. This rope volume is 4 *šar* (4 × 3,600) + 30 = 14,430 'units' of material to make the basket alone.

We defend here our conclusion that the quantities written in *šār* are meant to be and have to be taken seriously. A thousand years after the *Ark Tablet* was written these numbers in *Gilgamesh XI* became fanciful expressions to convey great magnitude, although an intervening scribe might have back-calculated certain measures in the attempt to reconcile textual variants. The important issue – which crops up several times in the *Ark Tablet* text – is that quantities of a raw material are given solely as totals with the standard units only implied. Here we have found that out of the two likely choices – *sūtu* or *gur* – for the standard volume measure behind numbers in *šār*, only *sūtu* gives meaningful results.

Given the shape and size of the Ark's basketwork hull, we substantiate this claim about the accuracy and nature of the numbers by comparing the amount of material that *should* be used in such a construction – which we call V$_{\text{CALCULATED}}$ – with the amount given in the text – which we call V$_{\text{GIVEN}}$

To perform this calculation we need two additional items of information. The first is the thickness of the woven rope basketry. Although this is not given in the cuneiform text, a clue comes from the (partly restored) 'ropes . . . for [a boat]' (line 10), implying, very plausibly, a type of rope peculiar to boat-making whose thickness was no doubt standard. The text also tells us the ropes were to be made by someone other than the shipwright, presumably a 'boat-rope' artisan, who would manufacture rope of a type independent of the size of coracle it was for. We assume that the thickness of rope used to make a *guffa* was always independent of its size, so that the width of the rope ordered would not scale up with the final size of the boat. Indeed, the descriptions of traditional *guffas* show that their structural rigidity depends on the internal framework, so that the basket is just a skin of convenient material to support the applied waterproofing layer. Assyrian sculptures mentioned in Chapter 6 prefer skins to rope for the hulls of their *guffas*.

This means the basket body of the Ark is constructed using standard materials and techniques, and, although it is nearly seventy metres across, the walls are still seen as having the same thickness as conventional-sized coracles. The most likely standard width of rope used is one *finger*, which is supported by early photographs of Iraqi *guffas* (e.g. 'Building the peculiar round boat . . .'), which show that the rope used was about one finger in thickness. This is supported by another calculation below about bitumen.

A new Iraqi coracle has just been finished. The rope's thickness can be seen to be roughly the thickness of a finger (or a toe). High-quality stereo photographs of this type from the 1920s preserve important information which often is otherwise unobtainable. Close-up of modern reed basket-work.

The second piece of information we need is the cross-sectional curve of the walls. These should have an outward camber at the base to resist hydrostatic pressure, and this is what is seen on the photographs of actual *guffas*. There the curvature of the walls is seen to lie somewhere between a straight-sided cylinder and the semicircle of the outer half of a torus (ring-doughnut). Therefore, we believe that it would not be far off the mark to assume it was exactly halfway in-between, and approximate the curvature by a semi-ellipse whose width is a quarter of its height. This means the walls of our reconstructed Ark – the sides of which are one nindan high – bulge out from the base by one-quarter of a nindan at their maximum diameter, thus:

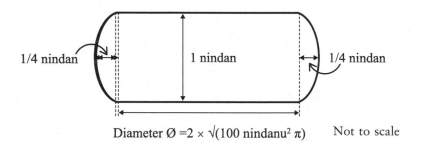

Diameter $\emptyset = 2 \times \sqrt{(100 \text{ nindanu}^2 \, \pi)}$ Not to scale

As is approximately true of real *guffas*, the walls are symmetrical about the mid-transverse plane, meaning the Ark would look the same if it was turned over, top-to-bottom. The important corollary to this is that the area of the roof is identical to the area of the base.

Rope calculations
The first step for rope volume used is to calculate the total surface area 'A' of the vessel. This is area of the base 'B', plus the area of the roof 'R', plus the area of the walls 'W'.

We are given $B = 12,960,000$ *fingers*^{2}, and have assumed that $R = B$. To calculate the area of the walls W we need Pappas's

First Centroid Theorem: *The surface area W of a surface of revolution generated by rotating a plane curve about an axis external to it and in the same plane is equal to the product of the arc length L of the curve and the distance D travelled by its centroid (centre of gravity): W = L × D.*

Here, the plane curve is the semi-elliptical shape of the walls, and its length is just half of the circumference of the full ellipse of which it is a part. Calculating the circumference of a general ellipse is a nightmare of complexity, but for the specific case we use here – one whose major axis of length '*a*' is twice as long as its minor axis – we have a neat formula to use called *Ramanujan's Approximation* which is correct to three places of decimals:

Ramanujan's Approximation

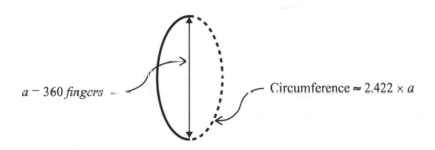

$a = 360$ *fingers* — Circumference $\approx 2.422 \times a$

Here, *a* is simply the height of the walls, 360 *fingers*, and we are only interested in half of the circumference, which gives us $L \approx$ ½ × 2.422 × 360 = 436 *fingers*.

The other component we now need is D, the length travelled by the centroid as the semi-ellipse is rotated to form the walls of the Ark. This is the length of a circle swept out by a radius equal to that of the base of the Ark plus the additional distance from the edge of the base to the centroid. We know the base of the Ark is a circle of area one *ikû*, so (from 'Area = $\pi \times$ Radius^2') we can calculate its radius '*r*' to be:

$$r = \sqrt{(\text{Base Area } B/\pi)} = \sqrt{(12{,}960{,}000/\pi)} \approx 2{,}031 \text{ \textit{fingers}}$$
(working to the nearest whole *finger*.)

The distance '*d*' of the centroid of a semi-elliptical arc to the axis of the ellipse is given by:

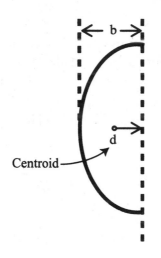

$d = 2b/\pi$
and *b* we define as 1/4 nindan
so: $d = 57$ *fingers*

Centroid

Using the familiar rule for circles 'Circumference = $2\pi \times$ Radius', we are now in a position to calculate D, the circumference of the circle travelled by the centroid:

$$D = 2\pi \times (r + d) = 2\pi \times 2{,}088 \text{ \textit{fingers}} \approx 13{,}119 \text{ \textit{fingers}}.$$

Finally, this gives the area of the walls W as:

$$W = L \times D = 436 \text{ \textit{fingers}} \times 13{,}119 \text{ \textit{fingers}} \approx 5{,}719{,}880 \text{ \textit{fingers}}^2;$$

giving the total area of the Ark as:

$$A = B + R + W = 12{,}960{,}000 + 12{,}960{,}000 + 5{,}719{,}880 \approx$$
$$31{,}639{,}880 \text{ \textit{fingers}}^2$$

We now assume that the ropes are whipped tightly enough to each other that they are densely packed and their cross-section can be taken as square with negligible error. Similarly, since the basket is very thin compared to its area, we can calculate its volume by just multiplying its area by its thickness of one finger, again with negligible error.

Thus our calculated volume ($V_{CALCULATED}$) of rope needed to make the basketwork of the Ark is:

$V_{CALCULATED} = 1$ *finger* (thickness) $\times$ 31,639,880 *fingers*^{2} = 31,639,8800 *fingers*^{3} or, dividing by 2,160 to give units of *sûtu*:

$$V_{CALCULATED} = 14,648 \text{ } s\hat{u}tu.$$

The given volume (V_{GIVEN}) of rope according to Enki is:

$$V_{GIVEN} = 14,430 \text{ } s\hat{u}tu$$

which differs from our calculated figure by just a little under 1½ per cent. This is a striking result, and we take it as evidence to support assumption that the quantities given in the *Ark Tablet* are factual.

We can work out the length of rope represented by $V_{CALCULATED}$ by dividing it by the assumed cross-sectional area of the rope:

$$\text{Length of Rope} = 31,639,880 \text{ } fingers^3/1 \text{ } finger^2 = 31,639,880$$
$$fingers = 527 \text{ km.}$$

As pointed out earlier, this is roughly the distance from London to Edinburgh!

The Babylonian reckoning

The very closeness of the figures $V_{CALCULATED}$ and V_{GIVEN} leads one to question how the Babylonians might have made their calculation of the quantity needed.

We believe the answer lies in the fact that one *ikû* is *defined* as an area equivalent to that of a square of ten nindan × ten nindan, thus making it easy to visualise the area in terms of such a square. This proposition seems to us reinforced by Enki's actually saying:

> *Draw out the boat that you will make*
> *On a circular plan;*
> *Let her length and breadth be equal,*

especially given the circle-in-its-square school diagram illustrated on p. 127 above.

The Babylonians found it difficult to do accurate arithmetic involving circular measures due to their imprecise value for π. If we assume that for the sake of ease of calculation they visualised the one-*ikû* base of the Ark as a square, then the walls will now be four panels, each ten nindan long by one nindan high, and this would be topped off by a square roof identical to the base. A trivial calculation of the area of this shallow biscuit-tin shape allows us to give the volume of material needed to make it by multiplying it by one *finger* thickness, as is done for the Ark above. If we call the volume 'V_{SQUARE}' we find:

$$V_{SQUARE} = 14,400 \ s\bar{u}tu.$$

This is four *šár* exactly, a difference of 0.2 per cent from V_{GIVEN}!

When first encountered, the 'plus 30' in the figure V_{GIVEN} seems like an insignificant if not inexplicable quantity, but the above calculation underscores its critical importance, for without it, it could be argued that the intention *was* to make a square-based vessel, but the extra thirty *sūtu* shows this cannot be the case.

However, the 'square-based' method was almost certainly how the Babylonian scribes 'back engineered' their figure for the volume involved given the shape. We can see this by doing the calculation for the volume of fibre needed for a circular-based vessel with straight vertical sides – a cylinder. As a circle has the smallest circumference which encloses a given area, the length of these walls will be less than the 'square based' value, resulting in an overall volume smaller than V_{SQUARE} by about 2 per cent. As we saw from our figure for $V_{CALCULATED}$, the extra area provided by the bulge in the walls slightly overcompensates for this 2 per cent, and empirical knowledge of this may have led the Babylonians to formulate a rule of thumb for such volume calculations of the type, 'Calculate the volume for a square-based vessel then add an extra bit on'

The 'extra bit' is what we believe the role of the thirty *sūtu* in V_{GIVEN}'s '4 *šār* + 30' to be. Whether or not such a procedure as this was actually used by the ancient Mesopotamian shipwrights, it is easy to see how it would have been useful in the typical scribal tasks of calculating the amount of rope needed to manufacture a particular size of vessel, as well as the quantity of bitumen needed to waterproof it.

The obvious question which then follows is how did they arrive at a number for that 'extra bit'? For the Ark this figure is '30 *sūtu*', so a natural assumption is that this is thirty times some real amount used for regular *guffas*. One way of pursuing this idea is to apply the above techniques to a *guffa* whose diameter is thirty times smaller than that of the Ark.

The diameter of this craft would then be:

$$4{,}062 \ fingers/30 = 135.4 \ fingers,$$

that is, a little over two metres. The walls of the Ark would not scale down in the same way, as their height is determined by practicality, as must have been true for the different sizes of *guffas*. The 'square-based' version of this would obviously have walls

10 *nindanu*/30 = 120 *fingers* long. We can now check what height of wall would give a difference (extra bit) of one *sūtu* between the round *guffa* and its square-based approximation, and see if this would be a practical size for this boat.

A slightly more involved calculation shows this height to be 34.4 *fingers*, about 58 centimetres. That is, this mini-Ark would have a diameter about four times the height of its walls, a proportion which seems reasonably safe and practical for a boat ferrying goods and people in calm water. Indeed, the photographs of traditional *guffas* being built show boats with very similar dimensions.

Given the simplicity of Enki's exhortation to build a boat 'as big as a field', it seems unlikely that this measurement is seen as being a regular *guffa* scaled up by a factor of 900 (= 30^2). However, this is possibly how the figures were arrived at in the scribal exegesis of the story. It is known that boats of the period came in standard sizes thought to be related to their cargo capacity, and it may have been either noticed or calculated that some measures for the Ark could be derived from those of a standard boat of one-thirtieth the diameter of the Ark.

3. FITTING THE INTERNAL FRAMEWORK

In parallel with the description of building a traditional *guffa* given in Hornell, the next stage of construction comes in where the main structural framework is fitted (lines 13 and 14). These are called ribs on the *Ark Tablet*, and are simply described as being 'set in', with no clue as to the exact process or their arrangement, or even of the material from which they are made.

The only hard rib information concerns dimensions: the length is given as ten nindan (sixty metres), while they are 'as thick as a *parsiktu*-vessel'. A *parsiktu* is a volume unit equal to sixty *qa*, deriving from the name of the wooden vessel used to measure out grain in approximately sixty *qa* amounts. That thickness is meant here rules out understanding *parsiktu* in this instance in its common meaning as a volume unit. It must refer to the seldom-mentioned measuring vessel itself. As explained, we take its usage in this context as hyperbole corresponding to our 'as thick as a barrel', designed to be an awe-inspiring superlative showing on the spot how much bigger the ribs of the Ark are when compared to those of a normal-sized vessel. Clearly we are meant to understand some approximate size from this statement, so the obvious question here is 'how thick *is* a barrel?'

A traditional square grain measure from Japan.
Most such objects seem to be round.

Traditional grain measures come in a variety of sizes and shapes, the most common being a squat cylinder whose width is about the same as its height. If as a working model we take this to be the shape of a *parsiktu* with an interior volume of 60 *qa* and stout walls 2 *fingers* thick, then the width across its mouth would be about 29.5 *fingers*, or 49 cm. However, given the lack of evidence for cooperage in Old Babylonian times, it seems much more likely that the shape of vessel used as a grain measure would be a simple box shape, like that shown in the above picture.

Only one known cuneiform text actually quotes the size of a *parsiktu*-vessel, and then only hypothetically. Significantly for the composition of the *Ark Tablet*, this is a school tablet with a problem in which the schoolchild has to calculate the depth of a 60-*qa parsiktu*-vessel which is four unspecified units 'across'. Since they don't mention 'sides' as they usually do in such problems, this is is likely to be a square-topped box, with the 'across' being the diagonal from corner to opposite corner. The units can really only be 'stacked hands' of ten *fingers*. Of course the problem does not take into account the thickness of the walls of a real measuring box, but if we again estimate this to be two *fingers* then an elementary calculation ($40/\sqrt{2}$) tells us its width along each side is 32.3 *fingers*, or 54 centimetres (and, solving the schoolboy problem, 18.2 *fingers* deep if you include the assumed thickness of the walls).

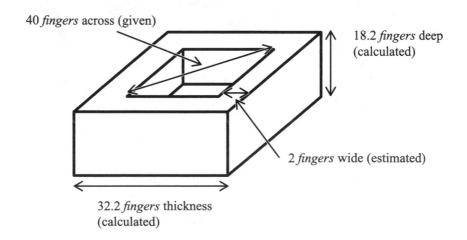

40 *fingers* across (given)

18.2 *fingers* deep (calculated)

2 *fingers* wide (estimated)

32.2 *fingers* thickness (calculated)

The '60 qa' parsiktu-vessel reconstructed from a school problem text.

This is not so far from the quoted estimate for a cylindrical measuring vessel, and means we can take 'as thick as a *parsiktu*' to mean roughly one cubit (~fifty centimetres) thick no matter what the *parsiktu*'s shape. The fact that the ribs were not described as one *cubit* thick indicates the use of the term *parsiktu* as an informal and easy-to-grasp literary device rather than an exact measure. The ribs of the Ark are thus ten nindan long and about thirty *fingers* wide.

As to their cross-sectional shape the cuneiform text is silent, but this is no doubt implicit in the name 'rib', which must have had a technical usage in boat-building. We can work out all we need to know from the corresponding elements in the traditional *guffa*, described by Hornell as 'lathes', meaning they have a thin rectangular cross-section. They are made of a resilient wood, and are sown into the basketwork of the hull under tension as the main source of rigidity in this structure. They run from the gunwales down the walls and across the base of the boat, but they are not all directed at the centre. Instead, each one of a series is offset from the angle of the wall so that they run parallel across the base to one side of the centre. These ribs are then interwoven with a second series set at 90° to the first, like so:

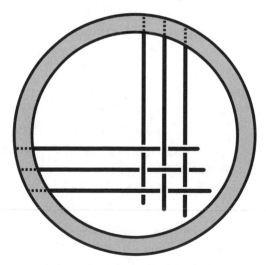

Plan view of the Ark with two series of ribs set in at 90°.

As more of these pairs of series at 90° are set in around the circumference, they not only strengthen the walls but build up a floor structure as well, which is later reinforced by pouring bitumen between the ribs. The scheme above uses six ribs from our total of thirty, so another four such sets need to be laid in, each rotated around the circumference by 360°/5 = 72° with respect to each other. Hornell tells us that the number used on the largest of the traditional *guffas* was twelve to sixteen, so the Ark uses about twice as many.

The curved walls have been shown above to be about 436 *fingers* long from top to bottom, so each 10-nindan-long rib will run down the wall and then approximately 8½ nindan along the base of the boat. The gap between ribs at the wall will be a quite large one of seven metres or so.

As these ribs in a normal-size *guffa* are thin springy strips of wood, the implication is that giant ones here are also intended to be wooden. Although there are no trees from the Ancient Near East of sufficient size for these to be carved from one piece, plank-sized sections can be scarf-jointed together, and, if the resulting ribs also had a shallow enough depth, they would be sufficiently flexible to interlace like the regular lathes. Given the comparative fragility of the basket walls, however, it seems improbable that such ribs could be fitted without damaging the hull unless they were pre-shaped into long, laid-back 'J' shapes.

Importantly, unlike the thickness of the shell of the boat (and, as we shall see later, its waterproofing) – where no concession was made to its exaggerated size – these structural elements do scale up in comparison to those of a regular *guffa*, in both size and number. The practical aspects of handling such huge structures seem to have had no interest to the authors, and no information is given as to how or with what they were to be installed into the hull.

In his description of *guffa*-building, Hornell tells us that between these main ribs shorter upright lathes the height of the walls are sewn to the inside of the basket to provide additional rigidity. These elements are not explicit in our description, but perhaps this absence is explained through the following step.

4. SETTING UP THE DECK AND BUILDING THE CABINS

At this stage there are no supports for the roof of the coracle basket, which must be assumed to have been woven along with the rest of the boat. The next lines of the *Ark Tablet* address this in typically succinct fashion, describing the installation of a vast number of stanchions as support for an interior floor and the fitting of wooden cabins so that the occupants had upper and lower decks. The presence of more than one deck is the second way in which the Ark differs from simply being a scaled-up *guffa*.

The supports are half a nindan long and – in parallel to the previous line about the ribs – 'half (a *parsiktu*) thick', and they are described as being 'made firm' within the boat (lines 15–16). If for simplicity we assume them to have a square cross-section then this would have an area of about 15 *fingers* x 15 *fingers* = 225 *fingers*² each. Although the greatest dimension of these elements is described as a length, their vertical nature is inescapable through the use of the term 'stanchion' (*imdu*, from the verb 'to stand'). Other uses of this term cited in the *Chicago Assyrian Dictionary* I/J assure us that these supports are intended to be made of wood. The *Ark Tablet* tells us that one *šār*, i.e. 3,600, are to be installed. Although this sounds more like an arbitrarily large number, it turns out that this number would actually take up only a little over 6 per cent of the one-*ikû* floor space of the Ark, which is similar to the proportion of any building's floor space taken up by supporting walls. Indeed, if this number is intended to be anything other than a literary device (as seems probable to us), these supports must have been thought of as having a placement designed to bear the load of the structures on the upper deck, rather than simply being arrayed across the floor like a forest.

Although this upper floor or deck is not mentioned as such in the text, we are assured that this is the purpose of the supports by their height – which is half the height of the Ark, by their shape, and by their number, which would be adequate for the purpose. We are next told that cabins have been constructed 'above and below', and it is possible that the flooring of the upper cabins was simply meant to be understood as the upper deck, resulting in an economy of description. This floor level would bisect the internal space of the craft into two roomy decks each about three metres high.

Such boat cabins are usually described as being wooden, but this probably meant having a wooden framework with woven basketwork walls, an idea reinforced by the root of the verb used for their construction – *rakāsu* – which involves the idea of 'tying'. The cabins complete the structural elements of the Ark, and result in a cross-section for the vessel which may be schematised thus:

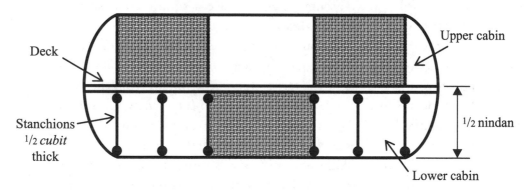

The Ark showing its stanchions, deck, and upper and lower cabins.

Obviously the framework of the cabins on the upper deck will have the function of supporting the already-completed roof of the Ark. If the internal floor was extended until it could be fixed to the external walls, this would also increase the structural strength and more than make up for the absence of the shorter supports expected between the ribs. So the presence of a deck and roof results in a more robust craft.

Caulking the Ark

The next step toward the completion of the boat is the water-proofing of both outside and inside faces of all external walls. This is done with the two types of bitumen – *iṭṭû*-bitumen and *kupru*-bitumen – with a final coating of oil. Before we move on to what the tablet says about this procedure, it will be of benefit to look at what is known generally about the two bitumen agents.

There are two useful resources here. The first is Leemans 1960, which looks at tablets dealing with the waterproofing of boats, and tentatively deduces the following information, valid for the Old Babylonian period to which the *Ark Tablet* dates:

1. *iṭṭû*-bitumen was moist; *kupru*-bitumen was harder and more mastic;
2. *iṭṭû*-bitumen is used as a liquid for some tasks, and its liquid form is produced in a kiln;
3. for caulking boats, large amounts of *kupru*-bitumen are used in comparison with *iṭṭû*-bitumen;
4. For caulking, *iṭṭû* bitumen could be used on a rough *kupru*-bitumen base to improve its quality;
5. *iṭṭû*-bitumen was used on top of *kupru*-bitumen, on cabins and on the inside.

The second source is Carter 2012, where analysis shows that ancient bitumen samples used in caulking were never just pure bitumen but included organic and mineral components in amounts suggesting they had been deliberately added, perhaps as tempering agents. In addition, quite large quantities of oil are accounted for in boat-building but for an unknown use, although it is assumed waterproofing of ropes might be involved.

Now we turn to what the *Ark Tablet* has to say about waterproofing. The process outlined in the text is entirely reasonable for caulking a normal-size boat, with the quantities proportionally adjusted to accommodate the vast surface area involved.

However, there are significant differences from the individual details adduced from the two references above. This part of the tablet is heavily abraded with a number of incomplete lines, but enough remains to clearly see the nature and order of the steps involved, which appear to throw new light on how bitumen was processed for caulking boats.

5. CALCULATING THE BITUMEN NEEDED FOR WATERPROOFING

Here, as before, Atra-hasīs's 3,600 measures are to be taken seriously. The first step is to work out how much bitumen will be needed to complete the process, and in lines 18 and 19 we are told that Atra-hasīs apportioned one *finger* thickness of *ittû*-bitumen, for the inside and outside of the hull. This is where the area calculations we looked at earlier come into their own. As the bitumen will be applied in a uniform layer, one need only work out the area of the boat, multiply it by two for the inside and outside, and then multiply it by the thickness of the coating. However, as the boat itself is one *finger* thick the work has already been done, and the amount of *ittû*-bitumen needed is twice the volume of fibre needed to make the hull, which was four *šar*-and-a-bit, so something over eight *šar*. This is exactly the sort of calculation a scribe accounting for boat-building materials would have to make, and the sort of problem that would be practised diligently in the scribal school.

Line 20 tells us that the interior cabins have already been coated with one *finger* thickness of liquid *ittû*-bitumen, thus focusing our attention on the critical task of waterproofing the hull.

6. LOADING THE KILNS AND PREPARING THE BITUMEN

Lines 21 and 22 tell us that indeed eight *šar* of *kupru*-bitumen have been loaded into the kilns and one *šar* of *ittû*-bitumen is to be poured in as well. That is, we have our two x four *šar*-and-a-bit, as anticipated above. The eight *šar* will form the one-finger-thick base coat on the inside and outside of the vessel, while the remaining one *šar* will be applied as a thin protective top-coat to the outside. Notice, however, that although we are told we need one *finger* thickness of *iṭṭû*-bitumen for the inside and outside of the hull, we are actually loading almost entirely *kupru*-bitumen into the kilns as raw material (as well as a small proportion of *iṭṭû*-bitumen as a liquid – it is poured in).

This can probably be explained by lines 23, 24 and 25, which read: '*The* iṭṭû-*bitumen did not come to the surface [lit. up to me), (so) I added five fingers of lard, I caused the kilns to be loaded … in equal measure.*'

We interpret this as alluding to the process of fractionation. The *kupru*-bitumen with fresh bitumen was probably in its native form, solid and containing plant and mineral impurities, and heating it in the presence of oil releases the more-fluid *iṭṭû*-bitumen, which rises to the surface and can be 'creamed off' and used. Much like butter added to a frying pan, the lard transfers the heat to the solid bitumen, preventing it from burning and helping it to melt. The '*five fingers*' is certainly meant to represent a small quantity, used as a rendering aid, which was then added to all the kilns equally.

7. 'ADDING' THE TEMPER TO THE MIX?

We have reached a stage in the bitumen processing where we can assume that the pure liquid *iṭṭû*-bitumen has been skimmed off the top, leaving only the heavier *kupru*-bitumen remaining in the kiln. This will have concentrated in it the residue of the plant and mineral impurities from the original raw bitumen. The resulting mastic was presumably used to provide a tough outer layer, similar to that seen in samples of ancient bitumen caulking – which have the appearance of having had tempering agents artificially added. As tamarisk wood is commonly used as fire-wood, we interpret lines 26 and 27 = 'I completed … tamarisk wood and stalks'; as referring to increasing the temperature of the fires beneath the kilns in an effort to soften the *kupru* to make it suitable for application.

8. BITUMINISING THE INTERIOR

Work has now progressed from preparation of the bitumen to its application, and although line 28 is almost totally obliterated, we can tell it refers to coating the interior surface of the hull, by line 29, which can be read as 'going between her ribs'.

9. CAULKING THE EXTERIOR

Again, line 30 has been reduced to indecipherable traces, but it must have described covering the exterior surfaces with *iṭṭû*-bitumen, as this is mentioned in line 31. This base layer is a fine waterproof coat, which must be free from impurities and sufficiently plastic not to crack when the boat flexes. By lines 32 and 33 it is already in place, as a further protective coat is here being applied: '*I applied the exterior* kupru-*bitumen from the kilns, using the 120* gur *set aside by the workmen.*' This is obviously the remains of the initial *kupru*-bitumen after all the *iṭṭû*-bitumen has been extracted. It would form a stiff protective shell over the waterproofing coat of *iṭṭû*-bitumen.

This order of coatings is the second point which differs from the details from the references in Leemans 1960, which suggest that a crude layer of *kupru*-bitumen is put on first which is then overlaid with a finer layer of *iṭṭû*-bitumen to improve it. However, the account suggested here tallies more with the ethnographic accounts of Iraqi reed boat-building given in Ochsenschlager 1992, where the still-hot waterproofing bitumen layer is coated with river mud, which binds to it and forms a strong protective layer. The actual figure on the tablet for the amount of *kupru*-bitumen used is 'two *gur*', but the nature of Babylonian numbers allows the possibility that this two can be understood as representing any factor of sixty. A coating using two *gur* would be too thin to be meaningful, and a coat using 7,200 *gur* would use much more bitumen than we have. Interpreting the two as 120 *gur* equates to a thickness of exactly one-sixth of a *finger* when applied to the whole exterior of the Ark. Now 120 *gur* is equal to one *šār*, so it must be asked why the quantity reserved by the workmen is not given in this fashion. We believe it to be because – rather than a raw material – it is a finished product gathered from the kiln in vessels more appropriate to measurement in *gur*.

Another important thing to note is that although – as in the references – the amount of raw *kupru*-bitumen used (eight *šar*) was indeed much more than *iṭṭû*-bitumen (one *šar*), by the time the bitumen had been cooked and the final products manufactured, these quantities would have been completely reversed, with eight *šar* of *iṭṭû*-bitumen being used as opposed to one *šar* of *kupru*-bitumen as the dregs. That is, the text suggests that the relative proportions of these types of bitumen is not fixed, but can be altered through a basic industrial process involving heating, much like the relative proportions of ice and water.

10. EXTERIOR FINISHING – SEALING THE OUTER COAT

The final part of waterproofing and sealing the boat comes in lines 57–8, after a gap in which the Ark is loaded up with animals and supplies. The lines read: '*I ordered repeatedly a one-finger (layer) of lard for the* **girmadû** *out of the thirty* gur *which the workmen had put to one side.*' As discussed, we consider that the *girmadû* is the roller-tool for applying the lard, which is the final operation before the boat is, as it were, ready for what lies ahead.

We are grateful to Sir Peter Badge for confirmation that oil is often applied in the construction of traditional *guffas*, where it can soften and prevent cracking in the outer waterproof layer, the tough coating of *kupru* in the case of the Ark.

Utnapishti's Ark

We turn finally to the revealing construction data preserved within *Gilgamesh XI*. Here the scribes are working with walls at ten *nindanu*, which are ten times higher than in Atra-hasīs's Ark. One of the *Gilgamesh XI* tablets gives the bitumen quantity for waterproofing at nine *šar*, transmitting correctly the original Old

Babylonian quantity and not adjusting it in terms of the 'new' walls. (The other gives six.) However, this nine *šār* of bitumen is to serve for the whole cubic Ark. This means that if Utnapishti's craft is waterproofed with a standard thickness of one *finger* for the bitumen, simple calculation shows that there would not be enough to do the interior at all, and the exterior could only be waterproofed to a height of 6.5 nindan up the walls, incredibly close to the 6.66 or two-thirds that the 'oiling' by the *girmadù* covers.

To us this means that the Gilgamesh editor has used the given height of the walls and the given quantity of bitumen to calculate the coverage this would provide, and then edited this new data into the story. Otherwise the appearance of the 'two-thirds' here is rather hard to explain. Unfortunately, in *Gilgamesh* XI the thirty *gur* of lard for the *girmadûs* has ended up as two *šār* – a completely unfeasible amount – and here the scribe has been unable to make sense of this.

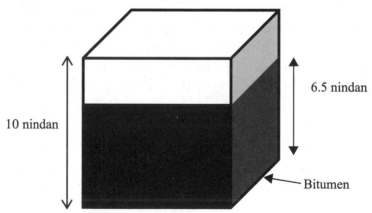

Ut-Napishtim's Ark coated with bitumen to about 2/3 its height.

Appendix 4

Reading the Ark Tablet

The fortified reader is now encouraged to have a look, line by line, at how the Babylonian cuneiform text translated and discussed in this book is actually written on the tablet. By now, this process cannot be as intimidating as it might once have sounded. As we have seen, it is up to Flood scholars to jump right in. Reading a new document from antiquity is always an exciting process, and this example is about as exciting as it gets.

The words of the Babylonian text of the *Ark Tablet* are largely recorded in Akkadian syllabograms, with some words given determinatives and others written with a Sumerian logogram.

First come the cuneiform signs in transliteration. Here the pronunciation of each syllabogram or syllable sign that makes up the Babylonian words is given in italic English letters; for example the first three signs, which are *i-ga-ar*.

Next comes the *translation* into English, the first word being 'wall'. Printed below that in smaller script (for anyone who might be really interested) is the 'joined-up' form of the Semitic Akkadian word, in this case *igāru*, as it appears in a modern dictionary of the language.

Words that are written with old Sumerian logograms or word signs are shown as they are in capital letters, and the Babylonian reading is supplied in the line underneath.

In this transliteration:
 x means one broken or unidentified sign
 x (x) means the traces might reflect two broken or
 unidentified signs rather than one

[x x] means space for two signs of which nothing survives and

[x (x)] means space for one or two broken or unidentified signs.

Lines 1–5: Atra-hasīs for Flood Hero

1   *i-ga-ar i-ga-a[r k]i-ki-iš ki-ki-iš*
Wall, wall! Reed wall, reed wall!
igāru, 'wall'; *kikkišu*, 'reed wall'

2   ᵐ*at-ra-am-ḫa-si-[i]s a-na mi-il-ki-ia qú-ul-[ma]*
Atra-hasīs, pay heed to my advice,
ana, 'to'; *milku*, 'advice'; *qâlu*, 'to pay attention to'

3   *ta-ba-al-lu-uṭ [d]a-ri-iš*
that you may live for ever!
balāṭu, 'to live; *dāriš*, 'for ever'

4   *ú-bu-ut* É *bi-ni* MÁ *m[a-a]k-ku-ra-am ze-e[r-ma]*
Destroy (your) house, build a boat; spurn property
abātu, 'to destroy'; É (ideogram) = *bītu*, 'house'; *banû*, 'to build', MÁ (ideogram) = *eleppu*, 'boat'; *makkūru*, 'property'; *zêru*, 'to despise'

5   *na-pí-iš-tam šu-ul-lim*
and save life!
napištu, 'life'; *šullumu*, 'to save'

Lines 6–12: Plan and Dimensions

6   MÁ *te-ep-pu-šu e-[ṣ]e-er-ši-ma*
Draw out the boat that you will make
MÁ (ideogram) = *eleppu*, 'boat'; *epēšu*, 'to make'; *eṣēru*, 'to draw'

7   *e-ṣe-er-ti ki-[i]p-pa-tim*
on a circular plan;
eṣirtu, 'design'; *kippatu*, 'circle'

8   *lu mi-it-ḫa-ar ši-id-da-[š]a ù pu-u[s-sa]*
Let her length and breadth be equal,
mitḫuru, 'to be the same'; *šiddu*, 'length'; *u*, 'and'; *pūtu*, 'breadth'

9   *lu-ú* ɪ (AŠ) IKU *ka-aq-qá-ar-š[a lu]-ꝛùꝛ* ɪ NINDAN
i-ga-r[a-tu-ša]
Let her floor area be one field, let her sides be one
nindan (high).
lū, 'let it be that'; ɪ is written AŠ; IKU (ideogram) = *ikû*, 'field'; 'acre';
qaqqaru, 'floor area'; *u*, 'and'; NINDAN (ideogram) = nindan, 'a
measure'; 'a rod'; *igāru*, 'wall', 'side'

10 *ka-an-nu aš-la-a ta-mu-u[r] ša* [MÁ]
You saw *kannu* ropes and *ašlu* ropes/rushes for [a
coracle before!]
kannu, 'rope'; *ašlu*, either 'rope' or 'rush'; *amāru*, 'to see'; *ša*, 'of'; MÁ
(ideogram) = *eleppu*, 'boat', 'coracle'

11 *li-ip-ti-il-kum* GIŠ ꝛárꝛ-ti pí-[t]i-il-tam*
Let someone (else) twist the fronds and palm-fibre for
you!
patālu, 'to plait'; GIŠ *arti*, 'foliage, fronds'; *pitiltu*, 'palm-fibre'

12 ŠÁR x 4 + 30 *ta-qab-bi-am li-[ku]-ul*
It will surely consume 14,430 (*sūtu*)!
ŠÁR (ideogram) = 3,600; 3 x 10 = 30; *qabû*, 'to speak'; *akālu*, 'to
consume, use up'

Lines 13–17: Atra-hasīs Builds the Boat

13 30 ṣe-ri i-na ŠÀ-ša a[d]-di
I set in place in thirty ribs
ṣe-ri: for ṣēlu, 'rib'; ina, 'in'; ŠÀ (ideogram) = libbu, 'heart, inside',
nadû, '(here) to set up, as of a reed hut'

14 ša 1 PI ik-bi-ru 10 NINDAN mu-r[a]-ak-šu
which were one *parsiktu-vessel* thick, ten nindan long;
ša, 'which'; PI (ideogram) = parsiktu, 'a measure'; kabāru, 'to be thick';
NINDAN (ideogram) = nindanu, 'a nindan'; mūraku, 'length'

15 ŠÁR im-di i-na ŠÀ-ša ú-ki-in
I set up 3,600 stanchions within her
ŠÁR (ideogram) = '3,600'; imdu, 'stanchion'; ina, 'in'; ŠÀ (ideogram)
= libbu, 'heart'; kunnu, 'to make firm'

16 ša ½ (PI) ik-bi-ru-ma ½ NINDAN mu-ˈraˈ-ak-šu
that were half (a *parsiktu-vessel*) thick, half a nindan
long (i.e. high);
ša, 'which'; understanding PI (ideogram) = parsiktu, 'a measure'; kabāru,
'to be thick'; NINDAN (ideogram) = nindanu, 'a nindan'; mūraku, 'length'

17 ar-ku-ús ḫi-in-ni-šá e-le-nu-um ˈùˈ ša-ap-lu!-um
I constructed her cabins above and below;
rakāsu, 'to tie, construct'; ḫinnu, 'cabin'; elēnum, 'above'; u, 'and';
šaplum, 'below'

Lines 18–33: The Waterproofing

18 1 ŠU.ŠI ESIR ki-da-ti-ša ap!-[r]u-ús
I apportioned one finger of bitumen for her outsides
ŠU.ŠI (ideogram) for ubānu, 'finger'; ESIR (ideogram) = iṭṭû, 'bitumen';
kidītu, 'outer surface'; parāsu, 'to apportion'

19　1 ŠU.ŠI ESIR *qí-ri-ib-ša* ⸢*ap*⸣-[*r*]*u-ús*

I apportioned one finger of bitumen for her interior;

ŠU.ŠI (ideogram) for *ubānu*, 'finger'; ESIR (ideogram) = *iṭṭû*, 'bitumen';

qerbu, 'interior'; *parāsu*, 'to apportion'

20　1 ŠU.ŠI ESIR *a-na ḫi-in-ni-ša aš*-[*t*]*a-pa-ak*

I had (already) poured out one finger of bitumen onto her cabins;

ŠU.ŠI (ideogram) for *ubānu*, 'finger'; ESIR (ideogram) = *iṭṭû*, 'pitch';

ana, 'for, onto'; *ḫinnu*, 'cabin'; *šapāku*, 'to pour'

21　*uš-ta-ar-ki*-ib ŠÁR x 8 ⸢ESIR.UD.DU.A⸣ [*i-n*]*a ki-ra-ti-ia*

I caused the kilns to be loaded with 28,800 (*sūtu*) of *kupru*-bitu[men] into my kilns

šutarkubu, 'to cause to be loaded'; ŠÁR (ideogram) = '3,600'; ESIR.UD.DU.A (ideogram) = *kupru*-bitumen'; *ina*, 'in'; *kīru*, pl. *kīrātu*, 'kiln'

22　*ù* ŠÁR ESIR *a-na li-ib-bi aš-pu-uk*

and I poured 3,600 (*sūtu*) of *iṭṭû*-bitumen within.

u, 'and'; ŠÁR (ideogram) = '3,600'; ESIR (ideogram) = *iṭṭû*, 'crude bitumen'; *ana*, 'to'; *libbu*, 'heart'; *šapāku*, 'to pour'

23　ESIR *ú-ul iq-r*[*i*]-*ba-am-ma*

The bitumen did not come to the surface (lit. up to me);

ESIR (ideogram) = *iṭṭû*, 'pitch'; *ul*, 'not'; *qerēbu*, 'to approach'

24　5 ŠU.ŠI *na-*⸢*ḫa*⸣-[*a*]*m ú-*⸢*re*⸣-[*e*]*d-di*

(So) I added five fingers of lard,

ŠU.ŠI (ideogram) for *ubānu*, 'finger'; *nāḫum*, 'lard'; *redû*, 'to add'

25　*uš-*⸢*ta-ar*⸣-[*k*]*i-ib* ⸢*ki*⸣-*ra-ti* x (x) *mi-it-ḫa-ri-iš*

I ordered the kilns to be loaded in equal measure;

šutarkubu, 'to cause to be loaded'; *kīru*, pl. *kīrātu*, 'kiln'; *mitḫāriš*,
'equally'

26 GI[Š].⌈ŠINIG GIŠ?⌉ x i
With tamarisk wood (?) and stalks (?)

GIŠ.ŠINIG (ideogram) = *bınu*, tamarisk'; GIŠ x i perhaps 'stalk'

27 x x x e? na? as tum i? bi? ma? *ba-ar¹-tam*
. . . [. . .] (= I completed the mixture(?))

28 x x x (x) MEŠ x in? bi?

MEŠ (ideogram) for plural

29 ⌈*il*⌉-*la-ku bi-rit* ⌈*ṣe-e-ri*⌉-*ša*
Going between her ribs;

alāku, 'to go'; *birīt*, 'between'; *ṣe-e-ri* for *ṣēlī*, 'ribs'

30 x nam? x x x . . . .
(indecipherable)

31 x x-ia i x x x ESIR x x
. . . . the *iṭṭû*-bitumen . . .

32 ⌈ESIR UD.DU⌉ *ki-du-*⌈*ú*⌉ [*ša k*]*i-ra-ti* x x x
I applied (?) the outside *kupru*-bitumen from the kilns,

ESIR.UD.DU (ideogram) = *kupru*-bitumen; 'outside'; *kīru*, 'kiln'

33 *e-zu-ub* 2 (x 60) G[UR] ⌈*ú-pa-az-zi-rù*⌉ *um-mi-*[*ia-ni*]
Out of the 120 gur-measures which the workmen had
put to one side.

Compare line 58; *ezub*, 'out of'; *puzzuru*, 'to put aside'; *ummi'ānu*,
'workman'

Lines 34–8: Boarding and Celebrations

34 ⸢uš⸣-ta-na-⸢al⸣ x x [x x (x)] x ri-a-ši
I lay myself down (?) . . . [. . .] . . . of rejoicing
nâlu, 'to lie down'; *ri ʾāšu*, 'to rejoice'

35 *a-na* MÁ ⸢i⸣-[ru-bu-ma] x x k[i-i]m-<tu>⸢sa⸣-al-la-at
My kith and kin [went into] the boat . . . ;
ana, 'to'; MÁ (ideogram) = *eleppu*, 'boat'; *erēbu*, 'to enter'; *kimtu*,
'family', 'kith'; *sallatu*, 'family', 'kin'

36 *ḫa-du-ú* x [x x x] ⸢ki?⸣ x x x *e-mu-tim*
Joyful . . . [. . . . . .] . . . . . . of my in-laws,
ḫadû, 'to rejoice; *emūtu*, 'family of the husband'

37 *ù za-bi-il* x [x x x x] x x *ù su? e? ri a? tum*
and the porter with . . . [. . . . . .] . . . and . . .
u, 'and'; *zābilu*, 'porter';

38 *a ki lum i* ⸢ik⸣ *k[a a]l [ša tu ú] ī ša aṭ ṭī*
They ate and drank their fill
ākilu, 'eater'; *akālu*, 'to eat'; *šātû*, 'drinker'; *šatû*, 'to drink'

Lines 39–50: Atra-hasīs Prays to the Moon God

39 *a-na-ku a-wa-t[um i-na* Š]À-*i[a ul] i-ba-aš-ši-ma*
As for me, there was no word in my heart, and
anāku, 'I'; *awatu*, 'word'; *ina*, 'in'; ŠÀ (ideogram) = *libbu*, 'heart';
ul, 'not'; *bašû*, 'to be'

40 x *na ti* x [x x x *l]i-ib-bi*
. . . [. . .] my heart;
libbu, 'heart'

41　x ab x x [x x x]-*ú-a*
　　. . . [. . .] . . . my [. . .]

42　ḫi-ni-it(?) x x [. . .] . . . -*i?-ti-ia?*
　　. . . [. . .] of my . . .

43　. . . áš-na/gi-an? . . . [. . .]-*e? ša-ap-ti-ia*
　　. . . [. . .] . . . of my lips
　　šaptu, 'lip'

44　. . . ne ra? bi . . . [. . .]-*it pi-qum aṣ-la-al*
　　. . . [. . .] . . . , I slept with difficulty;
　　pīqum, 'with difficulty' (colloquial for 'hardly at all'?); *ṣalālu*, 'to sleep'

45　˹*e-li*˺ *a-na ú-ri* ˹*ú*˺-[*sa-ap-pi* (?)]˹*a-na*˺ ᵈEN.ZU *be-li*
　　I went up on the roof and pr[ayed(?)] to Sin, my lord:
　　elû, 'to go up'; *ana*, 'to'; *ūru*, 'roof'; *suppû*, 'to pray'; ᵈEN.ZU,; the signs
　　EN.ZU in archaic reverse order spell ZU.EN for 'zu'en', the name of the
　　Moon God Sin; *bēlu*, 'lord'

46　˹GAZ?˺ *lìb?-bi?*˺ *li-ib-l*[*i la ta-ta-a*]*b-ba-al*
　　Let my heartbreak (?) be extinguished! [Do you not
　　disap]pear!
　　GAZ (ideogram) = *ḫīpu*, 'break'; *libbu*, 'heart'; *balû*, 'to be extin-
　　guished'; *tabālu*, 'to carry off'

47　x x x x x x ak? [x x x x] x-*ti?-bi ik-la*
　　. . . darkness

48　˹*i*˺-*na* x [x (x)]-*ia*
　　Into my [. . .] . . .

49　ᵈEN.ZU *i-na* GIŠ.G[U.ZA-*šu it-ta-m*]e *ga-ma-ar-tam*
　　Sin, from his thr[one swo]re as to annihilation

ᵈEN.ZU for Sin; *ina*, 'in', 'from'; GIŠ.GU.ZA (ideogram) = *kussû*, 'seat', 'throne'; *tamû*, 'to swear'; *gamartu*, 'annihilation'

50 *ù ar-m[u-tam i-na u₄-mi-im]* ⸢*e-ṭi*⸣*-i[m* (x x x)]
And desola[tion on (the)] darkened [day (to come)].
armūtu, 'desolation', *ūmu*, 'day', *eṭû*, 'dark'

Lines 51–2: The Wild Animals Come Aboard

51 *ù na-ma-aš-t[um i-na ṣe]-ri-i[m (. . .)]*
But the wild anim[als from the st]eppe [(. . .)]
u, 'and', or 'but'; *namaštu*, 'animals'; *ina*, 'from'; *ṣēru*, 'steppe'

52 ⸢*ša-na* MÁ! *lu-[ú* x x x x] x x x [x x x x]
Two by two the boat did [they enter] . . . [. . . . . .]
šanā, 'two by two'; MÁ (ideogram) = *eleppu*, 'boat'; *lū*, 'indeed did . . .'

Lines 53–8: Supplies for the Wild Animals

53 5 KAŠ *ar ma.?* x x *uš-t[a-* x x x x]
I had . . . 5 of beer (?) I . . . [. . .]
KAŠ (ideogram) = *šikāru*, 'beer'; *uš-ta-* . . . probably part of a verb in the first person sing.

54 11 12 ⸢*ú*⸣*-za-ab-ba-*⸢*lu*⸣ x (x) [x x x]
They were transporting eleven or twelve [. . . . . .]
zabālu, 'to transport'

55 3 Ú *ši-iq-bi u[k?-ta-*x x] x x x x
Three (measures) of *šiqbum* (?) I [. . .] . . . . . . ,
Ú = *šammu*, 'plant', determinative sign before plant names; *šiqbu*, if a useful plant, is unidentified; *uk-ta* . . . , part of a verb in the first person sing.

56   ¹/₃ *ú-ku-lu-ú* ⌜um?/dub? mu?/gu?⌝ [*kur*(?)]-*din*-⌜*nu*⌝
One-third (measure) of fodder, . . . and *kurdinnu* plant
(?).

ukulû, 'fodder'; *kurdinnu*, 'a malodorous plant.'

57   I ŠU.ŠI *na-ḫa-am a-na* ⌜*gi-ri*⌝-*ma-de-e* ⌜*aq?-ta?-na?-
bi?*⌝
I ordered several times (?) a one-finger (layer) of lard
for the *girmadû*

ŠU.ŠI (ideogram) for *ubānu*, 'finger'; *nāḫu*, 'lard'; *ana*, 'for'; *girmadû*,
application tool ; *qabû*, 'to order', 'to demand'.

58   *e-zu-ub* 30 GUR *ú-pá-az-zi-rù* LÚ.MEŠ *um-mi*-⌜*a*⌝-[*ni*]
out of the thirty gur which the work[men] had put to
one side.

ezub, 'out of' (rather than 'leaving aside'); *puzzuru*, 'to put aside';
LÚ.MEŠ, 'men' (determinative, not pronounced, omitted in parallel line
33); *ummi' ānu*, 'worker'

Lines 59–60: The Door is Sealed

59   ⌜*i*⌝-*nu-ma a-na-ku e-ru-bu-ma*
When I shall have gone into the boat,

inūma, 'when'; *anāku*, 'I'; *erēbu*, 'to enter'

60   *pi-ḫi pít ba-bi*-⌜*ša*⌝
'Caulk the frame of her door!'

peḫû, 'to caulk'; *pītu*, 'opening'; *bābu*, 'door'

Textual Notes to Appendix 4

7   *eṣirtu* is for *uṣurtu* A.

10   The final -a in *aš-la-a* is not to mark a long vowel but to confirm the accusative as shown by spacing; traces of -*ur* are slight but possible.

14   The stanchions are described by length from the point of view of preparation; once cut they will 'stand up'.

17   'Above and below' here means exactly that, rather than 'fore and aft' as these terms sometimes mean in Ark descriptions (George 2003, Vol. 2: 880).

18–20, 22–3   In these lines the *Ark Tablet* scribe consistently writes the sign ESIR, 'bitumen', which properly is A.ESÍR (LAGABxNUMUN), as A.LAGAB (i.e. without any small inside sign). This represents a kind of shorthand; the context leaves no doubt that it stands for ESIR. In line 21 he seems to write A.LAGABxBAD.

26   The word signs are read GIŠ.ŠINIG by the overall shape; the following word could refer to a second wood, but GIŠ.GIŠIMMAR.TUR! (wr. erroneously I), 'young date palm', is probably to be excluded.

32   ⌜ESIR UD.DU⌝ is more than possible but not certain, complicated by erasures here.

46   ⌜GAZ? *lìb?-bi?*⌝ – this reading, which is allowed by the traces, derives from *Old Babylonian Atrahasis* III ii 47 in identical context: *ḫe-pí-i-ma li-ib-ba-šu*, 'his heart was broken'. For the following restoration, see ibid. 39: *ib-ba-b]i-il ar-ḫu*, 'the moon disappeared'.

49   *gamartu*, 'annihilation', is said of the Flood in *Old Babylonian Schøyen*: iv 2 (George 2009: 22).

50   For some reason CAD A/2 294 doubts the authority of the lexical compilation that apparently equates *armūtu* with *namūtu*, 'desolation', 'wasteland', and questions its very existence, but the present context does much to support its re-election.

53   *ga-ar-ma-* is also possible but I do not know how to understand it.

54   The number '11' is written over a partial erasure; it is possible that the text should in fact be '12 12'.

55   I cannot find a plant Ú *šiK-bi anywhere, but unless the plan was to annoy Gilgamesh we cannot read Ú *igigallu* (IGI.GÁL.BI), the 'plant of wisdom'.

56   The plant *kurdinnu* is only lexically attested and all we know about it is that it reeked, but along with other animal fodder in the depths of a whacking great travelling zoo, who would be troubled by that? At any rate, the uncommon last word in this line, like *amurdinnu*, 'bramble (or similar)', ends in -*dinnu*.

59   For *girmadû* as 'roller' see p. 181–2 and note on p. 377.

In the latter stages of writing this book the writer has had the benefit of a first-rate resin cast of the *Ark Tablet* which was specially made in 2012 from the original by Mike Neilson, the British Museum cast maker. This has now been deposited in the cast collection of the Middle East Department, where it is freely available for inspection or collation. It is virtually indistinguishable from the original tablet.

Notes

Notes to Chapter 1: About this Book

P. 1   *one George Smith* . . . A readable account of the background to
this heart-stopping episode and the man himself is Damrosch
2006; Smith's own writings on all this (especially Smith 1875 and
1876) are by no means too antiquated to be worth a look today.

P. 2   *'Izdubar'* . . . Cuneiform signs, as we will see, can often be read
in more than one way, and the correct interpretation of 'Izdubar'
as *Gilgamesh* was only established about fifteen years later (in
great exhilaration) by Theophilus Pinches, one of Smith's successors as British Museum Assyriologist (Pinches 1889–90). Difficulties
in understanding this ancient and famous name persist to this
day; Andrew George devoted a twenty-page chapter of modern
cuneiform exposition to the question in George 2003, Vol. 1:
71–90.

P. 2   *E. A. Wallis Budge* . . . Quoted after Budge 1925: 152–3. Budge,
a very complex character, has been brought to convincing life in
Ismail 2011, with further insight by Reade 2011.

P. 4   *London, 1872* . . . An account of the occasion was published in
The Times newspaper on the following day, 3 December 1872,
while Smith wrote up the full details in two impressive articles
published by the host society as Smith 1873 and 1874.

P. 6   *where he had lived* . . . See Damrosch 2006: 75–6.

P. 7   *answering public enquiries* . . . In the author's department in the
British Museum (successively the Department of Western Asiatic
Antiquities, the Department of the Ancient Near East, and now
the Middle East Department), which covers the whole of the
Middle East, the demand for curatorial identification of objects
has come to diminish over recent years. In earlier times there were
frequent visits from auctioneers, dealers and collectors but the

significant progress that has been made in inhibiting the trade in antiquities illegally exported from the Middle East has meant that today we tend only to see objects with legitimate provenance.

P. 9 *a few interesting specimens* . . . Eight cylinder seals were purchased for the British Museum, now numbered BM 141632–141639.

P. 10 *what was emerging* ... He knew therefore that his Ark was round (discovering which, I nearly fell off my chair); he allowed me to describe it on television (a cameo appearance in *The Truth Behind the Ark*, Zigzag Films, 2010, produced by Alex Hearle), and he permitted me to discuss it with journalists (Maeve Kennedy wrote a full-page article in the *Guardian* newspaper, Friday 1 January 2010, entitled 'The animals walked round and round: Relic reveals Noah's Ark was circular', while Cathy Newman gave a brief account in the *National Geographic Magazine* for February 2011 under the title 'Hark the Round Ark').

Notes to Chapter 2: The Wedge between Us

P. 12 *The Wedge Between Us* . . . This title derives from a series of broadcasts on Radio 4 in 1992 designed to recruit Assyriologists from the public at large. Cuneiform studies today are as open-ended and exciting as Latin and Greek were in the eighteenth century and, as I argued then, should probably be introduced at secondary school on a national level, as there are so many marvellous tablets to be deciphered. So far this policy seems not to have been adopted.

P. 17 *other symbols for numbers* . . . Numbers evolved right alongside writing and quickly reached a remarkable level of sophistication, as clearly explained in Nissen, Damerow and Englund 1993.

P. 19 *The eye sees* . . . Interesting here are two rare specimens of cuneiform writing in *ink* where the Assyrian scribe accurately imitates the cuneiform signs as they look in clay when written with a stylus, but using a brush and ink; a photograph is given in Reade 1986: 217; see, for the implications, Finkel forthcoming (a).

P. 24 *destroy* . . . this verb has sometimes been translated 'flee', but the idea is that the boat is made out of the house materials.

P. 28 *spiky* . . . The Dutch word for cuneiform is *Spijkerschrift* which seems to me to convey incidentally much of the nature of cuneiform writing – if not some of its devotees – 'having spikes', 'being ill-tempered' or 'characterised by violent or aggressive methods'.

Notes to Chapter 3: Words and People

P. 31 *the city, Ur* . . . During the last invasion of Iraq, a high-flown American official, interviewed on the radio about damage to archaeological sites on which military installations had been imposed, referred to this city as 'Umm', evidently confusing one convention for 'I can't think what to say' with another.

P. 38 *the library at Alexandria* . . . For the likelihood that the Alexandrian library was influenced by that at Nineveh see Goldstein 2010.

P. 40 *Arlo Guthrie* . . . The quotation is from the original full recording of *Alice's Restaurant*, a work that cannot be beaten.

P. 43 *allow us to eavesdrop* . . . A good collection of letters from this point of view, all translated into English, is Oppenheim 1967.

P. 45 *Assyrian political treaty* . . . The whole text, from the reign of King Esarhaddon (680–669 BC), is translated in Parpola and Watanabe 1998 as no. 6; these are lines 643–5.

P. 46 *Shuruppak* . . . The long-running work of wisdom literature known to us as the *Instructions of Shuruppak* was handed down by a famous father, himself son of Ubar-Tutu, supposedly the last king to rule before the Flood; see Alster 2005: 63.

P. 47 *classic of Babylonian wisdom literature* . . . The *Dialogue of Pessimism*, as translated in Lambert 1960: 147.

P. 50 *could even read inscriptions* . . . This is the colophon that was added to many of Assurbanipal's library copies, making unambiguously clear the king's personal literary abilities; translation after Livingstone 2007: 100–101.

P. 52 *needed even less* . . . Recent works such as Charpin 2010; Wilcke 2000 and Veldhuis 2001 are good on this important subject.

P. 53 *hard it is to write religious history* . . . A. L. Oppenheim wrote in his influential book *Ancient Mesopotamia* that a history of Mesopotamian religion could never be written, which was all that was needed to goad his Harvard opposite T. Jacobsen into producing one called *Treasures of Darkness*. While a mass of documentary evidence relevant to cuneiform religion has since become available with detailed studies of specific rituals, aspects of temple administration or the history of individual gods, there has been no subsequent attempt at an overview.

P. 57 *for the whole universe* . . . This translation of the Sumerian is the work of Piotr Michalowski, quoted from his article about Sumerian liver divination, Michalowski 2006: 247–8.

P. 66 *but not always* . . . Invaluable here is Civil's 1975 overview of what can be learned from cuneiform dictionaries.

P. 70 *one unique discussion* . . . See Oppenheim 1974. This remarkable text seems hardly to have been appreciated for what it is.

P. 74 *drawings on clay* . . . See the examples in Finkel 2011.

P. 80 *Greeks learning Babylonian* . . . For lots about the remarkable 'Graeco-Babyloniaca' tablets see Geller 1997 and Westenholz 2007.

P. 81 *human diseases* . . . Discussed in Geller 2001/2002; the tablet of game rules is explicated in Finkel 2008.

P. 81 *have got away with quite a lot* . . . A good example is the so-called Greek invention of the gnomon or sun-dial, the construction of which is fully explained on a cuneiform tablet in the British Museum which was once in a library at Babylon. It is widely attributed to Anaximander but even Herodotus knew better; Pingree 1998: 130.

Notes to Chapter 4: Recounting the Flood

P. 84 *Many scholars* . . . The following interesting books, written long in advance of internet resources, have been concerned with this material: Frazer 1918; Riem 1925; Gaster 1969: 82–131; Westermann 1984: 384–406; Bailey 1989 and Cohn 1996. See also Dundes (ed.) 1988.

P. 86 *the biblical Flood itself* . . . The main writings then were Peake 1930; Parrot 1955; Mallowan 1964; Raikes 1966.

P. 86 *versatile pen* . . . Woolley 1954, 1982; Watelin 1934: 40–44; Moorey 1978.

P. 87 *in their footsteps* . . . It is with such matters that the internet is beyond challenge. I have looked at Anderson 2001; Wilson 2001.

P. 89 *if not beyond* . . . For echoes of post-cuneiform Gilgamesh see George 2003, Vol. 1: 54–70.

P. 89 *Atrahasis Epic* . . . Lambert and Millard 1969 is the first serious treatment; a fine translation with useful references is Foster 1993, Vol. 1: 158–201; important also are George and al-Rawi 1996, and the tablet published in Spar and Lambert 2005, referred to on p. 220 above.

P. 90 *have been excavated* . . . The tablet is CBS 10673, translated in Civil 1969: 142–5; discussed in Alster 2005: 32–3.

P. 90 *the god Enki* . . . The tablet is MS 3026, known to me only in photograph.

P. 91 *kings who lived before the Flood* . . . For more details, see Lambert and Millard 1969: 17–21; Alster 2005: 32.

P. 92 *a corking opera* . . . Mesopotamian mythology has, in fact, provided inspiration to composers such as George Rochberg, who wrote the song-cycle *Songs of Inanna and Dumuzi* for contralto and piano based on Sumerian poems. Similar influence on literature has been examined in Foster 2008 and Ziolkowski 2011.

P. 94 *fractious baby* . . . Useful quietening spells for this purpose are collected and translated in Farber 1989

P. 94 *Ipiq-Aya* . . . His story is told in van Koppen 2011.

P. 94 *I will try out the join* . . . The fragment C1 is BM 78942+; C2 is MAH 16064. Translations: Lambert and Millard 1969: 88–93 [source C]; Foster 1993: 177–9.)

P. 95 *how to accomplish it* . . . The tablet is MS 5108, translated in George 2009: 22.

P. 95 *the same lines* . . . See Chapter 13, p. 305.

P. 96 *from other versions* . . . The tablet is Aleppo Museum RS 22.421, translated in Lambert and Millard 1969: 132–3 (source H); Foster 1993, Vol. 1: 185.

P. 96 *University Museum, Philadelphia* . . . The tablet is CBS 13532, translated in Lambert and Millard 1969: 126–7 (source I); Foster 1993, Vol. 1: 184.

P. 96 *described in Chapter 3* . . . The tablet is BM 98977+, translated in Lambert and Millard 1969: 122–3 (source U); Foster 1993, Vol. 1: 184.

P. 96 *Daily Telegraph newspaper* . . . The tablet is DT 42, translated in Lambert and Millard 1969: 129 (source W); Foster 1993, Vol. 1: 194.

P. 96 *Penguin Classic* . . . Originally a slim, composite translation in Sandars 1960, which has been in every way replaced by George 1999.

P. 97 *something of an afterthought.* . . Translated in George 2003, Vol. 1: 704–9, which renders previous editions superfluous.

P. 100 *Berossus according to* . . . These two passages are quoted after Lambert and Millard 1969: 134–7. For a long time scholars had to be content with Cory 1832; later this was replaced by Jacoby 1958. An interesting study of Berossus is Gmirkin 2006, with whose conclusions I cannot agree; see Drows 1975; see now also De Breucker 2011. Geller 2012 has a highly original suggestion about the Berossus work, that it was first written in Aramaic, not Greek.

P. 102 *from the Koran* . . . Koranic translations into English given here are those of Haleem 2004

Notes to Chapter 6: Flood Warning

P. 112 *a message dream* . . . Mesopotamian dreams make very interesting reading in Oppenheim 1956; otherwise Butler 1998 and Zgoll 2006.

P. 113 *Tablet of Sins* . . . For this fragmentary but suggestive story see Finkel 1983a.

P. 116 *We are to conceive* . . . Lambert and Millard 1969: 11–12.

P. 118 *wetland marshes of southern Iraq* . . . Fulanain 1927; Salim 1962; Thesiger 1964, Young 1977 – with Nik Wheeler's excellent photographs – and Ochsenschlager 2004.

Notes to Chapter 7: The Question of Shape

P. 123 *No one had ever thought of that* . . . Florentina Badanalova has recorded an oral Bulgarian tradition in which 'Noah the cooper was told to build a *barrel* rather than an Ark, where he and his family and all the animals were to live while the Flood covered the

Earth for years instead of days'; Badalanova Geller 2009: 10–11.

P. 123 *and probably German* . . . For a history of European model Noah's Arks of painted wood see Kaysel 1992.

P. 127 *A circle within a square* . . . This Old Babylonian diagram of a circle within a tight-fitting square exemplifies how a circle might be said to possess equal length and breadth. It comes from a Babylonian teacher's geometrical textbook with drawings that is always on exhibition in the British Museum and tends to engender a shudder in visitors when they realise that it is 'something to do with maths.' A scribal tour de force, it is of about the same date as the *Ark Tablet*, and gives a sequence of about forty problem questions, each illuminated by a diagram. These show squares within squares, with circles, triangles and other divisions within them, and grow progressively more complex as the student works down the tablet, laboriously calculating the areas of the varous subdivided sections. To try all the classroom problems yourself consult Robson 1999: 208–217; Robson 2008: 47–50. Some of the most complex shapes in the textbook have no counterpart in our geometry and we have no convenient names for them in English although the Babylonians did (Kilmer 1990). On translating lines 6–9 of the *Ark Tablet* for the first time I thought at once of this particular diagram.

P. 129 *a hand reaching down* . . . According to one Jewish tradition God showed Noah with his finger how to make the Ark; another states that all the necessary information was included in the book called *Sefer Razi'el*, a copy of which was given to Noah by the angel Raphael.

P. 129 *Draw the design on the ground* . . . Miguel Civil told me of an unpublished Old Babylonian *Sumerian Schooldays* story that he had been working on which explains how the boys were taught cuneiform signs. They are drawn on a large scale in freshly swept sand in the courtyard for the pupils to copy down on their tablets before the signs got trodden on. Thus the lack of a *blackboard* was neatly circumvented by the *black-headed people*, as the Sumerians called themselves.

P. 130 *Jeffrey Tigay* . . . See Tigay 2002, and, for much useful textual information on the *Atrahasis* side, Shehata 2001.

P. 133   *coracles from India* . . . For coracles of the world, consult Badge 2009; Hornell 1938 and Hornell 1946.

P. 133   *standard works on ancient Mesopotamian boats* . . . For example, Salonen 1939; Potts 1997; Carter 2012 and Zarins 2008.

P. 133   *Legend of Sargon* . . . This legend has been well known since the nineteenth century, when George Smith and William Fox Talbot (pioneer Assyriologist and pioneer photographer) squabbled about the translation; the most recent treatment since Lewis 1980 is Westenholz 1997: 36–49.

P. 134   *I think we can conclude* . . . Since making this brilliant discovery I discovered from Carter 2012: 370 that M. Weszeli had already made the same point in 2009: 168.

P. 135   *a direct textual parallel* . . . Compare the final words of the *Ark Tablet*, 'Caulk the frame of her door!'

P. 135   *the smallest specimen ever made* . . . Chesney 1853: 640.

P. 136   *reed boats* . . . *skin-covered coracles* . . . Like the *Chicago Assyrian Dictionary* the historian A. K. Grayson (Grayson 1996), translated this passage as 'reed *rafts*' and '*rafts* (made of inflated) goatskins', but both interpretations are incorrect. Giant rafts were made of wood lashed together resting hovercraft-like on inflated animal-skin balloons but this is not what is meant by Shalmaneser's archivist. The Babylonian word for raft, only attested in the plural, is *ḫallimu*; ancient Mesopotamian rafts are often called by their modern Turkish name *kelek* in the literature. For notes by someone who knew about Iraqi rafts see Chesney 1850: 634–7.

P. 138   *which way was up* . . . Hornell 1938: 106 is rather sceptical concerning the reliability of the Herodotus account but Badge 2009: 172–3 defends his testimony with parallel practices from elsewhere, and I think does so rightly.

P. 139   Tigris *barcarii* . . . The observation that these men, listed in the *Notitia Dignitatum*, were *guffa* specialists is that of Reade 1999: 287 (see Holder 1982: 123).

P. 147   *boat called a ṭubbû* . . . Quoted after *Chicago Assyrian Dictionary* Ṭ 115, where the Babylonian tablet in which this otherwise unknown word occurs, here given in photograph, has recently been referred to (BM 32873); *ṭubbû* thus parallels *tēvāh* in another way, attested to twice in only one document!

P. 149   *conceivably even ultimately ancestral* . . . The origins of the word tub earlier than in Europe of the fourteenth century AD are lost to scholarly enquiry.

P. 149   *A remarkable kind of boat* . . . This and the following quotations are from Chesney 1853: 636–9.

P. 154   *Patai writes* . . . See Patai 1998: 5.

Notes to Chapter 8: Building the Arks

P. 163   *what a shipyard would do* . . . See Potts 1997: 126.

P. 168   *abbreviation, the sign PI* . . . This is not quite the same as our writing 'p' in '20p', even though 'p for *parsiktu*' is a good way to remember the word.

P. 169   *These types of wood* . . . For such matters see Powell 1992.

P. 172   *the cosmic Apsû* . . . See Horowitz 1998: 334–47.

P. 174   *Bitumen is thus applied* . . . For modern Iraqi boat-building bitumen practice see Ochsenschlager 1992: 52.

P. 175   *some scrappy records* . . . Leemans 1960.

P. 181   *a tool called girmadû* . . . This term is borrowed from Sumerian *giš.gìr-má-dù*, where giš is the determinative for 'wood', gìr means 'foot' and má means 'boat', although dù is a verb with many possible meanings. Its Sumerian origin is reflected in the mixed Sumerian and Akkadian-style spelling *gi-ir*-MÁ.DÙ.MEŠ in *Gilgamesh XI*: 79. Since it is a roller for applying a waterproof coating, the sign DÙ probably stands for the homonym DU$_8$, which means 'to seal', or 'to caulk'.

Notes to Chapter 9: Life on Board

P. 186   *category of 'clean'* . . . Foster 1993, Vol. 1: 178–9 sees Atra-hasīs as slaughtering these clean and fat animals but sacrifices were hardly needed to smooth the way for an activity carried out on direct divine orders.

P. 190   *two by two* . . . Anyone who stumbles across the early study of our *Middle Babylonian Nippur*, Hilprecht 1910: 49, 56–7, will find he has gratuitously restored the expression 'two of everything', but without any single part of any of the needed signs being preserved on the document!

P. 190   *I loaded aboard it* . . . This much-reiterated and possibly tension-building phrase in *Gilgamesh XI* may well be an indication of oral literary technique but grates now in printed context in much the same way as when politicians repeat a phrase like 'and the next thing we are going to do is . . .' five or six times while they think up a string of impressive-sounding promises. It is tantalising that we cannot know whether *Old Babylonian Atrahasis* 30–31, which begins in the same way as *Gilgamesh XI* 82–3, also concerned material wealth. I like to think that it did not.

P. 195   *occurred to me* . . . I later discovered, of course, that others have already done such things with the ark narrative, such as Parrot 1955: 15–22 (which is a first-rate book), Bailey 1989, Chapter 6, and especially Westermann 1984, but not reaching the same conclusions.

P. 197   *The statistics* . . . as retrievable from the internet.

P. 199   *Sumerian UR = Akkadian,* kalbu, *'dog'* . . . Words sometimes function differently between Sumerian and Akkadian; 'lioness', in Akkadian, is a specific noun, *nēštum*; in Sumerian 'lioness' is written with three cuneiform signs that etymologically mean 'female exalted dog', although the combination *means* 'lioness' not 'female exalted dog'. The etymology disappears into the word. To compare the order and content of the Mesopotamian 'living-things' lists in Urra = *hubullu* – which certainly aimed at completeness – with later classificatory systems would be very interesting.

P. 199   *what the entries would have been* . . . This translation depends on decades and mountains of philology by many valiant cuneiformists. The original tablets are available in the series *Materials for the Sumerian Lexicon* (MSL 8/1 and 8/2) and brilliantly accessible (in German) in Landsberger 1934; the English translations of all the words given here follow the *Chicago Assyrian Dictionary*. Older cuneiform sources exist than have been used here, as well as ancient explanations of the entries.

p. 207   *the right nuance* . . . Foster 1993, Vol. 1: 179 translates this, 'While one was eating and another was drinking.'

p. 208   *at least one was a vet* . . . There was veterinary as well as human medicine in ancient Mesopotamia, especially dedicated to horses. An ancient catalogue of cuneiform medical works now in the Oriental Institute Collection in Chicago puts horses and women in the same category!

P. 211   *laden with ripe meanings* . . . In addition to the discussion in George 2003, Vol. 1: 510–12, see George 2010.

Notes to Chapter 10: Babylon and Bible Floods

P. 214   *not the first time* . . . See Smith 1875: 207–22; Smith 1876: 283–9; Driver 1909; Bailey 1989: 14–22; Best 1999; George 2003, Vol. 1: 512–19. Westermann 1984: 384–458, on this whole thing, is a *tour de force* and absolutely fascinating.

P. 217   *most powerful writing* . . . Read it all at your leisure in George 1999: 88–99 or George 2003, Vol. 1: 709–13.

P. 219   *whole literary episode* . . . See George 2003, Vol. 1: 516–18.

P. 219   *the great flies* . . . According to Ann Kilmer, the wings of these flies might have some translucent connection with the rainbow image (Kilmer 1997: 175–80).

Notes to Chapter 11: The Judaean Experience

P. 224   *deriving from a shared ancestor* . . . This view has been promoted more than once by W. G. Lambert, who considers the story as common Middle Eastern property; see most recently Lambert 1994. Millard 1994 is careful on the subject. Finds of Gilgamesh tablets in 2nd millenium BC Middle Eastern sites such as Megiddo in Israel reflect the spread of cuneiform by Mesopotanian teachers as described on p. 74 above, not widespread familiarity with the full Gilgamesh Epic.

P. 228   *Nebuchadnezzar's Chronicle* . . . See Grayson 1975: 99–102. Such records were kept accessible long after their time. In Ezra 4, a sabotage letter sent to the Persian king Artaxerxes in Babylon by persons wishing to stop the rebuilding of the Temple in Jerusalem could well refer to this very Chronicle:

> . . . *we send and inform the king, in order that search may be made in the book of the records of your fathers. You will find in the book of the records and learn that this city is a rebellious city, hurtful to kings and provinces, and that sedition was stirred up in it from of old. That was why this city was laid waste* . . .

The answer confirmed that a:

> . . . *search has been made, and it has been found that this city from of old has risen against kings, and that rebellion and sedition have been made in it. And mighty kings have been over Jerusalem, who ruled over the whole province Beyond the River, to whom tribute, custom, and toll were paid.*

P. 231 *Before long* . . . There was a very considerable flurry of media interest and internet response to the Nebo-Sarsekim tablet. I myself got into hot water through trying to explain over the telephone how amazing Jursa's discovery was in quietly proving that one named individual mentioned in the Bible who was not a king really did exist, which ended up as *Curator claims Bible is true after all* headline; a second blunder was describing the size of the tablet as about 'equal to a packet of ten cigarettes', which provoked a different kind of outcry. The tablet has been treated by the discoverer in Jursa 2008; see also Becking and Stadhouders 2009.

P. 232 *Nebuchadnezzar's five highest-ranking officers* . . . These very high-ranking Babylonians were in the Middle Gate at Jerusalem as the city burned and the women screamed. The Judaean chronicler was anxious to name each with his title to establish responsibility for their blasphemous deeds for posterity. The unfamiliar names and words are recorded by ear and the recorder got flustered. The Court Calendar of Nebuchadnezzar, compiled in the king's seventh year (shortly before the first campaign), lists all high court officials by name and office. In this document (Jursa 2010: Da Riva (forthcoming)) nearly all the officials named by Jeremiah are to be found:

Nergal-Sharezer, *samgar*

In Babylonian he is Nergal-šar-uṣur, better known as Neriglissar, who himself twenty-six years later became king of Babylon, ruling from 560–556 BC by murdering his predecessor Amel-Marduk, Nebuchadnezzar's son and heir (and also his own brother-in-law). The Hebrew term *samgar* has sometimes been understood as a place name (hence the common translation 'of Samgar'), but it reflects the Babylonian *simmāgir*, 'district governor', which was Nergal-šar-uṣur's title at the time according to the Court Calendar.

Nergal-Sharezer, *rab mug*

This title, conventionally translated 'a high official', also reflects a real Babylonian word, *rab mungi*, the commanding officer for chariots and cavalry.

These separate titles, *simmāgir* and *rab mungi*, are erroneously applied in the Hebrew text to one name, Nergal-Sharezer; we know that Nebuchadnezzar's *rab mungi* at this time was called Nabu-zakir, and his name should properly have been entered here.

Nebo-Sarsekim, *rab sarīs*

The title conventionally translated 'chief officer' literally means 'chief eunuch', and is the Hebraised form of Babylonian *rab ša-rēši*, which was a high political title. As indicated above, we can identify Jeremiah's Nebo-Sarsekim *rab sarīs* with the Babylonian Nabu-šarrussu-ukin, *rab ša-rēši*, The Judaean chronicler again transcribed the unfamiliar name for posterity as best he could.

Nebuzaradan, *rab ṭabāḥīm*

In Babylonian this is Nabu-zer-iddin. His title is the equivalent of Babylonian *bēl* or *rab ṭābiḥī*. This title is found in the *Court Calendar* but the name of the official himself is broken away in the tablet. It means literally 'Chief Slaughterer', but we know from other texts that the 'slaughterers' were the royal guard. At Jerusalem he is very clearly in charge of Nebuchadnezzar's crack punitive war units.

The Court Calendar does mention a Nabu-zer-iddin in a different line of text, where he has the title *rab nuḫatimmī*, 'Chief Cook', with whom the Jeremiah official Nebuzaradan has sometimes been identified. This title can have nothing to do with warmongering, and the likelihood is that there were two people called Nabu-zer-iddin at the top in Babylon, rather than the 'Chief Cook' having been soon reappointed as 'Commander of the Royal Guard'. The Jeremiah passages seem to be in no doubt who Nebuzaradan was and what he did; he is the only official to be named in Jeremiah 52.

Nebushazban, *rab sarīs*
In Babylonian the name is **Nabu-šuzibanni**, but here again there has been a mix-up in the text. Since we know that **Nabu-šarrussu-ukin** was Nebuchadnezzar's *rab sarīs*, Nabu-šuzibannim must have had a different title, but he is not attested in the Court Circular and for the present we cannot identify him in a cuneiform source.

P. 237   *brief, nine-verse episode* . . . Before the Babylon Myth and Reality exhibition opened in November 2008 we had resolved to print the text of Genesis 11:1–9 on a panel because a preliminary 'public' survey had suggested that a majority of individuals were either altogether unfamiliar with the story or unaware that it occurs in the Old Testament. In the flurry of interviews that attended the first few days, a journalist read over the Tower of Babel quotation on the panel among other panel texts and agreed, apparently without irony, that we had a good team of writers at our disposal.

P. 239   *run out in the early stages* . . . The traveller in the Middle East today will commonly see inhabited houses where corner poles of scaffolding stick up high above the building as if the owner is planning on, or hoping for, another storey in due course.

P. 240   *issues of oil, barley* . . . For this extraordinary evidence that King Jehoiachin's party were alive and well in Babylon see Weidner 1939; Pedersén 2005a and Pedersén 2005b.

P. 241   *personal names* . . . Here the great expertise of Ran Zadok has borne fruit; for a useful survey of this work see Millard 2013.

P. 243   *little theological text* . . . see Pinches 1896: 1–3; Lambert 1964; Parpola 1995: 399.

P. 249   *Noah* . . . I like especially what Berossus has to say on this point (translation after Burstein 1978: 29):

> *Noah lived three hundred and fifty years after the deluge in happiness. He died after having lived nine hundred and fifty years. Let no one as a result of comparing life now and the fewness of the years which we live with that of the ancients think that what is said about them is false, judging that they did not live to such an age because no one now does. For they were dear to God and his own creatures; also as their food was more favourable to longer life, it is reasonable to suppose that they lived so great a number of years. Then also God permitted them to live longer because of their excellent character and the usefulness of their discoveries, astronomy and geometry, since, unless they lived six hundred years – for so long is the period of a great year – they could not have made accurate predictions.*

P. 251   *the Genesis Great Ages tradition* . . . For such literature see Hess 1994; Malamat 1994; Wilson 1994.

P. 251   *upright character and behaviour* . . . For traditions as to Noah's character, Lewis 1978 is interesting.

P. 251   *miraculous beginnings* . . . The unknown-parent-for-heroes device has been applied to major historical figures in many world literatures, and the specific topic of baby exposure is often central. Evidence for this is given in Lewis 1980, where some seventy passages are collected – aside from those in Babylonian and Hebrew – that make use of this idea, written in Arabic, Greek, Latin, Indian, Persian, German, Icelandic, English, Irish, Albanian, Turkish, Chinese, Malayan and Palaung.

P. 252   *acculturated to Babylonian life* . . . This point has been made about the Assyrians doing the same thing earlier in Parpola 1972: 34; Finkel (forthcoming [b]).

P. 253   *Great ages of man* . . . This tablet is ME40565 in the British Museum; see Finkel 1980: 65–8. It shows the ŠÁR signs discussed on p. 308.

P. 253   *curricular tablets* . . . A valiant study of these difficult texts, which are often in untidy beginner's script and full of errors, was published in Gesche 2000.

P. 254   This Baby Sargon tablet is ME47449 in the British Museum; see Westenholz 1997: 38–49.

P. 256   *people of the book* . . . See Jullien and Jullien 1995.

P. 256   *crystallising into permanence* . . . It is an interesting matter for reflection that the precarious Judaean religion which arrived out of the smoke of Jerusalem, surrounded by the mighty gods of the Egyptians and the Babylonians and all the other powers of the ancient Middle Eastern world, is the only one of them all to survive, as it has, into modern times.

P. 256   *round the country* . . . According to Jewish tradition, certain Judaeans were settled at this time at Nehardea, a walled town at the junction with the Euphrates and the Malka River, with a synagogue built using stones and earth brought from the Temple site; this, in due course, became one major centre of Talmudic scholarship and the seat of the Exilarch.

P. 257   *their documents* . . . An archive of more than one hundred cuneiform tablets from this crucial archive is to be published by Cornelia Wunsch and Laurie Pearce.

P. 259   *Survival of Babylonian ideas and practices* . . . loanwords: Kwasman (forthcoming); medicine: Geller 2004; divination by dreams: Oppenheim 1956; by necromancy: Finkel 1983b; textual exegesis; Lambert 1954–6; Lieberman 1987; Cavigneaux 1987; Frahm 2011: 369–83; Finkel (forthcoming [b]).

Notes to Chapter 12: What Happened to the Ark?

P. 261   *The map in question* . . . A recent book that covers some aspects of the Babylonian Map of the World is Horowitz 1998. Many writers who have discussed this map criticise its 'inaccuracies' or other supposed failings, which shows that they have never understood anything at all about it.

P. 262   *earliest known map of the world* . . . It should be pointed out that an early crossroads-type 'sketch map' on a mid-third-millennium-BC tablet from the site of Fara is considered by Frans Wiggermann to be a forerunner of this map; I am unconvinced; see Wiggermann 2011: 673.

P. 266   *writing something* . . . This duly appeared as Finkel 1995.

P. 266   *the following evening* . . . The date of the broadcast was 1 September 1995, my forty-fourth birthday! I feel it also necessary for some reason to record that I submitted the manuscript of this book into the hands of my publisher exactly eighteen years later, on 1 September 2013.

P. 269   *written with the determinative for river* . . . The word *marratu* is not the 'real' Babylonian word for sea; it was borrowed during the first millennium from a Chaldean dialect.

P. 269   *regions or districts* . . . See Horowitz 1988: 27–33.

P. 272   *Very Hairy One* . . . This type of character is known to guard important cosmic gates, and the whole family has been interestingly laid bare in Wiggermann 1992: 164–5.

P. 273   *(giant?) flightless birds* . . . Ostriches were well known in ancient Mesopotamia; they were often depicted and their shells put to good use from as early as the third millennium BC; here the point is likely to be that while everyone knew that some so-called birds couldn't actually fly, these *Nagû* III specimens were also on a giant scale, with unimaginable eggs . . .

P. 278   *ancient name Urartu* . . . See Mathkovič 1977

P. 280   *prefer Mount Niṣir* . . . The argument for Nimuš over Niṣir is based on the personal name Iddin-nimuš, supposedly of a workman of north Mesopotamian origin, in which the name of the mountain functions like that of a god (Lambert 1986). We know, however, that Niṣir was locally called Kinipa, and surely that is the form which would have been used in a local name.

P. 281   *Ashurnasirpal starts* . . . Quoted after Speiser 1928: 17–18.

P. 286   *Eutychius, Patriarch of Alexandria* . . . Quoted after Crouse and Franz 2006: 106.

P. 286   *Gertrude Bell described* . . . See Bell 1911.

P. 288   Translations after Grayson 1991: 204–5.

P. 288   *On my fifth* . . . and *Like a fierce bull* . . . Grayson and Novotny 2012.

P. 290   *contemporary Assyrian incantation* . . . This tablet is in a rather idiosyncratic script and does not resemble those of Assurbanipal in the Nineveh Library; it could well come from Sennacherib's period. It is part of an exorcistic manual against bad dreams and has not yet been published.

P. 291   *Mt Nipur* . . . This name is not to be confused with the southern Mesopotamian city of Nippur, already mentioned.

P. 291   *murdered their father Sennacherib* . . . On this murder and the identity of the culprits see Parpola 1980. Sennacherib was killed at Dur-Sharrukin, his father's new palace.

P. 293   *Traditions about* . . . Montgomery 1972 and Bailey 1989 can be recommended to anyone who is tempted to wander among these narratives.

P. 295   *an uncanny – and usually unexplained – resemblance* . . . On the similarity issue see most recently Zaccagnini 2012.

Notes to Chapter 13: What is the *Ark Tablet*?

P. 299   *we find this narrative* . . . As already mentioned, the length of the full Flood Story in *Gilgamesh XI* is undeniably disproportionate for the unfolding of the plot as a whole and its satisfactory dénouement. It can be seen as the device of telling a tale within a tale to keep the audience enthralled, but the length is nevertheless considerable for people who want to find out what happened in the end, and its inclusion might also mean that the redactors themselves just liked the story, and dropped it in with the minimum of alteration. Perhaps the whole of *Gilgamesh XI* formerly had an independent existence. We need new sources to bring new light, as always.

P. 301   *long convinced themselves* . . . Interesting remarks on this issue are given in Cooper 1992.

P. 306   *to interest inattentive schoolboys* . . . There is a closer parallel from the end of the first millennium BC when advanced pupils in a school at Babylon studying old and new cubit measurements were set to measure the dimensions of the giant ziggurat that could be seen from every vantage point of the city; see George 2008: 128, Fig. 109.

Notes to Appendices

P. 316   *Ancient Babylonian scholars* . . . A full discussion of what is otherwise known about this sign and many questions to do with the *eṭemmu* spirit is given in Steinert 2012: 309–11.

P. 317   *Tablet I* . . . I have translated these lines afresh, but with the benefit of many previous translations and discussions, for they have often been studied; Lambert and Millard 1969: 58–9; Foster 1993:165–6; George and Al-Rawi 1996: 149–50. The idea that Akkadian *eṭemmu* can mean both 'spirit' – as in 'ghost' – and 'human spirit', exactly like our own word, seems not to have been recognised, but it makes simple sense of this otherwise obscure passage.

P. 324   *The Descent of Ishtar* . . . quoted after Foster 1993: 404.

P. 326   *Ur-Shanabi* . . . For everything else that can possibly be needed concerning this name see George 2003, Vol. 1: 149–51.

P. 344   *the diameter of the Ark* . . . one might imagine that the larger size of the Ark derives from the substitution of a larger unit in a lighterman's song about boat building.

Bibliography

This bibliography includes all books and articles referred to or quoted in the main text and the notes.

Abdel Haleem, M.A.S., *The Qur'an: A New Translation*. Oxford World's Classics. Oxford, 2004.

Agius, D.A., *Classic Ships of Islam: From Mesopotamia to the Indian Ocean*. Leiden. 2007.

Alster, B., *Wisdom of Ancient Sumer*. Maryland, 2005.

Amiet, P., *La Glyptique Mesopotamienne Archaique*. Paris, 1961.

Anderson, W.W., *Solving the Mystery of the Biblical Flood*. [America], 2001.

Badalanova Geller, F., 'The Folk Bible', *Sophia* 3 (2009): 8–11.

Badge, P., *Coracles of the World*. Llanrwst, 2009.

Bailey, L.R., *Noah: The Person and the Story in History and Tradition*. South Carolina, 1989.

Barnett, R.D. and A. Lorenzini, *Assyrian Sculpture in the British Museum*. London, 1975.

Becking, B. (with H. Stadhouders), 'The Identity of Nabu-sharrussu-ukin, the Chamberlain. An Epigraphic Note on Jeremiah 39,3' ('Appendix on the Nebu(!)sarsekim Tablet' contributed by Stadhouders), *Biblische Notizen. Aktuelle Beiträge zur Exegese der Bibel und ihrer Welt* 140: 35–46.

Bell, G.L., *Amurath to Amurath*. London, 1911.

Best, R.M., *Noah's Ark and the Ziusudra Epic*. Florida, 1999.

Black, J.A., 'Sumerian', in J.N. Postgate (ed.), *Languages of Iraq Ancient and Modern*. Cambridge, 2007: 4–30.

de Breucker, G., 'Berossus between Tradition and Innovation', in K. Radner and E. Robson (eds), *The Oxford Handbook of Cuneiform Culture*. Oxford, 2011: 637–57.

Budge, E.A.W., *Assyrian Sculptures in the British Museum*. London, 1914.

—, *By Nile and Tigris*, Vols 1–2. London, 1920 [reprint: Hardinge Simpole, Kilkerran, 2011].

Budge, E.A.W., *The Rise and Progress of Assyriology*. London, 1925.

Burstein, S.M., *The Babyloniaca of Berossus: Sources from the Ancient Near East*, Vol. 1, fasc. 5. Malibu, 1978.

Butler, S.A.L., *Mesopotamian Conceptions of Dreams and Dream Rituals*. Alter Orient und Altes Testament, Vol. 258. Munster, 1998.

Carter, R.A., 'Watercraft', in D.T. Potts (ed.), *A Companion to the Archaeology of the Ancient Near East*, Vol. 1. Oxford, 2012: 347–72.

Cavigneaux, A. 'Aux sources du Midrash; l'herméneutique babyloni-enne', *Aula Orientalis* 5:243–55.

Charpin, D., *Reading and Writing in Babylon*. Cambridge, MA and London, 2010.

Chesney, F.R., *The Expedition for the Survey of the rivers Euphrates and Tigris carried on by Order of the British Government in the Years 1835, 1836 and 1837*. Vol. 2. London, 1850.

Civil, M., 'The Sumerian Flood Story', in Lambert and Millard 1969: 138–45, 167–72.

Civil, M., 'Lexicography', in S.J. Lieberman (ed.), *Sumerian Studies in Honor of Thorkild Jacobsen on his Seventieth Birthday, June 7, 1974*. Assyriological Studies 20. Chicago, 1975: 123–57.

Cohn, N., *Noah's Flood: The Genesis Story in Western Thought*. Yale, 1996.

Collins, P., *From Egypt to Babylon: The International Age 1550–500 bc*. London, 2008.

Cooper, J.S., 'Babbling On: Recovering Mesopotamian Orality', in M. E. Vogelzang and H.L.J. Vanstiphout (eds), *Mesopotamian Epic Literature: Oral or Aural?*' Lewiston, Queenston and Lampeter, 1992: 103–21.

Cory, I.P., *Ancient Fragments of the Phoenician, Chaldaean, Egyptian, Tyrian, Carthaginian, Indian, Persian and other Writers with an Introductory Dissertation: and an Enquiry into the Philosophy and Trinity of the Ancients*. Second edition. London, 1832.

Crouse, B. and G. Franz, 'Mount Cudi – True Mountain of Noah's Ark', *Bible and Spade* 19/4 (2006): 99-111.

Damrosch, D., *The Buried Book: The Loss and Rediscovery of the Great Epic of Gilgamesh*. New York, 2006.

de Graeve, M.-C., *The Ships of the Ancient Near East (c. 2000–500 B.C.)*. Orientalia Lovaniensia Analecta, Vol. 7. Leuven, 1981.

Da Riva, R., 'Nebuchadnezzar II's Prism (ES 7834): A New Edition', *Zeitschrift für Assyriologie und Vorderasiatische Archäologie*, forthcoming.

Drews, R., 'The Babylonian Chronicles and Berossus, *Iraq* 37 (1975): 39–55.

Driver, S.R., *The Book of Genesis*. London, 1909.

Dundes, A. (ed.), *The Flood Myth*. California, 1988.

Farber, W., *Schlaf, Kindchen, Schlaf! Mesopotamische Baby-Beschwörungen und -Rituale*. Mesopotamian Civilizations 2. Winona Lake, 1989.

Finkel, I.L., 'Bilingual Chronicle Fragments', *Journal of Cuneiform Studies* 32 (1980): 65–80.

Finkel, I.L., 'The Dream of Kurigalzu and the Tablet of Sins', *Anatolian Studies* 33 (1983a): 75–80.

Finkel, I.L., 'Necromancy in Ancient Mesopotamia', *Archiv für Orientfotschung* 29 (1983b): 1–16.

Finkel, I.L., 'A Join to the Map of the World: A Notable Discovery', *British Museum Magazine: The Journal of the British Museum Friends*, 23 (1995): 26–7.

Finkel, I.L., 'The Lament of Nabū-šuma-ukīn', in J. Renger (ed.), *Babylon: Focus mesopotamischer Geschichte, Wiege früher Gelehrtsamkeit, Mythos in der Moderne*. Saarbrücken, 1999: 323–41.

Finkel, I.L., 'The Game and the Play of the Royal Game of Ur', in I.L. Finkel (ed.), *Ancient Board Games in Perspective*. Papers of the 1991 Board Game Colloquium at the British Museum. London, 2008a: 22–38.

Finkel, I.L., 'The Babylonian Map of the World, or the *Mappa Mundi*', in I.L. Finkel and M.J. Seymour (eds), *Babylon: Myth and Reality*. London, 2008b: 17.

Finkel, I.L., 'Drawings on Tablets', *Scienze dell'Antichità* 17 (2011): 337–44.

Finkel, I.L., 'Assurbanipal's Library: An Overview', in K. Ryholt and G. Barjamovic (eds), *Libraries Before Alexandria*. Oxford, forthcoming (a).

Finkel, I.L., 'Remarks on Cuneiform Scholarship and the Babylonian Talmud', in U. Gabbay and Sh. Secunda (eds), *Encounters by the Rivers of Babylon: Scholarly Conversations between Jews, Iranians, and Babylonians in Antiquity*. Tübingen, forthcoming (b).

Forbes, R.J., *Studies in Ancient Technology*, Vol. 1. Leiden, 1955.

Foster, B., *Before the Muses*, Vol. 1. Maryland, 1993.

Foster, B., 'Assyriology and English Literature', in M. Ross (ed.), *From the Banks of the Euphrates: Studies in Honor of Alice Louise Slotsky*. Winona Lake, 2008.

Frahm, E. *Babylonian and Assyrian Text Commentaries*. Guides to the Mesopotamian Textual Record 5. Münster, 2011.

Frazer, J.G., *Folklore in the Old Testament*. London, 1918.

Fulanain, *Haji Rikkan: Marsh Arab*. London, 1927.

Gaster, M., *The Chronicle of Jerahmeel; or the Hebrew Bible Historiale. Being a Collection of Apocryphal and Pseudo-epigraphical Books (by Various Authors: Collected by Eleazar ben Asher, the Levite) Dealing with the History of the World from the Creation to the Death of Judas Maccabeus*. Oriental Translation Fund. New Series 4. London, 1899.

Gaster, T.H., *Myth, Legend and Custom in the Old Testament*. New York and London, 1969.

Geller, M.J., 'The Last Wedge', *Zeitschrift für Assyriologie* 87 (1997): 43–95.

Geller, M.J., 'West Meets East: Early Greek and Babylonian Diagnosis', *Archiv für Orientforschung* 18/19 (2001/2): 50–75.

Geller, M.J., *Akkadian Healing Therapies in the Babylonian Talmud*. Preprint, Max Planck Institute for the History of Science no. 259. Berlin, 2004.

Geller, M.J., 'Berossos on Kos from the View of Common Sense Geography', in K. Geus and M. Thiering (eds), *Common Sense*

Geography and Mental Modelling. Preprint, Max Planck Institute for the History of Science. Berlin, 2012: 101–9.

George, A.R., *The Epic of Gilgamesh: The Babylonian Epic Poem and Other Texts in Akkadian and Sumerian*. London and New York, 1999.

George, A.R., *The Babylonian Gilgamesh Epic*. Introduction, Critical Edition and Cuneiform Texts, Vols 1–2. Oxford, 2003.

George, A.R., 'Babylonian and Assyrian: A History of Akkadian', in J.N. Postgate (ed.), *Languages of Iraq Ancient and Modern*. Cambridge, 2007: 31–71.

George, A.R., 'The Truth about Etemenanki, the Ziggurat of Babylon', in I.L. Finkel and M.J. Seymour (eds), *Babylon: Myth and Reality*. London, 2008: 126–9.

George, A.R., *Babylonian Literary Texts in the Schøyen Collection*. Cornell University Studies in Assyriology and Sumerology, Vol. 10. Manuscripts in the *Schøyen* Collection, Cuneiform Texts IV. Maryland, 2009.

George, A.R., 'The Sign of the Flood and the Language of Signs in Babylonian Omen Literature', in L. Kogan (ed.), *Language in the Ancient Near East*. Winona Lake, 2010: 323–35.

George, A.R. and F.N.H. Al-Rawi, 'Tablets from the Sippar Library VI: Atra-hasis', *Iraq* 58 (1996): 147–90.

Gesche, P., *Schulunterricht in Babylonien im ersten Jahrtausend v. Chr.* Alter Orient und Altes Testament, Vol. 275. Münster, 2000.

Gmirkin, R.E., *Berossus, Genesis, Manetho and Exodus: Hellenestic Histories and the Date of the Pentateuch*. New York and London: 2006.

Goldstein, R., 'Late Babylonian Letters on Collecting Tablets and their Hellenistic Background', *Journal of Near Eastern Studies* 69 (2010): 109–207.

Grayson, A.K., *Assyrian and Babylonian Chronicles*. Texts from Cuneiform Sources, Vol. 5. New York, 1975.

Grayson, A.K., *Assyrian Rulers of the Early First Millennium BC I (1114–859 bc)*. The Royal Inscriptions of Mesopotamia. Assyrian Periods, Vol. 2. Toronto, Buffalo and London, 1991.

Grayson, A.K., *Assyrian Rulers of the Early First Millennium BC II*

(858–745 bc). The Royal Inscriptions of Mesopotamia: Assyrian Periods. Vol. 3. Toronto, Buffalo and London, 1996.

Grayson, A.K. and J. Novotny, *The Royal Inscriptions of Sennacherib, King of Assyria (704–681 bc), Part 1.* Royal Inscriptions of the Neo-Assyrian Period 3/1. 2012.

Hess, R.S., 'The Genealogies of Genesis 1–11 and Comparative Literature', in R.S. Hess and D.T. Tsumura (eds), 'I Studied Inscriptions from before the Flood'. *Ancient Near Eastern, Literary and Linguistic Approaches to Genesis 1–11*. Winona Lake, 1994: 58–72.

Hess, R.S. and D.T. Tsumura (eds), 'I Studied Inscriptions from before the Flood'. *Ancient Near Eastern, Literary and Linguistic Approaches to Genesis 1–11*. Winona Lake, 1994.

Hilprecht, H., *The Earliest Version of the Babylonian Deluge Story and the Temple Library of Nippur*. The Babylonian Expedition of the University of Pennsylvania Series D: Researches and Treatises, Vol. 5, fasc. 1, 1910.

Holder, P.A., *The Roman Army in Britain*. London, 1982.

Hornell, J., 'The Coracles of the Tigris and Euphrates', *The Mariner's Mirror* [Quarterly Journal of the Society for Nautical Research] 24/2: April 1938: 153–9 [reprint: *British Coracles and Irish Curraghs with a Note on the Quffah of Iraq*, London, 1938].

Hornell, J., *Water Transport: Origins & Early Evolution*. Cambridge, 1946.

Horowitz, W., 'The Babylonian Map of the World', *Iraq* 50 (1988): 147–65.

Horowitz, W., *Babylonian Cosmic Geography*. Mesopotamian Civilisations 8. Winona Lake, 1998.

Ismail, M., *Wallis Budge: Magic and Mummies in London and Cairo*. Kilkerran, 2011.

Jacobsen, T., *The Sumerian King List*. Assyriological Studies 11. Chicago, 1939.

Jacobsen, T., *The Treasures of Darkness*. New Haven and London, 1976.

Jacobsen, T., *The Harps that Once . . .* New Haven and London, 1987.

Jacoby, F., *Die Fragmente der griechischen Historiker*, Vol. 3. Leiden, 1958.

Jullien, C. and F., *La Bible en Exil*. Civilisations du Proche-Orient 3. Religions et Culture 1. Paris, 1995.

Jursa, M., 'Nabû-šarrūssu-ukīn, und 'Nebusarsekim' (Jer. 39:3)', *Nouvelles Assyriologiques Brèves et Utilitaires* 1 (2008): 10.

Jursa, M., 'Der neubabylonische Hof', in B. Jacobs and R. Rollinger (eds), *Der Achamenidenhof: The Achaemenid Court*. Akten des 2. Internationalen Kolloqiuims zum Thema 'Vorderasien im Spannungsfeld klassicher und altorientalischer Überlieferungen'. Landgut Castelen bei Basel, 23–25 May 2007. Wiesbaden, 2010: 67–95.

Kaysel, R., *Arche Noah*. Schweizer Kindermuseum Baden, 1992.

Kilmer, A.D., 'The Mesopotamian Concept of Overpopulation and Its Solution as Reflected in the Mythology', *Orientalia* New Series 41 (1972): 160–77.

Kilmer, A.D., 'Sumerian and Akkadian Names for Designs and Geometric Shapes', in A.C. Gunter (ed.), *Investigating Artistic Environments in the Ancient Near East*. Washington, 1990: 83–6.

Kilmer, A.D., 'The Symbolism of the Flies in the Mesopotamian Flood Myth and some Further Implications', in F. Rochberg-Halton (ed.), *Language, Literature and History: Philological and Historical Studies Presented to Erica Reiner*. New Haven, 1987: 175–80.

Kwasman, T., 'Loanwords in Jewish Babylonian Aramaic: Some Preliminary Observations', in M.J. Geller and S. Shaked (eds), *Babylonian Talmudic Archaeology*, Leiden, forthcoming.

Lambert, W.G., 'An Address of Marduk to the Demons', *Archiv für Orientforschung* 17 (1954–6): 310–21.

Lambert, W.G., *Babylonian Wisdom Literature*. Oxford, 1960a.

Lambert, W.G., 'New Light on the Babylonian Flood', *Journal of Semitic Studies* 5 (1960b): 113–23.

Lambert, W.G., 'The Reign of Nebuchadnezzar I: A Turning Point in the History of Ancient Mesopotamian Religion', in W.S. McCullough (ed.), *The Seed of Wisdom: Essays in Honor of T. J. Meek*. Toronto, 1964.

Lambert, W.G., 'Berossus and Babylonian Eschatology', *Iraq* 38 (1976): 171–3.

Lambert, W.G., 'Niṣir or Nimuš?' *Revue d'Assyriologie* 80 (1986): 185–6.

Lambert, W.G., 'A New Look at the Babylonian Background of Genesis', in Hess and Tsumura (eds), 1994: 96–113.

Lambert, W.G. and A.R. Millard, *Atra-Ḫasīs: The Babylonian Story of the Flood*. Oxford, 1969.

Landsberger, B., *Die Fauna des alten Mesopotamien nach der 14. Tafel der Series HAR-RA = HUBULLU*. Leipzig, 1934.

Landsberger, B., *The Fauna of Ancient Mesopotamia*, First Part. Materialen zum sumerisches Lexikon, Vol. 8/1. Rome, 1960.

Landsberger, B., *The Fauna of Ancient Mesopotamia*, Second Part. Materialen zum sumerisches Lexikon, Vol. 8/2. Rome, 1962.

Leemans, W.F., Review of Forbes 1955, *Journal of the Economic and Social History of the Orient* 3 (1960): 218–21.

Lewis, B., *The Sargon Legend: A Study of the Akkadian Text and the Tale of the Hero Who was Exposed at Birth*. American Schools of Oriental Research Dissertation Series 4. Cambridge, 1980.

Lewis, J.P., *A Study of the Interpretation of Noah and the Flood in Jewish and Christian Literature*. Leiden, 1978.

Lieberman, S. 'A Mesopotamian Background for the So-called Aggadic "Measures" of Biblical Hermeneutics?' *Hebrew Union College Annual* 58 (1987): 157–225.

Livingstone, A., 'Ashurbanipal: Literate or Not?' *Zeitschrift für Assyriologie* 97 (2007): 98–118.

Lynche, R., *An Historical Treatise of the Travels of Noah into Europe: Containing the first inhabitation and peopling thereof. As also a breefe recapitulation of the Kings, Governors, and Rulers commanding in the same, even unto the first building of Troy by Dardanus*. Done into English by Richard Lynche, Gent. London, 1601.

Malamat, A., 'King Lists of the Old Babylonian Period and Biblical Genealogies', in R. S. Hess and D.T. Tsumura (eds), 'I Studied Inscriptions from Before the Flood'. *Ancient Near Eastern, Literary and Linguistic Approaches to Genesis 1–11*. Winona Lake, 1994: 183–99.

Mallowan, M.E.L., 'Noah's Flood Reconsidered', *Iraq* 26 (1964): 62–82.

Marinković, P., 'Urartu in der Bibel', in S. Kroll, C. Gruber, U. Hellwag,

M. Roaf and P. Zimansky (eds), *Biainili-Urartu*. The Proceedings of the Symposium held in Munich 12–14 October 2007. *Acta Iranica*, Vol. 51. Louvain, 2012.

Michalowski, P., 'How to Read the Liver – in Sumerian', in A. K. Guinan, M. deJ. Ellis, A.J. Ferrara, S.M. Freedman, M.T. Rutz, L. Sassmannshausen, S. Tinney and M.W. Waters (eds), *If a Man Builds a Joyful House: Assyriological Studies in Honor of Erle Verdun Leichty*. Leiden, 2006: 247–57.

Millard, A.R., 'A New Babylonian "Genesis" Story', in Hess and Tsumura (eds), 1994: 114–28.

Millard, A.R., 'Transcriptions into Cuneiform', in Geoffrey Khan (ed), *Encyclopedia of Hebrew Language and Linguistics* Vol 3, 2013: 838–47.

Montgomery, J.W., *The Quest for Noah's Ark*. Minneapolis, 1972.

Moorey, P.R.S., *Kish Excavations 1923–1933*. Oxford, 1978.

Nissen, H., P. Damerow and R.K. Englund, *Archaic Bookkeeping: Writing and Techniques of Economic Administration in the Ancient Near East*. Trans. P. Larsen. Chicago, 1993.

Ochsenschlager, E.L., 'Ethnographic Evidence for Wood, Boars, Bitumen and Reeds in Southern Iraq: Ethnoarchaeology at al-Hiba', *Bulletin on Sumerian Agriculture* 6 (1992): 47–78.

Ochsenschlager, E.L., *Iraq's Marsh Arabs in the Garden of Eden*. Philadelphia, 2004.

Oppenheim, A.L., *The Interpretation of Dreams in the Ancient Near East with a Translation of an Assyrian Dream-Book*. Transactions of the American Philosophical Society. New Series 46/3 (1956).

Oppenheim, A.L., *Letters from Mesopotamia: Official, Business and Private Letters on Clay Tablets from Two Millennia*. Chicago, 1967.

Oppenheim, A.L., 'A Babylonian Diviner's Manual', *Journal of Near Eastern Studies* 33 (1974): 197–220.

Oppenheim, A.L., *Ancient Mesopotamia*, revised edition. Chicago, 1977.

Parpola, S. 'A Letter from Šamaš-šum-ukīn to Asarhaddon', *Iraq* 34 (1972): 21–34.

Parpola, S., 'The Murder of Sennacherib', in B. Alster (ed.), *Death in*

Mesopotamia. Papers read at the XXVI[E] Rencontre Assyriologique Internationale. Mesopotamia 8. Copenhagen, 1980: 171–86.

Parpola, S., 'The Assyrian Cabinet', in M. Dietrich and O. Loretz (eds), *Vom Alten Orient zum Alten Testament. Festschrift fur Wolfram Freiherrn von Soden*. Alter Orient und Altes Testament 240. Neukirchen-Vluyn, 1995: 379–401.

Parpola, S. and K. Watanabe, *Neo-Assyrian Treaties and Loyalty Oaths*. State Archives of Assyria 2. Helsinki, 1998.

Parrot, A., *The Flood and Noah's Ark*. Translated from the French by Edwin Hudson. Studies in Biblical Archaeology 1. London, 1955.

Patai, R., *The Children of Noah: Jewish Seafaring in Ancient Times*. With Contributions by J. Hornell and J.M. Lundquist. Princeton, 1998.

Peake, H., *The Flood: New Light on an Old Story*. London, 1930.

Pedersén, O., *Archive und Bibliotheken in Babylon: Die Tontafeln der Grabung Robert Koldeweys 1899–1917*. Abhandlungen der deutschen Orient-Gesellschaft 25. Saarbrücken, 2005a.

Pedersén, O., 'Foreign Professionals in Babylon: Evidence from the Archive in the Palace of Nebuchadnezzar II', in W.H. van Soldt (ed.), *Ethnicity in Ancient Mesopotamia: Papers Read at the 48th Rencontre Assyriologique Internationale, Leiden, 1–4 July 2002*. Leiden, 2005b: 267–72.

Peters, J.P., *Nippur, or Explorations and Adventures on the Euphrates*. The Narrative of the University of Pennsylvania Expedition to Babylonian in the Years 1888–1890, Vol. 1. Pennsylvania, 1899.

Pinches, T.G., 'EXIT GIŠṬUBAR!' *The Babylonian and Oriental Record* 4 (1889–90): 264.

Pinches, T.G., 'The Religious Ideas of the Babylonians', *Journal of the Transactions of the Victoria Institute* 28 (1896): 1–3.

Pingree, D., 'Legacies in Astronomy and Celestial Omens', in S. Dalley (ed.), *The Legacy of Mesopotamia* (1998): 125–37.

Potts, D., *Mesopotamian Civilization: The Material Foundations*. London, 1997.

Powell, M.A., 'Timber Production in Presargonic Lagaš', in J.N. Postgate (ed.), *Trees and Timber in Mesopotamia: Bulletin on Sumerian Agriculture*, Vol. 6. Cambridge, 1992: 99–122.

Raikes, R.L., 'The Physical Evidence for Noah's Flood', *Iraq* 28 (1966): 62–3.

Reade, J.E., 'Archaeology and the Kuyunjik Archives', in K.R. Veenhof (ed.), *Cuneiform Archives and Libraries*. Papers read at the 30ᴱ Rencontre Assyriologique Internationale Leiden, 4–8 July 1983. 1986.

Reade, J.E., 'An Eagle from the East', *Britannia* 30 (1999): 266–8.

Reade, J.E., 'Retrospect: Wallis Budge – For or Against?' in Ismail 2011: 444–63.

Riem, J., *Die Sinflut in Sage und Wissenschaft*. Hamburg, 1925.

Robson, E., *Mesopotamian Mathematics 2100–1600 BC: Technical Constants in Bureaucracy and Education*. Oxford Editions of Cuneiform Texts, Vol. 24. Oxford, 1999.

Robson, E., *Mathematics in Ancient Iraq*. Princeton, 2008.

Salim, S.M., *Marsh Dwellers of the Euphrates Delta*. London School of Economics Monographs on Social Anthropology no. 23. London, 1962.

Salonen, A., *Die Wasserfahrzeuge in Babylonien*. Studia Orientalia, Edidit Societas Orientalis Fennica VIII.4. Helsinki, 1939.

Sandars, N.K., *The Epic of Gilgamesh*. Penguin Books, 1960.

Schnabel, P., *Berossus und die babylonisch-hellenistische Literatur*. Leipzig and Berlin, 1923.

Shehata, D., *Annotierte Bibliographie zum altbabylonische Atramhasīs-Mythos Inūma ilū awīlum*. Göttinger Arbeitshefte zur Altorientalischen Literatur, Vol. 3. Göttingen, 2001.

Smith, G., 'The Chaldean Account of the Deluge', *Transactions of the Society of Biblical Archaeology* 2 (1873): 213–34.

Smith, G., 'The Eleventh Tablet of the Izdubar Legends: The Chaldean Account of the Deluge', *Transactions of the Society of Biblical Archaeology* 3 (1874): 534–87.

Smith, G., *Assyrian Discoveries: An Account of Explorations and Discoveries on the Site of Nineveh during 1873 and 1874*. London, 1875.

Smith, G., *The Chaldean Account of Genesis containing the Description of the Creation, the Fall of Man, the Deluge, the Tower of Babel, the Times of the Patriarchs, and Nimrod; Babylonian Fables and the Legends of the Gods; from the Cuneiform Inscriptions*. London, 1876.

Spar, I. and W.G. Lambert (eds), *Cuneiform Texts in the Metropolitan Museum of Art*, Vol. II. Literary and Scholastic Texts of the First Millennium B.C. New York, 2005.

Speiser, E.A., 'Southern Kurdistan in the Annals of Ashurnasirpal and Today', *Annals of the American Schools of Oriental Research* 8 (1928, for 1926–7): 1–42.

Stevens, E.S., *By Tigris and Euphrates*. London, 1923.

Streck, M.P., 'NiŞIR', *Reallexikon der Assyriologie* 9 7/8 (2001): 589–60.

Thesiger, W., *The Marsh Arabs*. London, 1964.

Tigay, J., *The Evolution of the Gilgamesh Epic*. Philadelphia, 1982.

van Koppen, F., 'The Scribe of the Flood Story and his Circle', in K. Radner and E. Robson (eds), *The Oxford Handbook of Cuneiform Culture*. Oxford, 2011: 140–66.

Velduis, N., 'Levels of Literacy', in K. Radner and E. Robson (eds), *The Oxford Handbook of Cuneiform Culture*. Oxford, 2001: 68–89.

Watelin, L.C., *Excavations at Kish*, Vol. 4. Paris, 1934.

Weidner, E.F., 'Jojachin, König von Juda, in babylonischen Keilschrifttexten', *Mélanges syriens offerts à Monsieur Rene Dussaud*, Vol. 2. Bibliothèque Archéologique et Historique 30 (1939): 923–35.

Westenholz, A., 'The Graeco-Babyloniaca Once Again', *Zeitschrift für Assyriologie und Vorderasiatische Archäologie* 97 (2007): 262–313.

Westenholz, J.G., *Legends of the Kings of Akkade: The Texts*. Mesopotamian Civilizations 7. Winona Lake, 1997.

Westermann, C., *Genesis 1–11: A Continental Commentary*. Trans. J.J. Scullion. Minneapolis, 1984.

Weszeli, M., 'Schiff und Boot. B. in Mesopotamischen Quellen des 2. und 1. Jahrtausends', *Reallexikon der Assyriologie* 12. Berlin, 2009: 160–71.

Wiggermann, F.A.M., *Mesopotamian Protective Spirits: The Ritual Texts*. Cuneiform Monographs 1. Groningen, 1992.

Wiggermann, F.A.M., 'Agriculture as Civilization: Sages, Farmers and Barbarians', in K. Radner and E. Robson (eds), *The Oxford Handbook of Cuneiform Culture*. Oxford, 2011: 663–89.

Wilcke, C., *Wer las und schrieb in Babylonien und Assyrien*.

Sitzungberichte der Bayersichen Akademie der Wissenschaften Philosophisch-historische Klasse 200/6. Munich, 2000.

Wilcke, C., *The Sumerian Poem Enmerkar and En-suhkeš-ana: Epic, Play, Or? Stage Craft at the Turn from the Third to the Second Millennium B.C. with a Score-Edition and a Translation of the Text.* American Oriental Series Essay 12. New Haven, 2012.

Wilson, I., *Before the Flood: Understanding the Biblical Flood Story as Recalling a Real-Life Event.* London, 2001.

Wilson, R.R., 'The Old Testament Genealogies in Recent Research', in R.S. Hess and D.T. Tsumura (eds), 'I Studied Inscriptions from before the Flood'. *Ancient Near Eastern, Literary and Linguistic Approaches to Genesis 1–11.* Winona Lake, 1994: 200–23.

Woolley, C.L., *Excavations at Ur.* London.

Young, G. and N. Wheeler, *Return to the Marshes.* London, 1977.

Zaccagnini, C., 'Maps of the World', in G. B. Lanfranchi, D. M. Bonacossi, C. Pappi and S. Ponchia, *Leggo! Studies Presented to Frederick Mario Fales on the Occasion of His 65th Birthday.* Wiesbaden, 2012: 865–73.

Zarins, J., 'Magan Shipbuilders at the Ur III Lagash State Dockyards (2062–2025 B.C.)', in E. Olijdam and R.H. Spoor (eds), *Intercultural Relations between South and Southwest Asia: Studies in Commemoration of E.C.L. During Caspers (1934–1996).* BAR International Series 1826. 2008: 209–29.

Zgoll, A., *Traum und Welterleben im antiken Mesopotamien.* Alter Orient und Altes Testament 333. Munster, 2006.

Ziolkowski, T., *Gilgamesh Among Us: Modern Encounters with the Ancient Epic.* Cornell, 2011.

Acknowledgements

Great expressions of gratitude are due to the late Douglas Simmonds, who first introduced me to the extraordinary document that forms the subject of this book and allowed me unrestricted access to decipher it at my leisure and follow wherever it led. Mark Wilson has been my invaluable friend and counsellor throughout and an admirable Appendix-writer. Mark Geller sent me elusive papers and, like Jenny Balfour Paul and Leander Feiler, was immensely supportive. Sue Kirk read early drafts at just the right time. Marion Faber and Roger Kaysel sent me wonderful background resources about European toy Noah's Arks and I owe to Małgorzata Sandowicz especially her timely view of the Ararat rainbow.

Dan Chambers of Blink Films has taken up the story recounted here in an altogether different medium which is, as this book goes to press, just underway under the command of Nic Young. Technical input about guffas and guffa building in the early stages came from Tom Vosmer and Sir Peter Badge.

British Museum colleagues have been wonderful, especially Jonathan Tubb, my Keeper, Hannah Boulton and Patricia Wheatley. Jon Taylor, St John Simpson, Lisa Baylis and Nigel Tallis each came unhesitatingly to the rescue with late and last-minute images.

I am delighted to thank Gordon Wise, my agent, for doing so much to advance progress on this book, and as for Rupert Lancaster, Maddy Price and Camilla Dowse at Hodder, no one can have ever embarked on such a voyage through such waters in better company. Their navigation has been truly inspiring to me.

Most of all, let me conclude, I thank my dear Joanna, who awarded me the title.

Text Acknowledgements

M.A.S. Abdel Haleem: extracts from *The Qur'an. A New Translation* (Oxford World's Classics, 2004); **Andrew George (translator):** extracts from *The Epic of Gilgamesh* (Allen Lane The Penguin Press, 1999), reproduced by permission of the translator and Penguin Books Ltd; **James Hornell:** extracts from *Water Transport: Origins & Early Evolution* (Cambridge University Press, 1946), © Cambridge University Press, translated with permission; **W. G. Lambert & A. R. Millard:** extracts from *Atra-Nasis: The Babylonian Story of the Flood* (Oxford University Press, 1969), reproduced by permission of Eisenbrauns; **A.L. Oppenheim:** extracts from 'A Babylonian Diviner's Manual' from *Journal of Near Eastern Studies* 33: 197-220 (University of Chicago, 1974).

Every effort has been to trace or contact all copyright holders. The publishers would be pleased to rectify any errors or omissions brought to their attention at the earliest opportunity.

Picture Acknowledgements

© Alamy: 5 (colour section)/ photo Robert Harding Picture Library, 9 (colour section, bottom), 15 (colour section, top)/ photo Mary Evans Picture Library. © Alinari Archives Florence: 297/ photo George-Tatge-Archivio Seat. © Ashmolean Museum, University of Oxford: 309 (detail, bottom AN1923.444). Author Collection: 1 (colour section, top and bottom right), 6 (colour section, middle and bottom), 97, 137 (top), 140, 142/ photos E.S. Drower (née Stevens), 144/ photo J.P. Peters, 145, 152/ photo J.P. Peters, 156, 183, 337 (top and details bottom left and middle). © bpk Bildagentur für Kunst, Kultur und Geschichte, Berlin: 11 (colour section, top) & 255/ photos Vorderasiatisches Museum, SMB Olaf M. Teßmer. © Bridgeman Art Library: 7 & 11 (colour section, both bottom)/ photos Christie Images, 9 (colour section, top)/ photo De Agostini Picture Library/ G.Dagli Orti, 124/ photo Look and Learn, 296 (top)/ photo Newberry Library, Chicago, Illinois, USA. © The Trustees of the British Museum: 1 (colour section, middle left), 3, 4 (colour section, top BM 120000), 5 (DT 42), 7 (colour section, top BM As1921,1208.1), 8 (colour section, top BM 1997,0712.28), 12 &13 (colour section BM 92687), 49 (BM 78158), 76 (BM 34580), 119 (BM 133043), 127 (detail BM 15285), 137 (middle), 147 & 148 (BM 32873), 184 (1870,0709.241), 229 (BM 21946b), 230 (BM 114789), 244 (BM 47406), 246 (BM 25636), 253 (BM 40565), 254 (BM 47449), 262 & 268 (BM 92687), 273 (detail BM 92687), 289, 296 (bottom), 316 (BM 47817). Courtesy of the John J. Burns Library Boston College, Jesuitica Collection: 204 (top). © Dale Cherry: 16 (colour section), 107, 235. © Corbis: 4 (colour section, bottom). © Getty Images: 10 (colour section) & 157/ photos De Agostini, 236/ photo Universal

Every reasonable effort has been made to contact the copyright holders, but if there are any errors or omissions, Hodder & Stoughton will be pleased to insert the appropriate acknowledgement in any subsequent printing of this publication.

Index

Page references in *italic* indicate illustrations.

A Note About the Author

Dr. Irving Finkel is Assistant Keeper of Ancient Mesopotamian script, languages, and cultures at the British Museum. He is the curator in charge of cuneiform inscriptions on tablets of clay from ancient Mesopotamia, of which the Middle East Department has the largest collection—some 130,000 pieces—of any modern museum.